Osage Language and Lifeways

Osage Language and Lifeways

CAMERON PRATT
STEPHANIE RAPP
MARCIA HAAG
DYLAN HERRICK

University of Oklahoma Press : Norman

Financial support for publication was provided by the University of Oklahoma's Office of the Vice President for Research and Partnerships, the Office of the Provost, the Dodge Family College of Arts and Sciences, and the Department of Modern Languages, Literatures, and Linguistics.

Library of Congress Cataloging-in-Publication Data

Names: Pratt, Cameron, 1972– author. | Rapp, Stephanie, 1949– author. | Haag, Marcia, 1951– author. | Herrick, Dylan, 1971– author.
Title: Osage language and lifeways / Cameron Pratt, Stephanie Rapp, Marcia Haag, Dylan Herrick.
Description: Norman : University of Oklahoma Press, 2025. | Includes index. | Summary: "A pedagogical grammar of the Osage language that includes a significant cultural component"— Provided by publisher.
Identifiers: LCCN 2024038868 | ISBN 9780806195292 (hardcover) | ISBN 9780806195629 (paperback)
Subjects: LCSH: Osage language—Grammar. | Osage Indians—Social life and customs.
Classification: LCC PM2081 .P73 2025 | DDC 497/.52545—dc23/eng/20241231
LC record available at https://lccn.loc.gov/2024038868

The paper in this book meets the guidelines for permanence and durability of the Committee on Production Guidelines for Book Longevity of the Council on Library Resources, Inc. ∞

Copyright © 2025 by the University of Oklahoma Press, Norman, Publishing Division of the University. Manufactured in the U.S.A.

All rights reserved. No part of this publication may be reproduced, stored in a retrieval system, or transmitted, in any form or by any means, electronic, mechanical, photocopying, recording, or otherwise—except as permitted under Section 107 or 108 of the United States Copyright Act—without the prior written permission of the University of Oklahoma Press. To request permission to reproduce selections from this book, write to Permissions, University of Oklahoma Press, 2800 Venture Drive, Norman, OK 73069, or email rights.oupress@ou.edu.

Contents

Introduction	1
Cameron Pratt	1
Stephanie Rapp	3
Marcia Haag and Dylan Herrick	4
How to use this book	5
Chapter 1 The Sounds and Spelling of Osage	8
Osage pronunciation	8
Writing and pronouncing Osage vowels	9
Writing and pronouncing Osage consonants	12
Quick guides to APA and 𐓇𐓘𐓓𐓘́𐓓𐓘 𐓂́𐓘 pronunciation	14
Chapter 2 The Basic Sentence	21
Subject markers for the third-person	22
Aspect	22
Evidentials	25
Chapter 3 More about Sentences: Adding Objects and Adjectives	30
Adding an object	31
Adding adjectives to phrases	32
Adjectives as predicates	33
ħα [ðe] *that*	35
Chapter 4 More about Sentences: Adding Time Expressions and Locations	39
Adding expressions of time	39
Adding a place	40
When the shape of a place matters	41
Yes-no questions	43
Numbers	44

Chapter 5	Verb Classes and the Pronouns *I*, *You*, *He*, *She*, and *It*	49
	The third-person singular subjects: *he*, *she*, and *it*	50
	The pronouns *I* and *you*	51
	The a-ða verb class	51
	The br-šc "brush" verb class	52
	The special cases of ⁵ʌ [wa] and ᴏ [o] verbs in the a-ða verb class	54
	The special cases of verbs that are in more than one class	55
Chapter 6	Continuous Aspect, Singular Pronouns, and the Verb ʰnʼ [ðį]	58
	The first-person continuous aspect markers	59
	The second-person continuous aspect markers	62
	A review of continuous aspect markers	64
	The verb ʰnʼ [ðį] *be*	65
Chapter 7	Plural Subject Pronouns and the Future Marker	70
	Completive aspect	71
	Continuous aspect	74
	Variations of completive and continuous aspect	77
	The future marker ᴆʌ [hta]	79
Chapter 8	Question Words, I-Stem Verbs, and Strong-Stem Verbs	82
	Using question words	83
	I-stem verbs	88
	Strong-stem verbs	90
	Verbs that belong to two classes	91
Chapter 9	Object Pronouns	96
	Object pronouns	97
	Using subject and object pronouns together	101
	Using plural forms of object pronouns	104
Chapter 10	Stative Verbs	109
	Stative verbs	110
	Words for feelings	114
	Using ⌐ńɑ [níe] *hurt, in pain*	116
	Using just the aspect marker with common stative verbs	117
Chapter 11	Osage Lifeways	120
	Blankets	121
	Talking about family members	123
Chapter 12	Commands and Negation	127
	Commands	128
	Negation	129
Chapter 13	Habitual and Durative Aspects and Freestanding Pronouns	135
	Marking habitual and durative aspects with adverbials	136

The connectors ᏂᎯᏍᏀ [ðáha] and ᎯᏍᏀ [áha]	139
Freestanding pronouns	140

Chapter 14 Motion Verbs — 147
- How to think about movement in Osage — 148
- Movement toward *here* — 148
- Arrival *here* — 150
- Movement toward *there* — 151
- Arrival *there* — 153
- Bringing and taking with ᏀᏂᏂ́ [aðį́] *have* — 154

Chapter 15 Connectors and Nasal-Stem Verbs — 160
- Clauses joined by word order (no connector) — 161
- Clauses joined with connectors — 163
- Examples of Osage connected sentences — 165
- Learn the difference: ᏀᏃᏂ́ [ažį́], ᏀᏃᏂ [ąži], ᏀᏃᏂ [aži] — 168
- Nasal-stem verbs — 168

Chapter 16 Using the ᏀᏂ [ki] Pronouns — 173
- ᏀᏂ́ [kí] *to or for someone (else)* — 174
- ᏀᏂ [ki] *do to or for one's own* — 176
- ᏀᏂ [hki] *do to or for oneself or each other* — 179

Chapter 17 Building Words with Prefixes — 185
- The prefixes Ꮒ, ᴏ, Ꭺ́ [i, o, á] — 186
- ᏃóᏓα [žóle] *accompaniment with* — 189
- Special Siouan instrumental prefixes — 190

Chapter 18 More about Plurals — 201
- Joining noun phrases — 202
- Words that name quantity — 203
- The adverbs ᏎᎯᏓᏂ́ [wálį] and ᏂᏂᏃ [xci] — 205
- ᎪᏃᏂ́ [ecí] *there is, there are, be or exist here/there* — 206
- Position markers — 207

Chapter 19 More about Word Formation: Causatives, ᏎᏀ [wa], and Compounding — 212
- Causatives — 213
- The third-person pronoun ᏎᏀ [wa] — 217
- Verbs into Nouns — 219
- Making new nouns using compounding — 219

Chapter 20 Final Topics: Useful Expressions, Verbs for Speaking, Relative Clauses — 222
- Evidential marker Ꭺ́ᏇᎠ [áape] — 223
- Expressions for *again*, *possibly*, and *if* — 224
- Verbs for speaking — 225

Relative clauses	228
How do we go forward from here?	229
Appendix A. APA Dialogues and Stories	231
Appendix B. Verb Classes	241
ˊʌzʌzɑ Ռɑ-English Glossary	245
English-ˊʌzʌzɑ Ռɑ Glossary	261
Index	277

Introduction

This book is a collaboration, and each of us would like to start by saying a few words about how we began working on this book and what it means to us.

Cameron Pratt

My 𐒰𐓘𐓓𐒰́𐓓𐒰 family lineage is as follows: 𐒻𐓂𐒷𐓆𐒼𐓂𐒰𐓏 (Great-Grandfather) Henry Pratt (Roll #736), 𐓏𐒼𐓆𐒼ó𐒰𐓏 (Great-Grandmother) Josephine Pratt (Roll #737), 𐒻𐓂𐒷𐓆𐒼𐓂 (Grandfather) George Pratt (Roll #739), and 𐓏𐒷𐓏𐒰𐒷𐓂 (Father) Michael Sylvester Pratt of the 𐒻́𐓆𐒷𐓂𐒻̈ 𐒻́𐓆𐒼𐒰𐓂. Our clan is the 𐒰𐓏𐓆𐒼́𐒷𐓏𐒼𐓂 𐒻́𐓆𐒼𐒰𐓂𐒼𐓏, which is translated as "the Men of Mystery." This clan is more commonly known as the 𐒻𐓆 𐓂𐒻𐓆𐒼𐒰𐒼𐓂𐒼𐓏 Thunder clan or Thunder People. Ψő𐒷𐒰𐓂𐓏 𐒰𐓘𐓓𐒰́𐓓𐒰 𐓓𐒰́𐓓𐒰 𐒻𐒰𐒷̃ 𐓂𐒼𐒼𐒰́, my Osage name is Jesus's Hair. This is a family name made by 𐒻𐓂𐒷𐓆𐒼𐓂𐒰𐓏 Henry Pratt and was given to his youngest son Henry Pratt Jr. (Hanky). Grandfather George wanted my father to give the name to me. I have four children: Ryan Armstrong-Pratt, Marissa Pratt, Henry Pratt, and Michaela Pratt. My wife is Nicole (Tallchief) Pratt, my mother is Judith Robinson, and my grandmother is Vina (Washington) Pratt.

Around the age of twenty, a relative extended an invitation to attend a 𐓎𐓂𐒼ó𐓓𐒰 (Osage Native American Church ceremony). This ceremony marked the beginning of a journey that I have been on for more than thirty years. As a student of 𐓎𐓂𐒼ó𐓓𐒰, I heard and saw that 𐒰𐓘𐓓𐒰́𐓓𐒰 ñ𐒰 (Osage language) was an inseparable part of the ceremony. I feel fortunate to have heard it spoken there over the years, particularly in prayers.

The word 𐓎𐓂𐒼ó𐓓𐒰 means *teach yourself* or *teach one another*. It has captivated me in life and driven me to learn more. My desire to be a good student of 𐓎𐓂𐒼ó𐓓𐒰 is what led me to study and learn 𐒰𐓘𐓓𐒰́𐓓𐒰 ñ𐒰. My first language teacher was my father and, after him, my 𐒰𐓘𐓓𐒰́𐓓𐒰 uncles and aunts. They all spoke the language and encouraged the younger generation to 𐒰̃𐒼𐒼̈ (do one's best). They were my first 𐒰𐓘𐓓𐒰́𐓓𐒰 ñ𐒰 𐒰𐓏𐒼ó𐓓𐒰 (Osage language teachers). Even though I sometimes felt uncomfortable trying to speak, they made it all right to stumble along.

I attended my first official 𐒰𐓘𐓓𐒰́𐓓𐒰 ñ𐒰 classes at the White Hair Memorial, and here I met a true Osage lady, Stephanie (Kenworthy) Rapp. Later, I gained her permission to address her as 𐓷𐓣𐓤𐓪 (Aunt) Stephanie. At that point, 𐓷𐓣𐓤𐓪 had been studying the language for many years. At the beginning of this book project, I knew I was going to need someone who possessed a deeper knowledge of the language to 𐓘𐓣𐓤𐓪 (counsel) with about the particulars of Osage grammar. I knew 𐓷𐓣𐓤𐓪 was a person with this knowledge, and I knew she was a hard worker who had a passion for learning and teaching. Most important, she possessed a kind, gentle, and patient nature. Knowing all that, I asked her to join me in this endeavor. She has been a crucial contributor to this book, working tirelessly and helping push it forward. I will always be grateful that we crossed paths in this life.

Sometime after taking classes at White Hair, I heard the Osage Nation was going to have language classes in Pawhuska. Soon after it opened its doors, I began attending classes, and eventually this led to me working for the program. Here, I got the chance to study the language more in depth, and as my knowledge of the language grew, I developed a strong feeling of responsibility for making the language move forward. I saw an opportunity for a children's class, and I was allowed to start teaching the first language class in the program that was designed specifically for children. At the time, Denise Keene, then director of the Osage Nation Head Start program, was the only other person I knew of who had included 𐓷𐓘𐓲𐓘𐓬𐓘 𐓣𐓟 in her program's curriculum, and I would like to thank her for her efforts.

During my early years with the language program, I had the privilege of consulting with Kaw language specialist Justin T. McBride and the late Osage language specialist Carolyn Quintero. I was impressed by their ability to talk about the complexities of 𐓷𐓘𐓲𐓘𐓬𐓘 𐓣𐓟 so clearly. They were early inspirations for my study of linguistics. I'm grateful to Chief Jim Gray and then-chief John Red Eagle, who wrote letters of support for my linguistic training at the University of Oklahoma. They were strong supporters of the Nation's language revitalization effort and had the foresight to realize that an Osage person with this training could make a positive contribution to the program. I would also like to thank the Osage Nation Elder's Committee for their vote of approval when we started work on this book.

Once accepted to OU, I was welcomed and supported by my academic advisor and linguistics professor, Dr. Marcia Haag. She has been patient, kind, and understanding of my desire to make a positive contribution to my Osage people in revitalizing 𐓷𐓘𐓲𐓘𐓬𐓘 𐓣𐓟. Her work with the Choctaw people to publish two grammars of their language gave her the experience that has guided our work. Further, her understanding of indigenous people's history of the Americas has made her a sympathetic ally to their language revitalization efforts. She has become a friend, respected mentor, and colleague.

While attending OU, I continued to work for the Language Department. At the time, we were developing the Osage orthography, and I wrote a paper on its development for one of my classes. A portion of the information presented in that paper was incorporated into the Unicode application that was submitted to the international Unicode Consortium. The contribution I made was the addition of diacritics. These are marks that indicate when vowels are long, short, or accented, and when consonants are pre- or post-aspirated—all crucial to understanding the sounds of Osage. Another argument I made for the inclusion of the diacritics was that it would increase the viability of its usage at an academic level and would thus increase the sovereignty of the Osage orthography. That sovereignty is now being demonstrated in the writing of 𐓷𐓘𐓲𐓘𐓬𐓘 𐓣𐓟 in this book. The Osage alphabet was approved by the consortium and added into Unicode in June 2016.

My understanding of how to represent Osage sounds in writing can mostly be blamed on a coauthor of this book, Dr. Dylan Herrick. Dylan was another of my linguistics professors who became a friend and then a colleague. Most of my foundational understanding of speech sounds has come from the courses I took under Dylan. While in Norman for classes, our friendship developed from our lunch meetings at his house, where we discussed a variety of topics that included needed areas of linguistic study on 𐒴𐒰𐒵𐒷𐒵𐒰 ń𐒰, home remodel projects, gardening projects, hobbies, and our families. Dylan is one of the best teachers I have ever encountered. He possesses the ability and talents to explain abstract linguistic concepts with clarity and wit, and this has left a positive impact on me as someone who strives to improve my ability to teach.

I would like to recognize my late 𐓏𐒼𐒰𐒻𐒷𐓂 for the teachings he gave me growing up, his stories about life such as the "four stages of a man's life," and his communication of our history and ways. He told me, "If you make a decision and stick with it, you'll win." His words coupled with the lifelong example my mother, Judy Robinson, set for being a loving, fair, kind, and hardworking person have led me to my successes. I want to thank my wife, Nicole Pratt (𐓂𐒻𐒿𐒺𐒰𐒷𐓂), for her support as I studied for my degrees. The time I have given to 𐒴𐒰𐒵𐒷𐒵𐒰 ń𐒰 has taken time away from our family. She has believed all this will serve a greater purpose for our people. As my grandchildren and future generations read this book, my personal wish is that it will instill a sense of pride and strengthen their connectedness to the 𐒴𐒰𐒵𐒷𐒵𐒰 people. Lastly, I would like to thank all the 𐒴𐒰𐒵𐒷𐒵𐒰 people and others, past and present, with good intentions and motives to make 𐒴𐒰𐒵𐒷𐒵𐒰 ń𐒰 move forward in this modern world. You are appreciated.

Stephanie Rapp

Growing up in the 1960s and attending our dances and dinners, I was fortunate to hear the Osage language spoken by those who heard and learned the language from first-language speakers. I did not know or understand what was being said by our elders, but I did know that I wanted to learn and someday speak 𐒴𐒰𐒵𐒷𐒵𐒰 ń𐒰. Like most young people I did not realize how precious our language was and what it might mean to lose it.

When I became an adult, I began to study the language and attend whatever classes were being taught at the time. There were very few materials—some of them were written or recorded very long ago, and others were written for linguists. The older speakers were becoming fewer, and eventually there were very few who had spoken Osage as a child. Each time one of our elders passed, some of our language passed as well.

I found that the more I studied, the more I wanted to learn. I would spend my evenings studying and researching the Osage language. I recall one evening, as I was working on the language, my husband came into the room and asked, "Is this going to be a book someday?" One of my former teachers, who has also studied in the way that I have, said to me, "We have good and understanding spouses because so much of what could be family time is taken up by our language."

When the Osage Nation created the Language Department, I was asked to be a teacher. I was hesitant at first but could see the need for teachers. I wanted to share what I had learned with others.

Several years ago, I was told that Cameron Pratt and his OU colleagues Dr. Marcia Haag and Dr. Dylan Herrick were starting a serious book project and that he might ask me to join them with this endeavor. When he did, I was very happy to say yes. We have learned from one another and have become good friends along the way. I am grateful to have contributed to this collaboration on this book to help revitalize the Osage language.

My great-great-grandfather, 𐓏𐓇𐓘𐓜𐓣𐓤𐓘 (Roll #190), was chief of the Osage tribe in 1906 right before Oklahoma became a state. I come from a family that has had four Gray Horse drumkeepers: Stephen Cody Tucker, John Webster Williams Sr., Curtis Oren Bear, and John Joseph Hall. My daughters and granddaughters participate in the 𐓏𐓘𐓤𐓘𐓣𐓤𐓘.

As we finish our work, I would like to imagine that my grandchildren will see this book alongside other native language books in bookstores, libraries, and museums.

I would like to thank my daughters and grandchildren for their encouragement for the past five years. I want to thank my teachers from long ago—Harry Red Eagle Jr., Edward Red Eagle Sr., Kenny Bighorse, Dr. David Nagle, and Dr. Mograin Lookout. I miss hearing them speak 𐓏𐓘𐓘𐓣𐓘. I want to thank my lifelong friend Janis Carpenter. She has always shared and talked with me about our 𐓏𐓘𐓣𐓘. She is my advisor and my "sister" 𐓏𐓘𐓤𐓘.

Last but not least, I want to thank Dr. Marcia Haag, Dr. Dylan Herrick, and Cameron Pratt for wanting my help with this book. It has been a pleasure working on, researching, and studying 𐓏𐓘𐓘 with these three very accomplished linguists. Dr. Haag and Dr. Herrick were very enthusiastic to learn what Cameron 𐓏𐓣𐓤𐓘 and I could share with them pertaining to our language and our culture. I will always appreciate their having sought me out for this very important endeavor.

Marcia Haag and Dylan Herrick

We met Cameron Pratt when he was an undergraduate at the University of Oklahoma majoring in linguistics. Cameron was an older student with four children who commuted from Pawhuska to Norman, a round trip of over five hours. We were impressed with his determination to learn linguistics so that he could understand his birth language, Osage, with the goal of teaching it, analyzing it, writing about it, and collaborating with everyone from community members to linguists. Naturally, a few years after his graduation, when Cameron contacted us again, we did not hesitate to join him in a project to write a pedagogical grammar of Osage. Although we both have considerable experience in describing Native American languages, none of those languages had been in the Siouan family. But linguists are never happier than when we have a new language to learn, so we set out with great excitement and great confidence that we would do our part in bringing forth this important book.

So began our collaboration, the *kiistó*. Cameron immediately realized that he could not manage all of the intricacies of Osage without another speaker. He sought out one with a reputation for being knowledgeable and dedicated: Stephanie Rapp. We held our breaths as we waited for her to agree to long hours, frustration, endless revisions, and the patience to teach the language to two English speakers who tended to immediately forget what they had learned. Because this kind of work had to be done together, the Osage members of the kiistó needed to travel to Norman regularly. This meant exhausting hours-long sessions, an overnight stay, and more work the next morning. But we made all that forced togetherness into something we looked forward to: dinner at a particular Thai restaurant and bagels and coffee the next morning before clearing the table and getting out the laptop. The pandemic forced us to meet virtually, which we somewhat surprisingly became efficient at.

We are deeply gratified to see this book come out. It has been our privilege to study and analyze this most interesting language. While many other linguists could have performed our role, only Cameron and Stephanie could have made their crucial contribution.

Besides our Osage partners, we have a number of people to thank. First, we would like to thank the undergraduate assistants who helped us, who learned the alphabet, attended meetings, transliterated our examples, and made glossaries: Madison Doyle, Brayden Autrey, Joe Bouchard, Noah Coen, and Jacob Mattke. Second, we thank the Osage Nation Foundation for providing a grant to help support this book. Third, we thank the University of Oklahoma. Financial support was provided by the Office of the Vice President for Research and Partnerships, the Office of the Provost, the Dodge Family College of Arts and Sciences, and the Department of Modern Languages, Literatures, and Linguistics. Fourth, we thank our colleagues Justin T. McBride and Jill Greer for their detailed and helpful comments throughout this project. The editorial staff at OU Press have been unfailingly supportive from the very beginning.

And finally, we need to thank our spouses and children for their patience and for their understanding. To Marcia's husband, Eddie Baron, we thank you for your patience with the loud and exuberant language discussions that our group brought to the kitchen table and for all the bagels and coffee you prepared for our meetings. To Dylan's family, we thank Susan Skapik, Eloise Herrick, and Beatrice Herrick for putting up with our late-night Zoom meetings and for accepting how working on the book took away from time together as a family.

How to Use This Book

We have designed this book with three different groups in mind: teachers and their students, those who want (or need) to study Osage on their own, and linguists, particularly those who are interested in Native American languages.

For teachers, we have designed a book with carefully ordered topics that lead quickly to knowing how pronounce Osage, how to create and understand full sentences, and how to read and write in the Osage alphabet. Our intent is to provide enough material for at least the equivalent of a two-semester college course. By adding supplementary material or by placing a strong focus on providing conversation and writing practice, we believe that our book can be used to provide three semesters of material, perhaps more. And by adjusting the pace of the course, it can also be used in high school or community classes.

For teachers and students, especially those who are working on their own, we have done our utmost to frame our explanations in clear language, limiting our use of linguistic jargon whenever possible, and including numerous example sentences to help illustrate our points. Even those who skip the grammar can still learn a considerable amount of Osage from this book. A student could make great progress simply by practicing, memorizing, and minimally modifying the sentences that appear in each chapter.

Indeed, each chapter begins with a short dialogue or story that contains useful, natural language. They have been written by the authors who are Osage speakers with the aim of presenting commonly used language and providing small windows into their life experiences. Our intent is for students to memorize these passages without trying to analyze them. The example sentences within the chapter, on the other hand, are designed to illustrate the topics as we introduce them. At times we will encounter expressions, words, or grammar that won't get explained until later. This is particularly true with the dialogues, which should be practiced and memorized, but not analyzed.

While our book is designed to stand on its own, we believe that it will be most useful when used in collaboration with other existing books and resources for Osage. In particular, we have taken great care to make our book as consistent as possible with Carolyn Quintero's *Osage Dictionary*. Without Carolyn Quintero's *Osage Dictionary* and *Osage Grammar*, none of what we have done here would be possible. We strongly recommend using her dictionary as a supplement to our book, particularly in terms of building vocabulary, because it is a rich source of information and example sentences. Where possible, we have tried to make our spellings consistent with hers. (La Flesche's 1932 work, *A Dictionary of the Osage Language*, may also be useful, though it has been subsumed and updated by Quintero's work, and students would also have to master its particular system of spelling.)

For linguists, our book provides a strong collection of empirical data as well as a solid introduction to the core principles of Osage grammar. While we have avoided the use of linguistic jargon to the fullest extent possible, the language we use should still be suitably descriptive for linguists to map our explanations to more technical ones. In a few places, we have added short notes at the end of the chapter for clarification.

In addition, to make this work accessible to linguists who may not have the time to master the Osage alphabet, we have provided Americanist Phonetic Alphabet (APA) transcriptions for all the dialogues, example sentences, and words in the glossary. From the seventh chapter on, the APA for the dialogues has been moved to an appendix. We do not, however, provide interlinear glossing or a morpheme breakdown for our sentences, as that was viewed as too distracting and potentially off-putting for those who have not studied linguistics. A second appendix illustrates ten of the verb classes that we present in the book.

Along these lines, one of our many goals is to teach the Osage alphabet. It is crucial to note that the Osage alphabet has ways of indicating where an accent falls, whether a vowel is long or short or nasal, and whether a consonant has an h-like sound preceding or following it. Knowing this information is absolutely critical to a language learner. Mistakes or omissions of any of these things can lead to saying something either incorrectly or incomprehensibly, or even saying something completely unintended. While native speakers, by virtue of knowing the language completely, could get by without all of these distinctions in their spelling system, language learners cannot. For this reason, we see their use as essential to any introductory materials for teaching Osage.

When using the Osage alphabet, we follow the usual conventions for punctuation and capitalization. Note that we do not do this when using the APA since punctuation and capitalization can change the intended sound for an APA symbol.

All of the lexical words in our book appear in the glossary in their basic form. And all the words that appear in our example sentences appear in the vocabulary section at the end of each chapter (and in the glossary). Grammatical words, however, present an entirely different problem because they rarely map clearly or successfully to any words in English. For this reason, we have included most of the grammatical words in the index but not the glossary.

We also need to acknowledge that some communities, families, and people have different words, turns of phrases, or ways of saying things. We respect all of them, though, for reasons of space we cannot include all the possible variations that exist.

CAMERON PRATT
STEPHANIE RAPP
MARCIA HAAG
DYLAN HERRICK

CHAPTER 1

The Sounds and Spelling of Osage

Oǧóǧna [ohkíhkie] *conversation*

šįmižį:	Ʃʌ৮á, Mary ᴢʎᴢα ʌʀńα.	**šįmižį:**	hawé, Mary žáže abríe
		Girl:	Hello, my name is Mary.
	DʎDʌ ᴢʎᴢα ʌ₲ᴇńα?		táatą žáže ašcíe
			What's your name?
šįtožį:	John ᴢʎᴢα ʌʀń.	**šįtožį:**	John žáže abrí
		Boy:	My name is John.
šįmižį:	O৮ńǧnα ђʎᴄſ ʌ₲ᴂʌ.	**šįmižį:**	owíhkie ðáalį akxa
		Girl:	It's good to talk to you.
	৮ʌᴄáɤαʎ੪α ń৮ńђα ÐʌᴍNǦḁá.		walézeaace iiwíðe hta mįkšé
			See you in class!
šįtožį:	Ʃо৮á, ń৮ńђα ÐʌᴍNǦḁá.	**šįtožį:**	howé iiwíðe hta mįkšé
		Boy:	Yes, I will see you.

We will start every chapter with a short dialogue or conversation. These dialogues are to be memorized and practiced, not analyzed. They will often have language that we have not yet explained, and the English we give may not match as precisely as in our examples. Some dialogues will be followed by a short paragraph like this, and others will not. Here, note that Mary introduces herself before asking John's name. For many Osage people, it would feel jarring to ask someone's name without introducing yourself first. Another point is that the boy uses Ʃо৮á [howé] and ʌʀń [abrí], which is considered men's speech. A woman would be more likely to use ʎ̃ [ą́ą] or ʌƩá [ąhą́į] instead of Ʃо৮á [howé] and ʌʀńα [abríe] instead of ʌʀń [abrí].

Osage pronunciation

When we hear people talk, one of the first things we notice is their accent and dialect. Do they use different words from us (e.g., *soda* vs. *pop*)? Do they pronounce things differently (*pie* vs.

"*pah*")? Are they not native speakers (*this one* vs. "*zis wan*")? In Osage, this is no different. In the introduction to his 1932 *A Dictionary of the Osage Language*, Francis La Flesche wrote, "In all words in the Osage language, the most important item to be considered is the accent." With this in mind, we begin our book with an overview of how to pronounce and spell the sounds of Osage.

Where possible, we introduce each Osage sound by giving a similar sound from English or Spanish. It is important to recognize, however, that Osage sounds are not the same as those of other languages; they need to be thought of as belonging solely to Osage. For those familiar with the spelling system in Quintero's *Osage Dictionary*, which follows the Americanist Phonetic Alphabet (APA), we have included APA spellings in addition to the letters of the Osage Alphabet in the guides below. We'll begin by looking at the vowel sounds and then work through the consonants.

Writing and pronouncing Osage vowels

Osage has three different types of vowels: regular vowels, long vowels, and nasal vowels. In addition, vowels may be accented or unaccented. The best way to learn the Osage sounds is to imitate your teacher, an experienced Osage speaker, or recordings of the language. If that is not possible, the pronunciation guide presented here provides a solid introduction to the sounds of Osage and how to write them in the Osage Alphabet.

Regular vowels

The regular vowels are written and pronounced as follows: Ո like the *ea* in *heat*, U like the *ou* in *soup*, ɑ like the *e* in *beg*, O like the *o* in *hope*, ʌ like the *a* in *father*, and ʌ like the *i* in *hi*. To get a sense of these sounds, try saying the English words *heat* or *feet*, *soup* or *Susan*, *egg* or *eight*, *hope* or *go*, *father* or *nod*, and *hi* or *buy*, and then repeating the underlined vowel sound.

In the pronunciation guide below, the first column is labeled ʌzáza ńɑ [wažáže íe] *Osage language*, and it lists the uppercase and lowercase letters of the Osage alphabet. The second column, labeled *sounds like*, provides a rough approximation of the sound of the Osage letter. Sometimes there is no English equivalent, and in these cases, we have given a brief explanation after the pronunciation guide. The third column gives an Osage word that contains the Osage sound that we are looking at, and this word is written in the Osage alphabet and followed by an APA spelling. In each case, the sound in question is indicated in **bold**. The next column, *English meaning*, provides a rough, though not exact, meaning from English, and the last column contains the APA equivalent of the Osage letter. If possible, you should listen to recordings of these sounds or ask a skilled Osage speaker or teacher to pronounce these words for you.

Pronunciation guide for the regular vowels

ʌzáza ńɑ	Sounds like	ʌzáza ńɑ word	English meaning	APA
Ո ո	*ea* in *heat*	ńɑ [íe]	*word*	[i]

U u	*ou* in *soup*	𐓘𐓶𐓬𐓘 [xúða]	*eagle*	[u]
ɑ ɑ	*e* in *beg*	ɑ́ᴅʌ [étą]	*therefore*	[e]
O o	*o* in *hope*	𐓸ó𐓸o [ðóðo]	*greasy*	[o]
ʌ ʌ	*a* in *father*	ᒐʌ́ᴅʌ [hápa]	*corn*	[a]
ʌ̇ ʌ̇	*i* in *hi*	ʌʖ𐓶ʌ́ [akxái]	*aspect (see chapter 2)*	[ai]

Note that the bolded vowel in each of these examples is written with an accent mark (´) like the **ń** in **ńɑ** [íe], to show that it is an accented vowel. We discuss accent marks in more detail below.

Long vowels

The next set of words illustrate the *long* vowels, which are written with the same basic letters as above, but include a length mark (¯) over the vowel. In Osage, the long vowels typically sound very similar to the regular vowels, but the length mark indicates that the vowel is pronounced for a longer amount of time than the regular vowel. This is different from English, where *long* and *short* vowels sound different, for example, in *seed* (long) and in *said* (short). The Osage long vowels are written as follows: **n̄** like the *e* in *he*, **Ū** like the *ue* in *Sue*, **ɑ̄** like the *ey* in *they*, **Ō** like the *o* in *so, and* **Ā** like the *a* in *pa*. If the vowel is both long and accented, as in ʖɑ̋ [hkée] *turtle*, it is marked with a double accent mark (˝) instead of the length mark (¯). We will discuss vowels and accent marks more below. In English, we can hear something like regular and long vowels when we listen carefully to the vowels in words like *seat* and *sea*. In *sea*, the vowel is longer in duration than it is in *seat*. Try pronouncing the following words, but make sure to pronounce the vowels in bold for a longer duration.

Pronunciation guide for the long vowels

𐓷ʌᴢ́ᴢɑ ńɑ	Sounds like	𐓷ʌᴢ́ᴢɑ ńɑ word	English meaning	APA
N̄ n̄	*e* in *he*	𐓸n̄ᒐó [ðiihǫ́]	*your mother*	[ii]
Ū ū	*ue* in *Sue*	𐓸ūᴢ́ʌ [ðuužá]	*wash*	[uu]
ɑ̄ ɑ̄	*ey* in *they*	ɜɑ̄ᒐ̋ [hceehį́į]	*yarn belt*	[ee]
Ō ō	*o* in *so*	ŌᒐÓ [oohǫ́]	*cook*	[oo]
Ā ā	*a* in *pa*	ᴘĀ𐓶Ó [paaxó]	*hill, mountain*	[aa]

Nasal vowels

Osage also has another group of vowels, called *nasal* vowels, and they can be either regular (short) or long. These vowels are similar to the sounds above, but they have a clear nasal twang and are written with a small dot (˙) and pronounced as follows: **ʌ̇** like the *o* in *on* or *Tom*, **n̄˙** like the *ee* in *seen* or *seem*, **Ȯ** like the *o* in *tone* or *home*, **Ȧ** like the *i* in *sign* or *time*, and **Ȯ** like the *oi* in *coin* or *join*. Again, these vowels can also use the marks for being accented or long. To help familiarize yourself with these sounds, try saying the English words and then repeating just the vowel sound.

Pronunciation guide for the nasal vowels

𐓏𐓘𐓓𐓘́𐓓𐓘 𐓘́𐓘	Sounds like	𐓏𐓘𐓓𐓘́𐓓𐓘 𐓘́𐓘 word	English meaning	APA
𐓣 𐓣˙	*ee* in *green*	𐒻𐓣́˙ [míį]	*sun*	[į]
𐓂 𐓂˙	*o* in *tone*	𐓐𐓂́𐒹𐓘́ [ðǫǫpá]	*two*	[ǫ]
𐓘 𐓘	*o* in *on*	𐒻𐓎́𐒹𐓘 [hą́ąpa]	*day*	[ą]
𐓘 𐓘	*i* in *sign*	𐒻𐓂𐓏𐓘́𐒻𐓲𐓣 [hową́įki]	*where?*	[ąį]
𐓂 𐓂	*oi* as in *coin*	𐒻𐓵𐓂𐓘́ [sitǫ́į]	*yesterday*	[ǫį]

Nasal vowels, although they exist in English, are often tricky for us to hear and pronounce when we need to. Try practicing these sounds by repeating the words in the pronunciation guide. Exercise 1, at the end of this chapter, also gives some advice on how to get better at pronouncing the nasal vowels.

Spelling the Osage vowel sounds

Because Osage has regular, long, and nasal vowels, and because these vowels can be either accented or not accented, each vowel can be spelled a number of ways (sixteen ways, actually, if we include both uppercase and lowercase letters). A vowel like 𐓣 can be regular and accented 𐓣́, regular but not accented 𐓣, long and accented 𐓣̋, long but not accented 𐓣̄, nasal and accented 𐓣̇́, nasal but not accented 𐓣̇, long nasal and accented 𐓣̋̇, and finally, long nasal but not accented 𐓣̄̇. This is summarized below for uppercase 𐓣. Note also that we have included the APA symbol for each spelling of 𐓣 in brackets, like this: [i].

Eight ways to spell 𐓣

	Regular	Long
Accented	𐓣́ [í]	𐓣̋ [íi]
Not accented	𐓣 [i]	𐓣̄ [ii]
	Nasal	Long nasal
Accented	𐓣̇́ [į́]	𐓣̋̇ [į́į]
Not accented	𐓣̇ [į]	𐓣̄̇ [įį]

Not every vowel has this many spellings. For example, 𐓘 and 𐓬 are almost never spelled with the nasal dot, and 𐓘 and 𐓂 have the nasal dot built in.

More about writing accents, nasal vowels, and long vowels

This book views the Osage alphabet's accent marks, nasal vowels, and long vowels as essential tools for studying Osage. While a native speaker knows intuitively how to pronounce each word, a learner does not. Thus, as students of the language, we must memorize how each vowel is pronounced, and the accent marks play a crucial role in allowing us to do this successfully.

There are, however, two cases where we will not use accent marks. The first is with words that have only a single short vowel such as 𐒹𐓘 [pa] *snow* or 𐓓𐓣 [zi] *yellow*. The second is with commonly used short words that are needed for the grammar, such as ᐱᐳᐱ [apa] or ᐱᏇᎷᐱ [akxai] (discussed in chapter 2). You can read more about this in the notes at the end of this chapter.

Writing and pronouncing Osage consonants

Osage has many consonants, and several of them are very similar to English. In order to make this introduction a bit more manageable, we have broken the consonant sounds into four groups: *m-n-l-w* sounds, *p-t-k* sounds, *s-z-h* sounds, and *combined* sounds. Of these, the *combined* sounds are the most different from English, so we have left those for the end.

Pronunciation guide for group one consonants (m-n-l-w)

ᔓᐱzᘂza ńa	Sounds like	ᔓᐱzᘂza ńa word	English meaning	APA
ᛞ ᛞ	*m* in *me*	ᛞ́íᴏᏢᐱ [míįǫpa]	moon	[m]
ᘂ ᘂ	*n* in *neat*	ᘂňᏇa [náake]	run	[n]
ᘔ ᘔ	*l* in *leek*	ᘔáʀᐱ [lébrą]	ten	[l]
ᔓ ᔓ	*w* in *we*	ᔓᐱǩó𝗓a [wakǫ́ze]	teacher	[w]

The sounds *m-n-l-w* require little explanation. If you pronounce them as you do in English, you will be doing a very good job.

Pronunciation guide for group two consonants (p-t-k)

ᔓᐱzᘂza ńa	Sounds like	ᔓᐱzᘂza ńa word	English meaning	APA
Ᏸ ᵽ	*p* in *spy*	Ᏸᐱ [pa]	snow	[p]
𝐃 𝐃	*t* in *sty*	𝐃ő𝗣ᐱ [tóopa]	four	[t]
Ꮶ Ꮶ	*k* in *sky*	Ꮶᐱᕼa [káxa]	creek	[k]
Ꮐ Ꮐ	*ch* in *chip*	Ꮐő𝗣ᐱ [čóopa]	a small amount, few	[č]
Ᏼ ᵹ	*ts* in *its*	Ᏼáψa [céγe]	bucket, kettle, pot	[c]
Ꭱ Ꭱ	*br* in *breeze*	Ꭱáʗᕼᐱ [bráaska]	flat	[br]

The *p-t-k* sounds are both easy and difficult at the same time. While they are similar to English sounds, they have been described as medial sounds, halfway between *p~b*, *t~d*, and *k~g*. Fortunately, the Osage alphabet provides a wonderful way to remind us of this. Look closely at the Osage letters. You can see that the *p* sound, Ᏸ, actually looks like a combination of *p* and *b*. The same is true of the *t* and *d* sounds. The *t* sound, 𝐃, looks like a combination of a capital *T* and a capital *D*. The *k* sound, Ꮶ, looks like a *k* that also has the descending hook part of a *g*. When we get to the *ch* [č] sound, Ꮐ, you can almost see this as a combination of *C* and a curvy *h* (like the *ch* in chip). For the *ts* [c] sound, Ᏼ, the top part looks like the Osage *t* sound, 𝐃, which has been combined with the mirror image of an *S* (and which sounds like the *ts* in *its*). Finally, the *br* sound, Ꭱ, looks sort of like a combination of a *b* (or the Osage Ᏸ) and *R*. We hope these images help you remember the Osage letters and their pronunciations. Now let's move on to the group three sounds.

Pronunciation guide for group three consonants (s-z-h)

𐒻𐓟𐓓𐒰́𐓓𐒰 𐓣́𐒰	Sounds like	𐒻𐓟𐓓𐒰́𐓓𐒰 𐓣́𐒰 word	English meaning	APA
𐓂 𐓂	*th* in *they*	𐓂𐓂𐒰́𐓓𐒰 [ðiðáce]	your father	[ð]
𐒿 𐒿	*s* in *say*	𐒿𐓟𐓬𐒰 [sápe]	black	[s]
𐓋 𐓋	*z* in *zoo*	𐓋𐓟 [zi]	yellow	[z]
𐓆 𐓆	*sh* in *shoe*	𐓆𐓟𐓬𐒰 [šáhpe]	six	[š]
𐓐 𐓐	*g* in *beige*	𐓐𐓟 / 𐓐𐓣́𐓤𐓟 [žį́] / [žį́ka]	little, small	[ž]
𐓷 𐓷	(heavy *h*)	𐓷𐒹́𐓂𐒰 [xúða]	eagle	[x]
𐓶 𐓶	(soft *g*)	𐓟𐓷́𐓶𐒰 [náɣe]	ice	[ɣ]
𐓞 𐓞	*h* in *hello*	𐓞𐒰𐓟́𐒰 [hawé]	hello	[h]

Among this third group, most of the sounds should be familiar to us, but there are three sounds that we need to discuss further. First, the letter 𐓂 sounds like the *th* in English words like *the* or *they*, but when we say this sound in English, the tip of the tongue sticks out just a bit beyond our teeth. In Osage, the tip of the tongue stays just behind the teeth. Second and third, the letters 𐓷 and 𐓶 are difficult to describe in terms of English. They are similar to a heavy *h* sound, but the tongue is almost the same shape as when we make a *k* or *g* sound, without touching the roof of the mouth. If you are familiar with Spanish, 𐓷 (heavy *h*) is very similar to Spanish *j* in *caja* (box), and 𐓶 (soft *g*) is very similar to Spanish *g* in *hago* (I do). Not all speakers make both 𐓷 and 𐓶, and many only use 𐓷. If you are in a class, ask your teacher to discuss and pronounce these sounds. You may also be able to find recordings online at websites for the Osage Language Program or the Sam Noble Museum of Natural History Native American Languages Archive.

The final group of sounds are perhaps best thought of as sound combinations. The sounds *p* [p], *t* [t], *k* [k], and *ts* [c] combine with the sounds 𐓞 (the *h* [h] sound) and (') (called a glottal stop). The glottal stop (') is sort of like a "catch in the throat," and it is heard in English in the middle of the word *uh-oh* (where the hyphen is). There are also some sequences of two Osage letters such as 𐓬𐓆 [pš] and 𐓬𐓷 [px]. These sound combinations take some practice to get used to, especially for native speakers of English. For these sounds, it is especially important to listen to a good speaker or to recordings.

Pronunciation guide for group four sounds (sound combinations)

𐒻𐓟𐓓𐒰́𐓓𐒰 𐓣́𐒰	Sounds like	𐒻𐓟𐓓𐒰́𐓓𐒰 𐓣́𐒰 word	English meaning	APA
𐓱 𐓱	*h* + *p*	𐓆𐒰́𐓱𐒰 [šáhpe]	six	[hp]
𐓰 𐓰	*h* + *t*	𐓞𐓓́𐓰𐒰 [hóohta]	animal noise, thunder	[ht]
𐓵 𐓵	*h* + *k*	𐓞𐓣́𐓵𐒰 [híihka]	ankle	[hk]
𐓳 𐓳	*h* + *ts*	𐓂𐓋𐒰́𐓳𐓟 [ožéhci]	bathroom	[hc]
𐓳 𐓳	*ts* + *h*	𐒰𐓳𐓣́ [achí]	arrive here	[ch]
𐓬' 𐓬'	*p* + '	𐓂𐓬'𐒰́𐓂𐒰 [op'áða]	steam, fog on water	[p']
𐓵' 𐓵'	*k* + '	𐒻𐒰𐓵'𐓓́ [wak'ó]	woman	[k']
𐓳' 𐓳'	*ts* + '	𐒻𐒰́𐓳'𐒰 [wéc'a]	snake	[c']
𐓬𐓆 𐓬𐓆	*p* + *sh*	𐓬𐓆𐒰 [pša]	pound it!	[pš]
𐓵𐓆 𐓵𐓆	*k* + *sh*	𐓵𐓆𐓓́𐓤𐒰 [kšóka]	second son	[kš]

ᏰᏘ ᏰᏘ	p + heavy h	ᏸᏘᏠᏂᎪᏃᏁ [pxáðaži]	confused	[px]
ᎠᏘ ᎠᏘ	t + heavy h	ᎠᏘᏠᏒᎪ [txáha]	until, from	[tx]
ᏛᏘ ᏛᏘ	k + heavy h	ᏛᏘᏠᎪᏃᏁ [kxážį]	third son	[kx]

The first four sounds can be made by pronouncing an *h* [h] and then saying the next sound (*p* [p], *t* [t], *k* [k], or *ts* [c]). If these sounds come at the beginning of a word, the *h* is often not heard. The fifth sound, ℨ, is made by adding an *h* [h] sound after *ts* [c] (pronounced like *ts* plus *h* and *not* pronounced like *t* plus *sh*). The next three sounds are made by pronouncing a *p* [p], *k* [k], or *ts* [c] and then a "catch in the throat" or by making a "sharp beginning" to the next vowel sound. The sounds ᏸᏕ [pš] and ᏛᏕ [kš] are made by pronouncing a *p* [p] or a *k* [k] followed by *sh* [š], similar to the start of the word *pshaw*. Finally, the sounds ᏸᏘ, ᎠᏘ, and ᏛᏘ are made with a *p* [p], *t* [t], or *k* [k], followed by a loud or heavy *h* [h] sound. Again, if possible, try listening to and imitating the recordings or ask your teacher for help pronouncing these sounds.

Quick guides to APA and 𐓏𐒰𐓓𐒰𐓓𐒰 𐓆𐒰 pronunciation

For your convenience, here are two lists you can bookmark and return to as needed. The first is an alphabetized list of APA pronunciations along with the Osage letter that makes that sound. It does not include *all* APA sounds—just the ones that are used in this book. The second is a list of Osage letters and combinations with their pronunciations. This information is all found in previous sections in this chapter, but it is arranged here for easy reference. Remember, an apostrophe (') indicates a glottal stop (like the hyphen in *uh-oh*).

Quick guide to APA pronunciation

APA	Sounds like	𐓏𐒰𐓓𐒰𐓓𐒰 𐓆𐒰
[a]	*a* in *father*	𐒰 𐒰
[aa]	*a* in *pa*	𐒰̄ 𐒰̄
[ą]	*o* in *on*	𐒰̨ 𐒰̨
[ai]	*i* in *hi*	𐒰𐓘 𐒰𐓘
[ąi]	*i* in *sign*	𐒰̨𐓘 𐒰̨𐓘
[br]	*br* in *breeze*	𐒴 𐒴
[c]	*ts* in *its*	ℨ ℨ
[c']	*ts* + '	ℨ' ℨ'
[ch]	*ts* + *h*	ℨ ℨ
[č]	*ch* in *chip*	Ꮆ Ꮆ
[ð]	*th* in *they*	Ᏺ Ᏺ
[e]	*e* in *beg*	Ꭰ ɑ
[ee]	*ey* in *they*	Ꭰ̄ ɑ̄
[h]	*h* in *hello*	Ꮛ Ꮛ
[hc]	*h* + *ts*	ℨ ℨ
[hk]	*h* + *k*	Ᏼ Ᏼ
[hp]	*h* + *p*	Ᏸ Ᏸ

APA	Sounds like	Osage
[ht]	h + t	Đ đ
[i]	e in heat	∩ ∩
[ii]	e in he	∩̄ ∩̄
[į]	ee in green	∩̨ ∩̨
[k]	k in sky	Ƙ ƙ
[k']	k + '	Ƙ' ƙ'
[kš]	k + sh	Ƙʂ ƙʂ
[kx]	k + heavy h	Ƙᐧ ƙᐧ
[l]	l in leek	ι ι
[m]	m in me	൝ ൝
[n]	n in neat	∠ ∠
[o]	o in hope	O o
[oo]	o in so	Ō ō
[ǫ]	o in tone	O̓ o̓
[ǫi]	oi as in coin	⊙ ⊙
[p]	p in spy	Þ þ
[p']	p + '	Þ' þ'
[pš]	p + sh	Þʂ þʂ
[px]	p + heavy h	Þᐧ þᐧ
[s]	s in say	ς ς
[š]	sh in shoe	ʂ ʂ
[t]	t in sty	D D
[tx]	t + heavy h	Dᐧ Dᐧ
[u]	ou in soup	U u
[uu]	ue in Sue	Ū ū
[w]	w in we	ɼ ɼ
[x]	(heavy h)	ᐧ ᐧ
[ɣ]	(soft g)	Ψ ψ
[z]	z in zoo	7 7
[ž]	g in beige	Ƶ ƶ

Quick guide to 𝄃ᴧzÁzɑ ńɑ letters and combinations with pronunciation

𝄃ᴧzÁzɑ ńɑ	APA	Sounds like
Λ ʌ	[a]	a in father
Λ̓ ʌ̓	[ą]	o in on
Λ̄ ʌ̄	[aa]	a in pa
Λʌ	[ai]	i in hi
Λ ʌ	[ąi]	i in sign
Я я	[br]	br in breeze
Ϭ Ϭ	[č]	ch in chip
α α	[e]	e in beg
ᾱ ᾱ	[ee]	ey in they
ʆ ʆ	[h]	h in hello

∩ ∩	[i]	*e* in *heat*
∩' ∩'	[į]	*ee* in *green*
∩̄ ∩̄	[ii]	*e* in *he*
Ƙ Ƙ	[k]	*k* in *sky*
Ƙ' Ƙ'	[k']	*k* + '
Ƙʂ Ƙʂ	[kš]	*k* + *sh*
Ƙ⋔ Ƙ⋔	[kx]	*k* + heavy *h*
Ƙ̄ Ƙ̄	[hk]	*h* + *k*
ᴌ ᴌ	[l]	*l* in *leek*
ᴍ ᴍ	[m]	*m* in *me*
ᴌ ᴌ	[n]	*n* in *neat*
O o	[o]	*o* in *hope*
O' o'	[ǫ]	*o* in *tone*
Ō ō	[oo]	*o* in *so*
⊙ ⊙	[ǫi]	*oi* as in *coin*
Þ þ	[p]	*p* in *spy*
Þ' þ'	[p']	*p* + '
Þʂ þʂ	[pš]	*p* + *sh*
Þ⋔ þ⋔	[px]	*p* + heavy *h*
Þ̄ þ̄	[hp]	*h* + *p*
Ꞇ ꞇ	[s]	*s* in *say*
ʂ ʂ	[š]	*sh* in *shoe*
D ᴅ	[t]	*t* in *sty*
D⋔ ᴅ⋔	[tx]	*t* + heavy *h*
Đ đ	[ht]	*h* + *t*
Ƨ ƨ	[c]	*ts* in *its*
Ƨ' ƨ'	[c']	*ts* + '
Ƨ̄ ƨ̄	[hc]	*h* + *ts*
Ƨ ƨ	[ch]	*ts* + *h*
ħ ħ	[ð]	*th* in *they*
U u	[u]	*ou* in *soup*
Ū ū	[uu]	*ue* in *Sue*
ɥ ɥ	[w]	*w* in *we*
⋔ ⋔	[x]	(heavy *h*)
Ψ ψ	[ɣ]	(soft *g*)
⁊ ⁊	[z]	*z* in *zoo*
ⱬ ⱬ	[ž]	*g* in *beige*

∩Ƙ'ʉƨɑ [ík'uce] *practice*

What follows is a set of exercises to help you practice speaking and pronouncing and a short list of useful Osage phrases. We have placed the most useful words from this chapter in the vocabulary (ȟα [íe]) section of chapter 2, though some words (question words, conjunctions, family members) have been moved to more relevant chapters.

Exercise 1. Pronouncing nasal vowels

For many of us, the nasal vowels i̇, o̊, and ʌ̇ are a bit tricky to hear and pronounce, but there is a simple exercise to help us hear and feel the difference between the nasal vowels and the regular vowels. Again, try saying the English example words above, but this time, pinch your nose shut as you say them. When you get to the nasal vowel examples in *seen*, *green*, *tone*, *home*, *on*, and *Tom*, do the words suddenly sound different? If so, you're making an excellent nasal vowel! Now try saying just the vowel while pinching your nose shut. Can you still make it sound nasal? Does it sound normal when you say the regular vowels *seat*, *suit*, *set*, *soda*, and *sod?* Practice saying the regular vowels and then the nasal vowels with your nose plugged. Then practice the vowels without your nose plugged and listen for the difference.

Exercise 2. Spelling vowels

Look at the table illustrating the eight ways to spell ȟ. Practice writing these out by hand. Now try spelling ʌ in these eight different ways. Next try this with the vowel O.

Exercise 3. Practicing the Osage alphabet

Handwrite each Osage letter on the left edge of a page. Practice saying the sound out loud and write the Osage letter as you pronounce the sound. Do this at least three times. Practice this each day until you feel comfortable writing the Osage letters. If you want, you can do this with the APA symbols too.

Exercise 4. Spelling and vocabulary

Go through each pronunciation guide one by one. Practice pronouncing the words. Start slowly and repeat each word a few times until you can pronounce them smoothly. Then, practice spelling the words. You can start with the APA if you find that helpful at first but be sure to also practice writing the words in the Osage alphabet too.

Exercise 5. Vocabulary and pronunciation A

In this exercise, person A asks how to say an English word in Osage, and person B responds with the Osage word. Try this with a classmate, or if you are not in a class, read both parts.

    A: ʃȟ̇ko ꜱDʌ̇ᴘɑ ʟʌᴘɑ___ ꜱʌzʌ́zɑ ȟɑ?   háakǫ štáace nąpe ___ wažáže íe
                                                                                 How do you say ___ in Osage?

    B: ___.   ___.

A: 𐒰𐓂 á𐓤𐓂𐓧. ši ékia
                    Say it again.
B: ___.   ___.

For example:

A: 𐓏𐓘𐓤𐓪 𐓤𐓘𐓟𐓤𐓘 𐓧𐓘𐓬𐓘 <u>eagle</u> 𐓟𐓘𐓓𐓘𐓓𐓘 ńa?
B: 𐒻𐓎𐓏𐓟𐓧.
A: 𐒰𐓂 á𐓤𐓂𐓧.
B: 𐒻𐓎𐓏𐓟𐓧.

Now try this with the other words from the pronunciation guide below. Whenever you want to learn a new word in Osage, you can use 𐓏𐓘𐓤𐓪 𐓤𐓘𐓟𐓤𐓘 𐓧𐓘𐓬𐓘 ___ 𐓟𐓘𐓓𐓘𐓓𐓘 ńa? to ask your teacher.

Exercise 6. Vocabulary and pronunciation B

In this exercise, the languages are reversed, and you are given an Osage word and asked what it means in English. Note that the word for English could be either ĩ𐓤𐓘𐓟𐓧𐓘𐓂 ńa [įįštáxį íe] or 𐓏𐒻𐓏𐓧𐓒𐓤𐓧 ńa [húhaska íe], and we have only used ĩ𐓤𐓘𐓟𐓧𐓘𐓂 ńa here.

A: 𐓏𐓘𐓤𐓪 𐓤𐓘𐓟𐓤𐓘 𐓧𐓘𐓬𐓘 ___ ĩ𐓤𐓘𐓟𐓧𐓘𐓂 ńa? háakǫ štáace nąpe ___ įįštáxį íe
      How do you say _____ in English?
B: ___.

For example:

A: 𐓏𐓘𐓤𐓪 𐓤𐓘𐓟𐓤𐓘 𐓧𐓘𐓬𐓘 𐓨𐓯 ĩ𐓤𐓘𐓟𐓧𐓘𐓂 ńa?
B: Sun.

Exercise 7. Vocabulary and pronunciation C

In this exercise, instead of asking a question, a teacher is telling a student to say an Osage word in English.

Teacher: ___ 𐓟𐓘𐓓𐓘𐓓𐓘 ńл.   ___ wažáže ía
                                        Say ___ in Osage.
Student: ___.   ___.

For example:

Teacher: <u>Corn</u> 𐓟𐓘𐓓𐓘𐓓𐓘 ńл.   <u>corn</u> wažáže ía
                                         Say <u>corn</u> in Osage.
Student: 𐓏𐓘𐓬𐓧.   hápa
                                         Corn.

Exercise 8. What's your name?

Follow the pattern in the dialogue below and ask others what their name is. Note that where some speakers use ᴢʌᴢɑ [žáže], others prefer ᴢʌᴢɳ [žáži], and we have included both options in the dialogue below.

A: ____ ᴢʌᴢɑ ʌʀɳ́ɑ.   ____ žáže abríe
                                My name is ____.
     ᴅʌ́ᴅʌ ᴢʌᴢɑ ʌ§ᵋɳ́ɑ?   táatą žáže ašcíe
                                What's your name?
B: ____ ᴢʌᴢɳ ʌʀɳ́ɑ.   ____ žáži abríe
                                My name is ____.

Exercise 9. What's his/her name?

Now try asking about someone else's name following the dialogue below.

A: ᴅʌ́ᴅʌ ᴢʌᴢɑ ʌЋɳ́ɑ?   táatą žáže aðíe
                                What's his (or her) name?
B: ____ ᴢʌᴢɑ ʌЋɳ́.   ____ žáže aðį́
                                His (or her) name is ____.

Notes for Chapter 1

A. Spelling

Where possible, we have followed the spelling system in Carolyn Quintero's *Osage Dictionary*. Her dictionary is written using the Americanist Phonetic Alphabet (APA). One area where we differ slightly from the *Osage Dictionary* is in our use of accents. We do not use accent marks on words with a single short vowel or on short two-syllable words that play a grammatical role. This second group includes words such as the subject markers like ʌʞЋʌ [akxa] and ʌᴘʌ [apa], aspect markers like ᴘɑ [pe], ʌʞЋʌ [akxa], or ʌʞЋʌ [akxai], or evidential markers like ᵋɑ [che] (see chapter 2). We do use accent marks on one-syllable words with a long vowel. This is because the accent mark also tells us that the vowel is long. Some speakers or families may use different accents than what is found in the *Osage Dictionary*, and accents can sometimes change, especially in morphologically complex words or phrases or when speaking quickly.

B. Spelling vowels in the APA

Note that in the APA system, long vowels are indicated by doubling the vowel: [i] is regular, and [ii] is long. Nasal vowels such as Ơ are spelled with a small hook, written like this (˛), under the vowel; [ǫ] is a nasal vowel, [o] is not a nasal vowel. The diphthongs ʌ [ai], ʌ [ąi], and ⊙ [ǫi] can be spelled by combining [a], [ą], or [ǫ] with [i] or [į]. Since the APA is a spelling system for sounds, we do not capitalize or use punctuation marks like commas or periods.

Finally, in spelling nasal vowels in the Osage alphabet, the nasal dot can be very difficult to see when the vowels 𐓣 or 𐓪 are followed by the consonants 𐓡, 𐓟, 𐓐, 𐓵 or 𐓩.

C. Notes about the sounds of Osage

We follow Quintero in using the sound [u], but this sound is better described as a high central vowel that often alternates with a front rounded, or even unrounded, vowel or diphthong. At times, this makes spelling challenging since, for example, the [u] in a word like [kúǫ] *come here* might be pronounced often with a sound like [i], [ü], or [y]. This makes it sound much more like [kyǫ́] than [kúǫ]. In cases like these, we have tried to spell words as they appear in the dictionary, unless the alternative is extremely common.

For linguists, the APA symbols may give more information about sounds. For example, [x] and [ɣ] are velar fricatives. It is not clear whether the distinction between these sounds is voicing, stridency, or something else.

There is a fair amount of variation in the pronunciation of vowels. For example, accented [ą́] often sounds like a nasal schwa, like the vowel in *hunt*, and final unaccented [e] and [a] are often pronounced as schwa (though many speakers don't hear it that way). The Osage alphabet has a symbol for this schwa vowel, but it is not often used and does not appear in the *Osage Dictionary*, so we have not included it here. The vowel ɑ likely ranges between [e] and [ɛ], with Cameron Pratt and Stephanie Rapp expressing a slight preference to illustrate it in English with words like *beg* or *egg* rather than *tale* or *vague*.

Nasal vowels also exhibit variation, with [ą] and [ǫ] often sounding like each other. Many oral (non-nasal) vowels are also sporadically spoken with nasalization.

Based on looking at archival recordings, the accent in Osage appears to be based on a pitch change (a lowering, after the accented vowel) without a change to loudness. Without doing an instrumental analysis, changes to length are more difficult to assess.

Finally, the letter ɑ [ei̯] is also a part of the Osage alphabet, but it is so rare that we have not included it here. One place where it occurs is in 𐓍ɑ́ [méi̯], an alternative form of 𐓍ᴧ𐓐ɪ́ [maðį́] *walk*.

Chapter 2

The Basic Sentence

Oⱪńⱪna [ohkíhkie] *conversation*

ȿńDoʒn˙:	ꓶᴧᴖά, Dᴧꓡά?	šítoži:	hawé tąhé
		Boy:	Hello! Everything well?
ȿńⱶnʒn˙:	Dᴧꓡά.	šímiži:	tąhé
		Girl:	Everything is well.
ȿńDoʒn˙:	ꓡʎko˙ ꙅᴧʚά?	šítoži:	háako ðaašé
		Boy:	How are you doing?
ȿńⱶnʒn˙:	Ɑᴆʎ, ʎᴧᴄп όʎo˙ ᴧꓡά.	šímiži:	ehtá, wáli ówo ąhé
		Girl:	Well, I've been really busy.
ȿńDoʒn˙:	ʎпʚʎń, ńᴄȫᴆᴧ!	šítoži:	wiškí, íinoohpa
		Boy:	Me too, take care!
ȿńⱶnʒn˙:	άko˙.	šímiži:	éko
		Girl:	All right!

Nowadays, when we see our acquaintances, the most common greeting is ꓶᴧᴖά, Dᴧꓡά? [hawé tąhé], and the most usual response is Dᴧꓡά [tąhé]. Another good greeting is ꓡʎko˙ ꙅᴧʚά? [háako ðaašé]. If this is the first question asked, Dᴧꓡά [tąhé] would still be a good answer. In the dialogue, the girl responds with "I've been really busy" because she's already answered ꓶᴧᴖά, Dᴧꓡά? [hawé tąhé] with Dᴧꓡά [tąhé], so it makes sense to say a bit more. Finally, άko˙ [éko] is a good way to show agreement with someone. For family members or people you live with, you might simply say Dᴧꓡά [tąhé] when you first see someone.

ńa ʎᴧⱪńᴄᴧꙅɑ [íe wahkílaace] *grammar*

When we learn another language, we must begin to think in our new language. You might think we could simply match up an English word with one that means something similar in Osage. But this is not the case! Instead, we must learn the way the Osage language views the world.

To make a basic Osage sentence, we will need to learn three important ways of thinking about what things mean. These three ideas convey information about the physical position of the subject, the way events unfold in time, and the speaker's confidence in the truth of what he or she is saying. Osage uses words called *subject markers* to give certain information about the subject. The way events unfold in time is called *aspect*, and the term *evidential* is used to express the speaker's confidence in the truth of a sentence. In Osage, we include these three ideas as a necessary part of our sentences. In English, we can also include these meanings, but we don't have to. The rest of this chapter presents these three crucial parts of Osage sentences.

Subject markers for the third-person: the physical position of the subject

The first thing an Osage speaker must determine is whether the subject of the sentence is *present* or *distant*, whether it is *stationary* or *moving*. These physical positions are marked with what we call *subject markers*. The two most important subject markers in Osage are ʌƙʌʌ [akxa] and ʌᏢʌ [apa]. These are used when the subject is third-person. (In grammatical terms, *first-person* refers to *I* or *we*, *second-person* refers to singular and plural *you*, and *third-person* refers to someone or something else—for example, *my father, the woman, the buffalo*, or pronouns like *he, she, it*, or *they*.)

When a subject is present and stationary we use ʌƙʌʌ [akxa], and we use ʌᏢʌ [apa] when a subject is distant, out of sight, or moving, for example, from one place to another. This means that if a subject is present but moving, ʌᏢʌ [apa] would be used.

The examples below show how they are used in sentences. Please remember that the context and speaker choices can change the nuance.

(1) Ո̓ᎠᏞᎿՈ **ʌƙʌʌ** ᏎʌɦÓ Ꮲɑ.
  i̧htáci **akxa** waaðǫ́ pe
  My father sang. (My father is present and stationary, while I'm talking.)

(2) Ո̓ᎠᏞᎿՈ **ʌᏢʌ** ᏎʌɦÓ Ꮲɑ.
  i̧htáci **apa** waaðǫ́ pe
  My father sang. (My father is not present, while I'm talking.)

Subject markers are used when a subject is *definite* or pointed out. We will learn about *indefinite subjects* in chapter 18.

Aspect: the way an event unfolds in time

The next important thing an Osage speaker must mark is the *way* something occurs. Has it been completed? Is it ongoing? Does it happen all at once? Does it happen over and over? The grammar term for this is *aspect*, and the Osage language indicates aspect with small words, or *aspect markers*, that come at the end of the sentence. The two most important aspects in Osage are *completive* and *continuous*, which we introduce below. Later chapters will introduce other aspect markers.

The completive aspect ᑊᗄ [pe]

The completive aspect is marked with ᑊᗄ [pe]. This marker is the most basic of the Osage aspect markers, and it is often understood even if it is not said out loud. It shows that an event or action has finished. This event or action does not have to be in the past as long as it has reached completion.

To better understand this, let's look at two sentences that are about a buffalo running. Notice the difference in meaning when we change the subject marker but keep the completive aspect marker. Keep in mind that when we speak English we would not include all the information that we must have in Osage.

(3) ᔓᓭ ᐱᧆᐁᐣ ᒐᨖᧆᐣ ᑊᗄ.
hcée akxa ną́ąka **pe**
The buffalo ran.
OR The buffalo has run. (*LITERALLY* The buffalo is present, and it is no longer running.)

(4) ᔓᓭ ᐱᑊᐣ ᒐᨖᧆᐣ ᑊᗄ.
hcée apa ną́ąka **pe**
The buffalo ran.
OR The buffalo has run. (*LITERALLY* The buffalo is somewhere out of sight, and it is no longer running.)

Notice that Osage does not need tense markers like we must have in English. Aspect markers and time words do the work of tense in Osage.

Notice also that there is no specific word for *the* in 3 and 4. The subject marker lets us know to use *the* in English.

Finally, in examples 3 and 4 the verb ᒐᨖᗄ [ną́ąke] *run* changes to ᒐᨖᧆᐣ [ną́ąka]. If a verb ends in ᗄ [e], that ᗄ [e] will change to ᐣ [a] when followed by ᑊᗄ [pe]. We will see this in other examples.

(5) ᑕᐣᗞᓯ ᓫᐣᨖᗄᔕᑊ ᐱᧆᐁᐣ ᓲᐣᑒᐣ ᑊᗄ.
sitǫ́į žįkážį akxa hiiðá **pe**
Yesterday the child swam.
(Yesterday, the child, who is present, swam.)

In example 5 ᐱᧆᐁᐣ [akxa] tells us that there is a child present, ᑊᗄ [pe] tells us the action is completed, and ᑕᐣᗞᓯ [sitǫ́į] tells us when it happened, so we know it was in the past.

We will show other ways that ᑊᗄ [pe] can be used in coming chapters.

The continuous aspect

The continuous aspect is somewhat more complicated than the completive aspect, and it has many more forms. It is used to show that an action continues, whether it is in the present or the past, as in *the birds are flying* or *the birds were flying*. It may also be used to state a general fact, such as *birds fly*.

The forms of the two major continuous aspect markers are very much the same as those of the subject markers. They have an interesting history, which is worth pointing out here because it affects the way the Osage language is used nowadays. Traditionally, men and women spoke somewhat different variations of language. Women would often finish their sentences with the marker ħɑ [ðe], which is discussed below in the section on *evidentials*. Men did not. The aspect marker ΛƘʌΛ [akxa] was used by men, while ΛƘʌΛ ħɑ [akxa ðe], shortened to ΛƘʌΛ [akxai], was used by women. Men used the aspect marker ΛÞΛ [apa], while women used ΛÞΛ ħɑ [apa ðe], which became ΛÞΛ [apai]. In the recent past, we have seen two situations: some men still only use ΛƘʌΛ [akxa] and ΛÞΛ [apa], but today, generally, everyone uses both, and they have evolved in their meanings. ΛƘʌΛ [akxa] is used when making a general statement about something in the world, such as *it's hot* and ΛƘʌΛ [akxai] is used when something is or was happening at the moment. It is also interpreted as being more emphatic. Modern speakers will use both forms in most situations. You will very rarely need to make a distinction between them, and you should expect to hear both. In our examples we will use both forms to help you get accustomed to them.

The continuous aspect markers ΛƘʌΛ [akxa] and ΛƘʌΛ [akxai] also foreground the subject or bring it to the front of our attention. This is partly why they are very often given in English using present tense.

On the other hand, ΛÞΛ [apa] and ΛÞΛ [apai] are used when an action takes place out of the speaker's sight or if the subject is moving, as with the subject markers. The words ΛÞΛ [apa] and ΛÞΛ [apai] will often be put into English using past tense.

Using ΛƘʌΛ [akxa], ΛƘʌΛ [akxai], ΛÞΛ [apa], and ΛÞΛ [apai]

The continuous aspect marker ΛƘʌΛ [akxa] or ΛƘʌΛ [akxai] is used when the action of the verb is continuing but the subject is stationary. ΛÞΛ [apa] or ΛÞΛ [apai] is used when the verb is continuing and the subject is in motion. In English we would most likely speak a simpler sentence and let the context take care of the more complicated details.

The continuous aspect marker *follows* the verb, just as ÞɑՈ [pe] does.

(6) ƘΛ⁴Λ ΛÞΛ ∠ӽƘɑ **ΛÞΛ**.
hkáwa apa ną́ąke **apai**
The horse is running. (The horse is either out of view or moving, and it is running.)

In example 6, the verb ∠ӽƘɑ [ną́ąke] *run* takes the ΛÞΛ [apa] aspect marker because running involves motion.

(7a) ⁴ΛƘ'ó **ΛƘʌΛ** ⁴ӽħó **ΛƘʌΛ**.
wak'ó **akxa** waaðǫ́ **akxai**
The woman is singing. (The woman who is present is continuing to sing.)

(7b) ⁴ΛƘ'ó **ΛƘʌΛ** ⁴ӽħó **ΛƘʌΛ**.
wak'ó **akxa** waaðǫ́ **akxa**
The woman sings. (The woman who is present sings but may or may not be singing right now.)

In example 7a we would again say 𝋓𐒼ʼó 𐓂𐓄𐓘 [wak'ó akxa] as *the woman*, and because she is continuing to sing but not move, we use the aspect marker 𐓂𐓄𐓘 [akxai]. If the singing is not happening right now, such as in 7b, we might use 𐓂𐓄𐓘 [akxa].

Notice what the subject markers and aspect markers tell us in the following sentences.

(8) 𐓍ą́pa ðe iló̜eží **akxa** owísi **pe**.
 há̜a̜pa ðe iló̜eží **akxa** owísi **pe**
 Today the cat jumped.
 OR Today the cat has jumped. (Today the cat is present and no longer jumping.)

(9) 𐓍ą́pa ðe iló̜eží **apa** owísi **apai**.
 há̜a̜pa ðe iló̜eží **apa** owísi **apai**
 Today the cat is jumping.
 OR Today the cat has been jumping. (Today the cat is somewhere moving and it continues to jump.)

In example 8, even though we are talking about *today*, the jumping has already been completed. 𐓂𐓄𐓘 [akxa] tells us that the cat is not moving now, so again, in English we would use past tense: "Today the cat jumped."

In example 9 the subject marker 𐓘𐓄𐓘 [apa] tells us that the cat is moving, and the aspect marker 𐓘𐓄𐓘 [apai] tells us that the jumping continues.

In example 10 we have a time word, 𐓏𐓈𐓘 [sitó̜į] *yesterday*, that can only refer to the past, but we have a continuous aspect 𐓘𐓄𐓘 [apai] and a moving subject marker 𐓘𐓄𐓘 [apa]. Remember that in Osage, time words will often tell us that an event is in the past, present, or future.

(10) **sitó̜į** iló̜eží **apa** owísi **apai**.
 sitó̜į iló̜eží **apa** owísi **apai**
 Yesterday, the cat was jumping. (Yesterday, the cat somewhere continued to jump.)

Here, we use *was jumping* to show that the jumping both continued and was in the past.

We could also say this sentence using the aspect marker 𐓘𐓄𐓘 [apa]. The meaning would be very similar, but perhaps with a somewhat less emphatic sense.

(11) **sitó̜į** iló̜eží **apa** owísi **apa**.
 sitó̜į iló̜eží **apa** owísi **apa**
 Yesterday, the cat was jumping.

Evidentials: confidence in the message

The third important thing in an Osage sentence has to do with how much confidence the speaker has in the truth of what he or she says. This is common in many languages of the world. Does the speaker know something because he did it? Because she heard it from someone else? Because it's common knowledge? Because he suspects it's true but can't be sure? Osage grammars call markers that show this judgment *evidentials*.

The most frequent Osage evidential marker is what the grammars call *declarative*. The declarative evidential marker is ƕα [ðe], meaning the speaker is simply asserting that something is true. The completive aspect marker ᖷα [pe] is a reduced form of ᐱᖷ ƕα [api ðe], where the ƕα [ðe] *is the evidential marker*. This means that when we use ᖷα [pe], the declarative marker is already built into the meaning. Similarly, as discussed earlier, the continuous aspect marker ᐱᏰᐱᐱ [akxai] is reduced from ᐱᏰᐱᐱ ƕα [akxa ðe], and ᐱᖷᐱ [apai] is reduced from ᐱᖷᐱ ƕα [apa ðe]. Sentences with ᐱᏰᐱᐱ [akxai] and ᐱᖷᐱ [apai] have the declarative built into them as well. When we use ᐱᏰᐱᐱ [akxa] and ᐱᖷᐱ [apa] as aspect markers, the declarative evidential is understood.

We have used *it's true that* in the English below, but there are many other ways to say ƕα [ðe] in English.

(12) ꜱⁿᴅó ꜱᐱƕńᴏᴅ⋏ᐱƕα ᐱᖷᐱ ᴊńƕᐱ ƕα.
   sitǫ́į wađíopxaðe apa hiiðá ðe
   (It's true that) the student swam yesterday.

Notice that if we use ƕα [ðe] by itself without an aspect marker, as in example 12, it adds an emphasis to what the speaker is saying.

A second important evidential is one that indicates that the speaker has evidence that something is true but did not witness it. This marker is ᶻα [che]. Many times in conversation, Osage speakers finish their speaking turns with ᶻα [che]. Doing this may also make a statement more emphatic or stronger. Because of the many ways ᶻα [che] can be used, there are different ways to put it in English, and sometimes it may make sense to not put ᶻα [che] into English at all. We use *I have evidence that* below, but there are several other possibilities.

(13) ꜱⁿᴅó ꜱᐱƕńᴏᴅ⋏ᐱƕα ᐱᖷᐱ ᴊńƕᐱ ᶻα.
   sitǫ́į wađíopxaðe apa hiiðá che
   (I have evidence that) the student swam yesterday.

Notice again that there is no aspect marker in sentence 13. The emphasis is on the speaker having evidence.

Compare 12 and 13 with sentence 14, where we use ᖷα [pe] instead of ƕα [ðe] *or* ᶻα [che]. In this book, most sentences we use end in an aspect marker like ᖷα [pe], which has the declarative marker built in but does not add extra emphasis.

(14) ꜱⁿᴅó ꜱᐱƕńᴏᴅ⋏ᐱƕα ᐱᖷᐱ ᴊńƕᐱ ᖷα.
   sitǫ́į wađíopxaðe apa hiiðá pe
   The student swam yesterday.

ńꝜ'ᴜᶻα [ík'uce] *practice*

Exercise 1. How do you say this?

In this chapter, we introduced how to use the subject and aspect markers ᐱᏰᐱᐱ [akxa], ᐱᏰᐱᐱ [akxai], ᐱᖷᐱ [apa], and ᐱᖷᐱ [apai]. Look at the sentences below and state what they mean. There may be different ways to say them in English.

1. ᏘᏂᏔᏐᏃ ᏞᎠᏞ ᏏᎶᏇᏫ ᏞᎠᏞ.
   šįmįžį apa waaðǫ́ apa
2. ᏘᏂᎠᎣᏃ ᏞᎠᏞ ᏏᎶᏇᏫ ᏫᎠ.
   šįtožį apa waaðǫ́ che
3. ᏚᏂᎠᏫ ᏣᏞᏏᏞ ᏞᏣᏫᏞ ᎣᏏᏂᏚ ᎠᏫ.
   sitǫ́į hkáwa akxa owísi pe
4. ᏌᏫᎠᏞ ᏍᏫ ᏏᏞᏣ'ᏫᏫ ᏞᎠᏞ ᏏᎶᏫᏂ ᏞᎠᏏ.
   háąpa ðe wak'ó apa waachí apai
5. ᏏᏞᏣᏫᎠ ᏞᏣᏫᏞ ᏂᏫ ᏞᏣᏫᏞ.
   wakǫ́ze akxa íe akxai
6. ᏌᏫᎠᏞ ᏍᏫ ᎠᏫᏫ ᏞᎠᏞ ᎣᏏᏂᏚ ᏫᎠ.
   háąpa ðe htáa apa owísi che
7. ᏘᏫᏣᎠ ᏞᎠᏞ ᏔᏞᏣᏫᏫ ᏞᎠᏞ.
   šǫ́ke apa mąðį́ apai
8. ᏌᏫ ᏞᎠᏞ ᏌᏂᏣᏞ ᏞᎠᏞ.
   ho apa hiiðá apai
9. ᏚᏂᎠᏫ ᏌᏂᏣᏞ ᏞᎠᏞ ᏏᏞᏣᏫᏃ ᏞᎠᏞ.
   sitǫ́į níhka apa wakáaži apa
10. ᏚᏂᎠᏫ ᏏᏞᏣᏫᎠ ᏞᎠᏞ ᏏᎶᏇᏫ ᎠᏫ.
    sitǫ́į wakǫ́ze apa waaðǫ́ pe

Exercise 2. Subject and aspect markers

Go through the sentences in exercise 1, change the subject and aspect markers, and say what the new sentences mean. If a sentence uses ᏞᎠᏞ [apa], change it to use ᏞᏣᏫᏞ [akxa] or ᏞᏣᏫᏞ [akxai]. If it uses ᏞᏣᏫᏞ [akxa], change it to use ᏞᎠᏞ [apa] or ᏞᎠᏞ [apai]. The examples below illustrate how to do this. Remember to change both the subject and aspect markers.

ᏏᏂᏃᏣᎠ ᏞᎠᏞ ᏏᎶᏇᏫ ᏞᎠᏞ.	CHANGE TO	ᏏᏂᏃᏣᎠ ᏞᏣᏫᏞ ᏏᎶᏇᏫ ᏞᏣᏫᏞ.
wižǫ́ke apa waaðǫ́ apa		wižǫ́ke akxa waaðǫ́ akxai
ᏏᏞᏣᏫᎠ ᏞᏣᏫᏞ ᏂᏫ ᏞᏣᏫᏞ.	CHANGE TO	ᏏᏞᏣᏫᎠ ᏞᎠᏞ ᏂᏫ ᏞᎠᏞ.
wakǫ́ze akxa íe akxai		wakǫ́ze apa íe apai

Exercise 3. Evidentials

Use the sentences in exercise 1 and replace the aspect or evidential marker with ᏫᎠ [che], then do this with the declarative marker (remember that the declarative marker is built into ᎠᏫ [pe], ᏞᏣᏫᏞ [akxa], ᏞᎠᏞ [apa]) and state how the meaning changes.

ᏂᏫ [íe] *Vocabulary*

Words from the dialogue will often not appear in the vocabulary section, but they will appear in the glossary in their basic forms. Some dialogue words are not in their basic forms, and you will need to study the dialogue's English meaning to learn them.

Nouns

𐓮𐓘𐓬𐓜	hápa	corn
𐒻𐓐𐓪𐓰𐓣	ilóežį	cat
𐓤𐓜𐓮𐓜	hkáwa	horse
𐓤𐓟	hkée	turtle
𐔀𐓣	míį	sun
𐔀𐓣𐓂𐓬𐓜	míįǫpa	moon
𐓇𐓘𐓤𐓜	níhka	man
𐓂𐓮𐓂	óohǫ	a cook
𐓬𐓜𐓐𐓂	paaxó	hill, mountain
𐓮𐓘𐔀𐓰𐓣	šímižį	girl
𐓮𐓘𐒼𐓪𐓰𐓣	šítožį	boy
𐓮𐓂𐓤𐓘	šǫ́ke	dog
𐓬𐓜	htáa	deer or meat
𐓺𐓘𐔂𐓘	céɣe	bucket, pail, kettle, pot
𐓺𐓜	hcée	buffalo
𐓜𐓬𐒼'𐓂	wak'ó	woman
𐓜𐓬𐒼𐓂𐓯𐓘	wakǫ́ze	teacher
𐓜𐓬𐓐𐓂𐓡𐓘	wanǫ́bre	dinner, a meal
𐓜𐓬𐓺𐓣	waachí	a dance
𐓜𐓬𐓇𐓂𐓬𐓪𐓬𐓡𐓘	waðíopxaðe	student
𐓜𐓬𐓇𐓂𐓬𐓪𐓬𐓜	waðíopxai	student (variant)
𐓜𐓬𐒻𐓯𐓂𐓤𐓘	wižǫ́ke	(my) daughter
𐓪𐓂𐓬𐓜	xúða	eagle
𐓯𐓣𐒼𐓜𐓯𐓣	žįkážį	child

Verbs

In Osage, verbs belong to different verb classes. We explain the most common classes, called a-ða and brush (br-šc), in chapter 5 and other verb classes in later chapters. In the vocabulary section, we include the verb class, in parentheses, with the APA form of each verb.

𐓮𐓣𐓡𐓜	hiiðá (br-šc)	swim, bathe
𐓣𐓘	íe (a-ða)	talk, speak
𐓇𐓘𐒼𐓘	náąke (a-ða)	run
𐓪𐓮𐓣𐓰	owísi (a-ða)	jump
𐓮𐓬𐒼𐓯𐓰	wakáaži (a-ða)	drive
𐓮𐓬𐓐𐓂𐓡𐓘	wanǫ́bre (a-ða)	dine
𐓮𐓬𐓺𐓣	waachí (a-ða)	dance
𐓮𐓬𐓡𐓂	waaðǫ́ (br-šc)	sing

Adjectives

𐓡𐓜𐓐𐓣	ðáalį	good

Other Words

Ẳ	áa̧	yes (used by women)
ᴧᴊÁ	a̧háį̧	yes (used by women)
ᴊẮƺᴧᴣᴒ	há̧a̧hkaži	no (used by both men and women)
ᴊẮÞᴧ ћɑ	há̧a̧pa ðe	today
ᴊᴧᴝɑ́	hawé	hello
ᴊő	hóo	yes (used by men)
ᴊoᴝɑ́	howé	yes (used by men)
ꜱᴒᴅó	sitóį̧	yesterday

Notes for Chapter 2

Some grammars use the term *noncontinuative* for *completive* and *continuative* for *continuous*, but we would like to use the terms that are most common in language studies.

Chapter 3

More about Sentences: Adding Objects and Adjectives

Oǩíȟna [ohkíhkie]

ǩíᴡnᴢn·: ÐᴀꜱńᴄᴀÐʎʎᴧ ʌꞓǩᴧ ᴈn oʌꞓn̆ ᴍnǩꞕᴀ́.

ʃóꜱᴧǩn oꞕʌꞓn̆ ᴌnǩꞕᴀ́?

ǩńᴅoᴢn·: ÞóǩᴧÐʎʎᴧ oʌꞓn̆ ᴍnǩꞕᴀ́.

ǩńᴡnᴢn·: ʎᴧᴢʎᴢᴀ ǫńᴀ.

ǩńᴅoᴢn·: ʎnǫǩń, ʎᴧᴢʎᴢᴀ ᴢʎᴢᴀ NAME ᴧǫń.

ǩńᴡnᴢn·: ʎᴧᴢʎᴢᴀ ᴢʎᴢᴀ NAME ᴧǫńᴀ.

šįmižį: htaasílee htąwą áška ci oálįį mįkšé
Girl: I live near Tulsa.

hówą́įki oðálįį nįkšé
Where are you from?

šítoži: hpǫ́hka htąwą oálįį mįkšé
Boy: I live in Ponca City.

šįmižį: wažáže brįe
Girl: I'm Osage.

šítoži: wiškí wažáže žaže NAME abrí
Boy: Me too, my Osage name is NAME.

šįmižį: wažáže žaže NAME abríe
Girl: My Osage name is NAME.

Many Osage people have both an English name and an Osage name. This is similar for the names of some older, important places. Well-known places like Tulsa often have a separate Osage name like ÐᴀꜱńᴄᴀÐʎʎᴧ [htaasílee htąwą], Deer Crossing Town.

Ńa ʎᴧǩńᴄᴧᴈᴀ [íe wahkílaace]

In this chapter, we will learn how to make bigger sentences. We will learn to add people, things, time expressions, and places to make more natural and complete sentences.

We will also learn how to add adjectives to nouns.

Adding an object

In chapter 2, we learned about the most basic elements of a sentence. These include subject markers (like ᐊᏓᎻᎧ [akxa] and ᎠᏅᎧ [apa]), aspect markers, and evidentials. Now we will add another important thing—an object. Consider the following sentence:

(1) ᏏᎳᏦᏝᎠ ᎠᏓᎻᎧ ᏃᏅᎲᎷᏃᎢ ᏏᏂ ᏙᏰᎳ ᎠᎠ.
     wakóze akxa žįkáži wį óhką pe
     The teacher helped a child.

In this sentence, the subject is ᏏᎳᏦᏝᎠ [wakóze] *the teacher*, and the object is ᏃᏅᎲᎷᏃᎢ ᏏᏂ [žįkáži wį] *a child*. Notice that the object ᏃᏅᎲᎷᏃᎢ ᏏᏂ [žįkáži wį] comes before the verb ᏙᏰᎳ [óhką] *help*. Remember from chapter 2 that ᎠᏓᎻᎧ [akxa] is the subject marker that means *the teacher* is present, and ᎠᎠ [pe] is an aspect marker that indicates that the helping action is complete. (There is no separate evidential marker because with ᎠᎠ [pe] the evidential marker is built in.). Finally, in the object, ᏃᏅᎲᎷᏃᎢ ᏏᏂ [žįkáži wį], the word ᏏᏂ [wį] means *a*.

By way of review, let's look at some other sentences with the different aspect and evidential markers that we studied in chapter 2.

(2) ᎢᎠᎳᏒᏃ **ᎠᎠᎳ** ᏖᏂᏍᏙ ᏙᏰᎳ ᎠᎠ.
     įhtáci **apa** ðiihǫ́ óhką pe
     My father helped your mother.

This sentence uses **ᎠᎠᎳ** [apa] as the subject marker to indicate that the subject is out of sight or is up and moving around. Literally, it says, "My father, who is at a distance or moving, completed the act of helping your mother."

(3) ᏏᏂᏑᎷᏂ **ᎠᎠᎳ** ᏖᏂᏃᏙᏆ ᏙᏰᎳ **ᎠᎠᎳ**.
     wihcími apa ðižǫ́ke óhką **apai**
     My aunt is helping your daughter.

This sentence uses **ᎠᎠᎳ** [apai] as the aspect marker to indicate that the action is ongoing. Literally, it says, "My aunt, somewhere out of sight, is continuing to help your daughter."

(4) ᏏᏂᏎᎠᏦᏂ **ᎠᎠᎳ** ᏖᏂᏃᏂᏆᎠ ᏙᏰᎳ **ᏎᎠ**.
     wįcéki apa ðižįke óhką **che**
     My uncle helped your son. (I have evidence for it.)

This sentence uses **ᏎᎠ** [che] as an evidential marker to indicate that the speaker has evidence that the action happened. Literally, it says, "My uncle, somewhere, helped your son, and I have direct evidence for it."

Here is a similar set of sentences with a subject (ᏃᏅᎧᎳ [níhka] *the man*) and an object (ᎠᎲ [htáa] *the deer*) and with various subject markers, aspect markers, and evidentials.

(5) 𐒻𐒼𐒰 𐒰𐒼𐒷𐒰 𐒰𐒽 𐒲'𐒰𐒻𐒰 **𐒹𐒰**.
níhka akxa htáa c'éða **pe**
The man killed the deer.

Sentence 5 literally means "The man who is present killed the deer." Remember from chapter 2 that when we use 𐒹𐒰 [pe], the final 𐒰 [e] of a preceding verb like 𐒲'𐒰𐒻𐒰 [c'éðe] changes to [a]; 𐒲'𐒰𐒻𐒰 𐒹𐒰 [c'éða pe].

(6) 𐒻𐒼𐒰 𐒰𐒹𐒰 𐒰𐒽 𐒲'𐒰𐒻𐒰 **𐒰𐒹𐒰**.
níhka apa htáa c'éðe **apai**
The man is killing the deer.
LITERALLY The man who is out of sight or moving is in the act of killing the deer.

(7) 𐒻𐒼𐒰 𐒰𐒼𐒷𐒰 𐒰𐒽 𐒲'𐒰𐒻𐒰 **𐒰𐒼𐒷𐒰**.
níhka akxa htáa c'éðe **akxai**
The man is killing the deer.
LITERALLY The man is present in one spot and killing the deer now.

(8) 𐒻𐒼𐒰 𐒰𐒼𐒷𐒰 𐒰𐒽 𐒲'𐒰𐒻𐒰 **𐒲𐒰**.
níhka akxa htáa c'éðe **che**
The man killed the deer. (I have evidence for it.)
LITERALLY The man who is present killed the deer, and I have evidence for this.

Adding adjectives to phrases

Another way to make longer and more descriptive phrases is by modifying a noun with an adjective (e.g., *white* cat, *big* man, *bad* dog). In Osage, we put the adjective after the noun, literally *cat white*, *man big*, *dog bad*. Examples 9–14 use the adjectives 𐒲𐒼𐒰 [ska] *white*, 𐒿𐒻𐒰 [lą́ąðe] *big*, 𐒹𐒻𐒾𐒻 [hpíiži] *bad*, 𐒽𐒲𐒰 [žúuce] *red*, 𐒾𐒻 [zi] *yellow*, 𐒹𐒻𐒿𐒻 [htóho] *blue*, and 𐒻𐒽𐒿𐒻 [dáalį] *good*. Notice how in each case, the adjective comes after the noun.

(9) 𐒻𐒿𐒻𐒾𐒻 𐒲𐒼𐒰
  ilǫ́eží ska
  white cat
(10) 𐒿𐒻𐒻𐒻 𐒾𐒻
  haxį́ zi
  yellow blanket
(11) 𐒿𐒻 𐒹𐒻𐒿𐒻
  ho htóho
  blue fish
(12) 𐒿𐒰𐒼'𐒻 𐒻𐒽𐒿𐒻
  wak'ó ðáalį
  good woman

Adding Objects and Adjectives

If a phrase like this (a *noun phrase*) is the subject of a sentence, the subject marker comes after the adjective.

(13) 𐒻𐓐𐒼𐒰 𐒰𐓏𐒰 𐓀𐒼𐓡𐓀 𐓏𐒰𐓓𐓂𐒼𐒰 𐓓𐓎𐓂𐒷 𐓂𐓡𐓀 𐓊𐒰.
níhka lą́ąde akxa wažįka žúuce íiða pe
The big man saw the red bird.

(14) 𐓡𐓂𐒼𐒰 𐓊𐓂𐓓𐓂 𐒰𐓊𐒰 𐓐𐓂 𐓊𐓂𐓐𐓂 𐓂𐓡𐓂𐓀𐒼𐒰 𐓊𐒰.
šǫ́ke hpíiži apa ho htóho oðį́įka pe
The bad dog caught the blue fish.

Adjectives as predicates

In most sentences, there is a subject and a predicate, and the predicate is usually a verb, such as *the buffalo runs*, where *runs* is the predicate. In English, many sentences have an adjective as the predicate of a sentence. For instance, *the man is good* or *my horse is black*. When we use an adjective as a predicate in English, we need to include some form of the verb *be* (like *is* or *was*). In Osage, adjectives that are the predicate of a sentence do not need *be*. Instead, we only need to use a subject marker (like 𐓀𐒼𐓡𐓀 [akxa]) and an aspect marker (like 𐓀𐒼𐓡𐓀 [akxa] or 𐓊𐒰 [pe]). By doing this, we can turn phrases like those in 9–14 into sentences, as shown below.

When we use adjectives as predicates, our choice of aspect marker can make a difference in meaning, as illustrated below. If we use the subject marker 𐓀𐒼𐓡𐓀 [akxa], we mean that the subject is present and stationary. Now, we may choose either the aspect marker 𐓀𐒼𐓡𐓀 / 𐓀𐒼𐓡𐓀 [akxa / akxai] or 𐓊𐒰 [pe]. If we choose 𐓀𐒼𐓡𐓀 / 𐓀𐒼𐓡𐓀 [akxa / akxai], we emphasize the state of the subject right then. If we choose 𐓊𐒰 [pe], we are more likely to be talking about a condition that is stable or permanent.

(15a) 𐓡𐓂𐒼𐒰 **𐓀𐒼𐓡𐓀** 𐓊𐓂𐓓𐓂 **𐓀𐒼𐓡𐓀**.
šǫ́ke **akxa** hpíiži **akxa**
The dog is bad.

In 15a, we mean that the dog is here right now and behaving badly.

(15b) 𐓡𐓂𐒼𐒰 **𐓀𐒼𐓡𐓀** 𐓊𐓂𐓓𐓂 **𐓊𐒰**.
šǫ́ke akxa hpíiži pe
The dog is bad.

In 15b, we mean that the dog is bad all the time; it is a bad dog.

(16a) 𐒻𐓐𐒼𐒰 **𐓀𐒼𐓡𐓀** 𐒰𐓏𐒰 **𐓀𐒼𐓡𐓀**.
níhka akxa lą́ąde akxa
The man is big.

In 16a, we mean the man is right here and we are commenting on his being big.

(16b) 𐓘𐓂𐓩𐓤𐓘 𐓘𐓤𐓯𐓘 𐓘𐓂𐓧𐓘 𐓷𐓘.
níhka **akxa** lą́ądа **pe**
The man is big.

In 16b, we are just saying he is a big man and that's a fact about him. Remember that before [pe], if the final vowel of the verb or adjective is [e], it becomes [a].

When we choose the subject marker ᐱᐯᐱ [apa], we mean the subject is moving, at a distance, or out of sight. When we use ᐱᐯᐱ [apa] for the subject marker, we will typically use the aspect marker ᐱᐯᐱ / ᐱᐯᐱ [apa / apai].

(16c) 𐓘𐓂𐓩𐓤𐓘 **ᐱᐯᐱ** 𐓘𐓂𐓧𐓘 **ᐱᐯᐱ**.
níhka **apa** lą́ąðe **apai**
The man is big.

In this case, we are saying that the man is not present or at a distance.

(17a) 𐓨𐓘𐓮𐓣𐓤𐓘 **𐓘𐓤𐓯𐓘** 𐓮𐓤𐓘 **𐓘𐓤𐓯𐓘**.
mąscíka **akxa** ska **akxa**
The rabbit is white.

The rabbit is here, and we are commenting on its being white.

(17b) 𐓨𐓘𐓮𐓣𐓤𐓘 **𐓘𐓤𐓯𐓘** 𐓮𐓤𐓘 **𐓷𐓘**.
mąscíka **akxa** ska **pe**
The rabbit is white.

We are saying that it is a white rabbit.

(17c) 𐓨𐓘𐓮𐓣𐓤𐓘 **ᐱᐯᐱ** 𐓮𐓤𐓘 **ᐱᐯᐱ**.
mąscíka **apa** ska **apai**
The rabbit is white.

The rabbit is out of sight, and it is white.
Examples 18–21 may all be interpreted the same way, as explained above.

(18) 𐓷𐓘𐓰𐓩𐓤𐓘 𐓘𐓤𐓯𐓘 𐓻𐓂𐓮𐓟 𐓘𐓤𐓯𐓘.
wažį́ka akxa žúuce akxa
The bird is red.
(19) 𐓄𐓘𐓯𐓣 𐓘𐓤𐓯𐓘 𐓻𐓣 𐓷𐓘.
haxį́ akxa zi pe
The blanket is yellow.

(20) 𐓏𐓘𐓤𐓘𐓧 𐓄𐓘𐓬𐓘 𐓑𐓘.
hó akxa htóho pe
The fish is blue.

(21) 𐓏𐓘𐓤'𐓘 𐓘𐓄𐓘 𐓬𐓘𐓧𐓲 𐓘𐓄𐓘𐓧.
wak'ó apa ðáalį apai
The woman is good.

Adding adverbs

Adverbs are words like 𐓧𐓴𐓻𐓲 [lúži] *slowly* that modify the meaning of verbs. In Osage, we put adverbs right before the verb.

(22) 𐓣𐓧𐓪𐓘𐓻𐓲 𐓒𐓤𐓘 𐓘𐓄𐓘 𐓧𐓴𐓻𐓲 𐓨𐓘𐓬𐓲 𐓘𐓄𐓘.
ilóežį ska apa lúži mąðį́ apai
The white cat was walking slowly.

𐓬𐓘 [ðe] *that*

We have learned that we do not have to use a special word for *the* in Osage. When we want to make a noun phrase more specific, we can use 𐓬𐓘 [ðe], which is most easily thought of as *that*. Osage does not have a separate word that means *this*, so 𐓬𐓘 [ðe] can also mean *this* in some contexts. The word 𐓬𐓘 [ðe] may appear either at the beginning of a noun phrase or at the end, right before the subject marker. This is shown in the examples below.

(23) **𐓬𐓘** 𐓏𐓘𐓮𐓘𐓄𐓘 𐓘𐓤𐓘𐓧 𐓮𐓘𐓄𐓘 𐓘𐓤𐓘𐓧.
ðe wasápe akxa sápe akxa
That bear is black.

(24) 𐓏𐓘𐓮𐓘𐓄𐓘 **𐓬𐓘** 𐓘𐓤𐓘𐓧 𐓮𐓘𐓄𐓘 𐓘𐓤𐓘𐓧.
wasápe **ðe** akxa sápe akxa
That bear is black.

(25) **𐓬𐓘** 𐓣𐓧𐓪𐓘𐓻𐓲 𐓑𐓲𐓻𐓲 𐓘𐓄𐓘 𐓵𐓘𐓤𐓘 𐓘𐓄𐓘.
ðe ilóežį hpíiži apa ną́ąke apai
That bad cat is running.

(26) 𐓣𐓧𐓪𐓘𐓻𐓲 𐓑𐓲𐓻𐓲 **𐓬𐓘** 𐓘𐓄𐓘 𐓵𐓘𐓤𐓘 𐓘𐓄𐓘.
ilóežį hpíiži **ðe** apa ną́ąke apai
That bad cat is running.

𐓣𐓤'𐓶𐓲𐓘 [ík'uce]

Exercise 1. Modifying nouns with adjectives

Here is a list of Osage nouns and another of adjectives. Make as many noun phrases as you can with the words on these lists. Make sure they make sense!

Example: őžu zí [óožu zí] *yellow bowl*

Nouns		Adjectives	
ʔã́	hcée	ħã́ʟɿ·	ðáalį
ꞩΛÞΛ	hápa	ÞÓꞩO	htóho
őžu	óožu	ʟΛžñ̈	lažį́į̃
ʔáψɑ	céɣe	ʒп	zi
пʟóɑʒп·	ilǫ́ežį̇	žń̈ʞΛ	žį́ka
ꞩóʞɑ	šǫ́ke	ꞩΛÞɑ	sápe
ń̈ÞυʞѫΛ	ípukxa	ꞩʞΛ	ska
ꞩΛžń̈ʞΛ	wažį́ka	ʒń̈žūʔɑ	žížuuce
		žūʔɑ	žúuce
		ʟñ̈ħɑ	lą́aðe
		ꞩΛꞩúꞩυ	wasúhu
		ꞩΛꞩúꞩυžп	wasúhuži

Exercise 2. Adjectives as predicates

Use the phrases you created with nouns and adjectives in exercise 1 to create sentences by adding a subject marker (like ΛʞѫΛ [akxa]) and an aspect marker (like ΛʞѫΛ [akxai] or Þɑ [pe]).
Example:

őžu zí [óožu zí] *yellow bowl* becomes
őžu **ΛʞѫΛ** zí **ΛʞѫΛ**. [óožu **akxa** zí **akxai**] *The bowl is yellow.*

Exercise 3. Sentence practice—adding objects

Replace the object noun, underlined, in the examples below with a different noun to make new sentences. Write out at least ten new sentences and choose words so that the new meanings make sense! Go to the vocabulary sections and the glossary to find nouns to use.

1. ʟń̈ʞΛ ΛʞѫΛ <u>пʟóɑʒп·</u> ń̈ħΛ Þɑ.
   nihka akxa <u>ilǫ́ežį̇</u> ííða pe
   The man saw <u>the cat</u>.
2. Ñ̈ʞó ΛÞΛ <u>őžu</u> ħūžá ΛÞɑ.
   iihkó apa <u>óožu</u> ðuužá apai
   (someone's) Grandmother is washing <u>the bowl</u>.

Exercise 4. Objects and adjectives

Start with the sentences you made in exercise 3, and modify the nouns with adjectives, like you did in exercise 1.

Ųa

Nouns

ᒐᓬᕀᐁ	haxí	blanket
ᒐo	ho	fish
ñƙó	iihkó	my (ALSO his/her) grandmother (any side)
ᑎᑓᐞᔑᑎ	įhtáci	(our) father
ᒣᐞᕁᕁñƙᐞ	mąšcíka	rabbit
ᒣᐞᕁᕁñƙᐞᔑᑎ	mąšcíkaží	bunny
óᔑU	óožu	bowl
ᑓᓬᕀƙ'ᐞ ñᐅUƙᕁᐞ	htanák'a ípukxa	paper napkin
ħñᒐó	ðiihó	your mother
ħᑎᔑñƙα	ðižíke	your son (any; general term)
ħᑎᔑóƙα	ðižóke	your daughter (any; general term)
ᑌᐞᔑñƙᐞ	wažíka	bird
ᑌᑎᒱñƙᑎ	wicéki	my uncle (mother's brother)
ᑌᑎᒱñᑉᑎ	wihcími	my aunt (father's sister; any)

Verbs

ñħα	íiðe (i-stem)	see, find
ƙᐞᔑñ	kaaží (a-ða)	drive (something, e.g., a car)
óƙᐞ	óhką (a-ða)	help
oħñƙα	oðíįke (br-šc)	catch, hug
ᒱ'áħα	c'éðe (ðe-causative)	kill
ħūᔑᐞ	ðuužá (br-šc)	wash (dishes, a car, etc.; not one's own)

Note, we explain the verb classes a-ða and brush in chapter 5, i-stem verbs in chapter 8, and ðe-causatives in chapter 19.

Adjectives

ᑭᐞᑕƙᐞ	bráaska	flat
ᑕñħα	lą́ąðe	big
ᑕᐞᔑñ	lažíį	thin, skinny, slender
oᑓᐞᔭᐞ	ohtáza	pretty, beautiful
ᑭñᔑᑎ	hpíiži	bad
ᑕᐞᑉα	sápe	black
ᑕƙᐞ	ska	white
ᑓóᒐo	htóho	blue
ᑕᐞᑕñᑕᑎ	wasísi	energetic, strong
ᑕᐞᑕúᒐU	wasúhu	clean

𐓷𐓘𐓺𐓶𐓧𐓶𐓻𐓣	wasúhuži	dirty
𐓷𐓘𐓯𐓜𐓺𐓘	wašóše	brave
𐓷𐓘𐓷𐓘𐓧𐓣	wáwalį	stingy
𐓺𐓣	zi	yellow
𐓺𐓣𐓻𐓶𐓷𐓘 𐓟𐓤𐓜	zížuuce éko̧	orange
𐓻𐓣𐓤𐓘	žįká (often žį)	small
𐓻𐓷𐓘	žúuce	red

Adverbs

| 𐓧𐓶𐓻𐓣 | lúži | slowly |

Other Words

| 𐓷𐓣 | wį | a |

Notes for Chapter 3

The dialog uses both [abrį́] and [abrį́e]. This raises the question, "What is the difference between [abrį́] and [abrį́e]?" The simplest answer is that women are more likely to use [abrį́e]. Men are more likely to use [abrį́].

There is a lot of variation in the pronunciation of Osage [a] and [o]. While many speakers use [žįkážį] for child, the form [žįkóžį] is also heard quite often.

Chapter 4

More about Sentences: Adding Time Expressions and Locations

𐓂𐓥𐓣́𐓥𐓣𐓟 [ohkíhkie]

𐒻𐓵𐓘́𐓲𐓟:	𐓷𐓣𐓻𐓣́͘𐓤𐓟! 𐓤𐓶𐓪́͘!	**iðáce:** wižį́ke kuǫ́ **Father:** Son! Come here!
𐒻𐓻𐓣͘𐓤𐓟:	𐓡𐓘𐓷𐓟́, 𐒻͘𐓱𐓘́𐓲𐓣. 𐓵𐓘́𐓘𐓧𐓣͘ 𐓵𐓘𐓝𐓣́ 𐓝𐓟.	**iži̧ke:** hawé įhtáci ðáali̧ ðachí che **Son:** Hello, Father. It's good you're here.
𐒻𐓵𐓘́𐓲𐓟:	𐓵𐓣𐓣𐓡𐓪́͘ 𐓝𐓣 𐓵𐓟?	**iðáce:** ðiihǫ́ chi ðe **Father:** Has your mother arrived?
𐒻𐓻𐓣͘𐓤𐓟:	𐓡𐓪𐓷𐓟́. 𐒻𐓣𐓩𐓘́͘ 𐓘𐓬𐓘 𐓝𐓣 𐓝𐓟.	**iži̧ke:** howé iiną́ apa chi che **Son:** Yes, Mother has arrived.
𐒻𐓵𐓘́𐓲𐓟:	𐓵𐓘́𐓘𐓧𐓣͘.	**iðáce:** ðáali̧ **Father:** Good.

For family or people you live with, you might greet them with a simple 𐓡𐓘𐓷𐓟́ [hawé] or 𐓡𐓪𐓷𐓟́ [howé]. They would typically respond with 𐓡𐓘𐓷𐓟́ [hawé] or 𐓡𐓪𐓷𐓟́ [howé].

𐒻́𐓟 𐓷𐓘𐓥𐓣́𐓧𐓘𐓘𐓲𐓟 [íe wahkílaace]

In this chapter, we will learn how to add expressions of time, locations, and destinations to make more natural and complete sentences.

Adding expressions of time

In chapter 2, we introduced time expressions like 𐓡𐓘́𐓘͘𐓬𐓘 𐓵𐓟 [há̧apa ðe] *today* and 𐓮𐓣𐓰𐓪́͘𐓣͘ [sitǫ́į] *yesterday*. In Osage, we almost always put time expressions like this at the beginning of the sentence. Here are some more sentences with time expressions.

(1) 𐒰𐓂𐓈𐓘 𐓄̣𐓘́ 𐓊𐓐𐓜𐓊 𐓊𐓏𐓎𐓊 𐓊𐓘.
  sitǫ́į hkée akxa hiiðá pe
  Yesterday, the turtle swam.

(2) 𐓊𐓎𐓊𐓐𐓘 𐓡𐓘 𐓎̣𐓊 𐓊𐓐𐓘 𐓂𐓏𐓎𐓊𐓂 𐒿𐓘.
  háapa ðe htáa apa owísi che
  Today, the deer jumped. (I have evidence that it did.)

(3) 𐓡𐓘𐓄𐓌́𐒿𐓘 𐓊𐓎́𐓄𐓊 𐓊𐓐𐓊 𐒻𐓎́𐓄𐓊 𒿱'𐓘́𐓎𐓘 𐓊𐓐𐓊.
  ðekǫ́ǫce níhka apa súhka c'éðe apai
  Now, the man is killing a chicken.

(4) 𐓊𐓎́𐒿𐓘 𐓄̣𐓎́𐓎𐓂𐓝𐓎 𐓊𐓐𐓊 𒿱𐓎́𐓊𐓘 𐓂́𐓄𐓊 𐓐𐓘.
  háace šímiži apa hcíle óhką pe
  Last night, the girl helped the family.

Note that many people will pronounce 𐓊𐓎́𒿱𐓘 [háace] as 𐓊𐓎́𒿱𐓂 [háaci], and we will use both forms in this book.

Adding a place: using the location words 𐓂𐓄𐓌́𐓎́ [įkší], 𒿱𐓂 [ci], 𐓄𐓂 [ki], 𐓄𐓌𐓂 [kši], 𐓄𐓌𐓎́𐓎𐓊𐓊𐓊 [kšíhtaha], and 𓌘́𐓎𐓊𐓊𐓊 [éhtaha]

When we want to add a place, like a location or destination, to an Osage sentence, we typically put it after the subject and before the verb. In sentence 5, the destination *to the pond* (𐓊𐓎̂𓌘𐓊𐓊 𐓂𐓄𐓌́𐓎́ [niitáahpa įkší]) comes after the subject (𐓊𐓎́𐓄𐓊 𐓊𐓐𐓊 [níhka apa]) and before the verb (𐓝𐓊𐓡𐓎̂ 𐓐𐓘 [mąðį́ pe]). We see this again in sentence 6, where the location (*toward the school*) comes before the verb and after the subject.

(5) 𐓊𐓎́𐓄𐓊 𐓊𐓐𐓊 **𐓊𐓎̂𓌘𐓊𐓊 𐓂𐓄𐓌́𐓎́** 𐓝𐓊𐓡𐓎̂ 𐓐𐓘.
  níhka apa **niitáahpa įkší** mąðį́ pe
  The man walked **to the pond**.

(6) 𐓊𐓎́𐓄𐓊̣𐓝𐓎 𐓊𐓐𐓊 **𐓊𐓎̂𐓐𐓂́𐓊𐓄𐓊𐓂 𓌘́𐓎𐓊𐓊𐓊** 𐓊𐓎́𐓄𐓊 𐓐𐓘.
  žįkážį aapa **taapóskahci éhtaha** ną́ąka pe
  The child ran **toward the school**.

If the sentence has both an object and a place, we can choose to put either the object or the place closest to the verb. In 7a the place, *in the forest* (𐓎̂𐓎̂ 𒿱𐓂 [žą́ą ci]), comes immediately before the verb (𒿱'𐓎́𐓊𐓊 𐓐𐓘 [c'éða pe]) and after the object (*the deer*). In 7b the object (𐓎̂𐓊 [htáa] *the deer*) appears closest to the verb. We see the same thing with *toward the river* in sentences 8a and 8b.

(7a) 𐓊𐓎́𐓄𐓊 𐓊𐓐𐓊𐓊 𐓎̂𐓊 **𐓎̂𐓎̂ 𒿱𐓂** 𒿱'𐓎́𐓊𐓊 𐓐𐓘.
  níhka akxa htáa **žą́ą ci** c'éða pe
  The man killed the deer **in the forest**.

(7b) 𐓊𐓎́𐓄𐓊 𐓊𐓐𐓊𐓊 **𐓎̂𐓎̂ 𒿱𐓂** 𐓎̂𐓊 𒿱'𐓎́𐓊𐓊 𐓐𐓘.
  níhka akxa **žą́ą ci** htáa c'éða pe
  The man killed the deer **in the forest**.

(8a) šímižį wahóśce akxa htaapé **níižuuce kšíhtaha** kį́įða pe
 šį́mįžį wahóśce akxa htaapé **níižuuce kšíhtaha** kį́įða pe
 The small girl threw the ball **toward the river**.

(8b) šímižį wahóśce akxa **níižuuce kšíhtaha** htaapé kį́įða pe
 šį́mįžį wahóśce akxa **níižuuce kšíhtaha** htaapé kį́įða pe
 The small girl threw the ball **toward the river**.

If a sentence also has a time expression, that will usually come at the beginning of the sentence.

(9a) **Sitói** šítožį akxa ho wį **niitáahpa ci** oðį́įka pe
 sitóį šítožį akxa ho wį **niitáahpa ci** oðį́įka pe
 Yesterday, the boy caught a fish **in the pond**.

In sentence 9b we changed the order of the object and the place, but the time expression stayed at the beginning of the sentence. Also note that in ho wį [ho wį] *a fish*, wį [wį] is the word for *a*.

(9b) **Sitói** šítožį akxa **niitáahpa ci** ho wį oðį́įka pe
 sitóį šítožį akxa **niitáahpa ci** ho wį oðį́įka pe
 Yesterday, the boy caught a fish **in the pond**.

When the shape of a place matters: ikší [ikší], ci [ci], ki [ki], kši [kši], kšíhtaha [kšíhtaha], and éhtaha [éhtaha]

As we learn words for location, we will need to pause to explain the different ways that Osage talks about places. The important difference between Osage and English is that in Osage we often use a different word depending on the shape of the location we are describing. One very important difference is with the words that mean *to*, *in*, and *toward*. The words ikší [ikší], kši [kši], ci [ci], and ki [ki] are used for *to*, but ikší [ikší] and ci [ci] are also used for *in*. The word éhtaha [éhtaha] is used for *toward*. Let's look at some sentences to examine this a bit more.

If we go to a place that is thought of as *round* or *sitting*, such as a pond, we use ikší [ikší].

(10) hkáwa apa niitáahpa **ikší** mąðį́ apai
 hkáwa apa niitáahpa **įkší** mąðį́ apai
 The horse walked to the pond.

If we go somewhere that is considered *spread out*, such as a town or a river, we use kši [kši].

(11) 𐓎𐓘𐓮𐓘 𐓘𐓄𐓘 𐓆𐓂𐓵𐓎𐓘𐓮𐓣 **𐓅𐓮𐓣** 𐓨𐓘𐓇𐓣́ 𐓘𐓄𐓘𐓣.
hkáwa apa níižuuce **kši** mąðį́ apai
The horse walked to the river.

If we go to something that is considered *vertical* and *singular*, such as a building, we use 𐓇𐓣 [ci].

(12) 𐓏𐓣𐓈𐓂́ 𐓎𐓘𐓮𐓘 𐓘𐓄𐓘 𐓇𐓣 **𐓇𐓣** 𐓨𐓘𐓇𐓣́ 𐓘𐓄𐓘𐓣.
sitǫ́į hkáwa apa hci **ci** mąðį́ apai
Yesterday, the horse walked to the house.

If we go to something or somewhere that is considered multiple or plural, we use 𐓎𐓣 [ki].

(13) 𐓮𐓘́𐓇𐓣 𐓷𐓣́𐓨𐓣𐓵𐓣 𐓘𐓄𐓘 𐓷𐓘𐓇𐓣́ **𐓎𐓣** 𐓨𐓘𐓇𐓣́ 𐓘𐓄𐓘𐓣.
hą́ąci šímįžį apa waachí **ki** mąðį́ apai
Last night, the girl walked to the dances.

Osage learners can become confused because 𐓇𐓣 [ci] is also used when an English speaker means *in*, as long as the object is vertical and singular.

(14) 𐓮𐓘́𐓇𐓘 𐓷𐓣́𐓨𐓣𐓵𐓣 𐓘𐓎𐓦𐓘 𐓇𐓣 **𐓇𐓣** 𐓵𐓣́𐓮𐓘 𐓄𐓘.
hą́ące šímįžį akxa hci **ci** žį́įha pe
Last night, the girl slept in the house.

Similarly, a round or sitting location still needs 𐓣𐓅𐓮𐓣́ [įkší] even if in English we would say *in*.

(15) 𐓉𐓣́𐓂𐓄𐓘 𐓷𐓂́𐓄𐓘́ 𐓮𐓘𐓮𐓣́𐓄𐓘 𐓷𐓣́𐓨𐓣𐓵𐓣 𐓘𐓄𐓘 𐓆𐓣𐓇𐓘́𐓄𐓘 **𐓣𐓅𐓮𐓣́** 𐓮𐓣𐓇𐓘́ 𐓘𐓄𐓘𐓣.
mį́įǫpa ðǫǫpá haašíhta šímįžį apa niitáahpa **įkší** hiiðá apai
Two months ago, the girl swam in the pond.

The meaning of ά𐓇𐓄𐓮𐓮 [éhtaha] is fairly well expressed by English *toward*.

(16) 𐓮𐓘́𐓄𐓘 𐓇𐓘́𐓵𐓣 𐓮𐓘𐓮𐓣́𐓄𐓘 𐓎𐓘𐓮𐓘 𐓘𐓄𐓘 𐓷𐓘𐓇𐓘́𐓂𐓄𐓘𐓇𐓣 **éhtaha** 𐓨𐓘𐓇𐓣́ 𐓘𐓄𐓘𐓣.
hą́ąpa ðáabrį haašíhta hkáwa apa wacúhtahci **éhtaha** mąðį́ apai
Three days ago, the horse walked toward the barn.

Finally, **𐓅𐓮𐓣́𐓇𐓄𐓮𐓮** [kšíhtaha] is very similar to ά𐓇𐓄𐓮𐓮 [éhtaha], but it is used when describing a location that is long like a river.

(17) 𐓎𐓘𐓮𐓘 𐓘𐓄𐓘 𐓆𐓂𐓵𐓎𐓘𐓮𐓣 **𐓅𐓮𐓣́𐓇𐓄𐓮𐓮** 𐓨𐓘𐓇𐓣́ 𐓘𐓄𐓘𐓣.
hkáwa apa níižuuce **kšíhtaha** mąðį́ apai
The horse walked toward the river.

We will discuss motion verbs like *come* or *go* in chapter 14.

Yes-no questions

Yes-no questions in Osage rely heavily on context. Often a yes-no question in completive aspect replaces ᴘα [pe] with the evidential marker ħα [ðe]. The subject marker is also often left out of questions.

(18) ქɔ́ო̃ŋ̊ʌϲα ᴧᴘᴧ ᴌ̃ʜ̃ᴋʌ ᴘα.
šǫ́mįhkase apa ną́ąka pe
The coyote ran.

(19) ქɔ́ო̃ŋ̊ʌϲα ᴌ̃ʜ̃ᴋα ħα?
šǫ́mįhkase ną́ąke ðe
Did the coyote run?

This can also be seen in the dialogue between a father and son that introduces this chapter.

(20) ħñ̃ᴊó̃ ᴤп ħα?
ðiihǫ́ chi ðe
Has your mother arrived?

(21) ᴊó̧ά. ñ̃ᴌ̃ḱ ᴧᴘᴧ ᴤп ᴤα.
howé iiną́ apa chi che
Yes, Mother has arrived.

The son's response shows that he doesn't actually see her, but he has evidence because he perhaps heard her. This is marked with the evidential marker ᴤα [che]. We also see the ᴤα [che] evidential when the son first says to his father, ħ̃ᴧᴄп ħᴧᴤń̃ ᴤα [ðáalį ðachí che], "It's good you are here."

If a yes-no question is in continuous aspect, speakers also usually omit the aspect marker. Compare the statement in 22, which has the aspect marker ᴧᴋ̊ʌᴧ [akxai], with the question in 23.

(22) ქɔ́ᴢп ᴧᴋ̊ʌᴧ ᴢñ̃ᴊα ᴧᴋ̊ʌᴧ.
šǫ́žį akxa žį́įhe akxai
The puppy is sleeping.

(23) ქɔ́ᴢп ᴧᴋ̊ʌᴧ ᴢñ̃ᴊα?
šǫ́žį akxa žį́įhe
Is the puppy sleeping?

If the context is clear, the full question can be shortened even more, as in 24, which also leaves out the subject marker. Sentence 25 is even shorter, with only a verb.

(24) ქɔ́ᴢп ᴢñ̃ᴊα?
šǫ́žį žį́įhe
Is the puppy sleeping?

(25) ᴢñ̃ᴊα?
žį́įhe
Is he asleep?
OR Is he sleeping?

Some speakers have begun to use a rising pitch in their intonation to mark a yes-no question, similar to what we do in English, but this is not part of traditional Osage grammar.

Numbers

Here are the numbers one through ten.

𐓏𐓣𐓬𐓰𐓘	wį́xce	one
𐓍𐓂𐓒𐓜	ðǫǫpá	two
𐓍𐓘́𐓬𐓪	ðáabrį	three
𐓈𐓘́𐓒𐓧	tóopa	four
𐓆𐓘́𐓑𐓧	sáhtą	five
𐓄𐓘́𐓒𐓘	šáhpe	six
𐓒𐓘́𐓍𐓂𐓒𐓧	hpéeðǫǫpa	seven
𐓣𐓬𐓘𐓈𐓂́𐓒𐓧	hkietóopa	eight
𐓬𐓘́𐓑𐓧 𐓜𐓘 𐓏𐓣́𐓸𐓘	lébrą hce wį́įke	nine (ten minus one)
𐓬𐓘́𐓑𐓧	lébrą	ten

When we get to eleven, we join numbers with 𐓘𐓬𐓂 [álįį] *place upon*, often pronounced as [álį] when used in counting. This gives us something like *one placed on ten* for eleven, *two placed on ten* for twelve, and so on.

𐓬𐓘́𐓑𐓧 𐓘𐓬𐓂 𐓏𐓣𐓬𐓰𐓘	lébrą álįį wį́xce	eleven
𐓬𐓘́𐓑𐓧 𐓘𐓬𐓂 𐓍𐓂𐓒𐓜	lébrą álįį ðǫǫpá	twelve
𐓬𐓘́𐓑𐓧 𐓘𐓬𐓂 𐓍𐓘́𐓬𐓪	lébrą álįį ðáabrį	thirteen
𐓬𐓘́𐓑𐓧 𐓘𐓬𐓂 𐓈𐓘́𐓒𐓧	lébrą álįį tóopa	fourteen
𐓬𐓘́𐓑𐓧 𐓘𐓬𐓂 𐓆𐓘́𐓑𐓧	lébrą álįį sáhtą	fifteen
𐓬𐓘́𐓑𐓧 𐓘𐓬𐓂 𐓄𐓘́𐓒𐓘	lébrą álįį šáhpe	sixteen
𐓬𐓘́𐓑𐓧 𐓘𐓬𐓂 𐓒𐓘́𐓍𐓂𐓒𐓧	lébrą álįį hpéeðǫǫpa	seventeen
𐓬𐓘́𐓑𐓧 𐓘𐓬𐓂 𐓣𐓬𐓘𐓈𐓂́𐓒𐓧	lébrą álįį hkietóopa	eighteen
𐓬𐓘́𐓑𐓧 𐓘𐓬𐓂 𐓬𐓘́𐓑𐓧 𐓜𐓘 𐓏𐓣́𐓸𐓘	lébrą álįį lébrą hce wį́įke	nineteen

When we get to twenty, thirty, forty, and so on, we say something like *ten-two, ten-three, ten-four*. To say *twenty-one*, we say 𐓬𐓘́𐓑𐓧 𐓍𐓂𐓒𐓜 𐓘𐓰𐓣́ 𐓏𐓣𐓬𐓰𐓘 [lébrą ðǫǫpá ecí wį́xce] *ten-two and one*.

𐓬𐓘́𐓑𐓧 𐓍𐓂𐓒𐓜	lébrą ðǫǫpá	twenty
𐓬𐓘́𐓑𐓧 𐓍𐓂𐓒𐓜 𐓘𐓰𐓣́ 𐓏𐓣𐓬𐓰𐓘	lébrą ðǫǫpá ecí wį́xce	twenty-one
𐓬𐓘́𐓑𐓧 𐓍𐓘́𐓬𐓪	lébrą ðáabrį	thirty
𐓬𐓘́𐓑𐓧 𐓈𐓘́𐓒𐓧	lébrą tóopa	forty
𐓬𐓘́𐓑𐓧 𐓆𐓘́𐓑𐓧	lébrą sáhtą	fifty
𐓬𐓘́𐓑𐓧 𐓄𐓘́𐓒𐓘	lébrą šáhpe	sixty
𐓬𐓘́𐓑𐓧 𐓒𐓘́𐓍𐓂𐓒𐓧	lébrą hpéeðǫǫpa	seventy
𐓬𐓘́𐓑𐓧 𐓣𐓬𐓘𐓈𐓂́𐓒𐓧	lébrą hkietóopa	eighty
𐓬𐓘́𐓑𐓧 𐓬𐓘́𐓑𐓧 𐓜𐓘 𐓏𐓣́𐓸𐓘	lébrą lébrą hce wį́įke	ninety

Íkʼuce [íkʼuce]

Exercise 1. Adding time expressions

Look at sentences 5–8 and 10–17. Rewrite each sentence by adding or changing one of the time expressions below.

1. háąpa ðe [hą́ąpa ðe] today
2. hą́ące [hą́ące] last night
3. sitǫ́į [sitǫ́į] yesterday
4. ðekǫ́ǫce [ðekǫ́ǫce] now
5. hą́ąpa ðáabrį haašíhta [hą́ąpa ðáabrį haašíhta] three days ago
6. mį́įopa ðǫǫpá haašíhta [mį́įopa ðǫǫpá haašíhta] two months ago
7. mį́įopa haašíhta [mį́įopa haašíhta] last month

Example using sentence 7a: sitǫ́į, níhka akxa htáa **žą́ą ci** cʼéða pe.
                          sitǫ́į níhka akxa htáa žą́ą ci cʼéða pe

Exercise 2. Sentence practice—adding locations

Add a location to the sentences listed below. Make sure the location makes sense.

Locations
niitáahpa įkší   niitáahpa įkší
níižuuce kšíhtaha   níižuuce kšíhtaha
žą́ą ci   žą́ą ci

1. iiną́ apa mąðį́ pe.
   iiną́ apa mąðį́ pe
2. wižǫke akxa xúða íiða pe.
   wižǫke akxa xúða íiða pe (remember that *íiðe* changes to *íiða* before *pe*)
3. iðáce apa hiiðá apai.
   iðáce apa hiiðá apai
4. wécʼa apa hiiðá apai.
   wécʼa apa hiiðá apai

Exercise 3. Making yes-no questions

Give the following sentences in English. Then, convert them into yes-no questions and read them out loud. You may use a rising intonation to form the question. The examples are all in completive aspect, so you will want to either delete pe [pe] or replace it with ðe [ðe]. Next, convert the sentences into continuous aspect. Since the continuous aspect marker is optional in questions like this, keep the aspect marker for half the sentences, and remove it for the other half. You may optionally use subject markers.

1. ᒡᗅᏃᗇ ᏻᏂᏢᏁᏃᏁ ᎠᏡᎮᎠ ᒡᏂᏮᎠ ᗞᗇ.
   háace šímiži akxa hiiðá pe
2. ᒡᗅᗞᎠ Ꮒᗇ ᏻᏅᏮᗇ ᎠᏡᎮᎠ ᏞᗅᏮᎠ ᗞᗇ.
   háapa ðe šóke akxa náaka pe
3. ᏚᏁᎠᏫ ᏒᎠᏮᏫᏃᗇ ᎠᗞᎠ ᏻᏂᎠᏫᏃᏁ ᏫᏮᎠ ᗞᗇ.
   sitóį wakóze apa šítoži óhką pe
4. ᏻᏂᏢᏁᏃᏁ ᎠᏡᎮᎠ ᏃᏅᏢᗇ ᎠᏡᎮᎠ.
   šímiži akxa žíįhe akxai

Exercise 4. Making food

Using the model below, replace the bolded adjectives and food words and make six new sentences.

ᏆᏞᏅ ᎠᏡᎮᎠ **ᗞᏅ ᏞᏁᏮᏫ** ᏮᏅᎯᎠ ᗞᗇ. **ᗞᏅ ᏞᏁᏮᏫ** ᎠᏡᎮᎠ ᏮᏅᏞᏁ.
iiną akxa **htáa likó** káaya pe. **htáa likó** akxa ðáali.
Mom made meat gravy. The meat gravy is good.

Exercise 5. Numbers 1–10

The numbers one through ten are listed below in the vocabulary. Practice counting to ten out loud. Note that the numbers for seven and nine have short forms that are often more common than the long forms. Note that if you want to say something like two dogs or three cats, you say the number second: ᏻᏅᏮᗇ ᏮᏫᗞᎠ [šóke ðǫǫpá] or ᏁᏞᏫᎠᏃᏁ ᏮᏅᎯᏁ [ilóeži ðáabri].

ńa

Nouns

ᏮᏅᏃᗇ	hkáace	apple or fruit
ᏮᏅᏃᗇᏞᏅ	hkáacenii	juice
ᎷᏅᒡᏁ	máahi	knife
ᎷᎠᏮᏅ	mąhká	medicine
ᎷᎠᏮᏅᗞᎠ	mąhkáhpa	pepper
ᎷᎠᏮᏅᏚᎠ	mąhkása	coffee
ᎷᏅᏃᗇ ᏃᏅᏮᗇ	máze hcúke	spoon (metal)
ᏞᏅᏚᏮᎠᗇ	níiskue	salt
ᏞᏅᏁᗞᎠᗞᎠ	niitáahpa	pond
ᏞᏅᏃᎠᗇ	níižuuce	river
ᏫᒡᏫᏃᏁ	oohóhci	kitchen
ᎷᏅᏃᗇᏫᒡᗡ	mázeooho	oven
ᏫᏞᏫᏮᗇ	ónobre	food

	paazénii	milk
	hpáata	eggs
	súhka	chicken
	šǫ́mįhkase	coyote, fox, wolf, canine
	šǫ́žį	puppy
	taapóska(hci)	school (building)
	tóoska	potato
	htáa lįkó	meat gravy
	htaaníi	soup
	htaacé	windy
	htóolą	sandwich
	htóožu	meat pie
	ce	lake
	cexéskažį	cup
	wahúhka	fork
	waléze	newspaper, book, printed material
	wasápe	bear
	wašį́	bacon or fat
	wacúhta	animal
	wacúhtahci	barn
	wéc'a	snake
	wéžeelą	skillet
	žą́ą	forest, woods
	žąąníi	sugar

Verbs

	káaɣe (strong-stem)	make
	kį́įðe (a-ða)	throw
	mąðį́ (br-šc)	walk
	oohǫ́ (a-ða)	bake, cook, prepare
	ðaaché (br-šc)	eat

Note, we will explain the a-ða and br-šc verb classes in chapter 5 and the strong-stem verb class in chapter 8.

Adjectives

	hpa	bitter
	taazíhi	browned, fried
	ðóðo	greasy
	wahóšce	small
	žéelą	fried

Location words

ᎴᏍᎦᎸ ᎿᏂ	áška ci	near
ᎥᎠᏂᎭᎸ	éhtaha	toward
ᏂᎦᏍᎾ	įkší	in, to; see chap. 4
ᎦᏂ	ki	in, to; see chap. 4
ᎦᏍᏂ	kši	in, to; see chap. 4
ᎦᏍᎾᎠᎸ	kšíhtaha	toward
ᏃᏂ	ci	in, to; see chap. 4

Other words

ᏐᎯᏔᏂᏛ ᎠᎰᏎ	háąmądį htáwą	Hominy (city in Oklahoma)
ᏐᎰᏅ ᏔᎰᏋᏛ ᏐᏞᏍᎾᎠ	háąpa ðáabrį haašíhta	three days ago
ᏐᎰᏃα	háące	last night
ᏐᎰᏃᏂ	háąci	last night (variant)
ᏐᎰᏔα	háąðe	tonight
ᎹᎾᎧᎸ ᏐᏞᏍᎾᎠ	míįopa haašíhta	last month
ᎹᎾᎧᎸ ᏔᎦᎰᏎ ᏐᏞᏍᎾᎠ	míįopa ðoopá haašíhta	two months ago
ᏌᏂᎠᎰ ᎦᎰᏛᎸ ᏃᏘ	sitóį kootáha ce	the day before yesterday
ᏔᎠᎦᎰᏃα	ðekǫǫce	now

Notes for Chapter 4

Even though there are two vowels, the pronunciation of the command ᎦᏌᏚ [kúǫ] (*come here!*) that appears in the ᎣᎦᏅᎦᏂα [ohkíhkie] is often pronounced like a single syllable, much more like [kjǫ́] or [kyǫ́] or sometimes even [kíǫ].

Chapter 5

Verb Classes and the Pronouns
I, You, He, She, and *It*

𐓂𐓤𐓣́𐓤𐓬𐓣𐓟 [ohkíhkie]

In this dialogue, two friends are talking on the phone about the weather and their plans.

A: 𐓴𐓘́𐓄𐓟 ð𐓘 𐓨𐓘́𐓶𐓟 𐓴𐓘́𐓤𐓪?   háapa ðe máaye háako
How's the weather today?

B: 𐓨𐓘́𐓠𐓯𐓘́ 𐓘𐓤𐓬𐓟.   máąšcé akxai
It's hot and sunny.

𐓎𐓟 𐓣𐓤𐓬𐓣́ 𐓬𐓴𐓘́ ð𐓟.   ce įkší brée hta
I'm going to the lake.

𐓴𐓘́𐓨𐓘𐓬𐓣𐓷 ð𐓘́𐓷𐓘 𐓨𐓘́𐓶𐓟 𐓴𐓘́𐓤𐓪?   háamąðį htáwą máaye háako
How's the weather in Hominy?

A: 𐓵𐓣́ʼ𐓶, ð𐓘́𐓎𐓘́ 𐓘𐓤𐓬𐓟.   níižu htaacé akxai
It's raining and (it's) windy.

𐓷𐓘𐓷𐓘́𐓤𐓟 𐓷𐓣 𐓬𐓴𐓘́𐓎𐓟 ð𐓟 𐓨𐓣𐓤𐓬𐓘́.   waléze wį bráace hta mįkšé
I'm going to read a book.

B: 𐓷𐓘𐓷𐓘́𐓤𐓟 ð𐓣́𐓎𐓪!   waléze ðížo
Enjoy the book!

A: 𐓎𐓟 ð𐓣́𐓎𐓪!   ce ðížo
Enjoy the lake!

𐓣́𐓟 𐓷𐓘𐓤𐓬𐓣́𐓞𐓘𐓎𐓟 [íe wahkílaace]

In this chapter, we will learn about subject *pronouns*, words like *I, you, he, she,* and *it*. In Osage, the pronoun appears with the verb, sometimes *inside* the verb. Even though this works very differently from English, we will call these forms *pronouns*. As we learn how pronouns and verbs work together, we will learn about different *classes of verbs* such as the br-šc class and a-ða class. This will help us make more natural and useful sentences.

There are so many details about how pronouns and verb classes work in Osage that we can only start to introduce them in this chapter. For now, we will limit our focus to a small list of pronouns (*I*, *you*, *he*, *she*, and *it*) and a small set of verbs. The Osage pronouns we study in this chapter will all be singular. We will learn about the plural subject pronouns in chapter 7. All the verbs here will be active/doer verbs like *dance, jump, sing, run*. Some of them will have objects (look back to chapter 3 to recall what these are). We will learn about other verbs and verb classes in later chapters.

The third-person singular subjects: *he, she,* and *it*

To say a third-person subject like *he*, *she*, or *it* in Osage, we typically don't need to say anything at all. Instead, just using the basic form of the verb and an aspect marker will tell us that the subject is third-person. The context of the sentence lets us figure out if the subject is *he*, *she*, or *it*. For example, 𐒴𐓈𐒷𐓆 [waachí] is the basic dictionary form for the verb *dance*, and 𐒴𐓈𐒷𐓆 [waachí] can mean either *he dances*, *she dances*, or *it dances*. If needed, Osage does have emphatic pronouns, and we will examine these in chapter 13.

To see how this works, let's look at a few examples. Sentence 1a has a named subject, *that woman*, which acts as the context for 1b. Because of the context, we know that the subject of 1b is *she*. Again, we don't need a special word to say *she*. Instead, we just need a basic verb such as 𐒴𐓎𐓌𐒼 [waaðǫ́] and an aspect marker such as 𐓈𐓘𐒼 [akxai].

(1a) 𐒴𐓈𐒼'𐒼 𐓍𐓘 𐓈𐓅𐓈 𐒴𐓎𐒷𐓆 𐓈𐓅𐓈.
waxʼó ðe apa waachí apai
That woman is dancing.

(1b) 𐓍𐓘𐒼𐒼𐓆𐓘 𐒴𐓎𐓌𐒼 𐓈𐓘𐒼.
ðekǫ́ǫce waaðǫ́ akxai
Now *she* is singing.

In 2a, we are talking about a deer, so we do not need to name it again in 2b. We just need the basic verb and an aspect marker.

(2a) 𐒼𐓂𐓊𐒼 𐒼𐓆 𐓈𐓘𐒼 𐓊𐒴𐓆𐓂 𐓊𐓘.
sitǫ́į htáa akxa owísi pe
Yesterday the deer jumped.

(2b) 𐒻𐓆𐓅𐓈 𐓍𐓘 𐒾𐓆𐓘 𐓊𐓘.
háąpa ðe ną́ąka pe
Today *it* ran.

If we do not know what the context is for a sentence, then the subject can be interpreted as either *he*, *she*, or *it*.

(3) 𐒴𐓅𐒷𐓆 𐓈𐓅𐓈.
waachí apai
He or she (possibly it) is dancing.

Notice that we use aspect markers such as ᵽa [pe], ᴧᵽᴧ [apai], and ᴧʞʌᴧ [akxai] whether we name our subject, as we do in sentences 1a (ꜱᴧʞ'ó [wak'ó]) and 2a (ᵽʌ́ [htáa]), or not, as in sentences 1b, 2b, and 3.

In sum, to make a sentence using the subject pronouns *he*, *she*, or *it* in Osage, we simply need the basic verb and an aspect marker. The next section discusses how to use *I* and *you* in Osage.

The pronouns *I* and *you*

Before we can talk about how to say *you* and *I* in Osage, we have to learn about three things: Osage verb classes, the Osage pronouns for *I* and *you*, and more about how aspect is understood.

Let's start with verb classes. Osage verbs, like those of many other languages, are divided into different classes. Each class requires a different way to pronounce the verbs when the subject is *I* or when it is *you*. The two most common verb classes are called the **a-ða class** and the **br-šc class**. These classes take their names from the sounds found in the first- and second-person pronouns. We will learn about these two verb classes in this chapter.

Knowing the verb class will let us know which Osage pronouns to use and where to put them in the verb. For the **a-ða** class, we use **a** for *I* and **ða** for *you* (which is why it is called the **a-ða** class). For the **br-šc** class, we use **br** for *I* and **šc** for *you*. Most teachers we know call this the **brush** class to make it easy to pronounce and remember, and we will often do so too. The sections below explain more about where to put the pronouns into the verbs.

Finally, as with all Osage sentences, we need to consider how aspect works. In this chapter, we will focus on the completive aspect because it is simpler. We will discuss other aspects in later chapters.

The a-ða verb class

The **a-ða class** is one of the two most common verb classes in Osage. We will start by looking at two common verbs: ᴢʌ́ʞa [náąke] *run* and zʌ̃́ʃa [žį́įhe] *sleep*.

The first-person Osage pronoun ʌ [a]

In the a-ða class, the Osage pronoun that means *I* is ʌ [a]. In the examples below, ʌ [a] is prefixed or placed before the verbs ᴢʌ́ʞa [náąke] and zʌ̃́ʃa [žį́įhe] (giving us ʌᴢʌ́ʞa [anáąke] and ʌzʌ̃́ʃa [ažį́įhe]). We will learn some slightly different rules for verbs that begin with **o** [o] or ꜱᴧ [wa] below.

(4) ꜱnᵽó ʌᴢʌ́ʞa.
    sitóį **aná**ąke
    Yesterday **I** ran.

(5) ʃʌ́ᵽa ʌzʌ̃́ʃa.
    háące **aží**įhe
    Last night **I** slept.

Recall from chapter 2 that completive aspect, marked with ᏢᎪ [pe], told us that an action is finished or completed. However, notice that ᏢᎪ [pe] is not included in these sentences. This is because when we use first- and second-person pronouns the completive aspect is assumed and does not need to be included. In other words, with *I* and *you* sentences, leaving off ᏢᎪ [pe] means the sentence is completive.

The second-person Osage pronoun ᏂᏞ [ða]

To say *you*, we use the Osage pronoun ᏂᏞ [ða]. Using the same examples from above with *you*, notice that the second-person pronoun ᏂᏞ [ða] is again prefixed to the verb.

(6) ᏚᏂᎠᎾ́ ᏂᏞᏃᏁ́ᏦᎪ.
sitǫ́i **ða**ną́ąke
Yesterday **you** ran.

(7) ᎫЯ́ᏢᎪ ᏂᏞᏃЯ́ᏚᎪ.
hą́ące **ða**žį́įhe
Last night **you** slept.

The br-šc "brush" verb class

A second important verb class is the br-šc class, again, named for the first- and second-person subject pronouns ʀ [br] and ɞᏈ [šc]. The teachers we know all call this class the brush class, and we will do the same.

The first-person Osage pronoun ʀ [br]

In the brush class the first-person pronoun *I* is ʀ [br]. All verbs in the brush class have the sound Ꮈ [ð] in them. To make the first-person, the ʀ [br] replaces the sound Ꮈ [ð]. For example, ᛗᏞᎻɴ́ [mąðį́] becomes ᛗᏞʀɴ́ [mąbrį́] and ᏂᏌᏏɴ́ [ðuwį́] becomes ʀᏌᏏɴ [brúwį]. Since the Ꮈ [ð] sound often occurs inside brush verbs, this means that the Osage pronoun ʀ [br] is frequently *infixed*, or placed inside the verb.

(8) Ꮮɴ́ᏃᏌᏢᎪ ᛕɞɴ ᛗᏞʀɴ́.
níižuuce kši mą**br**į́ (from the verb mąðį́)
I walked to the river.

(9) ᎫЯ́ᏢᎪ ᏏЯ̄ʀɴ́.
hą́ące waa**br**ǫ́ (from the verb waaðǫ́)
I sang last night.

(10) ᏚᏂᎠᎾ́ ᛗᏞᛒ́ᏚᏞ ʀᏌᏏɴ.
sitǫ́į mąhkása **br**úwį (from the verb ðuwį́)
Yesterday **I** bought coffee.

The second-person Osage pronoun 𐒰𐒷 [šc] or 𐒰𐒠 [št]

In the brush class, there are two forms of the pronoun that means *you*. The one we use depends on the sound of the vowel that follows it. If the following vowel is [o] or [a], we will use 𐒰𐒠 [št]. If it is anything else ([e], [i], or [u]), it will be 𐒰𐒷 [šc]. As with 𐒰 [br] above, 𐒰𐒷 [šc] and 𐒰𐒠 [št] replace the sound 𐒰 [ð] in all the verbs. Again, this means that the Osage forms 𐒰𐒷 [šc] or 𐒰𐒠 [št] are frequently infixed, or placed inside the verb. Many speakers also pronounce 𐒰𐒷 [šc] as 𐒰𐒺 [šč].

(11) 𐓆𐓆𐓆𐓆𐓆 𐓆𐓆𐓆 𐓆𐓆𐓆𐒷𐓆.
 níižuuce kši mą**šcį**
 You walked to the river.
(12) 𐓆𐓆𐓆𐓆 𐓆𐓆𐒰𐒠𐓆.
 hą́ące waa**štǫ́**
 You sang last night.
(13) 𐓆𐓆𐓆 𐓆𐓆𐓆𐓆𐓆 𐒰𐒷𐓆𐓆𐓆.
 sitǫ́į mąhkása **šcúwį**
 Yesterday **you** bought coffee.

Remember that with *I* and *you* sentences, leaving off the aspect marker means the sentence is completive.

Third-person subjects: *he*, *she*, or *it*

Here are two sentences with a-ða and brush verbs in third-person. Because they are in third-person, they don't need a pronoun, but they do need an aspect marker such as 𐓆𐓆 [pe]. Compare 14 and 15 with the *I* and *you* sentences 4–13 above.

(14) 𐓆𐓆𐓆 𐓆𐓆𐓆𐓆 𐓆𐓆.
 sitǫ́į ną́ąka **pe**
 Yesterday he (or she) ran.
(15) 𐓆𐓆𐓆𐓆 𐓆𐓆𐓆𐓆 𐓆𐓆.
 hą́ące waaðǫ́ **pe**
 He (or she) sang last night.

A quick summary

Let's make a quick summary of what we have just learned.
 First, Osage has verb classes that use different sounds to say the pronouns *I* and *you*.
 Second, the a-ða verb class has the pronouns 𐓆 [a] for *I* and 𐓆𐓆 [ða] for *you*.
 Third, the brush verb class has the pronouns 𐓆 [br] for *I* and 𐒰𐒷 [šc] or 𐒰𐒠 [št] for *you*.
 Last, the completive aspect is unmarked when using first- and second-person singular pronouns. In other words, we leave 𐓆𐓆 [pe] out of the sentence when using the Osage pronouns *I* and *you*.

The special cases of 𐒻𐓇 [wa] and 𐓂 [o] verbs in the a-ða verb class

Osage very often has variations in the place where pronouns appear. Some of these are regular enough that we can group them together. We will look at verbs that begin with [wa] and with [o] below.

Another change that will sometimes happen is that the accent on a word will shift from its original syllable to another one. When that happens, we will mark it as in 16 and 20 below.

Verbs that begin with 𐒻𐓇 [wa]

Many Osage verbs in the a-ða group begin with the syllable 𐒻𐓇 [wa]. In most of these cases, we need to move the second-person pronoun 𐓭𐓇 [ða] to the syllable following the 𐒻𐓇 [wa]—we need to flip their positions (𐒻𐓇𐓘𐓻𐓘𐓒𐓂 [wakáaži] becomes 𐒻𐓇𐓭𐓘𐓻𐓘𐓒𐓂 [waðákaaži]). In other words, we need to infix 𐓭𐓇 [ða] after the first syllable 𐒻𐓇 [wa]. The 𐓇 [a] first-person marker remains prefixed to the beginning of the verb.

(16) 𐒻𐒰𐓀𐓍 𐓭𐒶 𐒰𐒻𐓇𐓘𐓻𐓘𐓒𐓂.
háapa ðe **á**wakaaži
I drove today.

(17) 𐒻𐒰𐓀𐓍 𐓭𐒶 𐒻𐓇𐓭𐓘𐓻𐓘𐓒𐓂.
háapa ðe wa**ð**ákaaži
You drove today.

(18) 𐒻𐒰𐓛𐒶 𐒰𐒻𐓇𐓀𐓒𐓆𐒶.
háace **á**wanǫbre
Last night **I** dined (ate a meal).

(19) 𐒻𐒰𐓛𐒶 𐒻𐓇𐓭𐓘𐓒𐓆𐒶.
háace wa**ð**ánǫbre
Last night **you** dined.

(20) 𐓟𐓂𐒰𐒻𐓇𐓘𐓛𐓂.
sitóį **a**wáachi
Yesterday **I** danced.

(21) 𐓟𐓂𐒰 𐒻𐓇𐓭𐓘𐓛𐓂.
sitóį wa**ð**áachi
Yesterday **you** danced.

Verbs that begin with 𐓂 [o]

Some Osage verbs in the a-ða group begin with 𐓂 [o]. In many of these cases, 𐓇 [a] and 𐓭𐓇 [ða] are both placed after 𐓂 [o]; 𐓂𐓻𐓇 [óhką] becomes 𐓂𐒰𐓻𐓇 [oáhką] for *I* and 𐓂𐓭𐓻𐓇 [oðáhką] for *you*.

(22) 𐓣𐓻𐓂 𐒻𐓻𐓘𐒻 𐒻𐓂𐒰𐓀𐒶𐓒𐓂 **ó𐓻𐓇** 𐒴𐒶.
iihkó akxa wihtáeží **óhką** pe
My grandmother helped my little sister.

(23) ᔑᏁᎠᏞᎠᏃᏁ ᎣᏞᏥᏞ.
wihtáežį oáhką
I helped my little sister.

(24) ᏂᏁᎠᏞᎠᏃᏁ ᎣᏂᏞᏥᏞ.
ðihtáežį oðáhką
You helped your little sister.

Note that in the words for *little sister*, many speakers pronounce the ᏞᎠ [áe] combination as ᎷᎢ [ái]; ᔑᏁᎠᏃᏁ [wihtáižį]. Some others say ᎷᎢ [é]; ᔑᏁᎠᏃᏁ [wihtéžį].

(25) ᎫᎷᎬᎡ ᔑᎷᏂᎢᏌᎢᎠᎡ ᎣᏞᎬᎡ.
háące wéðušupe oáce
Last night **I** looked for the keys.

(26) ᎫᎷᎢᏞ ᏂᎡ ᔑᎷᏂᎢᏌᎢᎠᎡ ᎣᏂᏞᎬᎡ.
háąpa ðe wéðušupe oðáce
Today, **you** looked for the keys.

Notice that in 22–26, the verbs all take objects (ᔑᏁᎠᏞᎠᏃᏁ [wihtáežį] *my little sister*, ᏂᏁᎠᏞᎠᏃᏁ [ðihtáežį] *your little sister*, and ᔑᎷᏂᎢᏌᎢᎠᎡ [wéðušupe] *keys*). Even when we use Osage pronouns, an object will appear in its usual place before the verb. This can be seen in sentences 10 and 13 as well.

The special cases of verbs that are in more than one class

There are some verbs, like ᎫᏂᏂᏞ [hiiðá] *swim*, that belong to both the a-ða and the brush verb class. Verbs like this use the pronouns for both classes at the same time. For example, *I swim* is ᏞᎫᏂᏥᏞ [ahíibra] with the [a] from the a-ða class and the [br] from the brush class. Similarly, *you swim* is ᏂᎫᏂᏥᎠᏞ [ðahíišta]. This is a topic that will come up again in later chapters.

ᎢᏥ'ᎤᎬᎡ [ík'uce]

Exercise 1. How do you say this?

Give the English meaning of these sentences. There may be more than one way to correctly say them.

1. ᏏᏁᎠᎥ ᎢᎢᎷ ᏞᏥᏂᏞ ᔑᏞᏥᎢ ᏂᎤᔑᎢ ᎠᎡ.
   sitǫ́į iiną akxa wašį́ ðuwį́ pe
2. ᎬᎢᏦ ᏞᏥᏂᏞ ᏞᎢᏃᎤᎬᎡ ᏥᏂ ᔑᏞᏥᎷᏃᏁ ᎠᎡ.
   hcíko akxa níižuuce kši wakáaži pe
3. ᎫᎷᎢᏞ ᏂᎡ ᎠᎷᏉᎢᏤᏥᎬᎡ ᎷᎠᏞᎫ ᎷᏞᏥᎢ.
   háąpa ðe taapóskahci éhtaha mąbrį́
4. ᎫᎷᎬᏁ ᏞᔑᎷᎬᏁ
   háąci awáachi

5. ᏅᎠᎼ ᎤᏍᎼᎡᏂ ᎫᏂ ᎪᏍᎪᏗᎡᏆ.
   sitǫ́į oohǫ́hci ci áwanǫbre
6. ᏃᏂᏋᎪᏀᏐ ᏂᎳᏓᎢ ᏓᏋᏂᎪ ᎤᏍᏂᏓ ᏉᏆ.
   žįkázį ðáalį akxa owísi pe
7. ᎠᏂᎸᎡᏂ ᎫᏂ ᎫᏂ ᏂᎪᏃᏁᎠᎠ.
   hą́aci hci ci ðažį́įhe
8. ᏍᎳᏋ'ᎣᏃ ᎣᎠᎪᏃᎪ ᏓᏋᏂᎪ ᎤᏍᎼᎡᏂ ᎫᏂ ᏍᎪᏂᎼᎣ ᏉᏆ.
   wak'ó ohtáza akxa oohǫ́hci ci waaðǫ́ pe
9. ᏋᎪᏍᎪ ᏋᎣᎠᎢ ᏍᎤᎵ ᎣᏋᎪ ᏉᏆ.
   hkáwa šį́htąą wį óhką pe
10. ᎪᏂᎠᎪᏉᎪ ᎪᎠᏂᎠ ᎤᏋᎣᎢ ᎪᎠᎤᏋᎳ.
    niitáahpa lą́ąðe įkší ahíibra
11. ᏃᏂᏋᎠᏀᏐ ᎪᎠᏀᎢᏯ ᏍᎵᎳ ᎣᏂᎠᏋᎪ.
    žįkážį lažį́į wį oðáhką
12. ᏃᎠᏯ ᏋᎣᎢ ᎪᏍᎳᏋᎠᏀᏐ.
    žą́ą kši áwakaaži
13. ᏅᎠᎼ ᎠᎠᏉᎤᏍᏋᎳᎡᏂ ᎫᏂ ᏍᎳᎠᏋᎳᎪᏀᏐ.
    sitǫ́į taapóskahci ci waðákaaži

Exercise 2. Practicing a-ða and brush verbs

Use the list of a-ða and brush verbs below. For each verb, list the basic verb and then put the pronouns for *I*, *you*, and *he/she/it* where they belong. Be sure to pay attention to the a-ða verbs beginning with ᏍᎳ and Ꭳ. Example:

ᎪᎠᏋᎪ [nąą́ke] run
    ᎳᎪᎠᏋᎪ   anąą́ke   I...
    ᏂᎳᎪᎠᏋᎪ   ðanąą́ke   you...
    ᎪᎠᏋᎪ   nąą́ke   he, she, or it...

Some a-ða verbs:			Some brush verbs:		
ᎪᎠᏋᎪ	nąą́ke	run	ᎠᏂᏂᎳ	hiiðá	swim, bathe
ᏍᎪᎡᏂ	waachí	dance	ᏂᎤᏍᏂ	ðuwį́	buy
ᎣᏋᎳ	óhką	help	ᏍᎪᏂᎼ	waaðǫ́	sing
ᏃᏁᎠᎠ	žį́įhe	sleep	ᏃᎳᏂᏁ	mąðį́	walk
ᏍᎪᏉᏋ	wanǫ́bre	eat, dine	ᏂᎳᎡᎠ	ðaaché	eat
ᎣᏍᏂᎪ	owísi	jump	ᏂᏁᎠᎠ	ðiištą́	be finished
ᏍᎪᏋᎪᏀᏐ	wakáaži	drive	ᏂᏁᎠᏉᎠ	ðiišúpe	unlock, open
ᎣᎡᎠ	océ	look for			

Exercise 3. Adding Locations and time expressions

Look at the list of words that you made in exercise 2. Choose ten of the *I* or *you* examples and use them to make ten sentences, where each sentence includes a place. Look at previous chapters to review some ways to add objects, adjectives, locations, and time expressions to sentences. Here is an example using ᏞᏞᏁ̋ᎦᎠ:

ᏚᎾ̋ᏃᎠ ᏃᎾ̋ ᏫᏍᏁ ᏞᏞᏁ̋ᎦᎠ.
háące žą́ą kši **a**ną́ąke
Last night **I** ran to the woods.

ńa

Nouns

ᏚᎾ̃ᏚᏫ̨Ꮮ	haaská	shirt
ᎠᎾ̄ᏰᎠ̋	htaapé	ball
Ꮓᾱ́	hcí	house
ᏏᎾᏰᏞᎠᏃᏁ̇	ðihtáežį	your little sister
ᏎᎠ̋ᏦᏁᏞᏁ̇	wéhkilį	traditional clothes
ᏎᎠ́ᏏᏌᏦᏌᏰᎠ	wéðušupe	keys
ᏎᏁᏰᏞᎠᏃᏁ̇	wihtáežį	my little sister

Verbs

ᒼᏞᏏᏁ̋	mąðį́ (br-šc)	walk
ᎣᏦᏁ̋ᏰᏞᏚᏞ	okíhpaahą (a-ða)	dress oneself
ᎣᏃᎠ̋	océ (a-ða)	look for, search for, hunt
ᏏᏁ̄ᏌᏰᏞ	ðiištá (br-šc)	be finished
ᏏᏌᏎ̋	ðuwį́ (br-šc)	buy
ᏃᏁ̋ᏚᎠ	žį́įhe (a-ða)	sleep

Adjectives

ᏣᏍ̋ᏰᏞ	čóopa	small amount, few (also a noun)
ᏌᏁ̋ᏰᏁ̄	šį́htąą	fat (chubby)
ᏃᎠ́ᏦᏞ	hcéka	new, fresh

Notes for Chapter 5

In this chapter, we have used the word *pronouns* for the bound affixes that are pronominals in Osage. We have done this for pedagogical reasons.

In our book we use the terms *a-ða* and *brush* to name the two most common verb classes. These terms come from classroom teachers we worked with, and we find them very useful.

Chapter 6

Continuous Aspect, Singular Pronouns, and the Verb ᏂᏅ [ðį]

ᎣᏫᏂᏫᎾ [ohkíhkie]

ᏂᏚᏏ:	ᏇᏞᏐᎥᎠᏁ!	**iihǫ́:** paahą́pi
		Mother: Everyone get up!
	ᏚᎴᏨᏏ ᏇᎮᎠᎴ ᏃᏤᎠ ᎤᎭᏏᎴ ᎴᎠᏫᎴᏏᎭ.	waší hpáata žóle ooáhą ątxąhé
		I am about to cook bacon and eggs.
	ᎹᎴᏫᎥᏏᎴ ᎠᎠ ᏫᎸᏫᎴ.	mąhkása tóe káaɣa
		Make some coffee.
ᏁᏂᎸᏚᎠ:	ᏏᎣᏎᎥ, ᏚᎠᏚᎤᎠ ᎠᎴᏉᎥᏏᏁ ᏇᎸᏫᎠ ᏍᏫᏁ.	**iðáce:** howé wacúe tazíhi hpáaxe ški
		Father: I'll make some toast also.
	ᎣᏂᎸᏫᎠ ᏚᎴᏨᎠᏐ ᎴᏫᎤ ᎹᎴᏂᎥ.	óðake waléze akú mąðį́
		Go get the newspaper.
ᏁᎴᏐᏇᎴ:	ᏚᎥᎠ, ᎥᏫᏁᎹᏐ.	**ilǫ́ǫhpa:** wíe ékimǫ
		Eldest son: I will do it.
ᏂᏚᏏ:	ᎤᏚᏅ ᏂᏅᏫᏚᎥ́.	**iihǫ́:** óohǫ ðiištą́
		Mother: The cooking is finished.
	ᏂᎠᏉᎠᎠ ᎥᏚᎴᏐᏉᎠ ᏇᎠ!	ðekǫ́ǫce ą́wanǫbre htai
		Let's eat now!

The eldest son has a special name, ᏁᎴᏐᏇᎴ [ilǫ́ǫhpa]. This is true for many other members of the family as well. We discuss this more in chapter 11.

ᎢᎠ ᏚᎴᏫᏂᎴᏃᎠ [íe wahkílaace]

In chapter 5, we learned how to use the pronouns for *I*, *you*, and *he*, *she*, and *it*. We learned two verb classes, a-ða and brush. And we learned how to use completive aspect when using these pronouns. In this chapter, we will learn how to use these pronouns when we need continuous aspect. Recall that we use continuous aspect when an action is ongoing rather than complete. We will also learn how to use ᏂᏒ [ðį] *be*.

To review, we have already used continuous aspect in previous chapters—for example, ᖉᴀ́ ᴧᴘᴧ ᘋᏇᏫᎠ ᴧᴘᴧ [hcée apa ną́ake apai] *the buffalo is running*. We used ᴧᴘᴧ [apai] or ᴧᴘᴧ [apa] when a subject was out of sight or moving from place to place, and ᴧᏵᏫᴧ [akxai] or ᴧᏵᏫᴧ [akxa] when the subject was in sight or not moving. These two forms are also used with *he*, *she*, or *it*, as in ᘋᏇᏫᎠ ᴧᴘᴧ [ną́ake apai] *he*, *she*, or *it is running*.

When we use continuous aspect with a first-person *I* or second-person *you* subject, the aspect marker needs to change to match the person (*I* or *you*). In general, the continuous aspect markers indicate what state something or someone is in. This may include information about what position the subject is in, such as standing, sitting, lying, or moving from one place to another. The aspect markers also give information about the time frame of an event. Typically, this means that we need to know the context of a sentence to best understand how to use and interpret the aspect markers.

As a bit of history about these aspect markers, they evolved from the general Siouan way of using the verbs for *sit*, *stand*, and *lie* to mean *be in some state*. So, a tree might be said to stand, while a river would lie. Eventually, speakers began to use these verbs to talk about states of being. So the continuous aspect markers may actually indicate the position of a subject, or they may have a broader meaning.

As you study the first- and second-person aspect markers, please note that their meanings are different from the meanings of the third-person aspect markers ᴧᏵᏫᴧ / ᴧᏵᏫᴧ [akxa / akxai] and ᴧᴘᴧ / ᴧᴘᴧ [apa / apai]. We discuss this more below.

The first-person continuous aspect markers

We are going to discuss three first-person aspect markers in this section: ᵱᏁᏉᏥᴀ́ [mįkšé], ᴧᴊᴀ́ [ąhé] (and its variant ᴧᏂᏒᴊᴀ́ [ąðįhé]), and ᴧᴅᏫᴧᴊᴀ́ [ątxąhé]. The one you are likely to hear most often is ᵱᏁᏉᏥᴀ́ [mįkšé], which is typically used to indicate that an action is ongoing *or* that the subject doing the action is in a lying or sitting position.

ᵱᏁᏉᏥᴀ́ [mįkšé]

In examples 1 and 2 there are two usual ways to interpret the aspect marker ᵱᏁᏉᏥᴀ́ [mįkšé]. In the first way, the speaker is emphasizing that the action occurs while he is or was sitting or lying. In the second way, the speaker is not emphasizing the position; instead, the emphasis is on the ongoing nature of the action. We can tell which meaning is being used based on the context of the conversation.

(1)   Ꮙᴧᘋᴀ́ᏃᎠ ᏉᏒ ᴏᴧᖉᎠ **ᵱᏁᏉᏥᴀ́**.
      waléze wį oáce **mįkšé**
      I am currently looking for a book.
      OR I am looking for a book while sitting.

Without any context, this sentence could mean either "I am looking for a book while I'm in a sitting position" or "I am in the ongoing act of looking for a book."

If the speaker were to say this while seated at a messy table piled high with books, looking for a particular book, the sentence might mean something more like "I'm sitting here looking for a book." However, if someone asks the speaker, "What are you doing?" the speaker could respond with the same sentence to mean "I'm looking for a book right now," emphasizing that the action is happening right then, and it wouldn't matter what position the speaker was in.

(2) ᎠᏩᏃᏇ ᎻᎦᏎ.
áwanǫbre **mįkšé**
I am currently eating a meal.
OR I am eating a meal while sitting.

This sentence could mean either "I am eating a meal in a sitting position" or "I am in the ongoing act of eating a meal."

In example 3, when an event is in the past but we have continuous aspect, ᎻᎦᏎ [mįkšé] is then interpreted as emphasizing the ongoing nature of the event. This sentence could mean "I was singing in a sitting position," or it could emphasize the ongoing nature of the singing without implying a specific position.

(3) ᏌᎠᏨ ᏩᎯᏬ ᎻᎦᏎ.
hą́ąci waabrǫ́ **mįkšé**
I was singing last night.

Context also allows us to understand when the action occurs. Sentence 4 can mean both "I am cooking" or "I was cooking." The emphasis is on the ongoing nature of the cooking. We can use the context of the conversation or time adverbs like ᏏᏙᎢ [sitǫ́į] *yesterday* or ᏌᎭᏛ ᏃᎠ [hą́ąpa ðe] *today* to indicate whether we mean present or past tense.

(4) ᎣᎣᎯᎧ ᎻᎦᏎ.
ooáhą **mįkšé**
I am cooking.
OR I was cooking.

Note that the verb ᎣᏊᏬ [oohǫ́] *cook* has special forms for *I* and *you*. For example, *I am cooking* is ᎣᎣᎯᎧ [ooáhą], and *you are cooking* is ᎣᏉᎯᎧ [ooðáhą].

ᎠᏎᎠ [ąhé]

The next first-person aspect marker we will discuss is ᎠᏎᎠ [ąhé]. Again, there are two usual ways to interpret this marker. First, it can mean that the subject is moving, or changing location. Second, it can also be used to indicate a state that has started sometime in the past and continues to the present, similar to *have been doing* in English.

(5) ᎠᎵᎧᎦ ᎠᏏᎥ.
    anáake **ahé**
    I am running.
    OR I have been running.

This sentence can mean either *I am running* (emphasizing that I am moving) or *I have been running* (indicating that the running started sometime in the past and continues until now).

In addition, if the event was in the past, ᎠᏏᎥ [ahé] can be thought of as *had been doing*, as in 6 and 7.

(6) ᏏᏙᏲ, ᎠᎵᎧᎦ ᎠᏏᎥ.
    sitóį anáake **ahé**
    Yesterday, I was running.
    OR Yesterday, I had been running.

(7) ᏏᏙᏲ, ᎠᏏᏂᏆ ᎠᏏᎥ.
    sitóį ahíibra **ahé**
    Yesterday, I was swimming.
    OR Yesterday, I had been swimming.

Remember that for many speakers, ᏏᏂᏏᎠ [hiiða] is a member of both the a-ða and the brush class, so ᎠᏏᏂᏆ [ahíibra] *I was swimming* has both the a-ða pronoun Ꭰ [a] and brush pronoun Ꮖ [br].

ᎠᏂᏍᏏᎥ [aðihé]

The marker ᎠᏂᏍᏏᎥ [aðihé] is the full form of ᎠᏏᎥ [ahé]. It is used the same way, but it adds an emphatic meaning that we might express with an exclamation point in English.

(8) ᎠᎵᎧᎦ ᎠᏂᏍᏏᎥ!
    anáake **aðihé**
    I am running!
    OR I have been running!

(9) ᏏᏙᏲ, ᎠᎵᎧᎦ ᎠᏂᏍᏏᎥ!
    sitóį anáake **aðihé**
    Yesterday, I was running!
    OR I had been running yesterday!

ᎠᎠᏟᎠᏏᎥ [atxahé]

The final first-person continuous aspect marker is ᎠᎠᏟᎠᏏᎥ [atxahé]. It is used when the subject is standing. It is also used to indicate that the subject is imminently going to do or is about to do something, in any position. Many speakers pronounce this with the accent in the middle as ᎠᎠᏟᎠᏏᎥ [atxáhe].

(10) ZᏂᏦᎪᏃᏁ· ᏏᏁ· ᎤᏞᏦᎶ **ᏞᎠᎪᎶᏍᎠ́**.
žįkáži wį oáhką **ątxąhé**
I am helping a child (while standing).
OR I'm about to help a child.

(11) ᏏᎱᎡᎤ́ **ᏞᎠᎪᎶᏍᎠ́**.
waabrǫ́ **ątxąhé**
I'm singing (while standing).
OR I'm about to sing.

This example indicates that the subject is *standing ready* or *standing by* to sing.

The second-person continuous aspect markers

ᏃᏁᏦᎬᎠ́ [nįkšé]

The second-person *you* has four distinct continuous aspect markers. The one you may hear most often is ᏃᏁᏦᎬᎠ́ [nįkšé]. This is used when the subject is in a sitting position, or, like ᏒᏁᏦᎬᎠ́ [mįkšé], it indicates that an action is ongoing. ᏃᏁᏦᎬᎠ́ [nįkšé] is also often used as an aspect marker when the speaker doesn't need to emphasize the position of the subject.

(12) ᏏᎶᏂᎤᏃᎤᎡᎠ **ᏃᏁᏦᎬᎠ́**.
waðánǫbre **nįkšé**
You are eating a meal (while sitting).
OR You are currently eating a meal.

This example can mean *you are eating a meal while sitting* or *you are in the ongoing act of eating* without implying that someone is sitting.

(13) ᏍᏃ̋ᏒᏁ ᏏᎶᏬᎠᎤ́ **ᏃᏁᏦᎬᎠ́**.
hą́ąci waaštǫ́ **nįkšé**
You were singing last night (while sitting).
OR You were singing last night.

Again, if a past time adverb is used, ᏃᏁᏦᎬᎠ́ [nįkšé] usually emphasizes the ongoing singing and does not necessarily imply a sitting position.

ᏂᎶᏬᎬᎠ́ [ðaašé]

The second-person continuous aspect marker ᏂᎶᏬᎬᎠ́ [ðaašé] is used when the subject is moving from one location to another or when the sense of *have been* or *had been* is needed. It is similar to the use of ᎶᏍᎠ́ [ąhé], the first-person version of this aspect.

(14) ᏏᎶᏂᎶᏒᏁ **ᏂᎶᏬᎬᎠ́**.
waðáachi **ðaašé**

You are dancing.
OR You have been dancing.

Sentence 14 means that the subject is moving around while dancing, or that the subject started dancing some time ago and has now recently finished.

(15) ᏒᏂᎠᎣ ᏏᎠᏍᎾᏍᎠᎸ **ᏏᎸᏍᎠ**.
sitǫ́į ðahíišta **ðaašé**
You were swimming yesterday.
OR You had been swimming yesterday.

Similarly, sentence 15 means that the subject was moving around swimming, or that the subject was swimming and had finished.

ᏏᎠᎠᏥᏍᎦᎠ [ðatxą́še]

The second-person continuous aspect marker ᏏᎠᎠᏥᏍᎦᎠ [ðatxą́še] is similar to ᎠᎠᏥᎠᏚᎠ [ątxąhé]. It is used to mean the subject is standing, but it can also indicate an action that is imminent.

(16) ᏫᎸᏍᎠᎣ **ᏏᎠᎠᏥᏍᎦᎠ**.
waaštǫ́ **ðatxą́še**
You are singing (while standing).
OR You are about to sing (imminently).

ᏃᏥᏍᎦᎠ [žą́kše]

The second-person continuous aspect marker for the lying position is ᏃᏥᏍᎦᎠ [žą́kše]. This marker is somewhat different from the others in that it is nearly always used to indicate that the subject is in a lying position. It does not have other uses.

(17) ᎤᏍᎴᏂ ᏏᎠᏃᏍᎤᎠ **ᏃᏥᏍᎦᎠ**.
hą́ąci ðažį́įhe **žą́kše**
You were sleeping last night (lying down).

Aspect markers in greetings

The following sentences show how the position aspect markers might be used in a simple greeting with ᎠᎠᎤᎠ [tąhé], *be well*.

(18) ᎤᎠᏫᎠ, ᎠᎠᎤᎠ ᏞᏂᏍᎦᎠ?
hawé tąhé nįkše
Hello, are you doing well?

(19) ᎠᏂᏧᎢ ᏡᏂᎩᏎᎢ.
   tạhé mịkšé
   I'm fine.
   OR I'm doing well.

This is the basic way. The speakers can be more specific by changing the aspect marker. If two friends meet on the street, they might use ᎠᎠᏂᎢᏧᎢ [ạtxạhé] and ᏔᎠᎠᏂᏥᎦᎠ [ðatxą́še] to recognize that they are standing.

(20) ᎠᏂᏧᎢ ᏔᎠᎠᏂᏥᎦᎠ?
   tạhé ðatxą́še
   Are you doing well? (You are standing.)
(21) ᎠᏂᏧᎢ ᎠᎠᏂᎢᏧᎢ.
   tạhé ạtxạhé
   I'm fine.
   OR I'm doing well. (I am standing.)

As we have seen above, the aspect markers indicating movement, ᎢᏧᎢ [ạhé] and ᏔᎠᎦᎢ [ðaašé] would most often be interpreted as *have been*.

(22) ᎠᏂᏧᎢ ᏔᎠᎦᎢ?
   tạhé ðaašé
   Have you *been* well? (Said regardless of position.)
   OR Are you well? (Said to someone who is moving from one location to another, for example, walking or running.)
(23) ᎠᏂᏧᎢ ᎢᏧᎢ.
   tạhé ạhé
   I *have been* well.
   OR I am well. (I am walking.)

A review of continuous aspect markers

We have learned many aspect markers, especially for continuous aspect. The following tables summarize the aspect markers for *I*, for *you*, and for *he*, *she*, and *it* that we introduced above. Exercise 2, at the end of this chapter, asks you to reorganize this information in a way that highlights some patterns found with *I* and *you* markers.

Continuous aspect marker for *I* (first-person)

ᏡᏂᎩᏎᎢ [mịkšé]	ongoing action: *am doing*	OR	subject is sitting or lying
ᎠᎠᏂᎢᏧᎢ [ạtxạhé]	action is imminent: *about to*	OR	subject is standing
ᎢᏧᎢ [ạhé]	*have been doing*	OR	subject is moving
ᎢᏔᏂᏧᎢ [ạðịhé]	*have been doing*	OR	subject is moving

Continuous aspect markers for *you* **(second-person)**

ᘯᏫᏆᏕᘈ [nįkšé]	ongoing: *are doing*	OR	subject is sitting
ᏃᎯᏦᏕᘈ [žákše]	ongoing: *are doing*	OR	subject is lying
ᏂᐱᎠᏊᎯᏕᘈ [ðatxáše]	imminent: *about to*	OR	subject is standing
ᏂᎯᏕᘈ [ðaašé]	*have been doing*	OR	subject is moving

Continuous aspect markers for *he, she, it* **(third-person)**

ᎪᏦᏊᎪ [akxa]	ongoing: *is doing*	OR	stationary or visible
ᎪᏦᏊᎪ [akxai]	ongoing: *is doing*	OR	stationary or visible
ᎪᏆᎪ [apa]	ongoing: *is doing*	OR	in motion, at a distance, or out-of-sight
ᎪᏆᎪ [apai]	ongoing: *is doing*	OR	in motion, at a distance, or out-of-sight

When we don't need to specify the position of a first- or second-person subject, or if the position is not important, we usually just use ᘕᏫᏆᏕᘈ [mįkšé] and ᘯᏫᏆᏕᘈ [nįkšé].

The positions marked in the continuous aspect markers only apply to the subject of a sentence. We don't mark the position of other elements in a sentence this way.

The verb ᏂᏫ˙ [ðį] *be*

We know that Osage does not have a verb that does all the things that the English verb *be* does. Recall from chapter 3 that neither verbs nor predicate adjectives use any form of *be* when we would need to do this in English. For example, ᘯᏫᏦᎪ ᎪᏦᏊᎪ ᘯᏊᏂᎪ ᏉᎪ [níhka akxa láąda pe] means *the man is big* in Osage. Importantly, notice that there is no Osage word in this sentence that means *is*.

However, sometimes a noun is the predicate of a sentence: for example, "The man is a teacher" or "You are a doctor." In these cases, Osage, like English and many languages, requires some word to hold the sentence together the way *be* does. In Osage, this verb is ᏂᏫ˙ [ðį] *be* or *exist*.

How to say *he, she,* or *it is* using ᏂᏫ˙ [ðį]

Look at the examples below. When using a third-person subject like *the man* in 24 or *he, she,* or *it* in 25 and 26, Osage uses the verb ᏂᏫ˙ [ðį] to say *is*. This verb does not need an aspect marker.

(24) ᘯᏫᏦᎪ ᎪᏦᏊᎪ ᏎᎪᏉᎣᏃᎪ **ᏂᏫ˙**.
    níhka akxa wakóze **ðį**.
    The man is a teacher.

(25) ᏎᎪᏉᎣᏃᎪ **ᏂᏫ˙**.
    wakóze **ðį**.
    He is a teacher.

(26) 𐓣𐓬𐓘𐓻𐓣 𐓛𐓣꞉
   šímiži ði
   She is a girl.

But this verb is interesting because there are three different forms for *I* and *you*, and speakers may use any of them.

How to say *I am* using 𐓬𐓣꞉ [bri̜], 𐓬𐓣꞉ [mi̜], and 𐓘𐓵𐓣́꞉ [aní̜]

There are three commonly used words that mean *I am* (a noun): 𐓬𐓣꞉ [bri̜], 𐓬𐓣꞉ [mi̜], and 𐓘𐓵𐓣́꞉ [aní̜]. The decision for which word to use is typically left to personal choice. Note that we sometimes hear 𐓬𐓣꞉ [bri̜] in a longer form: 𐓬𐓣́𐓘 [brı́e].

(27) 𐓏𐓘𐓻𐓘́𐓻𐓟 𐓬𐓣꞉ OR 𐓏𐓘𐓻𐓘́𐓻𐓟 𐓬𐓣꞉ OR 𐓏𐓘𐓻𐓘́𐓻𐓟 𐓘𐓵𐓣́꞉
   wažáže **bri̜** OR wažáže **mi̜** OR wažáže **aní̜**
   I am Osage.
(28) 𐓏𐓘𐓸'ó 𐓬𐓣꞉
   wak'ó **bri̜**
   I am a woman.

How to say *you are* using 𐓮̌𐓛𐓣꞉ [šci̜], 𐓵𐓣꞉ [ni̜], and 𐓛𐓘𐓵𐓣́꞉ [ðaní̜]

The most common words that mean *you are* are 𐓮̌𐓛𐓣꞉ [šci̜], 𐓵𐓣꞉ [ni̜], and 𐓛𐓘𐓵𐓣́꞉ [ðaní̜]. Again, these three words are largely interchangeable, and note that we sometimes hear 𐓵𐓣꞉ [ni̜] in a longer form: 𐓵𐓣́𐓘 [nı́e].

(29) 𐓐𐓪́𐓸𐓘 𐓮̌𐓛𐓣꞉ OR 𐓐𐓪́𐓸𐓘 𐓵𐓣꞉ OR 𐓐𐓪́𐓸𐓘 𐓛𐓘𐓵𐓣́꞉
   hpóhka **šci̜** OR hpóhka **ni̜** OR hpóhka **ðaní̜**
   You are Ponca.
(30) 𐓵𐓣́𐓸𐓘 𐓮̌𐓛𐓣꞉
   níhka **šci̜**
   You are a man.

There are also other ways that Osage speakers may say sentences like these in conversation, but we cannot cover them all in this book.

𐓣́𐓸'𐓶𐓻𐓟 [ík'uce]

Exercise 1. How do you say this?

Give the English for the following conversation between a child and a grandmother. Note that there may be more than one good way to do this.

(ŽįkážĮ) Ñǩó, óʌo ꚘʌᏓᏂ ᏃᏂα. (žįkážį) iihkó, óohǫ ðáalį nįe
(Ñǩó) Ã́, óʌo ꚘʌᏓᏂ ᖇᏂα. (iihkó) ą́ą óohǫ ðáalį brįe
ᏣᏆó, óʌaᎦᏄ ÞÃᎠᏞ ᏃᏂʌᏁ ᖇÚʌᏆ. sitǫ́į ówehci hpaata zíhi brúwį
(ŽįkážĮ) ÞÃᎠᏞ ᏞᏂᏞoᏃα ÕꚘʌʌᏞ ꚘʌᎠⱶʌᏆǩá? (žįkážį) hpáata nílǫze ooðáhą ðatxą́še
(Ñǩó) ᏆƔ́ǩᏞᏃᏁ, ÞÃᎠᏞ ᏃǮᏞᏞ ÕʌʌᏞ ʌᎠⱶʌʌá. (iihkó) hą́ąhkaži hpaata žéelą ooáhą ątxą́hé
(ŽįkážĮ) ꚘʌᏞᏂ! (žįkážį) ðáalį

Exercise 2

The tables summarizing the continuous aspect markers in this chapter are organized by person. Another useful way to look at these aspect markers is to organize them by position and time frame. Use information in this chapter to fill in the aspect markers and complete the tables below.

Continuous aspect markers for *I* and *you* (first- and second-person)

Position		time frame	aspect marker	English
sitting	OR	ongoing: *is doing*	ⴘᏆǩ₷á [mįkšé]	*I*
			_____	*you*
lying	OR	ongoing: *is doing*	_____	*I*
			_____	*you*
standing	OR	imminent: *about to*	_____	*I*
			_____	*you*
moving	OR	*have been doing*	_____	*I*
			_____	*you*

Continuous aspect markers for *he, she, it* (third-person)

Position		time frame	aspect marker	English
stationary, or visible	OR	ongoing: *is doing*	_____	*he, she, it*
			_____	*he, she, it*
in motion, or out of sight	OR	ongoing: *is doing*	_____	*he, she, it*
			_____	*he, she, it*

Exercise 3. Using forms of ꚘᏁ [ðį]

Using examples 24–30 as a model, give the Osage for the following sentences.

1. I am a man.
2. I am Ponca.
3. I am a teacher.
4. I am a girl.
5. You are a teacher.
6. You are Osage.

7. You are a woman.
8. You are a boy.
9. He is Ponca.
10. She is Osage.
11. He is a man.
12. She is a woman.
13. The woman is a teacher.
14. The boy is Osage.
15. The girl is Ponca.

Exercise 4. Eating, drinking, and cooking

Using the verbs for eat, drink, and cook, and the vocabulary for foods below, make ten sentences. Be sure to use a range of subjects such as *I*, *you*, *she*, or *the girl*, and make sure to use adjectives in at least five of your sentences.

ńa

Nouns

ÁSALOBRA	áwanǫbre	table
SOBRÍKE	hǫbríke	beans
KÍKXO	kíkxo	feast (noun)
ẞÁZA SÍẞZA	hkąące hįįšce	peach
ẞÁZA ZÚA	hkąące žúe	tomato
MÁŽXA	máąžąxe	onion
ÓWEHCI	ówehci	store
PAAZÉNII SAAKÍ	paazénii saakí	cheese
HPÉŽEHTOHO	hpéžehtoho	lettuce
HPÓHKA	hpǫ́hka	Ponca
TÓOLEŽI	tóoleži	carrot
HTANÁK'A	htanák'a	paper
HTAANÍI	htaaníi	soup
HCÉHEŽĮ	hcéhežį	dishes, plates, cups, bowls
WASKÚA SÁPA	waskúa sápe	blackberry
WACÚA	wacúe	bread (any kind)
WACÚA ÐUTÁAHPA	wacúe ðutáahpa	biscuit
WÉLEZE	wéleze	pen or pencil
WÉLI	wéli	oil, pork fat

Adjectives

CÚUTAŽI	cúutaži	raw
CÚUCE, SÚUTĄ	cúuce, súutą	ripe

Verbs

ᏏᎸᎩᎢ   ðaahtą́ (br-šc)   drink

Notes for Chapter 6

The verb ōᎢᏍᎯ [ooáhą] *I cook* is pronounced and spelled ōᎥᎢᏍᎯ [oowáhą] by many people, adding a [w] between the [o] and the [á]. This is true of many other words that have [o] and [á] together, especially at the beginning of a word. In this book, we will generally not add the [w].

Chapter 7

Plural Subject Pronouns and the Future Marker

Oǧóǧna

Four friends have met up at a house to chat over coffee.

1. **A:** ͞ʌƀʌϲʌ ᴅóɑ ƙʌ́ψɑ ᴆʌ.
2. **B:** ʌ/ʌ́, ͞ʌƀʌϲʌ ƙóʁʌ ͞ʌпƙɕɑ́.
3. **C:** ᴅóɑ ᴆʌ́ψɑ ᴆʌ ͞ʌпƙɕɑ́. . . . ͞ʌƀʌϲʌ ōɹóʹ ᴛ̃пɕᴅʌ́.
4. **D:** ͞ʌƀʌϲʌ ōzú ᴛ̃ɑ́ƙʌ.
5. **C:** Ōɕńzu ᴇɑ. ᴆɑ́ ᴆʌ̄zɑ́ᴌñ zʌ̄ᴌñ ƙóᴛ̃ʌ?
6. **A:** ͞ʌƀʌϲʌ ʌƙʌ̃ʌ ᴆʌ ɕʌᴌп ʌƙʌ̃ʌ.
7. **B:** ᴆʌ̄zɑ́ᴌñ ᴅóɑ ƙóʁʌ ͞ʌпƙɕɑ́.
8. **D:** ͞ʌƀʌϲʌ ϲƙúɑ ʌᴛ̃ʌ́ᴌп. zʌ̄ᴌñ ᴅóɑ ʌƙ'ú.
9. **C:** ͞ʌƀʌϲʌ ϲʌ́ʁɑ ɑ̃́ᴌʌ ʁʌ̃́ᴆʌ.
10. **A:** ͞ʌƀʌϲʌ ᴛ̃ʌ́ᴌп ʌƙʌ̃ʌ.

1. **A:** Let's fix some coffee.
2. **B:** Yes, I want coffee. (woman speaking)
3. **C:** I'll make some. . . . The coffee is ready.
4. **D:** Here is a coffee mug.
5. **C:** Let me pour for you. Who wants cream and sugar?
6. **A:** This coffee is really strong.
7. **B:** I want some cream.
8. **D:** I like sweet coffee. Give me some sugar.
9. **C:** I only drink mine black.
10. **A:** The coffee is good.

By this point in the book, we assume that you have mastered the Osage spelling system. For those of you who still use the APA spelling, we have numbered each line, and you can find the APA for this dialogue in an appendix at the back of the book. We continue to use the APA for the examples in each chapter.

Ƞa ʎʌƙńcʎꝭa

Up until now, all of our noun phrases and all our pronouns have been singular forms like *the woman*, *I*, or *he*. It is time to introduce some of the ways to make the Osage plural subject pronouns *we two*, *we plural*, *you plural*, and *they*. We will look at plural noun phrases in chapter 18. We will learn about object pronouns in chapter 9. Remember that Osage pronouns have different forms for completive and continuous aspect. After introducing the pronouns for these aspects, we provide a summary of all the pronouns we have learned, singular and plural, for a-ða and brush verbs. We then introduce how to use the future marker ÞΛ [hta].

Completive aspect: plural subject pronouns

For the first-person plural pronouns, Osage, like many other Native languages, makes a distinction between dual—*we two*, and plural—*we plural* (more than two). Second-person *you* does not make a distinction between dual and plural. Third-person plural *they* follows the same pattern as third-person singular *he*, *she*, or *it*.

We will also learn that there are two types of Þa [pe]. One is used for completive aspect, and the other is used to help mark plurals, and we will show how to distinguish them below.

First-person dual *we two*

The first-person dual pronoun, *we two*, is ʌ [ą], which is placed in front of the verb. In the case of *we two*, there is no difference in how we form the pronoun for a-ða and brush verbs. The variant ʌƙ [ąk] is used if the verb begins with o [o] or ʌ [a].

In sentences below, the dual, *we two*, is made by placing ʌ [ą] before the verb. In 4, we use ʌƙ [ąk] because the verb, ōꜱó [oohǫ́], begins with the sound o [o].

(1) **ʌcʌ́ƙa.**
ąną́ąke
We two ran.

(2) Zʌ́ ꝭη **ʌ**ᴏ́ʰη.
žą́ą ci ąmą́ði
We two walked in the forest.

(3) ᴌηᴅʌ́ÞΛ ꝭη **ʌ**ꜱńʰΛ.
niitą́ahpa ci ąhíiða
We two swam in the pond.

(4) Óʎa **ʌƙ**ǫ́ꜱǫ.
ówe ąkóohǫ
We two cooked vegetables.

Two types of ᴅɑ [pe]

We have learned to use ᴅɑ [pe] as a completive aspect for third-person subjects. When we use ᴅɑ [pe] as an aspect marker, we write it separately from the verb, like the other aspect markers. There is another important type of ᴅɑ [pe] that helps to mark the plural for first- and second-person subjects. When we use ᴅɑ [pe] to mark plural, we attach it to the verb. This helps to distinguish plural ᴅɑ [pe] from the ᴅɑ [pe] used to indicate completive aspect with third-person subjects.

First-person *we plural* (more than two)

Plural *we* is made by placing ʌ [ą], the same pronoun we saw above, in front of the verb, plus we add ᴅɑ [pe] at the end of the verb: [ą] + verb + [pe]. As noted above, we use ʌ [ą] for both a-ða and brush verbs, and we use ʌҟ [ąk] if the verb begins with o [o] or ʌ [a].

In verbs that end in ɑ [e], such as Ⱬñҟɑ [ną́ąke], the final ɑ [e] becomes ʌ [a] before any ᴅɑ [pe], whether it is for plural or for aspect.

(5) ʌⱫñҟʌᴅɑ
 ąną́ąka**pe**
 We (plural) ran.

(6) ᴅā ᴅóсҟʌꝫп ɑ́ᴆʌꜱʌ ʌ☞ʌꞪпᴅɑ.
 taapóskahci éhtaha ąmą́ðį**pe**
 We (plural) walked toward the school (house).

(7) Ɫñzūꝫɑ ꝫп ʌꜱñꞪʌᴅɑ.
 níižuuce ci ąhíiða**pe**
 We (plural) swam in the river.

(8) ꜱʌ́ᴅʌ ꜱʌꝫúɑ ʌҟő ꜱоᴅɑ.
 hápa wacúe ąkóoho**pe**
 We (plural) baked cornbread.

Second-person plural *you*

The second-person plural pronoun, *you*, is almost the same as the singular forms. This means we will use Ɦʌ [ða] for a-ða verbs and ҕꝫ / ҕᴅ [šc / št] for brush verbs. To make *you plural*, we add ᴅɑ [pe] to the end of the verb. To see this, compare the singular *you* examples, 9a and 10a, with the plural *you* examples, 9b and 10b.

Note that in the first-person plural forms, the pronoun appeared at the front of the verb. However, with second-person plural forms, the pronoun appears in the same place that it does with singular forms. This means that with some verbs like óҟʌ [óhką] *help*, the pronoun goes inside the verb as explained in chapter 5 and shown in example 12 below.

(9a) ꞪʌⱫñҟɑ.
 ðaną́ąke
 You (singular) ran.

(9b) 𐓷𐓘𐓣𐒼̜́𐓤𐓘𐒿𐓘.
   ðaną́ąkape
   You (plural) ran.

(10a) 𐓷𐓘𐓯𐓣́𐓭𐓂𐓘.
   ðahíišta
   You (singular) swam.

(10b) 𐓷𐓘𐓯𐓣́𐓭𐓂𐓘𐒿𐓘.
   ðahíištape
   You (plural) swam.

(11) 𐓫𐓣́𐓓𐓶𐒿𐓘 𐒼𐓯𐓣 𐓅𐓘𐓭𐒿𐓣́𐒿𐓘.
   níižuuce kši mąš**cį́pe**
   You (plural) walked to the river.

(12) 𐓓𐓣𐒼𐓘́𐓓𐓣̨ 𐓏𐓣̨ o𐓷𐓘́𐒼𐓘𐒿𐓘
   žįkážį wį o**ðáhkąpe**
   You (plural) helped a child.

Notice that in all these examples, 𐒿𐓘 [pe] plural is connected to the verb.

Since English does not distinguish between *you singular* and *you plural*, we will say *you plural* when that is what we mean. Often, we will only use *you* to mean *you singular*.

Third-person pronouns *he*, *she*, *it*, *they*

Third-person plural *they* is formed the same way as third-person singular *he*, *she*, or *it*. Recall from chapter 2 that third-person pronouns are not marked on the verb.

Osage speakers use context to know whether a third-person subject is singular or plural. If we were talking about a boy, then sentence 13 would mean *he spoke*. If we were talking about several boys, then 13 would mean *they spoke*.

(13) 𐓣́𐓘 𐒿𐓘.
   ía pe
   he, she, or they spoke.

As we learned in chapter 5, completive sentences with third-person subjects are finished with the aspect marker 𐒿𐓘 [pe]. It is important to note that because this is the aspect marker 𐒿𐓘 [pe] and not the plural 𐒿𐓘 [pe], we write it separately from the verb.

(14) o𐓷𐓣́𐓰𐓣 𐒿𐓘.
   owísi pe
   he, she, it, or they jumped.

(15) 𐒿𐓣 o𐒾𐓘́ 𐒿𐓘.
   hci ocá pe
   he, she, or they looked for the house.

(16) ᏃᏅᏰᎠᏂ ᏴᏁ ÓᏦᏅ ᏛᎠ.
žįkážį wį óhką pe
he, she, or they helped a child.

(17) ᏍᏁᎠᎡᎠᏂ ᎠᏰᎮᎠ ᏴᎠᏃᏅᏰᎠ ᏃᎠᏰ'Ó ᏛᎠ.
šį́tožį akxa wažį́ka nąk'ǫ́ pe
The boys (or the boy) heard a bird.

Context tells us whether the subject in 17 is *the boys* or *the boy*.

Summary: subject pronouns with completive aspect

Dual first-person subjects (*we two*) are made by placing the pronoun ᗋ [ą] or ᗋᏰ [ąk] before the verb.

Plural first-person subjects (*we plural*) are made by placing the pronoun ᗋ [ą] or ᗋᏰ [ąk] before the verb and attaching ᏛᎠ [pe] after it.

Second-person plural subjects are made by using the appropriate second-person singular pronoun *and* attaching ᏛᎠ [pe] to the end of the verb.

Third-person plural subjects, whether singular or plural, are made the same way we learned in chapter 5, with no marking on the verb. Completive aspect is made by using ᏛᎠ [pe], and to help us distinguish this from plural ᏛᎠ [pe], we write the aspect marker separately from the verb.

Continuous aspect: plural pronouns

Recall from before that the continuous aspect has several forms that are changed depending on whether the subject is first-, second-, or third-person. The forms also indicate the position of the subject (sitting, standing, lying, moving) and, depending on context, can be used to indicate meanings such as *have been doing*, *is doing*, or *about to do* (see chapter 6).

First-person dual subjects in continuous aspect, *we two*

As with completive aspect, first-person dual subjects (*we two*) are marked with the pronoun ᗋ [ą] or ᗋᏰ [ąk] placed in front of the verb. To indicate the continuous aspect, there are three aspect markers that can go with first-person dual subjects: ᗋᏂᏅᏰᏪᎠ́ [ąðįkšé], ᗋᏂᎠ́ [ąðé], and ᗋᎠᏂᎠ́ [ątxá]. Similar to what we saw in chapter 6, each of these new aspect markers can have multiple meanings depending on context.

ᗋᏂᏅᏰᏪᎠ́ [ąðįkšé]

If the subjects are sitting or lying, the aspect marker is ᗋᏂᏅᏰᏪᎠ́ [ąðįkšé]. The action may be in the present or past as long as it is ongoing.

(18) ᏌᏁᎬᎠ ᎠᏴᎠᎬᏅᏜᎠ ᗋᏂᏅᏰᏪᎠ́.
háace ą́wanǫbre ąðįkšé

Last night we two were eating (a meal).

OR Last night, we two were eating (a meal, while sitting or lying).

(19) ᏑᏃᎦ, ᎠᏫᎯᎣ ᎯᎵᏂᎩᏍᎬ.
sitǫ́į ąwáaðǫ ąðįkšé
Yesterday we two were singing.

OR Yesterday we two were singing (while sitting or lying).

ᎯᏂᎦ [ąðé]

The continuous dual aspect marker ᎯᏂᎦ [ąðé] is used when the subjects are moving, or it can indicate that the action was begun in the past and continues to the present (*we two have been doing*), such as we saw with ᎠᏍᎦ [ąhé] in chapter 6.

Remember from chapter 5 that sometimes the accent moves in a verb. This is the case with ᎧᎥᎠᎿᎣᏒᎦ [áwanǫbre] in example 20 below.

(20) ᎧᎥᎠᎿᎣᏒᎦ ᎯᏂᎦ.
áwanǫbre ąðé
We two have been eating (a meal).

OR We two were eating (a meal, while moving).

(21) ᏃᎯᏓᎳᏇᏢ ᏣᎾᏂ ᎠᎭᎯᏂᎢ ᎯᏂᎦ.
níitáahpa kši ąmáðį ąðé
We two are walking to the pond.

OR We two are walking to the pond (moving).

ᎯᎠᏆᎧ [ątxá]

If the subjects are standing, the aspect marker is ᎯᎠᏆᎧ [ątxá]. This marker may also indicate an act that is imminent (*about to*) even if the subjects are not standing.

(22) ᎥᎠᏤᎤᎦ ᏣᏣᎤᏂᎦ ᎯᏣᎣᏍᎣ ᎯᎠᏆᎧ.
wacúe skúðe ąkóohǫ ątxá
We two are about to bake cake.

OR We two are baking cake (standing).

(23) ᎣᏍᎣᏏᏂ ᏃᎢ ᎠᏫᎯᎣ ᎯᎠᏆᎧ.
oohǫ́hci ci ąwáaðǫ ątxá
We two are about to sing in the kitchen.

OR We two were singing in the kitchen (while standing).

First-person plural subjects in continuous aspect, *we plural*

First-person plural subjects (*we, plural, more than two*) are again marked with the pronoun Ꭿ [ą] or ᎯᏣ [ąk] placed in front of the verb. There are two aspect markers that can go with first-person plural subjects: ᎯᏣᎯᏂᎦ [ąkáðe] and ᎯᏣᎠᏆᎧ [ąkatxá].

ᎠᎩᎶᏔ [akáðe]

If the subjects are sitting, lying, or moving from one place to another, the aspect marker is ᎠᎩᎶᏔ [akáðe]. Following the pattern seen earlier, ᎠᎩᎶᏔ [akáðe] may also indicate *have been doing*.

(24) ᎠᏃᎢᏌ ᎠᎩᎶᏔ.
ąžįįhe ąkáðe
We (plural) have been sleeping.
OR We (plural) are sleeping.

(25) ᎠᏫᎶᎠ ᎠᎩᎶᏔ.
ąwáaðǫ ąkáðe
We (plural) have been singing.
OR We (plural) are singing (while sitting or lying).

ᎠᎩᎠᎠᎣᏗ [akatxą́]

If the subjects are in a standing position, the aspect marker is ᎠᎩᎠᎠᎣᏗ [akatxą́]. Again, this marker may also indicate the imminent action *about to*.

(26) ᎠᏫᎠᎷᎣᎣᎠ ᎠᎩᎠᎠᎣᏗ.
ąwanǫbre ąkatxą́
We (plural) are about to eat (a meal).
OR We (plural) are eating (a meal, while standing).

(27) ᏍᏂᎡᎠ ᎠᏔᎤᏌᎠ ᎠᎩᎠᎠᎣᏗ.
hįįce ąðúuža ąkatxą́
We (plural) are about to wash the dishes.
OR We (plural) are washing dishes (while standing).

(28) ᏃᏏᎩᎠᏃᎣ ᏫᎣ ᎠᎩᎣᎱᎠ ᎠᎩᎠᎠᎣᏗ.
žįkážį wį ąkóhką ąkatxą́
We (plural) are about to help a child.
OR We (plural) are helping a child (while standing).

Second-person plural subjects with continuous aspect, *you plural*

Second-person plural subjects take the aspect marker ᏉᎶᏍᎠ [paašé] for all positions and situations.

ᏉᎶᏍᎠ [paašé]

Second-person plural pronouns are the same as the singular forms. Thus, we only need to add ᏉᎶᏍᎠ [paašé] and remember which class the verb belongs to, a-ða or brush, as discussed in chapter 5.

(29) ᎶᐞᏃᏘᏌᎠ ᏆᏘᏋᎠ́.
ðažį́įhe paašé
You (plural) are sleeping.

(30) Ó↰ᴀᏫᏂ Ꮒ ↙ᴏᏋᏘᏦᎠ ᏋᏫÚ↰Ꮙ́ ᏆᏘᏋᎠ́.
ówehci ci họbríke šcúwį paašé
You (plural) are buying beans at the store.

Third-person plural subjects

As with the completive forms, context tells us whether a third-person subject is singular or plural. Any of the sentences below could also be interpreted with a singular subject.

(31) ᏓᏂᴅó ᏋóᏦᎠ ᏦᏈᏘᏘ́ ᏗᏆᏗ.
sitǫ́į šǫ́ke ðuxí apai
They were chasing dogs yesterday.

(32) ↙ᏘźᴜᏋᎠ ᏦᏋᏂ ᑦᏗᏦᏘ́ ᏗᏆᏗ.
níižuuce kši mą̌ðį́ apai
They are walking to the river.

(33) ᏋᏘᑦᏂᏃᏙ ᏂᎠ óᏦᏗ ᏗᏦᏘᏗ.
šį́mįžį ðe óhką akxai
They are helping that girl.

Summary: subject pronouns with continuous aspect

First-person dual subjects (*we two*) take the pronoun Ꮧ [ą] or ᏗᏦ [ąk] placed before the verb. The continuous aspect markers ᏗᏦᏂᏦᏋᎠ́ [ą̌ðįkšé], ᏗᏦᎠ́ [ą̌ðé], or ᏗᴅᏦᏘ́ [ątxą́] finish the sentence.

First-person plural subjects (*we, more than two*) take the pronoun Ꮧ [ą] or ᏗᏦ [ąk] placed before the verb. The continuous aspect markers ᏗᏦᏘᏦᎠ [ąkáðe] or ᏗᏦᏗᴅᏦᏘ́ [ąkatxą́] finish the sentence.

Second-person plural subjects (*you plural*) use the second-person pronoun that corresponds to the verb class, such as a-ða or brush. Finish the sentence with the continuous aspect marker ᏆᏘᏋᎠ́ [paašé].

Third-person plural subjects (*they*) are formed the same way as third-person singular. Finish the sentence with the continuous aspect markers ᏗᏦᏘᏗ / ᏗᏦᏘᏗ [akxa / akxai] or ᏗᏆᏗ / ᏗᏆᏗ [apa / apai].

Variations of completive and continuous aspect: examples using ↙ᏘᏦᎠ [ną́ąke] *run* and ᏦᏈᏘᏘ́ [ðuwį́] *buy* in all persons and aspects

The purpose of these lists is to show how aspect markers indicate who the subject is. We have illustrated this with *run* and with *buy*. Some of the positional meanings here are odd and likely wouldn't be used with *run* or *buy*; running while standing might be running in place on a treadmill. Running while lying down is hard to imagine.

Completive aspect in its variations

ᏓᏝᎦᎦᎠ [náąke] *run* (a-ða)

ᎠᏝᎦᎦᎠ	anáąke	I run
ᎭᎠᏝᎦᎦᎠ	ðanáąke	you run
ᏓᏝᎦᎠ ᏂᎠ	náąka pe	he, she, they run
ᎠᏝᎦᎦᎠ	ąnáąke	we two run
ᎠᏝᎦᎦᎠᏁᎠ	ąnáąkape	we (plural) run
ᎭᎠᏝᎦᎦᎠᏁᎠ	ðanáąkape	you (plural) run

ᎭᎤᏏᏂ [ðuwį́] *buy* (brush)

ᏒᎤᏏᏂ	brúwį	I buy
ᏎᎤᏏᏂ	šcúwį	you buy
ᎭᎤᏏᏂ ᏂᎠ	ðuwį́ pe	he, she, they buy
ᎠᎭᎤᏏᏂ	ąðúwį	we two buy
ᎠᎭᎤᏏᏂᏁᎠ	ąðúwįpe	we (plural) buy
ᏎᎤᏏᏂᏁᎠ	šcúwįpe	you (plural) buy

Continuous aspect in its variations

ᏓᏝᎦᎦᎠ [náąke] *run* (a-ða)

ᎠᏝᎦᎦᎠ ᎼᏂᎦᏎᎠ	anáąke mįkšé	I run
ᎠᏝᎦᎦᎠ ᎠᏎᎠ	anáąke ąhé	
ᎠᏝᎦᎦᎠ ᎠᎠᎭᎠᏎᎠ	anáąke ątxąhé	
ᎭᎠᏝᎦᎦᎠ ᏝᏂᎦᏎᎠ	ðanáąke nįkšé	you run
ᎭᎠᏝᎦᎦᎠ ᎭᎸᏎᎠ	ðanáąke ðaašé	
ᎭᎠᏝᎦᎦᎠ ᎭᎠᎠᎭᎠᏎᎠ	ðanáąke ðatxą́še	
ᎭᎠᏝᎦᎦᎠ ᏃᏝᎦᏎᎠ	ðanáąke žą́kše	
ᏝᎦᎦᎠ ᎠᎦᎭᎠ	náąke akxai	he, she, they run
ᏝᎦᎦᎠ ᎠᏁᎠ	náąke apai	
ᎠᏝᎦᎦᎠ ᎠᎭᎠ	ąnáąke ąðé	we two run
ᎠᏝᎦᎦᎠ ᎠᎭᏂᎦᏎᎠ	ąnáąke ąðįkšé	
ᎠᏝᎦᎦᎠ ᎠᎠᎭᎠ	ąnáąke ątxą́	
ᎠᏝᎦᎦᎠ ᎠᎦᎠᎭᎠ	ąnáąke ąkáðe	we (plural) run
ᎠᏝᎦᎦᎠ ᎠᎦᎠᎠᎭᎠ	ąnáąke ąkatxą́	
ᎭᎠᏝᎦᎦᎠ ᏁᎸᏎᎠ	ðanáąke paašé	you (plural) run

ᎭᎤᏏᏂ [ðuwį́] *buy* (brush)

ᏒᎤᏏᏂ ᎼᏂᎦᏎᎠ	brúwį mįkšé	I buy

ɹúʜɴ ʌɾʃɑ	brúwį ąhé	
ɹúʜɴ ʌⱴʜʌʃɑ	brúwį ątxąhé	
ꜧᴤúʜɴ ⱴɴꝃʜɑ	šcúwį nįkšé	you buy
ꜧᴤúʜɴ ꜧʌꜧɑ	šcúwį ðaašé	
ꜧᴤúʜɴ ꜧʌⱴʜʌꜧɑ	šcúwį ðatxaše	
ꜧᴤúʜɴ ᴤʌꝃꜧɑ	šcúwį žąkše	
ꜧUʜɴ ʌꝃʜʌ	ðuwį akxai	he, she, they run
ꜧUʜɴ ʌⱴʌ	ðuwį apai	
ʌꜧúʜɴ ʌꜧɑ	ąðúwį ąðé	we two buy
ʌꜧúʜɴ ʌꜧɴꝃʜɑ	ąðúwį ąðįkšé	
ʌꜧúʜɴ ʌⱴʜʌ	ąðúwį ątxą	
ʌꜧúʜɴ ʌꝃʌꜧɑ	ąðúwį ąkáðe	we (plural) buy
ʌꜧúʜɴ ʌꝃʌⱴʜʌ	ąðúwį ąkatxą	
ꜧᴤúʜɴ ᴅʌꜧɑ	šcúwį paašé	you (plural) buy

The future marker ᴅʌ [hta]

We have already seen that Osage does not mark the past and present tenses as English does. Instead, we use time words and context to tell us if something occurred in the past. But Osage does have a future marker. It is used when an event will occur any time after the moment of speech. It can be said as *will* or *going to*.

Notice that ᴅʌ [hta] appears after the verb. It is most often followed by a continuous aspect marker. This means the order will be *verb + hta + aspect*.

(34) ʃíᴤɑ ɹúᴢʌ ᴅʌ ᴍɴꝃʜɑ.
hįįce brúuža hta mįkšé
I am going to wash the dishes.

(35) ꝃʌʜ óʜɑᴤɴ ᴤɴ ʃɴɹɴꝃɑ ꜧᴤúʜɴ ᴅʌ ᴅʌꜧɑ.
kaasį ówehci ci hobríke šcúwį hta paašé
Tomorrow you (plural) will buy beans at the store.

(36) ʃʌᴅʌ ꜧɑ ꜧɴᴍnᴢɴ ʌꝃʜʌ ɴꝃó óꝃʌ ᴅʌ ʌꝃʜʌ.
hą́ąpą ðe šįmįžį akxa iihkó óhką hta akxai
Today the girl is going to help Grandma.

(37) ʃʌꜧɑ ꜧʌᴄɴ ʌᴢꜧʃɑ ᴅʌ ʌꝃʌꜧɑ.
hąąðé ðáalį ąžį́įhe hta ąkáðe
Tonight we will sleep well.

If we make a yes/no question, the marker ꜧɑ [ðe] can follow ᴅʌ [hta] rather than the aspect marker.

(38) ꜧɑꝃǿᴤɑ ʜʌꜧʌⱴᴏꝃɑ ᴅʌ ꜧɑ?
ðekǫ́ǫce waðánǫbre hta ðe
Are you going to eat now?

𐓂𐓤'𐓂𐓵𐓣 [ík'uce]

Exercise 1. How do you say this?

Give the Osage for these short English sentences, choosing the correct aspect markers.

1. I have been singing.
2. You (plural) danced last night.
3. We two bought vegetables yesterday.
4. He is swimming now.
5. We (plural) are about to eat (a meal).
6. Last night you were washing the dishes (while standing).
7. Yesterday we two caught a fish.
8. She bought coffee.
9. We (plural) cooked corn last night.
10. I helped Mother.

Exercise 2. How do you say this?

Give the English for these Osage sentences, including variations in meanings based on context.

1. Ó𐓷𐓣 𐒹𐓀𐓷𐓣𐓆. [ówe brúwį]
2. 𐓐𐓟𐓤𐓣 𐓣𐓷𐓣𐓏𐓪𐓬𐓣. [háace ąwáaðope]
3. 𐓀𐓘𐓵𐓮𐓎 𐓏𐓘𐓵𐓟. [mąąščí ðaašé]
4. 𐓇𐓎𐓑𐓣 𐓣𐓤𐓎𐓣. [žįįhe akxa]
5. 𐓏𐓘𐓵𐓯𐓬 𐓪𐓘𐓵𐓟. [waaštǫ́ paašé]
6. 𐓏𐓣𐓤𐓘 𐓣𐓤𐓬𐓑𐓬 𐓣𐓏𐓟. [wacúe ąkóohǫ ąðé]
7. 𐓣𐓏𐓘𐓷𐓪𐓰𐓣 𐓀𐓆𐓵𐓟. [awánǫbre mįkšé]
8. 𐓏𐓟𐓤𐓬𐓮𐓣 𐓬𐓘𐓪𐓷 𐓵𐓮𐓎𐓵𐓣 𐓏𐓣𐓏𐓑𐓘𐓵𐓟. [ðekǫ́ǫce hpáata šcúwį ðatxą́še]
9. 𐓇𐓎𐓑𐓣 𐓬𐓟. [žįįha pe]
10. 𐓒𐓆𐓬́ 𐓏𐓣𐓑𐓣𐓅𐓣𐓵𐓰𐓬𐓟. [sitǫį ðahíištape]

Exercise 3. How do you say this?

Use the verbs ó𐓤𐓣 [óhką] *help* and 𐓏𐓘𐓵𐓬 [waaðǫ́] *sing* to make complete sentences using all the pronoun and aspect forms we have studied so far. Look at the examples for 𐓈𐓎𐓤𐓣 [ną́ąke] *run* and 𐓵𐓬𐓎𐓆 [ðuwį́] *buy* for an example of how to do this.

Exercise 4. How do you say this?

Choose ten of the sentences you wrote in exercise 3 and change them to future tense using *hta*.

ńa

Nouns

𝒪𝓼𝒶𝒢𝑒	hápa wacúe	cornbread (general)
	hį́įce	dishes
	ówe	vegetables, groceries
	hpáze	evening
	céɣenii aðį́	drumkeeper
	hcíle	family
	wak'óhpa	first daughter
	wacúe skúe	cake (common variant)
	wacúe skúðe	cake
	wacúe wéli	frybread (general)
	wihé	second daughter

Verbs

	nąk'ǫ́ (a-ða)	hear
	ðuxí (br-šc)	chase

Other

	ihtǫ́į ðéha	future, the future
	kaasį́	tomorrow
	kaasį́tą	tomorrow (variant)
	mį́įðohta	noon, midday
	mį́įðohta ðiištá	afternoon
	hpahále	first, at the outset

Notes for Chapter 7

The form [pe] is associated with several morphemes. One of them is the completive aspect marker. Another marks the plural in several forms. Please note that in Quintero's *Osage Grammar*, [pe] is always attached to the verb, regardless of its function. Pedagogically, it makes sense to introduce each morpheme [pe] in its particular function. We have chosen to keep [pe] attached to the verb when plural but separate from the verb when an aspect marker. This allows us to treat [pe] like the other aspect markers. There is a relationship between [pe] and [api], but the technicalities make it beyond the scope of this beginner's text.

Chapter 8

Question Words, I-Stem Verbs, and Strong-Stem Verbs

ᎤᏂᏞᎾ

1. **ᏔᏂᏍᏓ:** ᎦᎶ, ᏪᎬᏆ ᎣᏟᏁ ᏁᏓᏍᎦᎵᎠ ᎷᏆᎵᏂᎠ ᎠᎵ?
2. **ᎦᎶ:** ᎡᏚᎩ, ᏍᎦᎠᏫᎦᎠ ᎦᏃᎢ ᎦᏝᎣᎦᎠᎠ?
3. **ᏔᏂᏍᏓ:** ᎹᎦᏛᎤᎠ ᏂᎦᎦᎠ ᏍᎸᎾᎢ ᏂᎢ ᎨᎣᏆ.
4. **ᎦᎶ:** ᏍᎧᎦᏂᏞ ᎤᎩᎤᎠᏥᎷ ᎦᏝᎣᎦᎠᎠ?
5. **ᏔᏂᏍᏓ:** ᎡᏚᎩ, ᎦᎶ, ᏍᎧᎦᏂᏞ ᎤᎩᎤᎠᏥᎷ ᎨᎣᏆ.
6. **ᏔᎵᎩ'ᎣᎠ:** ᏌᏍᎳᏃᎵ, ᏍᎧᎦᏂᏞ ᎤᎩᎤᎠᏥᎷ ᎨᎣᏆᎳᎷᎵᏂ.
7. **ᎦᎶ:** ᎠᎾᎵ, ᏌᏍᎶᎩᎳᏂ ᎷᎾᎢᎵᎦ.
8. **ᏂᎬᎠᎵ:** ᏌᏍᎦ ᏍᎸᎾᎢ ᎨᎣᏆ.
9. **ᎦᎶ:** ᎧᎳᎢᏂ, ᏔᏂᏃᎦᎾ, ᏌᏍᎪᎢ ᏂᎦᎠᎵ ᏪᎤᎦᏪᎷ ᎠᎵ ᎳᏂᎦᎦᎢ.

1. **Second daughter:** Grandma, are we going to the Gray Horse dances?
2. **Grandmother:** Yes, when do you want to go?
3. **Second daughter:** I want to go to the afternoon dance.
4. **Grandmother:** Do you want to dress?
5. **Second daughter:** Yes, Grandma, I want to dress.
6. **First daughter:** No, I don't want to dress.
7. **Grandmother:** Well then, take your shawl.
8. **First son:** I want to dance tonight.
9. **Grandmother:** Good, Sonny, I will iron your shirt.

For the dialogue above, note that when the grandmother asks, "Do you want to dress?" she is asking if anyone wants to wear appropriate clothes to be able to participate in the Gray Horse dances.

Ĺıa ⟨Osage title⟩

We learned how to make yes-no questions in chapter 4. Now we will learn how to use the Osage question words ᴅÄᴅʌ [táatą] *what?*, ᴅä [pée] *who?*, ᴊᴏ⟨⟩ᴀ̨ᴋɴ [howáįki] *where?*, and ᴊᴏ⟨⟩ʌ [hówa] *which?* There are other useful question words that begin with ᴊᴧ [háa] in Osage. They include ᴊᴧᴅꜛᴋ̨ᴘɴ [haatxą́ci] *when (in the past)?*, ᴊᴧᴅꜛᴋ̨ᴅʌ [haatxą́ta] *when (in the present or future)?*, ᴊᴧ̨ʟᴧ [háaną] *how many?*, and ᴊᴧ̨ᴋoᴅʌ [háakǫta] *why?* There are other words that begin with ᴊᴧ [háa] that don't have good English matches. We will introduce some of them later in the book. This chapter also introduces two new important verb classes, the i-stem and the strong-stem classes.

Using question words

Osage question words do not automatically appear at the beginning of a sentence as they do in English. Instead, they appear where the answer would be if the question were turned into a statement. If you ask a question about the subject of a sentence, the question word goes where the subject would go. If you ask about the object, it goes where the object would go, and so on. We illustrate and discuss this in the examples below.

Another point is that when asking questions, the subject markers ʌᴋꜛʌ [akxa] and ʌᴘʌ [apa] tend to be omitted, although it is not incorrect to use them. But if the question word itself is a subject, it never takes a subject marker.

Similarly, the completive aspect marker ᴘa [pe] is usually left out when asking questions in Osage. Other aspect markers, such as ʌᴋꜛʌ [akxai] or ʌᴘʌ [apai], may be used in questions.

Although the focus of this chapter is on questions, we must also think about answers. In conversation, people often reply to questions with a short phrase or even a single word. However, when we answer with a full sentence, we need to remember to use subject markers, and if the answer is in completive aspect, we need to use a completive aspect marker like ᴘa [pe] too. We have provided several examples below of how to answer a question with a full sentence.

Using the question word ᴅÄᴅʌ [táatą] *what?*

If we want to ask a question using *what*, we use ᴅÄᴅʌ [táatą]. Notice that in sentences 1a, 2a, and 3, ᴅÄᴅʌ [táatą] takes the place of the object, which is almost always right before the verb. Sentences 1b and 2b give answers to their respective questions.

(1a) ⟨⟩ńȟʌ **ᴅÄᴅʌ** ꜛυ⟨⟩ń?
níhka **táatą** ðuwį́
What did the man buy?

(1b) ⟨⟩ńȟʌ ʌᴋꜛʌ **ᴊÄᴘʌ** ꜛυ⟨⟩ń ᴘa.
níhka akxa **hápa** ðuwį́ pe
The man bought **corn**.

In 1b, 𝓙𐓘𐓑𐓘 [hápa] *corn* is the object of the sentence, it is what we were asking about, and it appears right before the verb. Note that this is also the position where 𐓈𐓘́𐓐𐓘 [táatą] appears in question 1a.

(2a) **𐓈𐓘́𐓐𐓘** 𐓜𐓠𐓤𐓲́𐓶𐓣𐓸?
 táatą šcúwį
 What did you buy?

(2b) 𐒻𐓣̃𐓰́𐓑𐓏𐓪𐓰𐓘 𐓣̨𐓶́𐓸.
 niikáapxoke brúwį
 I bought a **soda**.

In 2a, the subject is *you*, which is marked on the verb. Again, note that the question word 𐓈𐓘́𐓐𐓘 [táatą] appears where an object would appear, right before the verb.

(3) 𐒿𐓣𐓈𐓪́ 𐒻𐓣̃𐓤𐓘 **𐓈𐓘́𐓐𐓘** 𐓧𐓶𐓸́?
 sitǫ́į níhka **táatą** ðuwį́
 What did the man buy yesterday?

In sentence 3, 𐓈𐓘́𐓐𐓘 [táatą] appears right before the verb. Time words usually come first in Osage, so 𐒿𐓣𐓈𐓪́ [sitǫ́į] *yesterday* is at the beginning of the sentence.

In sentences 4 and 5, 𐓈𐓘́𐓐𐓘 [táatą] is the subject of the sentence, so it appears in the position where the subject would go. Since these are questions, the word 𐓈𐓘́𐓐𐓘 [táatą] should not have a subject marker.

(4a) **𐓈𐓘́𐓐𐓘** 𐓑𐓣́𐓲𐓶 𐓧𐓘̄𐓠𐓘́?
 táatą hpísu ðaaché
 What ate the acorns?

(4b) 𐒿𐓣̃́𐓤𐓘 𐓐𐓑𐓘 𐓑𐓣́𐓲𐓶 𐓧𐓘̄𐓠𐓘́ 𐓑𐓘.
 síka apa hpísu ðaachá pe
 The squirrel ate the acorns.

(5) 𐓧𐓘𐓤𐓸́𐓠𐓘 **𐓈𐓘́𐓐𐓘** 𐓑𐓣́𐓲𐓶 𐓧𐓘̄𐓠𐓘́ 𐓑𐓑𐓘́?
 ðekǫ́ǫce **táatą** hpísu ðaaché apai
 What is eating the acorns now?

In question 5, like in 3, the time word 𐓧𐓘𐓤𐓸́𐓠𐓘 [ðekǫ́ǫce] comes first in the sentence.

Using the Question Word 𐓑𐓘́ [pée] *who?*

Using 𐓑𐓘́ [pée] is just like using 𐓈𐓘́𐓐𐓘 [táatą]. In questions 6 and 7, 𐓑𐓘́ [pée] comes first because it is the subject.

(6a) **𐓑𐓘́** 𐓪𐓧𐓣́𐓑𐓘 𐓧𐓶𐓸́?
 pée oðíhtą ðuwį́
 Who bought the car?

(6b) 𐓈𐓣𐓤𐓘 𐓘𐓤𐓻𐓘 𐓇𐓻𐓣𐓵𐓘 𐓻𐓶𐓏𐓣𐓷 𐓬𐓘.
níhka akxa oðíhtą ðuwį́ pe.
The man bought the car.

Note that in 6b, *the man* is the subject of the sentence, so it needs a subject marker. Remember that the subject marker is not needed when asking a question in 6a.

(7a) **𐓬𐓟́𐓟** 𐓟𐓘𐓻𐓣𐓵 𐓤𐓟́𐓷𐓘?
pée haxį kóða
Who wants the blanket?

(7b) 𐓟𐓘𐓻𐓣́ **𐓦𐓤𐓟́𐓬𐓣𐓘**.
haxí **hkóbra**
I want the blanket.

In 7b, the subject is *I*, which is marked on the verb. We explain how to use verbs like *want* in more detail below.

When 𐓬𐓟́𐓟 [pée] is the object, as in 8a and 9, it goes in the object's usual place, right before the verb. Please note that formal English distinguishes between *who* and *whom*, as in 8a and 9, but Osage makes no such distinction.

(8a) 𐓷𐓘𐓤𐓟́ **𐓬𐓟́𐓟** 𐓣́𐓻𐓘?
wak'ó **pée** íiðe
Whom did the woman see?

(8b) 𐓷𐓘𐓤𐓟́ 𐓘𐓤𐓻𐓘 **𐓷𐓘𐓤𐓟́𐓺𐓟** 𐓣́𐓻𐓘 𐓬𐓘.
wak'ó akxa **wakóze** íiða pe
The woman saw **the teacher**.

In 8b, 𐓷𐓘𐓤𐓟́𐓺𐓟 [wakóze] *the teacher* is the object of the sentence.

(9) 𐓯𐓣𐓬𐓟́ **𐓬𐓟́𐓟** 𐓳𐓻𐓘́𐓦𐓘?
sitóį **pée** oðáhką
Whom did you help yesterday?

Again, in 9, note that the subject is *you*, which is marked on the verb, just like in 2 above.

Using the question word 𐓟𐓳𐓷𐓘́𐓤𐓣 [howáįki] *where?*

The question word 𐓟𐓳𐓷𐓘́𐓤𐓣 [howáįki] *where?* asks about a location, so it appears where location words go in a sentence. Recall from chapter 4 that location words can go before the verb or before the object of the verb, if there is one. Note that 𐓟𐓳𐓷𐓘́𐓤𐓣 [howáįki] appears before the object 𐓺𐓬𐓘́𐓷𐓟 [žǫhpáleze] *quail* in 10a but after the object 𐓳𐓤𐓟́ [šǫ́ke] *dog* in 11.

(10a) 𐓈𐓣𐓤𐓘 **𐓟𐓳𐓷𐓘́𐓤𐓣** 𐓺𐓬𐓘́𐓷𐓟 𐓳𐓤𐓟́ 𐓘𐓬𐓘𐓣?
níhka **howáįki** žǫhpáleze océ apai
Where is the man hunting quail?

(10b) ᒷᏂᏦᎪ ᎪᏞᎪ **ᏃᎳ́ ᎬᏁ** ᏃᎤᏢᎪᏞᎠ7Ꭰ ᎤᎬᎪ́ ᎪᏞᎪ.
   níhka apa **žą́ą ci** žǫhpáleze océ apai
   The man is hunting quail **in the forest**.

(11) ᏃᏁᏦᎪᏃᏂ ᏋᎤ́ᏦᎪ **ᏕᎤᏎᎪᏦᏁ** ń́ᏂᎪᏞᎪ?
   žįkážį šǫ́ke **howáįki** íiðe
   Where did the child see the dog?

(12) ĐᎶ́ **ᏕᎤᏎᎪ́ᏦᏁ** ń́ᏂᎪᏞᎪ?
   htáa **howáįki** íiðaðe
   Where did you see the deer?

In question 12, the subject is the pronoun *you*, which is marked on the verb ń́ᏂᎪᏞᎪ [íiðaðe].

Using the question word ᏕᎤ́ᏎᎪ [hówa] which?

The question word ᏕᎤ́ᏎᎪ [hówa] *which* needs to go with a noun, as in *which boy* or *which dog*. In Osage, we put ᏕᎤ́ᏎᎪ [hówa] after the noun we are questioning. We will see this pattern again with ᏕᎶ́ᏞᎪ [háaną] below.

(13a) **ᏋᏂᎼᏁᏃᏂ ᏕᎤ́ᏎᎪ** ᏕᎪ́ᎠᎪ ᏦᎤ́ᏂᎪ ᎪᏦᎪᎪ?
   šį́mįžį hówa hápa kǫ́ða akxai
   Which girl wants the corn?

(13b) **ᏋᏂᎼᏁᏃᏂ ᏞᎪᏃᎶ́ ᎪᏦᎪᎪ** ᏕᎪ́ᎠᎪ ᏦᎤ́ᏂᎪ ᎪᏦᎪᎪ.
   šį́mįžį lažį́į akxa hápa kǫ́ða akxai
   The thin girl wants the corn.

(14) ᏋᏂᎼᏁᏃᏂ **ᏎᏂᏦᎪ ᏕᎤ́ᏎᎪ** ᎠᎤ́ᎠᎤ ᎪᏦᎪᎪ?
   šį́mįžį **síka hówa** tǫ́pe akxai
   Which squirrel is the girl watching?

(15) **ĐᎤ́ᏃᎢ ᏕᎤ́ᏎᎪ** ᏋᏦᎤ́ᏋᎠᎪ?
   htóožu hówa škǫ́šta
   Which meat pie do you want?

Using the question words ᏕᎪᎠᎪᏂ́ᏕᏁ [haatxą́ci] when (in the past)? and
ᏕᎪᎠᎪᏂ́ᎠᎪ [haatxą́ta] when (in the present or future)?

As you recall, time expressions come first in a sentence, so ᏕᎪᎠᎪᏂ́ᏕᏁ [haatxą́ci] and ᏕᎪᎠᎪᏂ́ᎠᎪ [haatxą́ta] will appear there too. We use ᏕᎪᎠᎪᏂ́ᏕᏁ [haatxą́ci] to ask about the past and ᏕᎪᎠᎪᏂ́ᎠᎪ [haatxą́ta] to ask about the present or future.

(16a) **ᏕᎪᎠᎪᏂ́ᏕᏁ** ᏕᎪᏦ'Ꭴ́ ᏃᏁᏦᎪᏃᏂ ń́ᏂᎪ?
   haatxą́ci wak'ó žįkážį íiðe
   When did the woman see the child?

(16b) **ᏕᎶ́́ᏕᏁ** ᏕᎪᏦ'Ꭴ́ ᎪᏦᎪᎪ ᏃᏁᏦᎪᏃᏂ ń́ᏂᎪ ᎠᎪ.
   hą́ąci wak'ó akxa žįkážį íiða pe
   The woman saw the child **last night**.

In 17a, the future marker is not needed at the end of the sentence because 𝒥ⱭDᴀⱭDᴧ [haatxáta] already includes the idea of the future.

(17a) 𝒥ⱭDᴀⱭDᴧ ᐧⱭⱤÓ?
haatxáta waabrǫ́
When do I sing?

(17b) ᗰńᴑᴛᴧᵹᴀ DŐᑭᴧ ⱸᑎ ᐧⱭᵹDÓ Dᴧ ᴌᑎᵹᵹᴀ.
míiǫðaake tóopa ci waaštǫ́ hta nįkšé
You sing **at 4:00**.
OR You *will* sing at 4:00.

Because 17a asks about the future, our answer in 17b should use the future marker Dᴧ [hta].

(18) 𝒥ⱭDᴀᴋⱸᑎ ÓᴌᴑⱤᴀ ᵹⱸÚᐧᑎ?
haatxáci ónǫbre šcúwį
When did you buy food?

(19) 𝒥ⱭDᴀⱭDᴧ ᴑᵹńDᴧ ᵹ'ᴀᴄⱭᵹᑎ ⱸń?
haatxáta oðíhtą k'ásaaki chí
When does the train arrive?

We will discuss verbs of motion such as ᴧⱸń [achí] *arrive* in chapter 14.

Using the question word 𝒥ᴀᴌᴧ [háaną] *how much* or *how many*?

The question words *how much?* and *how many?* are always used with nouns, as in *how much milk* or *how many books*. We put 𝒥ᴀᴌᴧ [háaną] directly after the noun we are asking about. If the noun is a living thing (animate), we use 𝒥ᴀᴌᴧ Dᴧ [háaną pa]. Some modern speakers use 𝒥ᴀᴌᴧ Dᴧ [háaną pa] with everything.

Examples 20 through 22 all show objects. We will talk about using 𝒥ᴀᴌᴧ [háaną] with subjects when we discuss plural subjects again in chapter 18.

(20a) ⌒ᑎDÓ ᐧᴧᵹ'Ó ᗰᴀ𝟩ᴀᴄᵹᴧ 𝒥ᴀᴌᴧ Ó𝒥ᑎ?
sitǫ́į wak'ó **mázeska háaną** óhi
How much money did the woman win yesterday?

(20b) ᐧᴧᵹ'Ó ᴧᵹᴀᴧ Ʀóᵹᴧ ᴌÁⱤᴧ Ó𝒥ᑎ Dᴧ.
wak'ó akxa **bróka lébrą** óhi pe
The woman won **ten dollars**.

(21) ᴌńᵹᴧ ᴄńᵹᴧ 𝒥ᴀᴌᴧ Dᴧ ńᴛᴀ?
níhka **síka háaną pa** íiðe
How many squirrels did the man see?

In example 21, we use 𝒥ᴀᴌᴧ Dᴧ [háaną pa] because the noun phrase *squirrels* is animate.

(22) 𐓇𐓘𐓬𐓶𐓯𐓤𐓣𐓧 𐓉𐓘𐓧𐓣 𐓤𐓵𐓶𐓷𐓣𐓬𐓘?
wapúška háaną šcúwįpe
How many beads did you (plural) buy?

Using the question word 𐓉𐓘𐓤𐓪 [háakǫ] *how?*

The question word 𐓉𐓘𐓤𐓪 [háakǫ] can generally be used where we would use *how* in English. This kind of question is usually answered with several sentences, something you will get better at as you continue to practice and study Osage.

(23) 𐓉𐓘𐓤𐓪 𐓯𐓰𐓘𐓮𐓘 "corn" 𐓏𐓘𐓻𐓘𐓻𐓘 𐓣𐓘?
háakǫ štáace "corn" wažáže íe
How do you say "corn" in Osage?

(24) 𐓉𐓘𐓤𐓪 𐓬𐓰𐓸𐓻𐓶 𐓯𐓤𐓘𐓫𐓘?
háakǫ htóožu škáaye
How do you make meat pies?

Using the question word 𐓉𐓘𐓤𐓪𐓰𐓘 [háakǫta] *why?*

The question word 𐓉𐓘𐓤𐓪𐓰𐓘 [háakǫta] *why?* will generally come first in a sentence.

(25) 𐓉𐓘𐓤𐓪𐓰𐓘 𐓣𐓭𐓘𐓧𐓘?
háakǫta íðae
Why did you speak?

(26) 𐓉𐓘𐓤𐓪𐓰𐓘 𐓯𐓳𐓤𐓘 𐓘𐓤𐓭𐓘 𐓉𐓳𐓬𐓘 𐓘𐓤𐓭𐓘?
háakǫta šǫ́ke akxa hóohtą akxai?
Why is the dog barking?

I-stem verbs

There is an important subgroup of a-ða verbs called *i-stem verbs*. This verb class contains the very important verbs 𐓣𐓘 [íe] *speak* and 𐓣𐓭𐓘 [iiðe] *see*. These are called i-stem verbs because they begin with either a short 𐓣 [i] or a long 𐓣̄ [ii], and we must learn a few important points in order to use this class correctly.

Singular *I* and *you* pronouns

First, like the o-verbs that we studied in chapter 5, we place the pronouns for *I* and *you* inside of i-stem verbs, just after the i-sound.

The next thing we need to know is that we use the same pronoun, 𐓭𐓘 [ða], for the first- and second-person singular pronouns, *I* and *you*. Even though we use the same pronoun, we can tell these forms apart by where the accent falls. For example, in 𐓣𐓭𐓘 [iðáe] *I speak*, the second syllable is accented, and in 𐓣́𐓭𐓘 [íðae] *you speak*, the accent stays on the 𐓣́ [í]. Briefly, accented 𐓭𐓘́ [ðá] is used for *I*, and unaccented 𐓭𐓘 [ða] is used for *you*.

Many speakers pronounce the end of these words with the sound ʌ́ [ái] rather than ʌa [áe], as ᏂᏖʌ́ [iðái] and ńᏖʌ [íðai].

We two, *we plural*, and *you plural* pronouns

In the forms for *we two* and *we plural*, the pronoun is ʌᏃʌ́ [aną́]. It replaces the Ꮒ [i] (or ñ [ii]) at the start of the verb. For example, *we two speak*, from ńa [íe], is said as **ʌᏃʌ́a** [aną́e] and *we (plural) speak* is said as **ʌᏃʌ́aÞa** [aną́epe].

For *you plural*, we add Þa [pe] to the *you singular* form; ńᏖʌa [íðae] *you (singular) speak* becomes **ńᏖʌaÞa** [íðaepe] *you (plural) speak*.

These verbs will still need their aspect markers when relevant. Here are the forms for ńa [íe] *speak* in both completive and continuous aspect. Space does not allow for all the possible English meanings for each form. Please review chapters 2, 5, and 6 for explanations of how to use these forms.

Completive forms for ńa [íe] *speak*

ᏂᏖʌa	iðáe	I speak	(often pronounced ᏂᏖʌ́ [iðái])
ńᏖʌa	íðae	you (singular) speak	(often pronounced ńᏖʌ [íðai])
ńᏖʌaÞa	íðaepe	you (plural) speak	(often pronounced ńᏖʌÞa [íðaipe])
ńa	íe	he (or she or they) speaks	(pronounced ńʌ [ía] before Þa [pe])
ʌᏃʌ́a	aną́e	we two speak	(often pronounced ʌᏃʌ́ [aðą́i])
ʌᏃʌ́aÞa	aną́epe	we (plural) speak	(often pronounced ʌᏃʌ́Þa [aną́ipe])

Continuous forms (with their aspect markers) for ńa [íe] *speak*

ᏂᏖʌ́a ᵐᏂᏦ᚛á	iðáe mįkšé	I speak
ᏂᏖʌ́a ʌᴊá	iðáe ahé	
ᏂᏖʌ́a ʌDᏄʌᴊá	iðáe atxahé	
ńᏖʌa ᏃᏂᏦ᚛á	íðae nįkšé	you (singular) speak
ńᏖʌa Ꮒ⩲᚛á	íðae ðaašé	
ńᏖʌa ᏂʌDᏄʌ́᚛a	íðae ðatxą́še	
ńᏖʌa ʑʌ́Ꮶ᚛a	íðae žą́kše	
ńᏖʌa Þʌ⩲᚛á	íðae paašé	you (plural) speak
ńa ʌᏦᏄʌ	íe akxai	he (or she or they) speak
ńa ʌÞʌ	íe apai	
ʌᏃʌ́a ʌᏖá	aną́e aðé	we two speak
ʌᏃʌ́a ʌᏖᏂᏦ᚛á	aną́e aðįkšé	
ʌᏃʌ́a ʌDᏄʌ́	aną́e atxá	
ʌᏃʌ́a ʌᏦʌ́Ꮒa	aną́e akáðe	we (plural) speak
ʌᏃʌ́a ʌᏦʌDᏄʌ́	aną́e akatxá	

ñʰα [íiðe] *see* (or *find*)

The forms of ñʰα [íiðe] *see* are similar to those of ñα [íe]. The pronoun for both *I* and *you* is ʰʌ [ða], and again, we distinguish them by placing the accent on different syllables, ñʰʌʰα [iiðáðe] *I see* and **ñʰʌʰα** [**íi**ðaðe] *you speak*. In first-person plural, ʌʑʎ [aṇá] replaces ñ [ii]. Note that the verb *see* can also mean *find*. Here are the forms for ñʰα [íiðe] *see* or *find* in both completive and continuous aspect.

Completive forms for ñʰα [íiðe] *see* (or *find*)

ñʰʌʰα	iiðáðe	I see
ñʰʌʰα	íiðaðe	you see
ñʰʌʰʌᴘα	íiðaðape	you (plural) see
ñʰα (ñʰʌ ᴘα)	íiðe (íiða pe)	he/she/they see
ʌʑʎʰα	aṇáðe	we two see
ʌʑʎʰʌᴘα	aṇáðape	we (plural) see

Continuous forms

ñʰʌʰα ᵐᴜᵏ̧ᵴ́α	iiðáðe mikšé	I see
ñʰʌʰα ʌʄα	iiðáðe ahé	
ñʰʌʰα ʌᴅʰʌʄα	iiðáðe atxahé	
ñʰʌʰα ʑᴜᵏ̧ᵴ́α	íiðaðe nikšé	you see
ñʰʌʰα ʰʌ̃ᵴ́α	íiðaðe ðaąšé	
ñʰʌʰα ʰʌᴅʰʌ́ᵴ́α	íiðaðe ðatxášé	
ñʰʌʰα ʑʎᵏ̧ᵴ́α	íiðaðe žákše	
ñʰʌʰα ᴘʌ̃ᵴ́α	íiðaðe paašé	you (plural) see
ñʰα ʌᵏ̧ʰʌ	íiðe akxai	he (or she or they) sees
ñʰα ʌᴘʌ	íiðe apai	
ʌʑʎʰα ʌʰά	aṇáðe aðé	we two see
ʌʑʎʰα ʌʰᴜᵏ̧ᵴ́α	aṇáðe aðikšé	
ʌʑʎʰα ʌᴅʰʌ́	aṇáðe atxá	
ʌʑʎʰα ʌᵏ̧ʌ̃ʰα	aṇáðe akáðe	we (plural) see
ʌʑʎʰα ʌᵏ̧ʌᴅʰʌ́	aṇáðe akatxá	

Strong-stem verbs

Another important class of verb is the *strong-stem* class. This class contains useful verbs that we need for everyday speech.

In this class, if the first sound is Ꮖ, Ꭰ, Ꮡ [p, t, k], then the subject pronouns for *I* and *you (singular)* change. The subject pronoun for first-person singular *I* is Ꭷ [h], and the subject pronoun for second-person singular *you* is Ꭶ [š]. Both pronouns appear at the beginning of the verb, as shown below. Note that the first-person plural pronoun remains Ꭰ [ą].

Completive forms for ᎠᎧᏆᎠ [tǫ́pe] *watch* or *look at* and ᏆᎯᏍᎠ́ [paasé] *cut up*

ᏆᎧᏆᎠ	htǫ́pe	I watch it
ᎶᏆᎧᏆᎠ	štǫ́pe	you (singular) watch it
ᎶᏆᎧᏆᎠᏢᏆᎠ	štǫ́pa**pe**	you (plural) watch it
ᏆᎧᏆᎠ	tǫ́pe	he (or she or they) watches it
ᎠᏆᎧᏆᎠ	ątǫ́pe	we two watch it
ᎠᏆᎧᏆᎠᏢᏆᎠ	ątǫ́pa**pe**	we (plural) watch it
ᏆᎯᏍᎠ	hpáase	I cut it up
ᎶᏆᎯᏍᎠ	špáase	you (singular) cut it up
ᎶᏆᎯᏍᎠᏢᏆᎠ	špáasa**pe**	you (plural) cut it up
ᏆᎯᏍᎠ́	paasé	he (or she or they) cuts it up
ᎠᏆᎯᏍᎠ	ąpáase	we two cut it up
ᎠᏆᎯᏍᎠᏢᏆᎠ	ąpáasa**pe**	we (plural) cut it up

Continuous forms for verbs like these take the aspect markers, as explained in chapter 6 and as shown with the i-stem verbs above.

Verbs that belong to two classes

ᎢᏆᎠᏍᏅ [ípahǫ] *know* and ᎪᎢᏔᎠ [kǫ́ða] *want*

Recall from chapter 5 that some verbs belong to two classes. This means that they will use pronouns from both classes at the same time. ᎢᏆᎠᏍᏅ [ípahǫ] *know* and ᎪᎢᏔᎠ [kǫ́ða] *want* are strong-stem verbs that also belong to other classes.

ᎢᏆᎠᏍᏅ [ípahǫ] *know*

The verb ᎢᏆᎠᏍᏅ [ípahǫ] *know* belongs to both the i-stem and the strong-stem verb classes. We use the Ꭷ [h] and Ꭶ [š] pronouns from the strong-stem class, but place them after the Ꮎ [i] and before the Ꮘ [p].

ᎢᏆᎠᏍᏅ	í**h**pahǫ	I know
ᎢᎶᏆᎠᏍᏅ	í**š**pahǫ	you know

In the first-person plural, again the syllable ᎠᏃᎢ [ąną́] replaces Ꮎ [i], the way we do with i-stem verbs.

ᎠᏃᎢᏆᎠᏍᏅ	**ąną́**pahǫ	we two know

Ϝóħʌ [kǫ́ða] *want*

The important verb Ϝóħʌ [kǫ́ða] *want* is in both the strong-stem class and the brush class. Like other strong-stem verbs, it takes [h] for *I* and [š] for *you*. And like other brush verbs, the [ð] is replaced by [br] for *I* and [št] for *you*. Look at the following examples, repeated from the dialogue above.

(27) ꞌɅħα ꜱʌℇꞌ **Ϝóʀʌ**.
háąde waachí **hkǫ́bra**
I want to dance tonight.

For *I want*, notice that Ϝóħʌ [kǫ́ða] has an initial ꞌ [h], like a strong-stem verb, and replaces ħ [ð] with ʀ [br] to produce **Ϝóʀʌ** [**hkǫ́bra**], like a brush verb.

(28) ꜱáʁпᴄп᙭᙭ʌꞌɅ **ϛϜóϛᴅʌ**?
wéhkilį okíhpaahą **škǫ́št**a
Do **you** want to dress?

For *you want*, Ϝóħʌ [kǫ́ða] takes ϛ [š] initially and also replaces ħ [ð] with ϛᴅ [št].
For other forms like *he wants* or *she wants* or for the plural forms, Ϝóħʌ [kǫ́ða] follows the basic brush pattern, so no new changes are needed.

Using Ϝóħʌ [kǫ́ða] with nouns and verbs

We use Ϝóħʌ [kǫ́ða] in sentences with both nouns and verbs. Verbs do not need any special form; they appear directly before Ϝóħʌ [kǫ́ða]. We will discuss sentences like these again in chapter 15.

(29) ꜱʌℇúα Ϝóʀʌ ᴍпϜϛά.
wacúe hkǫ́bra mįkšé
I want bread.

(30) ꜱʌℇúα ħʌℇá Ϝóʀʌ ᴍпϜϛά.
wacúe ðaaché hkǫ́bra mįkšé
I want to eat bread.

(31) ꜱʌħó ʌϜóħʌ ʌħпϜϛά.
waaðǫ́ ąkǫ́ða ąðįkšé
We two want to sing.

ńϜuℇα

Exercise 1. Give the English meaning for this short story

ñϜó ʌϜħʌ пᴢóϜα σℇá ʌϜħʌ. ꜱʌℇꞌ ᴅóᴅα Ϝóħʌ ʌϜħʌ.
"ꜱʌℇꞌ ϛϜóϛᴅʌ ᴄпϜϛά?"
"ꞌɅϜʌᴢп. ꜱʌʀó ᴅʌ ᴍпϜϛά."

"𐓏𐓘𐓧𐓣𐓤𐓘 𐓯𐓘𐓷𐓣́?"
"𐓏𐓧̄𐓧𐓘 𐓯𐓘𐓰𐓘 𐓜𐓘 𐓷𐓯𐓣𐓷𐓘."

Exercise 2. Using i-stem verbs

𐓣́𐓧𐓘 [íixa] *laugh* is an i-stem verb. Look at the section on i-stem verbs above and give the forms for *I laugh, you laugh, she laughs, we two laugh, we (plural) laugh, you (plural) laugh,* and *they laugh.*

Exercise 3. Using strong-stem verbs

𐓤𐓘́𐓷𐓘 [káaɣe] *make* is a strong-stem verb. Look at the section on strong-stem verbs above and give the forms for *I make, you make, she makes, we two make, we (plural) make, you (plural) make,* and *they make.*

Exercise 4. Question words

Use the examples presented above as a model to form a question for each of the question words listed here: 𐓏𐓘́𐓧𐓘 [táatą] *what?*, 𐓄𐓘́ [pée] *who?*, 𐓯𐓘𐓷𐓘́𐓤𐓣 [howáįki] *where?*, 𐓯𐓘́𐓷𐓘 [hówa] *which?*, 𐓏𐓘𐓧𐓘́𐓤𐓛𐓣 [haatxą́ci] *when (in the past)?*, 𐓏𐓘𐓧𐓘́𐓧𐓘 [haatxą́ta] *when (in the present or future)?*, 𐓏𐓘́𐓫𐓘 [háaną] *how much* or *how many?*, 𐓏𐓘́𐓤𐓪𐓧𐓘 [háakǫta] *why?* Then, provide an answer for each of your questions.

Exercise 5. 𐓤𐓘́𐓧𐓘 [kǫ́ða] *want*

Review the section on 𐓤𐓘́𐓧𐓘 [kǫ́ða] and then put the following sentences into Osage.

1. I want to bathe.
2. Do you (singular) want to talk?
3. He wants to buy bacon.
4. We (plural) want to drink coffee.
5. They want to laugh.
6. I want a car.
7. You (singular) want firewood.
8. She wants a pretty blanket.
9. We two want ice cream.
10. You (plural) want soup.
11. They want ten dollars.

ńa

Nouns

𐓷𐓘́𐓤𐓘	bróka	dollar
𐓏𐓘̄𐓯𐓤𐓘́𐓷𐓣	haaskámį	shawl

ᴦʌ́ᴊаⲥʞʌ	mázeska	money
ⳑʌ́ᴪɑ ʞńᴘᴤɑ	náye kípše	ice cream
ⳑʌ́ᴪɑ ᴘʌ̄ᴊɑ́ⳑn̄	náye paazénii	ice cream
ⳑn̄ʞʌ́ᴘᴀ̇oʞɑ	niikáapxohke	soda, pop
oħńᴅʌ	oðíhtą	car
oħńᴅʌ ʞ'ʌ́ⲥʌ̄ʞn	oðíhtą k'ą́saaki	train
ᴘʌ̋ᴊɑ ᴢʌ̋	hpéece žą́ą	firewood
ᴘńⲥu	hpísu	acorns
ⲥńʞʌ	síka	squirrel
ɥʌʞóᴅʌᴈn	wahkótahci	church
ɥʌᴘúᴤʞʌ	wapúška	beads
ɥʌᴅóɑᴈn	watóehci	store
ɥʌᴅóᴈn	watóįhci	store (variant)
ɥɑ́ʞnⳑʼ	wéhkilį	dress
ᴢʌ̋ʞoɑ	žą́ąhkoe	trunk, box (variant)
ᴢʌ̋ʞoʞɑ	žą́ąhkoke	trunk, box
ᴢʌ̄ⳑńɑᴢʼ	žą̨ąníežį	candy

Verbs

ʃóᴅʌ	hóohtą (a-ða)	shout, bark, howl
ńᴘʌʃơ	ípahǫ (i-stem, strong)	know
nħʌ́ᴘɑ	iðáhpe (i-stem)	wait, wait for
ńħɑ	íiðe (i-stem)	find, see
ńᴀ̇ʌ	íixa (i-stem)	laugh
ʞóħʌ	kóða (strong, br-šc)	want
ᴘʌ̄ⲥɑ́	paasé (strong-stem)	cut (something up)
ᴅóᴘɑ	tópe (strong-stem)	watch, look at

Question words

ʃʌ́ʞơ	háakǫ	how?
ʃʌ́ʞơᴅʌ	háakǫta	why?
ʃʌ́ⳑʌ	háaną	how many?
ʃʌ̄ᴅᴀ̇ʌ́ᴅʌ	haatxą́ta	when (in the present or future)?
ʃʌ̄ᴅᴀ̇ʌ́ᴈn	haatxą́ci	when (in the past)?
ʃóɥʌ	hówa	which?
ʃoɥʌ́ʞn	hową́įki	where?
ᴘʌ̋	pée	who?
ᴅʌ́ᴅʌ	táatą	what?

Notes for Chapter 8

The form [pe] is usually left out when asking questions in Osage. This is because, as discussed in chapter 2, [pe] is a shortened form of [apiðe], which includes the declarative marker. Questions are inherently in the interrogative mood, not the declarative.

Quintero's *Osage Grammar* uses the term *forticizing stop-stem verbs* to describe verbs like [tǫ́pe] *watch*. The teachers we know usually call verbs like this *strong-stem verbs*. To both simplify jargon and better match how these verbs are currently taught, we use the term *strong-stem verbs* in this book.

Verbs like [ípahǫ] *know* and [kǫ́ða] *want* are sometimes called *doubly inflected* verbs.

Chapter 9

Object Pronouns

ᎣᏏᏲᏅᎠ

1. ᎣᏂᏔᎣᎠᎳ ᏂᏅᏣᎠᏫ ᏃᎴᏂ ᎵᏟᏐᎵ, ᎦᏂᏠ ᎠᎠᎵ ᎠᏎᎯᎠ ᏎᎵᏍᎣᎲᎠ ᏂᎢ ᎠᎵ ᎠᎠᎵ.
2. ᏃᏁᏏᎠ: ᏞᎣᎠᎠᎶᏐᏁ. ᏃᎣᏎᎪᏁ ᎠᎯᎠᎠ ᏎᎵᏍᎣᎲᎠ ᎵᏓᏛᎠ ᎠᎵ ᎵᏝᎠᎠᏄᎭ?
3. ᏃᎵᎮ'ᎣᎠᎵ: ᎦᏂᏣ ᎵᎭᎣᎠᎵᎠ 7ᎵᎦᎣᏟ ᎦᎠᏫᎠᏞᏁ ᎵᏂᏁ ᏂᎮᎵ ᏏᎣᏎᏞᎠ ᎵᏎᎵᏍᎣᎲᎠ ᎠᎵ ᏂᎢ?
4. ᏅᏞᎣᏞᎵ: ᎠᏐᏞᎵ ᎣᏐᎣ᷄ ᎠᎠᎵ?
5. ᏅᏃ᷄: ᎠᏐᎵ ᏞᏁᎬᎣ ᏎᎵᎦᎤᎠ ᏆᏁᏍᎦᎤ.
6. ᏃᎵᎮ'ᎣᎠᎵ: ᎭᎵᏟ!
7. ᏅᏞᎣᏞᎵ: ᏎᎢᏟ ᎵᏐ᷄!
8. ᏃᏁᏏᎠ: ᎣᏂᎣᎭᎵᎦ ᏏᎢᏟᎵ ᎵᎪᎵᎠ ᎠᎵ?
9. ᏅᏃ᷄: ᎣᏂᎣᎭᎵᎦ ᎠᎣᎠᎵ ᎠᎵ ᎵᎪᎵᎠ ᎠᎵ ᎵᎪᏪᎵ. ᎠᎯᎠᎠ ᏎᎵᏍᎣᎲᎠ ᎣᏂᎣᎭᎵᎦ ᏣᎠᎠᎵ ᎵᎪᏪᎵ.
10. ᏁᎭᎵᏎᎠ: ᎣᎠᏪᎵ ᏏᎵᏎᏁᎭᎠᎠᎵ.

1. After the afternoon dance, the family will be going to supper.
2. **Second daughter:** I'm hungry. Where will we eat supper?
3. **First daughter:** Are we going to eat with our family or with the Hominy drumkeeper?
4. **First son:** What are they cooking?
5. **Mother:** Meat gravy and frybread.
6. **First daughter:** Good!
7. **First son:** I really like that!
8. **Second daughter:** What time will we go?
9. **Mother:** When it's 4:00, we will leave. Supper is at 5:00.
10. **Father:** Everybody be ready.

As can be seen from this dialogue, eating is an important part of the dances. Getting to eat with someone who plays an important role in the dances, like the drumkeeper, would make the day even more special.

Ña ʌʞńcʌ̃ɞa

In this chapter we will learn about object pronouns: *me*, *you*, *him*, *her*, *it*, *us*, and *them*. We will also learn how to use object pronouns in combination with subject pronouns. So we will be able to make sentences such as *the woman helped me*, which has *me* as an object pronoun, and also *you helped me*, which has both *you* as a subject pronoun and *me* as an object pronoun.

Object pronouns

Since the object pronouns have many forms, we will introduce them one by one before making a table of them. Some pronouns will have special forms.

Just like the subject pronouns, Osage object pronouns usually appear at the beginning of the verb. If the subject pronoun would be placed inside the verb, like with óʞʌ [óhką] *help*, the object pronoun will appear in the same place the subject pronoun would go. To help make these points clear, the object pronouns have been bolded in the examples below.

The object pronoun ʌ [ą] *me*

In example 1 below, the verb is Dópa [tópe] *look at, watch*, and the pronoun is ʌ [ą] *me*, which attaches to the beginning of the verb root.

(1) ÑÐʌ̃ɞɳ ʌʞʌʌ **ʌDópa** ʌʞʌʌ.
    įhtáci akxa **ą**tópe akxai
    My father was watching **me**.

The verb óʞʌ [óhką] *help* infixes pronouns (see chapter 5.) Notice the difference in sentences 2a and 2b. The pronouns are different, but they are in the same position. Also note that the accent stays on the ó [o] of the verb with the object pronoun in 2a but moves to the subject pronoun ʌ́ [á] in 2b.

(2a) Ñʞó ʌʞʌʌ ó**ʌ**ʞʌ Ðа.
     iihkó akxa ó**ą**hką pe
     My grandmother helped **me**.

(2b) Ñʞó oʌ́ʞʌ.
     iihkó o**á**hką
     I helped my grandmother.

The object pronoun ʜɳ [ði] *you*

Here are similar sentences with the second-person (singular) object pronoun ʜɳ [ði] *you*.

(3) ჹóʞa ʌʞʌʌ **ʜɳ**ᴜʌ́ʞ'o Ðа.
    šóke akxa **ði**nák'ǫ pe
    The dog heard **you**.

(4) 𐓑𐓂𐓤𐓘́ 𐒼𐓏𐒰 𐓂𐓷𐓎𐒼𐓘̨́ 𐒰𐓏𐒰.
ðiihǫ́ apa óðihką apai.
Your mother is helping **you**.

Singular third-person objects: *him, her, it*

Just as we do not have a pronoun for third-person singular subjects, we do not have a pronoun that goes on the verb for third-person singular objects like *him*, *her*, or *it*. This is very different from English, and it can be confusing. Usually, context allows us to understand the meaning. But there are also two common ways to clarify the meaning of a sentence with a third-person singular object, and we will show them below.

Let's begin with a full sentence, one with both a subject and object, and then examine how we can understand its meaning when we omit one or both of its noun phrases. Chapter 13 discusses how to use freestanding third-person pronouns.

(5a) 𐓷𐒰𐒼'𐓘́ 𐒰𐒼𐓷𐒰 𐓓𐓎𐒼𐓘́𐓓𐓎 𐓷𐓎 ó𐒼𐓘̨ 𐓀𐒰.
wak'ó akxa žįkáži wį óhką pe
The woman helped a child.

If we replace the subject 𐓷𐒰𐒼'𐓘́ [wak'ó] with *she*, we get the sentence in 5b.

(5b) 𐓓𐓎𐒼𐓘́𐓓𐓎 𐓷𐓎 ó𐒼𐓘̨ 𐓀𐒰.
žįkáži wį óhką pe
She helped a child.

If we want to then say *she helped him* (or *her*) because we have someone specific in mind, we have two options. We can put something in the object position, as in 5c. Most often this will be 𐓑𐓘́ [ðée] *that one*. The other option is to not use a pronoun at all, as in 5d. This would then mean *she helped him* (or *her* or *it*).

(5c) **𐓑𐓘́** ó𐒼𐓘̨ 𐓀𐒰.
ðée óhką pe
She helped **that one** (him, her).

(5d) Ó𐒼𐓘̨ 𐓀𐒰.
óhką pe
She helped **him** (or *her* or *it*).

If we mean that she helped people in general, and we don't have anyone particular in mind, we use a special pronoun, 𐓏𐒰 [wa]. This pronoun has many uses in Osage, and one of the most important is to give the meaning of some indefinite thing—folks or stuff. 𐓏𐒰 [wa] goes in the place where pronouns appear on the verb.

(5e) Ó𐓏𐒰𐒼𐓘̨ 𐓀𐒰.
ówahką pe
She helped **folks.**

We will discuss this use of ꜱᴀ [wa] again in chapter 19.

Plural object pronouns

Osage pronouns for plural objects are more complicated than the singular forms. The pronouns for plural *you* and *us* consist of two parts, one that appears at the beginning of the verb and one at the end. For example, the pronoun for *us* has ꜱᴀ [wa] before the verb and ᴀᴘᴨ [api] after the verb.

An additional complication, particularly when we use both subject and object pronouns together, is that there are multiple meanings possible. Some meanings can be distinguished by using different aspect markers, but in many cases, we will need context to help us understand the intended meaning.

ꜱᴀ . . . ᴀᴘᴨ [wa . . . api] *us*

Osage distinguishes between *we two* and *we plural* for subject pronouns; however, there is only one plural first-person object pronoun, ꜱᴀ . . . ᴀᴘᴨ [wa . . . api], which means *us*. In most cases, the ᴀ [a] in ᴀᴘᴨ [api] will be deleted. This happens in example 6 where, instead of óꜱᴀȟᴀᴀᴘᴨ [ówahką̈api], we have óꜱᴀȟᴀᴘᴨ [ówahką̈pi].

(6) Įᴆᴀᵶᴨ ᴀᴘᴀ óꜱᴀȟᴀᴘᴨ ᴆᴀ ᴀᴘᴀ.
    į̈htáci apa **ówahką̈pi** hta apai
    My father will help **us**.

Another point is that object pronouns often vary slightly when we use completive rather than continuous aspect, as shown in the sentences below.

Remember from chapter 2 that when a sentence is in completive aspect and when the subject is in third-person, we need to use the ᴘᴀ [pe] aspect marker. When a sentence is in completive aspect, the plural marker ᴀᴘᴨ [api] will become ᴘᴀ [pe]. This would seem to require two ᴘᴀ's [pe], one to help form the plural and another for aspect. However, in Osage, we use a single ᴘᴀ [pe] to both form the plural and serve as the aspect marker. When this happens in this book, we will attach ᴘᴀ [pe] to the verb and understand that it indicates both a plural object and completive aspect.

(7) Ōᴢʀ́ ᴀȟ̈ᴛᴀ ꜱᴀᴢʀ́ȟ'ᴏᴘᴀ.
    iiną́ akxa **waną́k'ǫpe** (not [waną́k'ǫpi pe].)
    Mother heard about **us**.

Sentence 7 is in completive aspect with a third-person subject ōᴢʀ́ [iiną́], so the sentence will end with the aspect marker ᴘᴀ [pe]. But the object pronoun is plural ꜱᴀ . . . ᴀᴘᴨ [**wa . . . api**], so the ᴀᴘᴨ [api] will become ᴘᴀ [pe] too. We only say one ᴘᴀ [pe], which we will interpret as plural, and we will understand that this is also in completive aspect.

When we use continuous aspect as in example 8, the aspect markers will tell us what the subject is, so we will have to rely much less on context.

(8) ȟakǫ́ȥa iiná akxa **wanák'ǫpi** akxai
    ðekǫ́ǫce iiną́ akxa **waną́k'ǫpi** akxai
    Now Mother hears **us**.

ȟn ... api [ði ... api] *you plural*

We make *you plural* with ȟn ... api [ði ... api]. ȟn [ði] appears in the place where pronouns go on the verb, and api [api] comes after the verb stem, just as we did with wa ... api [wa ... api].

In 9, like in 7 above, pe [pe] indicates both the plural object and completive aspect.

(9) iiná akxa **ðinák'ǫpe**.
    iiną́ akxa **ðiną́k'ǫpe**
    Mother heard **you (plural)**.

Example 10 illustrates the continuous aspect. The *pi* plural marker appears as well as the aspect marker.

(10) iiná akxa **ðinák'ǫpi** akxai.
    iiną́ akxa **ðiną́k'ǫpi** akxai
    Mother hears **you (plural)**.

wá [wá] *them*

Plural third-person objects need to be marked. They take the pronoun wá [wá], which carries an accent. How can we tell the difference between this and the unaccented wa [wa] we discussed above? Here are some examples of sentences with indefinite wa [wa] and plural object wá [wá].

(11a) šítoži akxa ho ðǫǫpá ðuuzá pe.
    šį́toží akxa ho ðǫǫpá ðuuzá pe
    The boy took two fish.

In 11b, wá [wá] tells us that the boy took the two fish we are referring to.

(11b) šítoži akxa **wáðuuza** pe.
    šį́toží akxa **wáðuuza** pe
    The boy took **them**.

In 11c, unaccented wa [wa] tells us that the boy took something or other.

(11c) šítoži akxa **waðúuza** pe.
    šį́toží akxa **waðúuza** pe
    The boy took **stuff**.

Special forms

When any 𐓷𐓘 [wa] pronoun, accented or unaccented, appears on a verb that begins with the sound 𐓣 [i] (an i-stem verb, see chapter 8), it will change to 𐓷𐓟́ [wé] and the 𐓣 [i] disappears. (If the i-sound is long, then we use 𐓷𐓟́ [wée].) We show this with the common verb 𐓣́𐓭𐓘 [íiðe] *see*. The distinction between a plural object and the indefinite can only be made by context.

(12) 𐓮𐓪́𐓤𐓘 𐓘𐓷𐓣 𐓷𐓟́𐓭𐓘 𐓘𐓷𐓣.
sǫ́ke apa **wéeðe** apai
The dog sees **them**.
OR The dog sees **stuff**.

(13) 𐓵𐓣́𐓭𐓤𐓘 𐓘𐓷𐓣 𐓷𐓟́𐓭𐓘 𐓘𐓷𐓣.
níhka apa **wéeðe** apai
The man sees **them**.
OR The man sees **stuff**.

Using subject and object pronouns together

Now that we have both subject and object pronouns, we can begin to say very important things like *I see you* and *you are helping us*.

You may have already wondered, if both the subject pronouns and the object pronouns are placed right before the verb root, what will happen if we need to use both of them?

Order of pronouns

Even though Osage places the subject before the object in a sentence, the usual order of the pronouns on the verb is *object, subject*. However, there are several special cases that we will also examine.

You-me: *you* (subject)—*me* (object)

We have highlighted the pronouns to show how the object 𐓘 [ą] *me* comes before the subject 𐓭𐓘 [ða] *you*.

(14) **𐓘𐓭𐓘́𐓵𐓘𐓤'𐓪?**
ąðánąk'ǫ
Did **you** hear **me**?

In sentence 15, we know the a-ða verb ó𐓤𐓘 [óhką] *help* infixes pronouns after the initial o [o].

(15) **O𐓘́𐓭𐓘𐓤𐓘.**
oą́ðahką
You helped **me**.

Note that when ο [o] is followed by ʌ [a] or ʌ̨ [ą], most people pronounce a short ꜣ [w] between them, like οꜣʌ̃ʌƀʌ [ową́ðahką]. Sometimes, the [o] even changes to match the [ą], giving us the pronunciation ʌ̨ꜣʌ̃ʌƀʌ [ąwą́ðahką] for some people.

In 16, οԵꜛka [oðį́ike] *hug* is in the brush class, so its subject is ᑫꜱ [šc] *you*, which comes after the object, ʌ̨ [ą] *me*.

(16) Oʌ̨ᑫꜱꜛka.
 oą́šcįike
 You hugged **me**.

In example 17, ᴅόᴘa [tǫ́pe] *look at* is in the strong-stem class, so its subject, *you*, is ᑫ [š].

(17) ʌ̨ᑫᴅόᴘa ᴢꜛᑫά.
 ąštǫ́pe nįkšé (or, in place of [nįkšé], another form of continuous aspect)
 You're looking at **me**.

A special form for *me*

When a verb is in the i-stem class, like ńᴘʌʃơ [ípahǫ] *know* and ńꜛa [íiðe] *see*, it will have a special form for the *me* pronoun: ʌᴢʌ̃ [ąną́]. This pronoun will also cause the initial n [i] to be deleted.

(18) ʌᴢʌ̃ʌ̃ꜛa.
 ąną́ðaðe
 You see **me**.
(19) ʌᴢʌ̃ᑫᴘʌʃơ.
 ąną́špahǫ
 You know **me**.

ꜣn [wi] *I* (subject)—*you* (object)

In Osage we have a special form for when the subject is *I* and the object is *you singular* or *you plural*. This pronoun ꜣn [wi] takes the place of both subject and object. It can only be used for *I-you*; it cannot be used for *you-me*. Very often the accent will be moved to the ꜣn [wi] pronoun, as we see in example 20.

(20) ᑕnᴅό οꜣńƀʌ.
 sitǫ́į owíhką
 Yesterday **I** helped **you (singular or plural)**.
(21) ƀaƀόꜱa ńꜣnꜛa ꟼꜛᑫά.
 ðekǫ́ǫce íiwiðe mįkšé (or, in place of [mįkšé], another form of continuous aspect)
 Right now **I** see **you (singular or plural)**.

When we have brush verbs, we use both ᏏᏁ [wi] and the ᏒR [br] pronoun.

(22) ᎣᏏᏁRᏁᏦᎠ.
   owíbriįke
   I hugged **you (singular or plural)**.

Similarly, strong-stem verbs use both ᏏᏁ [wi] and the Ꭻ [h] pronoun.

(23) ᏂᏏᏁᎠᎧᏐ ᎹᏁᏦᎦᎠ.
   iwíhpahǫ mįkšé
   I know **you (singular or plural)**.

Plural forms *you-us* and *you-them*

The plural object for *us*, ᏏᎶ...ᎶᎠᏁ [wa...api], appears in its full form in continuous aspect. The you subject-marker, ᏂᎶ [ða], stays unchanged.

(24a) ᎫᎮᎠᎶ ᏂᎠ ᎣᏏᎶᏂᏦᎶᎠᏁ ᏞᏁᏦᎦᎠ.
   háąpa ðe owaðáhkąpi nįkšé
   Today you are helping **us (plural)**.
(24b) ᎫᎮᎠᎶ ᏂᎠ ᎣᏏᎶᏂᎶᏦᎶ ᏞᏁᏦᎦᎠ.
   háąpa ðe owáðahką nįkšé
   Today you are helping **them**.

ᎶᎠᏁ [api] becomes ᎠᎠ [pe] in completive aspect.

(24c) ᏎᏁᎠᎤ ᎣᏏᎶᏂᏦᎶᎠᎠ.
   sitǫ́į owaðáhkąpe
   Yesterday you helped **us**.

Verbs from the i-stem class will change ᏏᎶ [wa] to ᏏᎠ̃ [wée] in the manner we have seen in other ᏏᎶ [wa] pronouns.

(25a) **ᏏᎠ̃ᏂᎶᏂᎶᎠᏁ** ᏞᏁᏦᎦᎠ.
   wéeðaðapi nįkšé
   You see **us**.
(25b) ᏎᏁᎠᎤ **ᏏᎠ̃ᏂᎶᏂᎶᎠᎠ**.
   sitǫ́į **wée**ðaðape
   Yesterday you saw **us**.

Some people pronounce this as ᏏᎠ̃ᏂᎠ̄ᎠᎠ [wéeðaape].
When we have a third-person subject, we only have the object pronoun.

(25c) 𐓈𐓘𐓬𐓘𐓬𐓣 𐓘𐓬𐓣.
    wéeðapi apai
    He sees **us**.

As we know, verb stems ending in α [e] will change that sound to ʌ [a] before ÞΑ [pe] or ʌÞΩ [api]. So forms of óħα [íiðe] will change the final stem vowel to ʌ [a] whenever the plural marker is attached, just as it changes when ÞΩ [pe] marks third-person completive aspect.

Using plural forms of object pronouns

Plural forms: using *we* and *you*

Recall that the subject pronoun for *we* is ʌƙ [ąk] or ʌ [ą]. This means that it can be confused with ʌ [ą] *me*. But one way that Osage handles this problem is to change the rule about the object pronoun coming before the subject. When the subject is *we*, ʌƙ [ąk] or one of its variants will come first, before the object pronoun, except when that pronoun is 𐓈ʌ [wa], as we will see below. In many, but not all, verbs with infixed pronouns, ʌƙ [ąk] will appear first, as we see in examples 26–27, with óƙʌ [óhką] *help*.

From chapter 6, recall that Osage distinguishes between dual and plural *we* in subject pronouns. The aspect of the sentence is very important here. In completive aspect, dual *we two* takes the form of ʌ [ą] or ʌƙ [ąk], while plural *we* is ʌ . . . ÞΩ [ą . . . pe] or ʌƙ . . . ÞΩ [ąk . . . pe]. In the next two examples, remember that ħΩ [ði] is the object pronoun for *you*.

(26a) **ʌƙóħΩƙʌ.**
    ąkóðihką
    We two (dual) helped **you**.

(26b) **ʌƙóħΩƙʌÞΩ.**
    ąkóðihkąpe
    We (plural or dual) helped **you (singular or plural)**.

In completive aspect, we have a problem in interpreting example 26b. Because we can only have one ÞΩ [pe] on the verb, and because *you plural* is ħΩ . . . ʌÞΩ [ði . . . api], we will have to use context to know if this verb means *we two helped you (plural)*, *we (plural) helped you (singular)*, or *we (plural) helped you (plural)*.

We do not have this problem in continuous aspect because the aspect marker tells us what the subject is. Remember that continuous aspect markers come in several variations; we are giving one variation in these examples.

(27a) ʌƙóħΩƙʌ **ʌħΩƙʂá.**
    ąkóðihką **ąðįkšé**
    We two (dual) are helping **you**.

(27b) ʌƙóħΩƙʌ **ʌƙʌħα.**
    ąkóðihką **ąkáðe**
    We (plural) have been helping **you**.

(27c) ΛƙóħΩƙΛÞՈ **ΛħΩƙᚦá**.
 ąkóðihkąpi **ąðįkšé**
 We two (dual) are helping **you (plural)**.

(27d) ΛƙóħΩƙΛÞՈ **ΛƙΛħɑ**.
 ąkóðihkąpi **ąkáðe**
 We (plural) have been helping **you (plural)**.

A second complication with Λ [ą] is that it means both *we* and *me*. With many verbs, the meaning will sometimes have to be clarified either by context or by using continuous aspect, which tells us the subject.

(28a) **ΛㄥΛƙ'ơ** Þɑ.
 ąnąk'ǫ́ pe
 He heard **me**.

(28b) **ΛㄥΛƙ'ơ Þɑ**.
 ąnák'ǫ**pe**
 We heard him.

Sentences 28a and 28b will sound the same, but we write them differently to help us distinguish their meanings.

(28c) **ΛㄥΛƙ'ớ** ΛƙʌΛ.
 ąnák'ǫ akxai
 He hears **me**.

(28d) **ΛㄥΛƙ'ơ Λħá**.
 ąnák'ǫ **ąðé**
 We two hear him.

(28e) **ΛㄥΛƙ'ơ ΛƙΛÞʌƙ**.
 ąnák'ǫ **ąkatxą́**
 We hear him.

Verbs in the i-stem class again use the form ΛㄥΛ́ [ąną́], which again can mean either *we* or *me*. In continuous aspect, we know which meaning is intended because the subject is also indicated by the aspect marker, as in 29b and 29d.

(29a) ՐՈÞó **ΛㄥΛ́ħΛ** Þɑ.
 sitǫ́į **ąną́**ða pe
 Yesterday she saw **me**.

(29b) ħakóʕɑ **ΛㄥΛ́ħɑ** ΛÞΛ.
 ðekǫ́ǫce **ąną́**ðe apai
 Now she sees **me**.

(29c) ՐՈÞó **ΛㄥΛ́ħΛÞɑ**.
 sitǫ́į **ąną́**ðape
 Yesterday **we** saw him.

(29d) 𐓏𐒰𐓤𐓓𐒷𐒰 𐓘𐓒𐓣𐓏𐒰 𐓘𐓤𐒰𐓈𐓶𐓻.
ðekǫ́ǫce ąną́ðe ąkatxą́
Now **we** see him.

Plural forms: using *you plural*

We have a similar pattern for *you plural* pronouns. When either the subject or object is plural, 𐓘𐓷𐓣 [api] or its completive form 𐓷𐒰 [pe] will appear on the verb. In completive aspect, context will determine the meaning of the verb when we have 𐒰 [ą] and 𐓏𐓣 [ði] as well as 𐓷𐒰 [pe], as in example 30b.

(30a) 𐓘𐓏𐒰𐓒𐒰𐓤'𐓪𐓷𐒰.
aðánąk'ǫ**pe**
You (plural) heard me.

(30b) 𐓘𐓏𐓣𐓒𐒰𐓤'𐓪𐓷𐒰.
aðínąk'ǫ́**pe**
We heard **you (plural)**.

With the right context, 30b could also mean *we heard you (singular)*. However, without such a context, the meaning *you plural* is usually the first meaning to come to mind for Osage speakers.

In continuous aspect, the aspect marker will always tell us what the subject is.

(30c) 𐓘𐓏𐓣𐓒𐒰𐓤'𐓪𐓷𐓣 𐓘𐓤𐒰𐓈𐓶𐓻.
aðínąk'ǫpi ąkatxą́
We hear you (plural).

Third-person subjects and 𐓷𐒰́ [wé]

Recall that the form 𐓷𐒰 [wa] can refer to an indefinite thing, and that accented 𐓷𐒰́ [wá] is *them*, and that 𐓷𐒰 [wa] can also be the first part of the pronoun for *us*, 𐓷𐒰 . . . 𐓘𐓷𐓣 [wa . . . api]. If 𐓷𐒰 [wa] in any form also precedes the sound 𐓣 [i], the 𐓷𐒰 [wa] will become 𐓷𐒰́ [wé].

Since the third-person subject is unmarked, there are many completive aspect forms that sound the same.

(31) 𐓷𐒰́𐓏𐒰 𐓷𐒰.
wéeða pe
They (or he or she) saw stuff.
OR They (or he or she) saw them.

(32) 𐓷𐒰́𐓏𐒰𐓷𐒰.
wéeðape
They (or he or she) saw us.

Again, we can clarify the object when the continuous aspect is used, although we cannot distinguish singular or plural subject.

(33) ᏍᎾᏫᎵᏓ ᎸᎠᎵ.
wéeðapi apa
They (or he or she) see us.

ᏫᏣ'ᏌᏋᎠ

Exercise 1. Give the English meaning for this short story

ᏍᎳᏎᎣᎳ ᎵᏣᎵ ᏍᎳᎠᎣ'ᎠᏋᏁ ᏋᏁ ᏣᎴᎠᎾᏁᎯ ᏍᎾ ᎥᏣᎵ ᎠᏆ. ᏣᎴᎠᎾᏁᎯ ᎵᏣᎵ ᏍᎳᎠᎣᎠ ᎵᎠᎵ.
"ᏍᎳᏎᎣᎳ! ᏍᎳᏣᏋᎤᏍᎯ? DᎯᎠᎵ ᏣᏋᎤᏍᎯ?"
"ZᾱᏗᏁᎠᏃᎯ ᏍᎯᎬᎤᏍᎯ."
ᏣᎴᎠᎾᏁᎯ ᎵᏣᎵ ᎥᏣᎵ ᎠᏆ.
"ᏍᎳᏎᎣᎳ ᏂᏣᏗᎯ ᏗᏁ!"

Exercise 2. Singular object pronouns

Look at sentences 1–5. Now use the verb oᏋᏆ [océ] *look for*, and make sentences using all the singular object pronouns.

Exercise 3. Plural objects pronouns

Look at sentences 6–13. Use the verb oᏋᏆ [océ] *look for*, or ᏂᏑᏍᎮ [ðuwį́] *buy*, and make sentences using all the plural object pronouns.

Exercise 4. Subject and object pronouns

Look at sentences 14–29. Using the verb ᏗᏣ'ᏬᏰ [nąk'ǫ́] *hear* (a-ða), make the following sentences:

1. I hear you.
2. You hear me.
3. We hear you (plural).
4. You hear us.
5. You hear them.

ᏫᎠ

Nouns

ᎯᏗᏣᏲᎠ	ánąąhkoe	floor, porch
ᎫᎧ	hą́ą	night
ᎫᎧᎠᎵ	hą́ąpa	day
ᎫᎣᎠᎧ	hóohtą	animal noise

ʞʌʎʌ	káxa	creek
ᒪƆᒐÓÐᴧ	lǫǫhóohtą	thunder
ᵐÃΨα	mą́ąγe	weather
ᒐᴧΨα	ną́γe	ice
ᒐñᴣU	níižu	rain
OÞ'ʎʈʌ	op'ą́ða	steam, fog on water
Oᴣᾰᴈɴ	ožéhci	bathroom
ÞΛ	pa	snow
ᴈńOʞ̧ʌ	hcíohka	room
५ʌᒐÚ	wahú	bone

Verbs

ʞ̧ōÞ५α̃	hkoopšé (a-ða)	run away, flee
OÞα̃	ohpé (a-ða)	enter, go in
ʈūᵴʎᑕU	ðuuwásu (br-šc)	clean, clean up

Adjectives

ᒐŎ̧	nǫ́ǫ	old, elderly
५ʌᒐÓʞ̧'ʌ	wahók'a	young

Other

ʎᒪñᒐʌ	álįįha	afterward
ᵐńOÞʌ ʎʞ̧ɴᒐʌ	mį́įǫpa áhkiha	next month
ᵐńOʈʌʞ̧α	mį́įoðaake	clock, o'clock, time of day (LITERALLY sun tells it)
ᵐńOʈʌʞ̧α ᒐʎᒪʌ	mį́įoðaake háaną	what time?

Notes for Chapter 9

The sequence ʈʌʈʌ [ðaða] in words like ५α̃ʈʌʈʌÞα [wéeðaðape] is often pronounced as a long ʈʌ̄ [ðaa].

Chapter 10

Stative Verbs

ᎣᏏᏲᏓ

1. **ᎤᏥ:** ᏌᎾᏐᏛᎢ ᎸᎨᏂᎵ ᏌᏞᏐᏥᎠ ᎠᎵ.
2. **ᎤᎵó:** ᏌᎠᏅᎲᎨᎠ ᎵᎨÓᎠᎸᏂ ᎵᎨÃᏇᎠ ᎠᎵ.
3. **ᎤᏥó:** ᏉᎸᎲ ᏥᎠ ᎨᎠ ᏱᎴᏑᎵᎻᏓ ᏋᎩᏂ ᎴᎴᏂᏥᎠ ᎠᎵ ᎵᎨᎠᎠᏪᏥᎵ.
4. **ᎤᏔᎵᎨᎠ:** ᏌᏁᏋᎾᏛᎵ, ᏫᎾᏚᎠᏕᎵᎠ ᎠÓᎠ ᏞᎴᎶᎤᎽᎤ ᏋᏉᏂ ᎨᎥᏂᎴᎵᏆ ÁᏃᎤ ᎸᏒᎾ ᏬᏁᏅᎠ.
5. **ᎤᏥó:** Ꮀ́ᎴᏂ ᎠᎵ ᎸᎨᏂᎵ.
6. **ᎤᎵó:** ᏂakőᎨᎠ, ᏉáᎠ ᏌᎴᏐᏥᎠ ᎦᏂᏍᎨá?
7. **ᎤᎴőᎠᎵ:** ᏌᎾᎠ, áᏋᏁᏬ.
8. **ᎤᏥó:** ᏌᎾᏐᏛᎵ, ᏉáᎠ ᏌᎠᏅᎲᎨᎠ Ꮩ'ᎾᎵᎦ?
9. **ᎨᏂőᏋᎵ:** ᏌᎾᎠ, áᏋᏁᏬ.
10. **ᎤᎵó:** ᏋᏅᏂᎨᏃ, ᏫᎾᏌᎠᎸᎨᎠ ᎴᎤᏑᎠᏋᎤ.
11. **ᏌᎸᏐᎠᎵ:** ᏫᎾᏌᎠᎸᎨᎠ ᏃᎶᎨᎠ ᎸᎴᏑᎠᏋᎤ.
12. **ᏌᏂᎤá:** ᏫᎾᏌᎠᎸᎨᎠ ᎠÓᎠᎤ ᎸᎴᏑᎠᏋᎤ.
13. **ᎤᏥó:** Ꮀ́ᎴᏂ. . . . ᎵᏋᏂᎴᏂᏋᎠᎸᎠ.

1. **Grandma:** Tomorrow is Giveaway.
2. **Mother:** Let's make our bundles.
3. **Grandma:** These are the blankets and shawls we are going to give away.
4. **Father:** I also have some money and tobacco to put on the drum.
5. **Grandma:** It'll be good.
6. **Mother:** Now, who is going to tie up the giveaway?
7. **Eldest son:** Me, I will do it.
8. **Grandma:** Tomorrow, who will carry the bundle?
9. **Second son:** Me, I will do it.
10. **Mother:** Girls, get your blankets ready.
11. **First daughter:** I have my red blanket ready.
12. **Second daughter:** I have my blue blanket ready.
13. **Grandma:** Good. . . . We are ready.

A bundle, 𐓷𐓘𐓷𐓘𐓷𐓘𐓷𐓘 [wapáaxce], consists of blankets, shawls, and other items that will be given away on Sunday, the last day of Ilonshka. Bundles are usually tied up in a piece of fabric or a sheet. People can also put the items in trunks (𐓵𐓘𐓵𐓘𐓵𐓘 [žą́ąhkoe]). The 𐓷𐓘𐓷𐓘𐓷𐓘 [waníðe] *giveaway items* are carried to the arbor and placed on the ground at the appropriate time, when the family's song ends. The family will then open the bundle and call names of the people they will give away items to.

𐓄𐓘 𐓷𐓘𐓷𐓘𐓷𐓘𐓷𐓘

Besides the verb classes that tell us which pronouns to use, Osage has a more general distinction between verbs that are considered *active* and those considered *stative*. This distinction is extremely common in Native American languages and, indeed, in the languages of the world. As the name suggests, stative verbs are those whose subject is experiencing some sort of state rather than doing something. We can often guess which verbs will be stative from their meanings, but sometimes verbs that seem like they should be stative are treated as active in Osage. There are also many concepts that are expressed by adjectives in English but that are stative verbs in Osage. For example, *sick* and *hungry* are adjectives in English but are stative verbs in Osage.

Stative verbs

Let us start by looking at a stative verb with a named subject, *the woman*. Here are example sentences that show the set of forms for the verb 𐓷𐓘𐓷𐓘𐓷𐓘 [húheka] *be sick*.

(1a) 𐓷𐓘𐓷'ó 𐓘𐓶𐓘𐓶 𐓷𐓘𐓷𐓘𐓷𐓘 𐓘𐓶𐓘𐓶.
    wak'ó akxa húheka akxai
    The woman is sick (and she is here).
    OR The women are sick.
(1b) 𐓷𐓘𐓷'ó 𐓘𐓐𐓘 𐓷𐓘𐓷𐓘𐓷𐓘 𐓘𐓐𐓘.
    wak'ó apa húheka apai
    The woman is sick (and she is elsewhere).
    OR The women are sick.

Remember that in third-person, singular and plural forms are the same. We distinguish them by context. Stative verbs most commonly take continuous aspect in Osage. Stative verbs usually do not have objects. The stative subject pronouns are as follows:

𐓘 [ą]	first-person *I*
𐓷𐓘 [wa]	first-person dual and plural *we*
𐓐𐓘 [ði]	second-person singular and plural *you*
(no pronoun used)	third-person singular and plural *he, she, it, they*

These subject pronouns are all illustrated in the sentences below.

Stative verbs and continuous aspect markers

Sometimes verbs are not used with an aspect marker. In chapter 5, when we used first- and second-person pronouns, the completive aspect is assumed and does not need to be included. With stative verbs, if we don't use an aspect marker with first- or second-person subjects (*I, we two, we plural, you singular,* or *you plural*), then we understand the aspect to be continuous. If we do use an aspect marker, we add different nuances to the sentence. When we use an aspect marker, we take advantage of the fact that it marks *position* to emphasize the position of the subject.

In examples 2a, 2b, and 2c, notice the difference in emphasis when we use a continuous aspect marker with the singular pronoun *I*.

(2a) 𐓘𐓷𐓶𐓲𐓘𐓤𐓘.
ąhúheka
I am sick.

We would use example 2a in a situation where we just wanted to declare the condition of being sick. This is because 𐓷𐓶𐓲𐓘𐓤𐓘 [húheka] is stative and so continuous by its nature and doesn't need the aspect marker to emphasize this.

(2b) 𐓘𐓷𐓶𐓲𐓘𐓤𐓘 **𐓉𐓂𐓤𐓯𐓟**.
ąhúheka **mįkšé**.
I am **sitting** here sick.

In 2b, adding the continuous aspect marker 𐓉𐓂𐓤𐓯𐓟 [mįkšé] emphasizes the position of the subject—sitting.

(2c) 𐓘𐓷𐓶𐓲𐓘𐓤𐓘 **𐓘𐓷𐓟**.
ąhúheka **ąhé**
I am sick while **moving around**.
OR I **have been** sick.

In 2c, someone might say this if speaking on the phone where she can't be seen and wants to indicate that she's still able to walk around. As we already learned, using 𐓘𐓷𐓟 [ąhé] could also be interpreted as *have been*, as in *I have been sick*.

Plural subjects with stative verbs

With plurals, the Osage language takes advantage of the fact that aspect markers give us information about *number*. This is what allows us to distinguish, for example, plural *you* from singular *you*.

𐓻𐓂 [ðí] is the stative pronoun we use for *you singular* and for *you plural*. As we saw above, if we do not use a continuous aspect marker with 𐓻𐓂 [ðí] as in example 3a, we understand that the aspect is continuous and that the subject is *you singular*. However, when we add the plural continuous aspect marker 𐓹𐓘𐓯𐓟 [paašé], as in 3b, we understand the subject as *you plural*.

(3a) **Ꮏꮒꮪꭴꮜꭿᏸꭸ.**
ðihúheka
You (singular) are sick.

(3b) **Ꮏꮒꭴꮜꭿᏸꭸ ᏆᎸᏋᎠ.**
ðihúheka **paašé**
You (plural) are sick.

In short, we tell the difference between singular and plural *you* by the presence of the aspect marker ᏆᎸᏋᎠ [paašé].

In 4a and 4b, we tell the difference between dual and plural *we* by the aspect markers ꭰꮢꮑᏸᎠ [ą̊ðįkšé] for dual and ꭰᏸᎧꮠ [ąkáðe] for plural. Note that the aspect for *sitting* will be the one we typically use for stative verbs. See chapter 6.

(4a) **Ꮙꮈꭴꮜꭿᏸꭸ ꭰꮢꮑᏸᎠ.**
wahúheka **ą̊ðįkšé**
We two are sick.

(4b) **Ꮙꮈꭴꮜꭿᏸꭸ ꭰᏸᎧꮠ.**
wahúheka **ąkáðe**
We (plural) are sick.

Example 5 shows again the use of the "standing" version of first-person plural ꭰᏸꭰᎠᏯᎢ [ąkatxái] to show position. This might be said in a context where several people are waiting in line to get into a clinic, and we want to emphasize that they are standing.

(5) **Ꮙꮈꭴꮜꭿᏸꭸ ꭰᏸꭰᎠᏯᎢ.**
wahúheka **ąkatxái**
We are **standing** here sick. (more than two and in a standing position)

Infixing verbs like ᏃᏆᎠꮒ [nǫhpéhi] and ᏆᏂᎦ [níhce]

The verbs ᏃᏆᎠꮒ [nǫhpéhi] *be hungry* and ᏆᏂᎦ [níhce] *be cold* are stative verbs whose subject pronouns appear inside the verb root. In other words, the pronouns are *infixed* into the verb.

(6) **ᏳꮖᏪꮒᏃ ꭰᏸᏯꭸ ᏃᏆᎠꮒ ꭰᏸᏯꭸ.**
šįmįžį akxa nǫhpéhi akxai
The girl is hungry.
OR **The girls are hungry.** (Typically used if the girls are present. We would use the subject marker ꭰᏆꭸ [apa] if the girls were somewhere else.)

In third-person, stative verbs generally take the continuous aspect marker ꭰᏸᏯꭸ [akxai] and ꭰᏆꭸ [apai]. Recall that these aspect markers indicate how distant or present the subject is rather than its position.

With other subjects, we place the stative pronoun inside the verb and use aspect markers to indicate dual and plural subjects. We have bolded the pronouns and aspect markers to show this in the sentences below.

(7a) ᎳᎣᏖᎠᏃᏍᏂ.
    nǫhpéa̧hi
    I am hungry.

(7b) ᎳᎣᏖᎠᏃᏍᏂ **ᏘᏂᏣᏋᎠ**.
    nǫhpéa̧hi **mi̧kšé**
    I am hungry **(sitting)**.

(8a) ᎳᎣᏖᎠᏢᏂᏍᏂ.
    nǫhpéðihi
    You are hungry.

(8b) ᎳᎣᏖᎠᏢᏂᏍᏂ ᎳᏂᏣᏋᎠ.
    nǫhpéðihi **ni̧kšé**
    You are hungry **(sitting)**.

(8c) ᎳᎣᏖᎠᏢᏂᏍᏂ ᏖᎠᏋᎠ.
    nǫhpéðihi **paašé**
    You (plural) are hungry.

(9a) ᎳᎣᏖᎠᏏᎳᏍᏂ ᎳᏢᏂᏣᏋᎠ.
    nǫhpéwahi **a̧ðįkšé**
    We two are hungry.

(9b) ᎳᎣᏖᎠᏏᎳᏍᏂ ᎳᏣᎷᏢᎠ.
    nǫhpéwahi **a̧káðe**
    We (plural) are hungry.

(10a) ᎳᏃᎳᎨᎠ.
    nía̧hce
    I am cold.

(10b) ᎳᏃᎳᎨᎠ **ᏘᏂᏣᏋᎠ**.
    nía̧hce **mi̧kšé**
    I am cold **(sitting)**.

(10c) ᎳᏃᎳᎨᎠ ᎳᏍᎠ.
    nía̧hce **a̧hé**
    I am cold **(moving around)**.

(11a) ᎳᏃᏏᎳᎨᎠ ᎳᏣᎷᏢᎠ.
    níwahce **a̧káðe**
    We (plural) are cold.

(11b) ᎳᏃᏏᎳᎨᎠ ᎳᏣᎳᎠᏲᏍᎠ.
    níwahce **a̧katxái**
    We (plural) are cold **(standing)**.

I-stem stative verbs

Stative verbs like ᎥᏖᎤᏃᎠ [ípuze] *be thirsty* have the same special pronoun forms as the other i-stem verbs (see chapter 8). Again, we have bolded the pronouns and aspect markers below to show how to use i-stem verbs.

(12a) **ᏁᎳᏁ**ᏖᎤᏃᎠ.
    a̧nápuze
    I am thirsty.

(12b) 𐒰𐓓𐒰́𐓣𐓲𐒷 𐓬𐓣𐔌𐒷́.
ąnápuze mįkšé
I am thirsty (**sitting**).

(13a) 𐒻́𐓮𐓣𐓲𐒷.
íðipuze
You are thirsty.

(13b) 𐒻́𐓮𐓣𐓲𐒷 𐓧𐓣𐔌𐒷́.
íðipuze nįkšé
You are thirsty (**sitting**).

(13c) 𐒻́𐓮𐓣𐓲𐒷 𐓬𐒰𐔌𐒷́.
íðipuze paašé
You (plural) are thirsty.

(14a) 𐓏𐒷́𐓣𐓲𐒷 𐒰𐓮𐓣𐔌𐒷́.
wéepuze ąðįkšé
We two are thirsty. (See chapter 9 for why this begins with [wée].)

(14b) 𐓏𐒷́𐓣𐓲𐒷 𐒰𐔌𐒰́𐓮𐒰.
wéepuze ąkáðe
We (plural) are thirsty.

(15) 𐒻́𐓣𐓲𐒷 𐒰𐔌𐓯𐒰.
ípuze akxai
He/she/they is/are thirsty.

Words for feelings

Osage has several words that mean things such as *like, love, enjoy, feel good*. Some of them are synonyms, meaning we can use whichever we choose and the meaning will be pretty much the same. Others have more special meanings.

Ki-stative verbs

Many words about feelings belong to a verb class called *ki-statives*. We will study 𐔌𐓣𐓷𐒰́𐓧𐓣 [kiðáli], 𐔌𐒻́𐓪𐓎 [kíhǫǫ], 𐔌𐒻́𐓲𐓪 [kízo], and 𐔌𐒻́𐓪𐔎𐓵𐒰 [kíoxta]. With ki-stative verbs, we only include the 𐔌𐓣 [ki] syllable for third-person subjects. First- and second-person subjects delete this syllable and use the usual stative subject markers.

𐔌𐓣𐓷𐒰́𐓧𐓣 [kiðáli] *be pleased, feel good, like*

This stative verb can be used in a general way to include being pleased about something, liking to do something, and liking things.

(16) 𐒰́𐓷𐒰𐓧𐓣.
ą́ðali
I'm glad.

In example 16, only 𐒰 [ą́] appears. The 𐓄𐓂 [ki] has been deleted.

(17) 𐓰𐒰́ 𐓏𐒷𐒰́ 𐓤𐓂𐓏𐒲𐒼𐓂.
htáa ðaaché **ki**ðáli̧ pe
He (or she) likes to eat meat.

In example 17, we use completive 𐓄𐒰 [pe] because we're describing a characteristic of someone.

(18) 𐓂𐒼𐓻𐓂́ 𐓏𐓂́𐓏𐒲𐒼𐓂?
waší **ð**íðali̧
Do **you** like bacon?

(19) 𐓧𐓷́𐓤𐒲𐓊𐓂, 𐓤𐒰́𐒷𐒰 𐒰́𐓏𐒲𐒼𐓂.
hą́ąhkaži hką́ące **á**ðali̧
No, **I** like fruit.

𐓤𐓂́𐓉𐓏̄ [kíhǫǫ] *like, love to do things*

This verb is a synonym of 𐓤𐓂𐓏𐒲𐒼𐓂 [kíðali̧] and is also a ki-stative verb.

(20) 𐓰𐒰́𐓰𐒰 𐓏𐓂́𐓉𐓏̄?
táatą **ð**íhǫǫ
What do **you** like?

(21) 𐓸𐓂́𐒼𐒰 𐒰𐒼𐓻𐒻𐒰 𐓧𐒰𐓊𐒰́𐓻𐒷 𐓅𐒼𐓂𐒴𐒼𐒰 **𐓤𐓂́𐓉𐓏̄** 𐓄𐒰.
hcíle akxa wažáže ónǫbre **kí**hǫǫ pe
The family loves Osage food.

𐓤𐓂́𐓻𐓊 [kízo] *enjoy, like, have a good time*

This verb is also a synonym of 𐓤𐓂𐓏𐒲𐒼𐓂 [kiðáli̧] and 𐓤𐓂́𐓉𐓏̄ [kíhǫǫ] and is also a ki-stative verb.

(22) 𐓏𐒰𐒰𐒷𐓂́ 𐓏𐒰́𐓊𐓊 𐒰𐓤𐒰𐓰𐓏𐒰́𐒻.
waachí **wá**zo ąkatxái
We are (**standing** here) enjoying the dances.

(23) 𐒼𐒰́𐓜𐒰 𐓏𐒰́𐒼𐓂 𐒰́𐓊𐓊 𐓎𐓂𐓤𐓻𐒻𐒰́.
máąye ðáali̧ **á**zo **mi̧**kšé
I'm sitting here enjoying the good weather.

(24) 𐓧𐓷́𐓰𐒰 𐓤𐓂́𐓤𐓻𐓊 𐓏𐓂́𐓊𐓊 𐓏𐒰?
hą́ąde kíkxo **ð**ízo ðe
Are **you** enjoying the feast tonight?

(25) 𐓤𐓂́𐓻𐓊 𐓄𐒰.
kízo pe
He/she/they had fun.

𐓄𐓂𐓇𐓈𐓘 [kíoxta] *cherish, love, like* (especially in family relationships)

This verb is used to talk about human relationships. It is not used to talk about things. This means that sometimes both the subject and the object take object pronouns—for instance, *I love you* in 26. In this case we use the pronoun 𐓏𐓂 [wi] *I-you* (see chapter 9).

(26) 𐓏𐓂𐓇𐓈𐓘.
 wíoxta
 I love **you.**

For *you love me*, we put the *me* pronoun first and accent it: 𐓘́ [ą́] followed by the *you* pronoun 𐓅𐓂 [ði].

(27) 𐓘́𐓅𐓂𐓇𐓈𐓘.
 ą́ðioxta
 You love **me.**

(28) 𐓂𐓎𐓐 𐓄𐓂𐓇𐓈𐓘 𐓑𐓘.
 iihǫ́ kíoxta pe.
 He (or she or they) loves his (or her or their) mother.

Using 𐓇𐓂́𐓘 [níe] *hurt, in pain*

In Osage we describe physical pain by naming the body part that hurts and a form of 𐓇𐓂́𐓘 [níe], which is a stative verb. The subject of 𐓇𐓂́𐓘 [níe] is the person in pain.

(29) 𐓈𐓐́𐓑𐓘 𐓘𐓇𐓂́𐓘.
 tóoce ąníe
 My throat hurts. (*LITERALLY* The throat hurts me.)

(30) 𐓆𐓘𐓄𐓈 𐓅𐓂𐓇𐓂́𐓘?
 žeká ðiníe
 Does **your** leg hurt?

(31) 𐓎𐓘́𐓄𐓈𐓆𐓂, 𐓋𐓂́ 𐓘𐓇𐓂́𐓘.
 hą́ąhkaži síi ąníe
 No, **my** foot hurts.

(32) 𐓂𐓇𐓘́ 𐓘𐓄𐓇𐓈 𐓏𐓘́𐓋𐓂 𐓇𐓂́𐓘 𐓘𐓄𐓇𐓈.
 iiną́ akxa wéeli níe akxai
 My mother's head hurts.

Another word we might use is 𐓑𐓂́𐓆𐓂 [hpíiži], which means *bad* but can also be a stative verb, *feel bad*. When we use it as a stative verb, it behaves the same as 𐓇𐓂́𐓘 [níe].

(33) 𐓑𐓘́𐓆𐓘 𐓘𐓑𐓂́𐓆𐓂.
 hcéze ąhpíiži
 My stomach feels bad.

We might expect ꝁꞏᴅʎꞏꞏ [kitáhe] *get better* to be stative, but it is an a-*ða* verb.

(34) ħaꝁö̀ꞏꞏ ʌꝁꞏᴅʎꞏꞏ ᴍꞏꝁꞏꞏá.
ðekǫ́ǫce **a**kitáhe mįkšé
Now **I**'m better.

Using just the aspect marker with common stative verbs

In casual conversation you may hear Osage speakers use the continuous aspect marker by itself, without the pronoun, for very common expressions such as *I'm hungry* or *I'm thirsty*. Because the aspect marker tells us the subject and stative verbs are most often in continuous aspect, this is a shorter way to say things in conversation.

(35) Ú̱ꞏᴅuꞏꞏ **ᴍꞏꝁꞏꞏá**!
ípuze **mįkšé**
I'm thirsty!
(36) ⌐oꞏꞏáꞏꞏ **ʌħꞏꝁꞏꞏá**!
nǫhpéhi **aðįkšé**
We two are hungry!
(37) ᴅʎꞏꞏá **ʌꞏꞏá**.
tąhé **ąhé**
I've been fine.

While examples 35–37 are fine in conversation, remember that it is more complete to use the subject pronouns—for example, ʌ⌐ʎꞏᴅuꞏꞏ [ąnápuze] or ʌ⌐ʎꞏᴅuꞏꞏ ᴍꞏꝁꞏꞏá [ąnápuze mįkšé] for *I'm thirsty*.

Ú̱ꝁ'uꞏꞏ

Exercise 1. Give the English meaning for this short conversation

ᴍöꞏ̌ꞏꞏa ʌꝁꞏʌ ꞏözᴅ ʌꝁꞏʌ. ꞏǫ́⌐ꞏ ʌ⌐ꞏ̌á. ⌐ú̱ʌꞏꞏ. ʌ⌐ʎꞏᴅuꞏꞏ. ꞏʌħꞏꞏ ơ⌐ꞏꞏ ʌꞏꞏá.
Ú⌐ʎꞏ ʌꝁꞏʌ ʌ⌐ʎꞏħꞏꞏ ʌꝁꞏʌ.
"ᴅʎꞏꞏá ⌐ꞏꝁꞏꞏá?"
"ꞏʎꞏ̌ꝁʌꞏᴅ. ʌꞏúꞏʌꝁʌ."
"ꝁꞏ̌ꞏꞏa⌐ꞏ ħú̱ħʌ⌐ꞏ? ꞏꞏꞏꞏ̌ꞏꞏa ꞏʌ ᴍꞏꝁꞏꞏá. ħʌꝁꞏᴅʌꞏꞏ ꞏʌ ⌐ꞏꝁꞏꞏá."

Exercise 2. How do you feel?

Practice saying how you feel. You should be able to say that you feel fine, sick, thirsty, cold, hungry, happy, sad, and more.

A: ꞏʎꞏ̌ꝁơ ħʌꞏ̌ꞏꞏá? How have you been doing?
B: ʌꞏúꞏʌꝁʌ. I am sick.

Exercise 3. Liking things

Practice asking and talking about what people like. Use the sentences below but change out the words in bold for new ones.

A:	DÍDΛ ℏńᴊŏ?	What do you like?
B:	ʞÍƵα ÍℏΛᴄΠ.	I like **fruit**.
	ʞÍƵα ℏńℏΛᴄΠ?	Do you like **fruit**?
A:	ᴊÍʞΛᴢΠ, **ᎦΛᏪń** ÍℏΛᴄΠ.	No, I like **bacon**.

Exercise 4. Using pronouns with stative verbs

Look at the examples starting with 2a, which illustrate the verb ᴊÚᴊαʞΛ *feel sick*. Now use all the stative pronouns and make sentences with ʞń7o *enjoy, like*.

Exercise 5. It hurts.

Look at the examples starting with 29. Then choose three body parts and use the verb ∠ńα *hurts* to say that those body parts are in pain.

ńα

Nouns

ᴊń	híi	teeth
ᴊńʞΛ	híihką	ankle
∠Λ∠Úᴊu	nąnúhu	tobacco
ÞΛ	hpa	nose
ÞΛᴊÚ	hpahú	hair
ᴄń	síi	foot
ᏪÍʞα	šáake	hand
ᴅŐƵα	tóoce	throat
Ƶá7α	hcéze	stomach
ᎦÍᴄΠ	wéeli	head
ᴢαʞΛ	žeká	leg

Verbs

ᴊÚᴊαʞΛ	húheka (stative)	be sick
ʞńᴊŏ	kíhǫǫ (ki-stative)	like, like to do things
ʞńoᏪᴅΛ	kíoxta (ki-stative)	like or love someone
ʞńᴅÍᴊα	kitáhe (a-ða)	get better
ʞńℏΛᴄΠ	kiðáli̧ (ki-stative)	be glad, be pleased, like
ʞń7o	kízo (ki-stative)	enjoy, like

ᏅᎢᎠ	níe (stative)	be hurt, in pain
ᏅᎯᏎᎠ	níhce (stative)	be cold
ᏅᎣᏮᎠᏍᏂ	nǫhpéhi (stative)	be hungry
ᏮᏂᏞᏂ	hpíiži (stative)	bad, feel bad
ᎠᎸᏍᎠ	tąhé (stative)	be fine

Notes for Chapter 10

The verbs [kiðáli̧] and [kíðali̧] *like, be pleased* are variants.

Chapter 11

Osage Lifeways

Oȟóⁿa

Author Stephanie Rapp has written some words of encouragement to our students. This is also a model of how to address a group of people.

1. 7ǟℓп ʜʌʜó𐑛ѕ𐑞ᴅп ƙóƦʌ.
2. ʜпzóʎ ʜпᴅʌаzп̄ ʜпʐóᴅᴏ ʜпzóƕа.
3. ᴆʌʜ́ℓа, ʜʌℓá7а ƕа па ᴅóа áƙпᴆɋа ƙóƦʌ.
4. Ӟ ʜʌzáza па ʐа ʜʌzáza óƙ'ʎ ɋƙп оƕʎ́ƙа ᴆʌ ʌƙѧʌ.
5. ʜʌzáza па ńƕʌ ƕпóᴆѧʌ ɋƙóɋᴅʌᴆп ƕʌʃʌ ʜʌℓá7а ƕа оƕпՋƙʌᴆп ᴆʌ ʌƙѧʌ.
6. ƕаƙóʐа оʌՋпℓʌƙа ᴍпƙɋа̄.
7. Stephanie Rapp п̄ɋᴅʌѧп zázа ʌƦп́а
8. ѧʋƕʌ́ᴆᴏᴍп̄ ʜʌzáza zázа ʌƦп́а.
9. Tulsa ᴆʌ́ʜʌ оʜʌℓп̄ ᴍпƙɋа̄.
10. ʃʌɋп́ᴆʌ ʌᴅʌ ᴆʌℓп́ℓа ᴆʌ́ʜʌ ƕʌᴅʌ́ ᴅа.
11. ʐп́zо ʜʌɋᴅʌ́ƙа ᴆʌ́ʜʌℓʌ ᴍпƙɋа̄.
12. ᴆʌℓʋ́ оℓп́ ʌℓп́ƙʌɋпа.
13. ʜпzóƙа ƕо̋́ᴅʌ п̄ᴅʌ́ƕа.
14. Zпƙʌ́ оʜʌՋпʃʎ ᴅо̋́ᴅʌ ʌƦп́ ᴍпƙɋа̄.
15. ƕа ʜʌℓá7а ʌƙѧʌ Zпƙʌ́ оʜʌՋпʃʎ ʜńᴆʌ ʜʌzáza па ƙпᴆп́ᴏ́ óƙ́ʎ ᴆʌ ʌƙѧʌ ʐа áƙᴏ́ ʌzʌ́ᴍп̄ ᴍпƙɋа̄.
16. ʜʌzáza па ᴆп́ᴏ́ ʜʌƙóƦʌ.
17. пᴆó ƕʌʃʌ ʜʌzáza па оƙп́ƙпа ɋп ʌ́ℓʌƙ́ʼо́ ƙóƦʌ ᴍпƙɋа̄.
18. ʜʌzáza ℓп́ƙʌɋп ʌᴅʌ ʜʌzáza па ʜʌzáza óƙ́ʎ ʌƙóᴆʌᴆп ɋо̄ɋóʜа ᴍʌƕп́ ƕа̋ ƙóƦʌ ᴆʌ ʌᴅʌ.
19. Ӟᴅʌℓʌ 7ǟℓп ʜʌɋƙ́ʌ ᴆʌ!

1. I wish to address all of you with respect.
2. Older sisters, younger sisters, older brothers, younger brothers.

3. First, I want to say a few words about this book.
4. It is going to tell you about the Osage language and Osage ways.
5. This book is going to help those of you who want to know and understand the Osage language.
6. Now I'm going to tell about myself.
7. Stephanie Rapp is my (English) name.
8. My Osage name is Xuðátǫmį̄.
9. I live in Tulsa.
10. The ones before me called it Htaasíle Htą́wą (Deer Tracks Town).
11. My clan is Hcížo Waštake.
12. I belong to the Gray Horse district.
13. I have two daughters.
14. I have four grandchildren.
15. I believe this book will help my grandchildren learn the Osage language.
16. I want them to learn the Osage language.
17. In the future, I want to hear the Osage language being spoken again.
18. Osage people want the Osage language and our Osage ways to go on forever.
19. Therefore, everybody, let's do our best!

Blankets

Blankets have been important to us for a long time, perhaps even before they gained value as a trade item. Woolen blankets in the style of those made by the Hudson Bay Company, Pendleton, or other companies are typically called 𐒻𐓎𐓐𐒻́ [haxí], and these are worn by both men and women. Blanket shawls (fringed blankets) are worn by women and are also called 𐒻𐓎𐓐𐒻́ [haxí]. Women also often wear lightweight shawls called 𐒻𐓈𐓍𐒼𐒻́𐒿𐒻́ [haaskámį].

There are many other words for blankets. Some, called 𐓇𐒻́𐓎𐓈𐓐𐓈𐒵𐒰 [míwaapaache], are only worn by women, and ó𐓐𐓎𐓐𐓈𐒵𐒰 [óhkihpaache] are worn by men. These blankets are generally made from broadcloth and often have ribbonwork or beadwork. Some blankets can also be embroidered or have yarnwork. We call a wraparound skirt 𐓏𐒻́𐓐𐓎𐓐𐒰𐒵𐓎𐒿 [wáakipetxą]. This is often made from lightweight materials like silk. In the old days, these were almost always black. Other Osage wraparound skirts are called 𐓏𐓈𐒵𐒰 [wáache] (often 𐓏𐓈𐒵𐒰́ [waaché]) and are made from 𐒻𐓈𐓐𐓂𐒻𐒿𐓎 [haaštáha], a woolen broadcloth.

Another word for blanket is 𐓇𐒻́ [mį], though this word is usually used for robes. The word O𐓇𐒻́𐓐𐒰 [omíže] is typically used for bedding, like sheets and blankets, throws, quilts, bedclothes, or even rugs and carpets. O𐓇𐒻́𐓐𐒰 [omíže] is also used for the bundle of blankets or pillows wrapped in a bedsheet and carried to 𐓐𐓎𐓐𐒻ó𐓐𐒰 [hkihkǫ́ze] Osage Native American Church meetings. The word for a saddle blanket is 𐓏𐓈𐓐𐓈𐓐𐓂 [wákaštǫ], and this word can also be used for a blanket that is folded up and used to pad a chair or even as a term for a cushion or pillow.

Although some people no longer do this, others we know follow traditions where the colors, patterns, and decorations for blankets given to children (when they are old enough) are determined by birth order. For one author's family, the eldest son will be given a red and blue blanket with a pattern where the red part, when worn, will cover the heart or the left side of the body. The second son would be given a completely red blanket, and the third son (and any after that) would be given an all-blue blanket. For daughters, the first daughter gets a red blanket, and all others get a blue blanket. Nowadays, people may get blankets of red or blue, regardless of their birth order, and each family may follow a different way of doing this.

The Gray Horse arbor near Fairfax, Oklahoma. Photo by Butch DeLong.

The Hominy Arbor in Hominy, Oklahoma. Photo by Butch DeLong.

Talking about family members

There's no finer way of linking Osage language and culture than to look at the structure of the 𐓇𐓘𐓶𐓒́ [wahǫ́ǫ] system. This system is the Osage way to address each other according to their position in families that demonstrates respect. It demonstrates our respect for and interconnectedness with family, community, and our natural world. Children who were raised in this system grew up knowing and understanding the positions and expectations given to everyone in the family. Birth order was very important. For example, firstborn children were given special treatment, and they also had extra roles and responsibilities. And we will see the importance of this in names for our kin.

We will learn how to talk about our parents, aunts, uncles, grandparents, siblings, children, and grandchildren. We will also mention how these words change when talking about someone else's relatives. Please remember that some families may follow slightly different traditions and use a few different words (or variations of these words) than we have used here.

Let's start with our mother and our mother's sisters. In Osage, we typically call our mother 𐓣𐓧𐓘́ [iiną́]. Our mother's older sister is usually called 𐓣𐓧𐓘́𐓸𐓛 [iináhtą], and we call her younger sister 𐓣𐓧𐓘́𐓵𐓯 [iináži]. Remember that 𐓸𐓛 [htą] means *big* and 𐓵𐓯 [ži] means *small*, so aunts on our mother's side are our *big* or *little mothers*.

Moving to our father and his brothers, we call our father 𐓣𐓸𐓘́𐓵𐓤 [įhtáci], and we typically call our father's older brother 𐓣𐓸𐓘́𐓵𐓤𐓸𐓛 [įhtácihtą] and his younger brother 𐓣𐓸𐓘́𐓵𐓤𐓯 [įhtáciži] (*big* or *little father*).

If a child were to lose either parent, they still have their big (or little) mother and father. This illustrates the interconnectedness and relationships of the 𐓇𐓘𐓶𐓒́ [wahǫ́ǫ] system and how it helps to ensure that no one will become 𐓇𐓘𐓶𐓒́𐓤𐓰 [wahǫ́įke] *an orphan, without family*.

Our aunts on our father's side are called 𐓇𐓣𐓸𐓵́𐓰𐓧 [wihcími], whether they are older or younger than our father. And our mother's brothers, regardless of birth order, are called 𐓇𐓣𐓸𐓘́𐓰𐓤 [wįcéki].

The words we use for our brothers and sisters depend on whether we are a man or a woman. As a man, we call our older brother 𐓇𐓣𐓵𐓘́𐓺𐓰 [wižį́ðe] (or 𐓇𐓣𐓵𐓘́𐓰 [wižíe] or 𐓇𐓣𐓵𐓘́ [wižį́]), and we call our younger brother 𐓇𐓣𐓴𐓒́𐓤𐓧 [wisǫ́ka]. And as a man, we call our older sister 𐓇𐓣𐓸𐓘́𐓰𐓤 [wihtą́ke] and our younger sister 𐓇𐓣𐓸𐓘́𐓯 [wihtéži]. As a woman, we call our older sister 𐓇𐓣𐓵𐓒́𐓧 [wižǫ́ą] (some say 𐓇𐓣𐓵𐓒́ [wižǫ́]) and our younger sister 𐓇𐓣𐓸𐓘́𐓯 [wihtéži]. And as a woman, we call our older brother 𐓇𐓣𐓵𐓘́𐓸𐓒 [wihcį́hto] and our younger brother 𐓇𐓣𐓴𐓒́𐓘𐓯 [wisǫéži].

Mothers and fathers use the same words for their sons and daughters. The firstborn son is called 𐓣𐓧𐓒́𐓸𐓧 [ilǫ́ǫhpa]. The firstborn daughter is called 𐓇𐓘𐓱'𐓒́𐓸𐓛 [wak'óhtą] (or 𐓇𐓘𐓱'𐓒́𐓸𐓧 [wak'óhpa], and some say 𐓧𐓧́𐓧 [míina]). The second-born son is called 𐓱𐓯𐓒́𐓤𐓧 [kšǫ́ka] (or 𐓱𐓯𐓘́𐓤𐓧 [kšą́ka]) and the second-born daughter is 𐓇𐓣𐓮𐓘́ [wihé]. For sons born third and after, people say 𐓱𐓯𐓘́𐓵𐓯 [kxáži] (or 𐓱𐓯𐓘́𐓤𐓧 [kxáke]). For the third-born daughter, we say 𐓧𐓴𐓘́𐓤𐓧 [asíka] (some say 𐓧𐓴𐓘́𐓸𐓧 [asíhpa]). And for the fourth-born daughter and beyond, we say 𐓧𐓴𐓘́𐓵𐓯 [asíži]. The general terms for children are 𐓇𐓣𐓵𐓘́𐓤𐓧 [wižį́ke] for sons and 𐓇𐓣𐓵𐓒́𐓤𐓧 [wižǫ́ke] for daughters.

Our grandfathers on either side of the family are typically called 𐓇𐓣𐓸𐓒́𐓱 [wihcíko] or 𐓸𐓒́𐓱 [hcíko], and our grandmothers (either side) are called 𐓣𐓱𐓒́ [iihkó]. Our grandchild, whether a boy or a girl, is usually called ꜱꞎꝫꞬꝰꞍ [wihcóšpa]. A more general way to say *grandchild* (more like *a* or *the grandchild*) is ᏃꞎꝄꞀ ꝊꜱꞀᏉꞎꞈ [žįká owáhkihą].

Within our family, we often use birth order names for each other rather than our given names. So, everyone might just call the firstborn son ꞈꞋꝌꝰꞀ [ilǫ́ǫhpa] and the firstborn daughter ꜱꞀᏏ'ꝌꝰꞀ [wak'óhtą]. This might be like people calling a child *Sonny* or a parent *Mom* or *Dad* in English, and we've tried to capture the sense of this in a few of our chapter dialogues.

The Hominy Roundhouse in Hominy, Oklahoma. Photo by Butch DeLong.

The Pawhuska Arbor in Pawhuska, Oklahoma. Photo by Butch DeLong.

Along these lines, a husband may call his wife *mother of* (name of the firstborn child), and a wife may call her husband *father of* (name of the firstborn child). So if the eldest child's name is Jesse, then the husband would call his wife "Jesse ñ𐓘ó" [iihǫ́] and the wife would call her husband "Jesse ɴħʌꜱα" [iðáce].

Another point is that Osage uses slightly different forms of these words to talk about other people's family members. For example, *my grandfather* is ˤɴꜱńꝁo [wihcíko], but *your grandfather* is ħɴꜱńꝁo [ðihcíko], and *his* or *her* (or *a* or *the*) *grandfather* is ɴꜱńꝁo [ihcíko]. We have organized the family words into a table below. Notice that the words in the *my* column often begin with *wi* (or *i̧*), the words in the *your* column begin with *ði*, and the words in the *his* or *her* column begin with *i*.

English	*my*	*your*	*his or her* (or *a/the*)
father	ɴᴅʌꜱɴ [i̧htáci]	ħɴħʌꜱα [ðiðáce]	ɴħʌꜱα [iðáce]
mother	ñʟʎ́ [iiná̧]	ħñ𐓘ó [ðiihǫ́]	ñ𐓘ó [iihǫ́]
uncle (father's elder)	ɴᴅʌꜱɴᴅʌ [i̧htácihta̧]	ħɴħʌꜱα [ðiðáce]	ɴħʌꜱα [iðáce]
uncle (father's younger)	ɴᴅʌꜱɴꜱɴ [i̧htáciži̧]	ħɴħʌꜱαꜱɴ [ðiðáceži̧]	ɴħʌꜱαꜱɴ [iðáceži̧]
aunt (mother's elder)	ñʟʎ́ᴅʌ [iináhta̧]	ħñ𐓘óᴅʌ [ðiihǫ́hta̧]	ñ𐓘óᴅʌ [iihǫ́hta̧]
aunt (mother's younger)	ñʟʎ́ꜱɴ [iináži̧]	ħñ𐓘óꜱɴ [ðiihǫ́ži̧]	ñ𐓘óꜱɴ [iihǫ́ži̧]
uncle (mother's brother)	ˤɴꜱάꝁɴ [wi̧céki]	ħɴꜱάꝁɴ [ði̧céki]	ɴꜱάꝁɴ [i̧céki]
aunt (father's sister; any)	ˤɴꜱńʍɴ [wihcími]	ħɴꜱńʍɴ [ðihcími]	ɴꜱńʍɴ [ihcími]
older brother (if a man)	ˤɴꜱɴ́ħα [wiží̧ðe]	ħɴꜱɴ́ħα [ðiží̧ðe]	ɴꜱɴ́ħα [iží̧ðe]
older brother (if a woman)	ˤɴꜱɴ́ᴅo [wihcíto]	ħɴꜱɴ́ᴅo [ðihcíto]	ɴꜱɴ́ᴅo [ihcíto]
younger brother (if a man)	ˤɴꜱóꝁʌ [wisǫ́ka]	ħɴꜱóꝁʌ [ðisǫ́ka]	ɴꜱóꝁʌ [isǫ́ka]
younger brother (if a woman)	ˤɴꜱóαꜱɴ [wisǫ́eži̧]	ħɴꜱóαꜱɴ [ðisǫ́eži̧]	ɴꜱóαꜱɴ [isǫ́eži̧]
son (any; general term)	ˤɴꜱɴ́ꝁα [wiží̧ke]	ħɴꜱɴ́ꝁα [ðiží̧ke]	ɴꜱɴ́ꝁα [iží̧ke]
daughter (any; general term)	ˤɴꜱóꝁα [wižǫ́ke]	ħɴꜱóꝁα [ðižǫ́ke]	ɴꜱóꝁα [ižǫ́ke]
grandchild (general term)	ˤɴꜱóϭᴘʌ [wihcóšpa]	ħɴꜱóϭᴘʌ [ðihcóšpa]	ɴꜱóϭᴘʌ [ihcóšpa]
grandfather (any)	ˤɴꜱńꝁo [wihcíko] OR ꜱńꝁo [hcíko]	ħɴꜱńꝁo [ðihcíko]	ɴꜱńꝁo [ihcíko]
grandmother (any)	ñꝁó [iihkó]	ħñꝁó [ðiihkó]	ñꝁó [iihkó]

This table is a good start for the words we use for family members, but there are still many other things to learn (like how to talk about cousins or in-laws). You can ask your teacher about these terms, or you can find many of them in Quintero's *Osage Dictionary* or her *Osage Grammar*. Please also remember that some people use slightly different words for their family members.

ñꝁ'υꜱα

Exercise 1. Name your own family

Make a list or draw a family tree of your family members, including your grandparents, parents, aunts, uncles, and siblings. Write down the Osage family term for each of them.

Princess Lulu Goodfox shows the correct way to wear a blanket shawl. Photo by Butch DeLong.

Chapter 12

Commands and Negation

ᎣᏏᏲᎾ

1. ᏅᎳᏈᏂᏣ ᎣᏈᏅᎠᏉᏗ ᎠᏐ ᎠᏉᏔᏗ.
2. **ᎤᏥᎤ́:** ᎠᎾᏅᎠᏗ ᏥᎦᏅ ᎠᏉᏐᏔᏣ ᎠᎠ.
3. **ᎤᏎᎤ́:** ᏇᎤᏥᏗ ᏓᎠᏗ ᏅᎳᏔᎤ᷄ ᎮᎤᏌᏗ Ꭰ̈ᎠᎦᎠᏗ ᎠᎠ.
4. ᏅᎳᏔᎯᎿᏂ ᎠᎠ ᎴᎤᏥᏣᏂᎠ ᎤᏥᎾᏬ ᎴᎤᏔᎠ, ᏅᎠᏥ᾽Ꭴ᷄ ᏅᎳᏔᎤ᷄ ᎾᏅᏗ ᏅᎠᏥ᾽Ꭴ.
5. ᎦᎠ́ᏦᎠ ᎣᏔᎾᏦᎠ ᏥᎳᏔᎤ᷄ ᏨᎤᏬᎠᏩᏥᎠ ᏅᎠᏥ᾽Ꭴ.
6. **ᎤᏥᎤ́:** ᏇᏃᎾᏦᎠ ᏅᎳᏔᎤ᷄ ᎾᏉᎠ ᏔᎤᏒᎠ Ꭰ̈ᎠᎦᎠᏗ ᎠᏐ ᎠᏉᏔᏗ.
7. **ᏅᎠᏥ᾽ᎣᏉᎠ:** ᏝᎴᏦᎠᏈᏔᎠ. ᏅᏇᎤᏥᏦᎠ ᏇᎠᏥᎠ ᏅᎠᏃ ᎠᎠ ᎠᏥᎤ́ᏣᎠᎴᎠ.
8. **ᎤᏥᎤ́:** ᏇᏃᎾᏦᎠ ᏅᎳᏔᎤ᷄ ᏔᎾᏓᎠᏗ ᎠᎠ ᏅᎠᏉᎴᏇᎠ ᎠᏥᎤ́ᏉᎠᏇ ᎠᏥᎤᎴᎠᏥᏦᎠ ᎠᎠ ᎠᏥᏐᏔᎠ.
9. **ᎤᏎᎤ́:** ᏇᏃᎾᏦᎠ ᎠᏉᏔᏗ ᏂᎠ ᎠᎤ́Ꭰ ᎣᏈᏓ ᏥᎳᏔᎤ᷄ ᏤᎠᏤᎠ ᏥᎾᏉᎠ ᏅᎳᏅᎳᏥ᾽Ꭴ ᎠᎠ.
10. ᏉᎳᏌᎳᎠ Ꭰ̆ ᏇᎠᏫᎠᎵᏃ ᎠᏔᏂ́ ᏔᎳᏐ᷆ ᏥᎾᏉᎠ ᏥᎳᏔᎤ᷄ ᏢᎠᏔᎠ ᎠᏥᎤ́ᏉᎠᏇ ᏅᎠ̆ᏒᎳ ᎠᏥᎤ́ᏔᎠ ᎠᎠ.
11. ᏇᏃᎾᏦᎠ ᏴᎠᏔᎠᏂ́ ᏴᎠᎴᏥᎠᏟ᾿ ᏣᎠᏂ Ꮒ᾿ ᏣᎠᏂᏔ́, ᎿᎳᎴᏂ ᎦᎠ́ᏦᎠ ᎣᏔᎾᏦᎠ.
12. ᏥᎳᏔᎤ᷄ ᏂᎴᏅᏉᎠ ᎠᏉᏔᏗ ᏣᎠ́ᏉᎠ Ꭰ̈ᏔᏬᏉᎠ ᏨᎤᏬᎠᏬᏥᎠ ᎴᎴᎴᏌᏴᎤ ᏣᎠᏂ ᏇᎠᏫᎠᎵᏃ ᎠᏃᎤ.

1. It's time again for Giveaway.
2. **Grandma:** Let's go to the arbor.
3. **Mother:** It's almost time for the singers to start.
4. When you dance, give to the visitors or women singers.
5. Shake hands and give them money.
6. **Grandma:** It's almost time for Grandpa's song.
7. **First daughter:** Get ready. When Grandpa starts dancing we will follow him out.
8. **Grandma:** When Grandpa's song ends we will gather together with our bundles.
9. **Mother:** Grandpa will say a few words and then call out the names we are giving to.
10. He will call the three drumkeepers first, and then our friends we want to show our appreciation to.
11. After Grandpa puts blankets and shawls on them, shake hands with everybody.
12. And then First Son and Second Son will both put money and tobacco on the drum.

In the dialogue, Grandpa has a song. Some people have been honored with their own song, and the song has been placed into an Osage dance. Having a song is a great honor, and a song can be passed on to another person.

𐓏𐓘 𐓤𐓘𐓸𐓘𐓮𐓟𐓧𐓘𐓮𐓘

Every language needs a way to give commands such as "Come here!" or "Don't eat that!" or "Let's eat!" In this chapter we will learn to make positive and negative commands. Some of these are "Come here!" or "Don't touch this!" We will also learn how to use *let*. For example, "Let him sing" or "Let's dance!"

Every language also needs ways to say that something is *not*—this is negation. We will learn a basic form of negation (*he is **not** running*) and also forms for *having none* and *being none* (for example, *there is **no** milk*).

Commands

Singular *you*

Positive Osage commands are made with the bare verb. Verbs that end in the sound 𐓘 [e], as in examples 1 and 3, 𐓧𐓘́𐓮𐓘 [ną́ąke] and 𐓨𐓣́𐓬𐓘 [tǫ́pe], will change that sound to 𐓘 [a] (as we have done before). Sometimes the accent is moved to the final syllable for emphasis, but this is not necessary.

Note that commands are not marked for aspect.

(1) 𐓧𐓘́𐓮𐓘́!
nąąká
Run!
(2) 𐓣𐓘𐓸𐓘́!
oąhką́
Help me!
(3) 𐓘́𐓨𐓣𐓬𐓘́!
ątǫpá
Look at me!

A command may be made more emphatic by putting 𐓵𐓟 [ði], a form of *you*, after the verb.

(4) 𐓣𐓤𐓟́𐓻𐓟 𐓵𐓟!
owísi ði
(You singular) Jump!

Plural *you*

The command for plural *you* is made by putting the plural marker 𐓬𐓟 [pi] after the verb.

(5a) 𐒰𐓶𐒻𐓏𐓊𐓈!
owísipi
(You plural) jump!

(5b) 𐓡𐒰𐒹𐓇𐓈!
ðaachápi
(You plural) eat!

The verb o𐒹𐒰 [océ] *look for* has special command forms o𐓊𐒷 [otá] and o𐓊𐒷𐓈 [otápi]. In general, verbs ending in 𐒹𐒰 [ce] change to 𐓊𐒷 [ta] in commands, and verbs ending in 𐒹𐒰 [hce] change to 𐓊𐒷 [hta].

(6) o𐓊𐒷!
otá
Look for it!

Negative commands are explained later in the chapter.

𐒹𐒰 [hce] and 𐓊𐒷 [htai] *let* and *let's*

Some commands are about allowing someone to do something. In English, we use *let*—for example, *let me sleep*. In Osage, we use [hce], placed after the verb. When we want to make sentences with *let's*, we use 𐒹𐒰 [hce] for two people and 𐓊𐒷 [htai] for more than two people.

(7) Á𐓶𐒰𐓍o𐓘𐒰 𐒹𐒰.
áwaǫbre hce
Let's eat! (the two of us)

(8) 𐓉𐒰𐓐𐒰𐓅𐒰 𐒰𐓡𐒷𐓊𐒰 𐓊𐒷.
mąhkása ąðáahtą htai
Let's drink coffee. (more than two of us)

(9) 𐓶𐒰𐓡ó 𐒹𐒰.
waaðǫ́ hce
Let him sing!

(10) 𐒰𐓶𐒷𐒹𐓊 𐒹𐒰.
awáachi hce
Let me dance!

Negation

Negation with forms of 𐒰𐓑𐓊 [aži]

The simplest way to negate a sentence is to place a form of the negator 𐒰𐓑𐓊 [aži] after the verb root. There are three forms: 𐒰𐓑𐓊 [aži] for second- and third-person subjects (you, he, she, it), 𐓉𐒰𐓑𐓊 [maži] for first-person subjects (I), and 𐓈𐒰𐓑𐓊 [paži] for plural subjects. Similar to what we have seen before, if a verb ends in the sound 𐒰 [e], it is replaced with the 𐒷 [a] in 𐒰𐓑𐓊 [aži].

We will write ᏘᏃᎻ [aži], ᏒᏘᏃᎻ [maži], and ᏇᏘᏃᎻ [paži] as part of the verb. Some people prefer to write these as separate words.

While we use the forms of continuous aspect for all persons, third-person negation does not take completive Ꮖα [pe]. This is one of the instances where the completive aspect is built in.

ᏘᏃᎻ [aži]

(11) ᏆᏇᏗᏃᎻ ᏘᏰᎷᏘ Ꮖᐠ ᏚᎻ ᏆᏒᏘᏃᎻ.
ịhtáci akxa htáa wį́ íiðaži
My father didn't find a deer.

(12) ᏆᏒᏘᏰ'ᏌᏋᏘᏃᎻ ᏗᎻᏰᏪα.
íðak'ucaži nįkšé
You are not studying.

ᏒᏘᏃᎻ [maži]

First-person singular subjects (I) have a special negator, ᏒᏘᏃᎻ [maži]. The final vowel of the verb is not deleted when ᏒᏘᏃᎻ [maži] is used.

(13) ᏘᏗᏋᎻαᏒᏘᏃᎻ.
aną́ąkemaži
I didn't run.

(14) ᏚᏘᏗα᜴α ᎻᏋᎻαᏒᏘᏃᎻ ᏘᏚα.
waléze bráacemaží ąhé
I haven't been reading the book.

ᏇᏘᏃᎻ [paži]

The plural marker ᏆᎻ [pi] is combined with ᏘᏃᎻ [aži] to form ᏇᏘᏃᎻ [paži]. This is used with all plural subjects.

(15) ᏚᏘᏗα᜴α ᏆᏇᎻᏘᏇᏘᏃᎻ ᏇᏘᏰα.
waléze štáacapaži paašé
You (plural) aren't reading the book.

(16) ᏓᏚα ᏚᏘᏒᏘᏗᏋᏇᏘᏃᎻ.
ówe waðálįpaži
We don't like vegetables.

(17) ᏃᏆᎻᏘᏃᎻ᜴ ᏘᎻᏒᏘ ᏚᏓᏚαᎻᏘᏇᏘᏃᎻ ᏘᎻᏒᏘ.
žįkáži akxa húhekapaži akxai
The children are not sick.

In example 17, we know that ᏃᏆᎻᏘᏃᎻ᜴ [žįkáži] is *children* because ᏇᏘᏃᎻ [paži] tells us that the subject is plural. In Osage, *child* and *children* are the same word, ᏃᏆᎻᏘᏃᎻ᜴ [žįkáži].

Negation with ᏂᏅᏨᎠ [ðįįké] and ᏂᏁᏨᎠ [ðįké]

Another important form of negation is made with the use of ᏂᏅᏨᎠ [ðįįké] and ᏂᏅᏨᎠ [ðįké]. (Some people say these as ᏅᏨᎠ [įįké] and ᏁᏨᎠ [įké].) These words only differ in the vowel: ᏂᏅᏨᎠ [ðįįké] has a long vowel ų [įį], but they do different work. Let's see how to use them.

ᏂᏅᏨᎠ [ðįįké] *have none, lack, not have any*

The stative verb ᏂᏅᏨᎠ [ðįįké] is used to mean that the subject lacks or doesn't have something. The final accent on ᏂᏅᏨᎠ [ðįįké] is moved when pronouns are present. This verb does not need a continuous aspect marker.

(18) ᎹᏌᏃᎠᏕᏨᏞ ᎪᏂᏅᏨᎠ.
mázeska ądį́įke
I have no money.
OR I don't have any money.

(19) ÓᏞᎣᏒᎠ ᏉᎪᏂᏅᏨᎠ.
ónǫbre wadį́įke
We have no food.

ᏂᏁᏨᎠ [ðįké] *none, no, not any, there is no*

The negator ᏂᏁᏨᎠ [ðįké] has a number of uses. It negates noun phrases, and while it is not a true verb, it can act like one and be the predicate of a sentence. Look at how ᏂᏁᏨᎠ [ðįké] is used with words like ᏇᎠ [pée] and ᎠᎸᎠᏞ [táatą] to form expressions like *no one, anyone, nothing,* and *anything.*

(20) ᏉᏁᏐᏮᎠ ᏞᏨᎥᏞ **ᏇᎠ ᏂᏁᏨᎠ** ᏐᏂᎸᏎᏁ.
wižǫ́ke akxa **pée ðįké** íiðaži.
My daughter did not see **anyone**.

(21) **ᎠᎸᎠᏞ ᏂᏁᏨᎠ** ᏒᏫᎦᏁᎹᏞᏁ.
táatą ðįké brúwįmaži
I did not buy **anything**.

(22) **ᏇᎠ ᏂᏁᏨᎠ**.
pée ðįké
No one (was there).

We also use ᏂᏁᏨᎠ [ðįké] for the English expression *there is no*. This kind of sentence takes no subject or aspect marker.

(23) ᏆᎸᏌᎠᏞᏅ **ᏂᏁᏨᎠ**.
paazénii **ðįké**
There's no milk.

Negative commands: *don't*

We use the negator 𐓧𐓘𐓤𐓟 [ðįké] plus the command marker 𐓘 [á] to make 𐓧𐓘𐓤𐓘 [ðįká] *don't!* This negator also has the variation 𐓘𐓤𐓘 [įká].

(24) 𐓁𐓘 **𐓧𐓘𐓤𐓘**!
íe **ðįká**
Don't talk!

(25) 𐓶𐓘𐓤𐓘 **𐓘𐓤𐓘**!
ɣaaké **įká**
Don't cry!

Just as with positive commands, we may add 𐓧𐓘 [ði] to a negative command to make it more emphatic.

(26) 𐓷𐓘𐓧𐓪 𐓘𐓤𐓘 **𐓧𐓘**!
waaðǫ́ įká **ði**
Don't **you** sing!

The plural form *don't* adds the plural marker 𐓷𐓘 [pi] to make 𐓧𐓘𐓤𐓘𐓷𐓘 [ðįkápi].

(27) 𐓧𐓘 𐓧𐓘𐓰𐓘 𐓧𐓘𐓤𐓘**𐓷𐓘**!
ðée ðaaché ðįká**pi**
Don't **(you plural)** eat that!

Future negation with 𐓘𐓰𐓘 𐓷𐓘 [aži hta] **and** 𐓧𐓘𐓤𐓘 𐓷𐓘 [ðįké hta]

We make future negation—*not going to*—using either 𐓘𐓰𐓘 [aži] or 𐓧𐓘𐓤𐓘 [ðįké]. We place the future marker 𐓷𐓘 [hta] after the negator and generally add a continuous aspect marker. We are translating Osage future negation with *not going to* rather than *won't* because *won't* in English suggests refusal.

It seems to be true that either 𐓘𐓰𐓘 [aži] or 𐓧𐓘𐓤𐓘 [ðįké] can be used, although there may be some situations when a speaker may prefer one to the other.

(28) 𐓇𐓘𐓪𐓰𐓘 𐓘𐓤𐓘 𐓪𐓘𐓤𐓘𐓰𐓘 𐓷𐓘 𐓘𐓷𐓘.
šítožį akxa oáhkaži hta apai
The boy is not going to help me.

(29) 𐓷𐓘 𐓱𐓘𐓰𐓘𐓪𐓘𐓰𐓘 𐓷𐓘 𐓪𐓘𐓤𐓘.
htáa bráachemaži hta mįkšé
I'm not going to eat meat.

(30) 𐓇𐓘𐓪𐓰𐓘 𐓘𐓷𐓘 𐓶𐓘𐓧𐓘 𐓧𐓘𐓤𐓘 𐓷𐓘 𐓘𐓷𐓘.
šįmižį apa híiða ðįké hta apai
The girl is not going to bathe.

(31) 𐓷𐓘𐓧𐓘𐓰𐓘 𐓧𐓘𐓤𐓘 𐓷𐓘 𐓰𐓘𐓤𐓘.
waðáachi ðįké hta nįkšé
You're not going to dance.

Commands and Negation

ñk'uȼa

Exercise 1. Do you understand?

What does this short conversation mean in English?

A: Doþĺ! Þāzáʐñ ħnǩá. ǩʌśńaʌȼn ʌʐórą ǩʌ̃ψa ǩórʌ.
B: Óʌaȼn ȼn ᴍʌǩń, Þāzáʐñ ǩúʌn ðʌ ᴍnǩ&á.
A: ʃʌ̃ǩʌzn. Oħńðʌ ʌǩázn ȼa.
B: ħʌ́ʐn. ʐoþáʌʃn.

Exercise 2. Composition

Write a composition in Osage of six sentences. Include at least one command and one form of negation.

Exercise 3. Commands

Give the Osage for these commands.

1. Sing now!
2. Don't look at me!
3. Don't cry! (you plural)
4. Let's help Mother.
5. Let him finish eating.

Exercise 4. Negative commands

Give the negative forms of each of these verbs, using ʌzn, ᴍʌzn, and þʌzn.

1. ńþʌʃơ
2. ðóþa
3. ʐʌ̃ǩa
4. ʌ̄ȼń
5. ħʌ̄ȼá

ńa

Nouns

ʌ̃ȼnðʌ	áhcihtą	arbor
ǩʌþʌ̄ǩa	brápxąąke	mosquito
ʃá̃oȼa	héeoce	monkey
nȼókʌ	įchóka	mouse

ҟᴧꜱñɑ⋔ᴣп	kaası̨exci	morning
ҟᴧꜱñɑ⋔ᴣп ꜱᴧᶜóꝚɑ	kaası̨exci wanǫ́bre	breakfast (morning meal)
ҟñҟñɑᴢп˙	kı̨́ikı̨iežı̨	butterfly
ᶜᴧᴘ⋔ᴧ̄ҟɑ	lápxa̧a̧ke	mosquito
ᵐᴧ́ҟᴧ	mą́ka	skunk
ᵐñѰᴧ	míɣa	duck
ᴅᴧ̄ꜱҟᴧ́	htaaská	sheep
ᴅᴧ́ᴅᴧ𝟽ɑ	htáhtaze	grasshopper
ꜱᴧᶜóꝚɑ	wanǫ́bre	dinner
⋔óҟᴧ	xóhka	singers and drummers

Verbs

ñҟ'ᴜᴣɑ	ík'uce (i-stem)	practice, study, try
ᴘᴧ́ᶜɑ𝟽ɑ	páaleze (strong-stem)	write
Ɦᴧᴣɑ́	ðaacé (brush)	call, pronounce, read
Ɜñҟɑ́	ðı̨iké (stative)	have none, lack, not have anything
Ѱᴧ̄ҟɑ́	ɣaaké (a-ða)	cry

Other

ɑ̃ᴅ⋔ᴧ́	éetxą	it is time to
ᴘɑ̃ Ɜñҟɑ́	pée ðı̨ké	not anyone, no one
ᴅᴧ́ᴅᴧ Ɜñҟɑ́	táatą ðı̨ké	not anything, nothing
Ɜñҟɑ́	ðı̨ké	none, no, not any, there is no

Notes for Chapter 12

We treat [aži] as an affix like *n't* in English in part because it deletes the final vowel of a preceding verb. Doing this also helps us keep [aži] separate from [ažı̨́] *believe* and [a̧ži] *but*. (See chapter 15.) Some might prefer to spell this out as a separate word.

Chapter 13

Habitual and Durative Aspects and Freestanding Pronouns

ᎤᎾᏞᎾᎦ

1. **ᎤᏥ:** DōᏀᎪᎠᎯ ᏃᏂᎦᏂᎦ ᏞᎦᏓᎵ ᏗᏞᎧᎦᎵ ᎣᎾᎠ ᎠᎵ ᏞᎦᏓᎵ.
2. **ᏗᏐᎴᎦ:** ᎠᎦᎯ, ᎠᎠᏓᎵ ᎠᏍᎯ ᏞᎦᏓᎵ.
3. **ᎤᏥ:** ᎠᎯᎠᎯ ᎬᎢᎷᏂ ᏞᎦᎵᏂᏛ ᎦᎠ ᎶᎠᏍᏂ ᎦᎠ, ᏣᎵᏂᎣ ᎠᎯᎠᎵᏂᎦᏂᏂ ᏞᎳᎤᏅ ᎦᎵᎤᏅᎵᎵ ᏞᎦᏂᏀᎶᎨᎠ.
4. ᏗᎾᎠᏀᏂ ᏞᎦᏓᎵ ᏄᎤᏂᎵ ᏯᎯᎪ ᎦᏂ ᏞᎦᏂᏂᏛ ᏞᎦᏓᎵ.
5. **ᏗᏐᎴᎦ:** ᏥᎵᎶᏂ.
6. **ᎤᏥ:** ᎠᎶᏌᎦ, ᎦᎠᎤᏆᏂᎦ ᎦᏂᏂ ᏞᎳᎤᏅ ᎠᎵ ᏞᎦᎠᎠᏄᎵ.
7. **ᏗᏐᎴᎦ:** ᎠᎶᏌᎦ ᏙᎠᎤ, ᎦᎶᏣᏃᎵᏀᎦ ᎠᎣᎠ ᎠᎦᎯ.
8. **ᎤᏥ:** ᏗᎦᎤᏝᏂ ᏞᎦᏓᎵ ᏙᎠᎵᎠᎦ ᎦᎠᎦᎠᏂᎵ ᎦᎠᎤᎨᎠ ᎠᎵ ᏞᎦᏓᎵ.
9. **ᏗᏐᎴᎦ:** ᏓᎠᏎᎦ ᏥᎵᎶᏂ ᎦᎠᎨᎳ ᎠᏂ ᎦᎠ.
10. **ᎤᏥ:** ᏒᎰᏂᎦ, ᏒᏂᏂᎳᎵ, ᏒᏂᏂᎳᎵ ᎳᎦᎠ ᎦᎠᎤᎨᎠ ᎠᎵ. ᎠᎷᎠ ᎠᎯᎠᎯ ᎲᎵᎶᏂ ᎠᎵ ᏞᎦᏓᎵ.
11. ᎠᎠ ᎠᎣᎷᏞᎦ ᎦᎠᎨᎠ ᎦᏂᏂ.

1. **Mother:** In the summer Sonny will go into the dance.
2. **Father:** It is time.
3. **Mother:** Let's gather up everything we have, and then decide what else we will buy.
4. Uncle has an eagle feather for him.
5. **Father:** Good.
6. **Mother:** We will buy him a roach headdress and drop feathers too.
7. **Father:** I have a roach spreader and some handkerchiefs.
8. **Mother:** Aunt will make his Osage clothes.
9. **Father:** She makes good ribbon work.
10. **Mother:** She is going to make leggings, breechcloth, and a tail piece for him. Therefore, his things will be good.
11. She will make his otter too.

When a boy or man is initiated into the Ilonshka, it is a very important occasion. This requires a lot of special preparation, including Osage clothes, giveaway items, and an Osage name.

In sentence eleven, ᴅóᴌʌ𝚔ɑ [htónąke] refers to an item of clothing made from an otter hide that is often worn at the dances.

ñɑ ⸝ʌ𝚔ńᴌʌꭉɑ

We have carefully studied the two major Osage aspects, completive and continuous. There are many other aspects in Osage and the languages of the world. This lesson will introduce the habitual and durative aspects, which are marked with a kind of adverb, similar to how we do this in English.

We have also studied two kinds of pronouns: those that mark the subject and those that mark the object of verbs. All these are attached to the verb. There are other kinds of pronouns in Osage that are not attached to verbs. Two uses of these freestanding pronouns are to mark possession (my, your, etc.) and to be able to hold conversations without using a whole sentence ("Who wants lunch?" "Me!"). There are even more pronouns that we will study in future chapters.

We will begin with the habitual and durative aspects and then turn to the freestanding pronouns.

Marking habitual and durative aspects with adverbials

Habitual aspects

One very important aspect is the one that indicates that an act happens habitually or repetitively. We will call this habitual aspect. This aspect is typically made with adverbials. Some English adverbs that mark this aspect are *always*, *a lot*, *over and over*, *usually*, *habitually*, *sometimes*, *often*, *used to*, *keep on*, and others.

There are four common Osage adverbials that mark this aspect: ᴌʌ [ną], ৪ᴅʌ [štą], ᴊʌꭉɲ [háachi], and ńʞɲᴊʌ [íkiha]. We discuss each of them along with their meanings below.

ᴌʌ [ną] (or ᴌʌ [na]) and ৪ᴅʌ [štą]

Two of the four most commonly used adverbials are ᴌʌ [ną] and ৪ᴅʌ [štą]. Rather than try to match these to English adverbs, it's best to understand that the difference between them is that ৪ᴅʌ [štą] indicates that the rate or intensity of the action is stronger than that indicated by ᴌʌ [ną]. For many Osage speakers, ᴌʌ [ną] means *sometimes* or *usually*, and ৪ᴅʌ [štą] means *always* or *a lot*. If we wanted to say *over and over* we could use either, but ᴌʌ [ną] would indicate *every so often* and ৪ᴅʌ [štą] would indicate *more frequently*.

These two adverbials appear *after* the verb and *before* the completive or continuous aspect marker, if one is used. When ᴌʌ [ną] is used with the completive ᴘɑ [pe], it is almost always written 𐒻𐓜𐓷𐒰 [nąpe]. When the aspect is continuous, instead of 𐒻𐓜 [ną] plus 𐓘𐓵𐓪𐓘 [akxa] we only use 𐒻𐓜 [ną], and 𐒻𐓜 [ną] plus 𐓘𐓵𐓪𐓘 [akxai] will appear as 𐒻𐓜 [nai].

(1) 𐓷𐓘𐕃𐓪́𐓈𐓘𐕋𐒻 𐓘𐓪́𐕎𐓪𐒼𐒻 **𐒻𐓜**.
    wahkǫ́tahci ąmą́ðį **ną**
    We walk to church **sometimes.**

(2) 𐒻̨𐕃𐓪́ 𐓘𐓵𐓪𐓘 𐓷𐓵𐓷𐒰𐓵𐓘 **𐒻𐓜**.
    iihkǫ́ akxa húheka **ną**
    My grandmother is **occasionally** sick.

(3) 𐓪́𐓷𐒰𐒻𐒼 𐒼𐒻 𐓪́𐓰𐓪𐕃𐒰 𐓘́𐕋𐓶𐓷𐕎 **𐒻𐓜** 𐒷𐓵 𐓘𐒼𐓘́𐕋𐒰.
    óweci ci ónǫbre ą́ðuwį **ną** hta ąkáðe
    We will **usually** buy food at the grocery store.

(4) 𐓷𐒻𐕎𐒰́𐒼𐒻 𐓘𐓵𐓪𐓘 𐒷𐓵𐒰 𐒻́𐕃𐒻𐓷𐓰𐓪𐓘𐒼𐒻 **𐒻𐓜**.
    wį́céki akxa hcíle íkihtǫpaži **ną**
    My uncle **doesn't** visit the family **regularly**.

In English, the simple present tense is very often used to talk about events that happen habitually. We see this in example 5a, where the English sentence means that my father grows corn all the time, or habitually. In Osage, we get this meaning by placing 𐒻𐓜 [ną] (or 𐒻𐓜𐓷𐒰 [nąpe]) after the verb.

(5a) 𐒻̨𐕋𐒰́𐒼𐒻 𐓘𐓵𐓪𐓘 𐓵𐓘́𐓷𐒰 ōžú **𐒻𐓜**.
     įhtáci akxa hápa oožú **ną**
     My father grows corn (habitually).

We can even put 𐕃𐒰𐓜 [štą] and 𐒻𐓜 [ną] together to get the sense of something happening all the time periodically, as in 5b, which means "My father grows corn all the time (𐕃𐒰𐓜 [štą]) and it happens regularly in the summer (𐒻𐓜 [ną])."

(5b) Dōkádą įhtáci akxa hápa oožú **štąnǫ**.
     tookétą įhtáci akxa hápa oožú **štąną**
     My father **always** grows corn in the summer.

(6) 𐒷𐓵𐒰 𐓷𐒻́𐕋𐒰 𐓘𐓵𐓪𐓘 𐕋𐒰𐓵𐒼𐒰́ 𐓘́𐕋𐓪𐓷𐒰 **𐒻𐓜𐓷𐒰**.
    hcíle wíhta akxa htaaská átǫpe **nąpe**
    My family **used to** raise sheep.

(7) 𐓷𐓘𐕃𐓪́𐓈𐓘𐕋𐒻 𐒼𐒻 𐓘́𐓷𐓘́𐕃𐓪 **𐕃𐒰𐓜**.
    wahkǫ́tahci ci ąwáaðǫ **štą**
    We sing at church **a lot.**

(8) 𐒻̨𐒻́ 𐓘𐓵𐓪𐓘 oohǫ́ **𐕃𐒰𐓜** 𐓘𐓵𐓪𐓘.
    iiną́ akxa oohǫ́ **štą** akxai
    My mother is **always** cooking.

(9) 𐓪𐓘𐕃𐒰́𐓵𐒰 𐕋𐓪́𐕋𐒰 **𐕃𐒰𐓜** 𐓘𐕋𐓪́.
    mąhkása bráahtą **štą** ąhé
    I'm **always** drinking coffee.

ᏉᎦᏂ [háachi] and ᎢᎩᏂᏌ [íkiha]

Two other common habitual aspect markers are the adverbs ᏉᎦᏂ [háachi] and ᎢᎩᏂᏌ [íkiha]. While ᏉᎦᏂ [háachi] has a meaning fairly close to that of ᏍᏓᎦ [štą], ᎢᎩᏂᏌ [íkiha] includes another shade of meaning that the others don't have. It means that something happens repeatedly, such as *every day*.

Another important point is that ᏉᎦᏂ [háachi] and ᎢᎩᏂᏌ [íkiha] come *before* the verb. This is because they are full words, not small adverbial particles like ᏃᏱ [ną] and ᏍᏓᎦ [štą].

(10) ᎣᏃᏆ ᏉᎦᏂ ᎧᎾᏫᏆ ᎠᎶᎠ.
 ónǫbre **háachi** káaye apai
 They **continually** make food.

(11) ᏉᎦᏂ ᏔᎠᏍᎣᏓᎦ.
 háachi ðahóohtą
 You **kept on** shouting.

Notice the difference in these examples.

(12a) ᎧᎠᏍᎾᏆᏱᏂ ᎠᏃᎦᎧ ᏍᏓᎦ.
 kaasįexci anąąke **štą**
 I run **a lot** in the morning.

(12b) ᎧᎠᏍᎾᏆᏱᏂ **ᎢᎩᏂᏌ** ᎠᏃᎦᎧ.
 kaasįexci **íkiha** anąąke
 I run **every** morning.

These words can also be used together with ᏃᏱ [ną] and ᏍᏓᎦ [štą], as in the following examples.

(12c) ᎧᎠᏍᎾᏆᏱᏂ **ᎢᎩᏂᏌ** ᎠᏃᎦᎧ ᏃᏱ.
 kaasįexci **íkiha** anąąke **ną**
 I **usually** run **every** morning.

(12d) ᎧᎠᏍᎾᏆᏱᏂ **ᎢᎩᏂᏌ** ᎠᏃᎦᎧ ᏍᏓᎦ.
 kaasįexci **íkiha** anąąke **štą**
 I run **a lot every** morning.

Durative aspects

Another kind of aspect is called *durative aspect*. It describes events or states that *last over time*. The English adverb for this aspect is *still*.

ᏍᎣ [šǫ] *still*

The adverbial particle ᏍᎣ [šǫ] behaves like ᏃᏱ [ną] and ᏍᏓᎦ [štą]—it appears after the verb and before any aspect marker. Durative aspects are a kind of continuous aspect (they continue over time), so we will generally use a continuous aspect marker at the end of the sentence.

(13) 𐒰𐒷𐒰𐒰𐒰́ **𐒰𐒰·** 𐒰𐒰𐒰𐒰𐒰́.
waaštǫ́ **šǫ** nįkšé
You are **still** singing.

(14) 𐒰𐒰𐒰𐒰𐒰 𐒰𐒰 𐒰𐒰𐒰𐒰𐒰𐒰 𐒰𐒰𐒰̋ **𐒰𐒰·** 𐒰𐒰𐒰.
wižíke apa hpahúska olį́į **šǫ** apai
My son **still** lives in Pawhuska.

(15) Ó𐒰𐒰 𐒰𐒰𐒰𐒰𐒰𐒰𐒰 **𐒰𐒰·** 𐒰𐒰𐒰𐒰𐒰́.
ówe wáhǫǫpaži **šǫ** ąkatxái
We **still** don't like vegetables.

𐒰𐒰· [šǫ] *while*

Another way that we can use 𐒰𐒰 [šǫ] is to join two smaller sentences to show that one event is happening *while* another is ongoing. The grammatical term for smaller sentences that make up a larger sentence is *clause*.

In both Osage and English, we may put either clause first. Use an aspect marker in both clauses.

(16) 𐒰𐒰́𐒰𐒰 𐒰𐒰𐒰 𐒰𐒰𐒰𐒰́𐒰𐒰 **𐒰𐒰·** 𐒰𐒰𐒰 𐒰𐒰𐒰𐒰̋𐒰𐒰 𐒰𐒰́𐒰𐒰𐒰.
hcíle apa wanǫ́bre **šǫ** apa ðažį́įhe žą́kše
While the family ate dinner, you slept.
OR You slept **while** the family ate dinner.

The connectors 𐒰𐒰𐒰𐒰 [ðáha] and 𐒰𐒰𐒰 [áha]

𐒰𐒰𐒰𐒰 [ðáha] *when* (at a point in time), *as soon as*

A connecting word (the grammar term is *conjunction*) that is closely related to the meaning of 𐒰𐒰 [šǫ] *while* is 𐒰𐒰𐒰𐒰 [ðáha] *when*. We use 𐒰𐒰 [šǫ] when two events are ongoing at the same time. We use 𐒰𐒰𐒰𐒰 [ðáha] to talk about two events that are related in time. At the time that one event happened, the other happened. Clauses connected with 𐒰𐒰𐒰𐒰 [ðáha] are completed events, marked with completive aspect, while clauses marked with 𐒰𐒰 [šǫ] are continuous.

Examine the difference in meaning between these two sentences.

(17a) 𐒰𐒰́𐒰𐒰 𐒰𐒰𐒰𐒰𐒰𐒰́ 𐒰𐒰 **𐒰𐒰𐒰𐒰** 𐒰𐒰𐒰𐒰́𐒰𐒰𐒰 𐒰𐒰𐒰𐒰𐒰 𐒰𐒰𐒰𐒰𐒰𐒰𐒰.
níižu ðiištą́ pe **ðáha** watǫ́ehci éhtaha áwakaži
As soon as it stopped raining, I drove to the store.

(17b) 𐒰𐒰𐒰̋𐒰𐒰 **𐒰𐒰·** 𐒰𐒰𐒰𐒰𐒰́ 𐒰𐒰𐒰́𐒰𐒰 𐒰𐒰𐒰 𐒰𐒰́𐒰𐒰 𐒰𐒰𐒰.
ažį́įhe **šǫ** mįkšé žįkážį apa škáce apai
While I was sleeping, the children were playing.

In example 17a, the emphasis is on the moment when it stopped raining. In 17b, the sleeping and the playing are going on at the same time.

ᎭᏒᎪ [áha] *whenever*

Another connecting word is ᎭᏒᎪ [áha], which corresponds very well to English *whenever*. It is used in the same situations as *whenever*—some unspecified time, which could be in the past, present, or future.

(18) Ɛá7α ᏁᏞñα **ᎭᏒᎪ** ÞᎨ7áᏞñ ᖇᎯᎠᏒ.
hcéze ąníe **áha** paazénii bráahtą
My stomach hurts **whenever** I drink milk.

(19) ᏄᏞᶄó7α ᏞᶄóᎠᎪᎠ ᎪᎠᏒ óᏄᏞᶄᎪᎠ ᎠᏒ **ᎭᏒᎪ** ᏞᶄóᏏᎪ ᏞᶄᎯᏏα.
wakóze ąkóhtapi apa ówahkąpi hta **áha** ąkóða ąkáðe
Our teacher will help us **whenever** we want.

Freestanding pronouns

Up until now, all of our pronouns have been affixed to the verbs they are used with. There are other important pronouns that work differently and are separate from the verb. Two of these kinds of pronouns are *possessives* (for example, *my* or *mine*) and *emphatics* (for example, *me!* or *you!*).

Possessive pronouns

ᏄñᎠᎪ [wíhta] *my, mine*

Let's start by looking at two sentences with ᏄñᎠᎪ [wíhta].

(20) ᶄóᶄα **ᏄñᎠᎪ** ᎪᶄᏏᎪ ᏏᏁᏏᏏᎠᎪᶄᎪ Þα.
šǫ́ke **wíhta** akxa ðiðáaxtaka pe
My dog bit you.

(21) Ꮏα ᶄóᶄα ᎪᶄᏏᎪ **ᏄñᎠᎪ** ᎪᶄᏏᎪ.
ðe šǫ́ke akxa **wíhta** akxa
That dog is **mine**.

In example 20, we see that the word for *my* (**ᏄñᎠᎪ** [wíhta]) appears after the noun ᶄóᶄα [šǫ́ke] and before the subject marker ᎪᶄᏏᎪ [akxa]. In 21, **ᏄñᎠᎪ** [wíhta] is the predicate of the sentence by itself along with the aspect marker. The other freestanding pronouns all work in a similar way, as shown below.

ᏏñᎠᎪ [ðíhta] *your, yours*

(22) ᏁᏞóαᏃᎠ **ᏏñᎠᎪ** ᎪᶄᏏᎪ ᎪᏏñᶄ'ᎠᏏᎪ Þα.
ilǫ́eži **ðíhta** akxa ąðík'iða pe
Your cat scratched me.

(23) Ƭa ncóazn ʌkʎʌ **ƭńƉʌ** ʌkʎʌ.
 ðe ilǫ́eži akxa **ðíhta** akxa
 That cat is **yours**.

ńƉʌ [íhta] (all third-person singular possessives)

(24a) ʞʎʮʌ **ńƉʌ** ʌkʎʌ ʞ'ʎcʎʞn Þa.
 hkáwa **íhta** akxa k'ąsaaki pe
 His/her horse is fast.

(24b) Henry ʞʎʮʌ **ńƉʌ** ʌkʎʌ ʞ'ʎcʎʞn Þa.
 Henry hkáwa **íhta** akxa k'ąsaaki pe
 Henry's horse is fast.

(25) Ƭa ʞʎʮʌ ʌkʎʌ **ńƉʌ** ʌkʎʌ.
 ðe hkáwa akxa **íhta** akxa
 That horse is **his/hers**.

ʌʞóƉʌ [ąkóhta] *our, ours* (dual)

(26) ℨn **ʌʞóƉʌ** ʌkʎʌ cʞʌ Þa.
 hci **ąkóhta** akxa ska pe
 Our (dual) house is white.

(27) ℨn ʌkʎʌ **ʌʞóƉʌ** ʌkʎʌ.
 hci akxa **ąkóhta** akxa
 The house is **ours (dual)**.

ʌʞóƉʌÞn [ąkóhtapi] *our, ours (plural)*

(28) ncóazn **ʌʞóƉʌÞn** ʌkʎʌ ʃʎÞʌ ʒʎcn ʒʎʃa ʌkʎʌ.
 ilǫ́eži **ąkóhtapi** akxa hą́apa záani žį́įhe akxa
 Our (plural) cat sleeps all day.

(29) Ƭa ncóazn ʌkʎʌ **ʌʞóƉʌÞn** ʌkʎʌ.
 ðe ilǫ́eži akxa **ąkóhtapi** akxa
 That cat is **ours (plural)**.

ƭńƉʌÞn [ðíhtapi] *your, yours (plural)*

(30) ʞʎʮʌ **ƭńƉʌÞn** ʌkʎʌ cʎÞʌ Þa.
 hkáwa **ðíhtapi** akxa sápa pe
 Your (plural) horse is black.

(31) Ƭa ʞʎʮʌ cʎÞa ʌkʎʌ **ƭńƉʌÞn** ʌkʎʌ.
 ðe hkáwa sápe akxa **ðíhtapi** akxa
 That black horse is **yours (plural)**.

ÍƉʌɒ [íhtapi] *their, theirs*

(32) OħńƉʌ **ÍƉʌɒ** ʌʖⱴʌ Ƨɑʖʌ ⱴꙅɒ ʌʖⱴʌ.
 oðíhtą **íhtapi** akxa hcéka xci akxa
 Their car is brand new.

(33) Ћɑ OħńƉʌ ʌʖⱴʌ **ÍƉʌɒ** ʌʖⱴʌ.
 ðe oðíhtą akxa **íhtapi** akxa
 That car is **theirs**.

Other freestanding pronouns

When we converse, we don't always have to use a full sentence. Sometimes a phrase or even a single word is what we need. Freestanding pronouns let us do this.

Think about the following English responses to the question "Who found the dog?"

(34a) Me.
 OR I did.
(34b) I found the dog.

The answer in 34a is a normal conversational response to this question. If someone answers as shown in 34b, we expect the pronoun *I* to be emphasized: *I* found the dog.

Osage freestanding pronouns can be used in a similar way, especially in conversation. In 35b, the pronoun ⅄ńɑ [wíe] is a freestanding pronoun that provides a simple answer to the question. Or it can appear at the beginning of a sentence to make a pronoun that does appear on the verb more emphatic (or brings a greater focus to the pronoun), as in example 36.

⅄ńɑ [wíe] *I, me*

(35a) Ƥɑ́ ʠóʖɑ ńჩɑ?
 pée šǫ́ke íiðe
 Who found the dog?
(35b) ⅄ńɑ.
 wíe
 Me.
 OR I did.
(36) **⅄ńɑ** ⅄ʌcóʀɑ ʖóʀʌ
 wíe wanǫ́bre hkǫbra
 I want to eat.
 OR **I'm** the one who wants to eat
 OR As for **me**, **I** want to eat.

It is very important to remember that in a sentence, freestanding pronouns such as ⅄ńɑ [wíe] cannot be used to replace the pronouns that are attached to the verbs (which we studied in earlier chapters). Rather, the emphatic pronouns are used in combination with the pronouns that are already used with the verbs, as example 36 shows.

𐓇𐓣́𐓘 [ðíe] *you and you plural*

𐓇𐓣́𐓘 [ðíe] can be used for *you* and *you plural*. We also have a modern plural form, 𐓇𐓣́𐓘𐓏𐓣 [ðíapi], which you may hear.

(37a) 𐒹𐓣́𐓨𐓣̧𐓻𐓣̧ 𐓘𐓤𐒰𐓘 𐓬𐓟́𐓟 𐓤𐓣́𐓪𐒼𐓯𐓘?
šį́mįžį akxa pée kíoxta
Whom does the girl love?

In everyday English, we rarely hear "whom," although it is grammatically correct.

(37b) 𐓇𐓣́𐓘.
ðíe
You.

(38) **𐓇𐓣́𐓘** 𐒹𐓣́𐓨𐓣̧𐓻𐓣̧ 𐓘𐓤𐒰𐓘 **𐓇𐓣𐓪́𐒼𐓯𐓘**.
ðíe šį́mįžį akxa **ðí**óxta.
The girl loves **you**.
OR **You** are the one the girl loves.

Notice again in example 38 that we still have to add 𐓇𐓣 [ði] *you* to the verb even though we use the freestanding 𐓇𐓣́𐓘 [ðíe].

We don't have a record of whether traditional Osage had a special freestanding form for *you plural* or not. If we need 𐓇𐓣́𐓘 [ðíe] to refer to a plural pronoun, we will mark that on the verb. And as mentioned above, nowadays some speakers say 𐓇𐓣́𐓘𐓏𐓣 [ðíapi], which would always mean *you plural*.

(39) **𐓇𐓣́𐓘** 𐒹𐓣́𐓨𐓣̧𐓻𐓣̧ 𐓘𐓤𐒰𐓘 **𐓇𐓣𐓪́𐒼𐓯𐓘𐓏𐓣**.
ðíe šį́mįžį akxa **ðí**óxta**pi**
The girl loves **you (plural)**.

𐒰𐓤𐓪́𐓘 [ąkóe] *we (dual and plural)* and *us*

𐒰𐓤𐓪́𐓘 [ąkóe] is used for *we two*, *we plural*, and *us*.

(40a) 𐓬𐓟́ 𐓷𐒰𐓻𐓪́𐓘 𐓯𐓤𐓪́𐓘 𐓤𐓪́𐓇𐒰?
pée wacúe skúe kǫ́ða
Who wants cake?

(40b) 𐒰𐓤𐓪́𐓘.
ąkóe
Us.
OR We do.

(41) **𐒰𐓤𐓪́𐓘** 𐓷𐒰𐓻𐓪́𐓘 𐓯𐓤𐓪́𐓘 **𐒰𐓤𐓪́𐓇𐒰 𐒰𐓤𐒰́𐓇𐓟**.
ąkóe wacúe skúe **ąk**ǫ́ða **ąk**áðe
We want cake.
OR **We** are the ones who want cake.

ǽ [ée] *he/him, she/her, it, that, they/their*

ǽ [ée] is used for all third-person pronouns, singular or plural.

(42a) Pǽ ɥʌƨúɑ ᴄҡúɑ ɥńᴆʌ ᴛ̄λƨá?
      pée wacúe skúe wíhta ðaaché
      Who ate my cake?

(42b) ǽ.
      ée
      Him/her/them.
      OR **He/she/they** did.

(43) ǽ ɥʌƨúɑ ᴄҡúɑ ɥńᴆʌ ᴛ̄λƨá ᴅɑ.
     ée wacúe skúe wíhta ðaachá pe
     She/he/they ate my cake.
     OR **He/she** is the one who ate my cake.
     OR **They** are the ones who ate my cake.

Dóɥʌ [tówa] *that one, those ones* (third-person)

Another important third-person pronoun is Dóɥʌ [tówa]. (Do not confuse this with Dóɑ [tóe] *some*.) Dóɥʌ [tówa] always refers to persons or objects whose identity is unknown or unimportant. Some ways of translating Dóɥʌ [tówa] are *that guy, those guys, those people, those things*. Unlike ǽ [ée], it takes a subject marker when it is the subject.

Context plays a crucial role in understanding and using these pronouns. Examples 44a–b include a context followed by an example sentence. Notice how the context helps us understand the meaning of the pronoun.

Context: I see that my grandmother made coffee. Someone asks if I or my grandmother made the coffee. I respond:

(44a) ǽ ᴍʌҡásʌ ҡáʏʌ ᴅɑ.
      ée mąhkása káaɣa pe
      She is the one who made coffee.

Context: We are at a gathering with a number of people, some of whom I don't know. Someone asks if there is coffee. I respond:

(44b) **Dóɥʌ** ʌᴅɑ ᴍʌҡásʌ ҡáʏʌ ᴅɑ.
      tówa apa mąhkása káaɣa pe
      That guy made coffee.

In 44a, we are emphasizing that a particular known person made coffee. That person does not need to be present, simply known in the current context. In 44b, it is less important to identify him or her, but the person needs to be in the area to be pointed out.

𐓂𐓰'𐓂𐓟𐓘

Exercise 1. Do you understand?

What does this short story mean in English?

𐒻𐒿𐓟́𐓘𐓻𐒷 𐓷𐒻́𐓩𐓘 𐓘𐓰𐒼𐒰 𐓷𐓘𐓛𐓯𐒼𐒰𐓻𐒷 𐓣𐓪, 𐓄𐓰𐒼𐒰𐓻𐒷 𐓣𐓪. 𐓷𐒰́𐓪 𐓛𐓚𐓻𐒷 𐓻𐒰́𐓪 𐓛𐓚. Ą 𐓷𐒰́𐓷𐓘𐓰𐒼 𐓣𐓪' 𐒰𐒼𐒰𐓘.
𐒻𐒿𐓟́𐓘𐓻𐒷 𐓷𐒻́𐓩𐓘 𐓘𐓰𐒼𐒰 𐓷𐒰𐓪𐒼𐒰́𐓪𐓘 𐒼𐒻́𐓪𐒰𐓷𐒰? 𐓂𐓘𐓷𐓚𐓪𐒻𐒷.

Exercise 2. Composition

Write a composition of six sentences in Osage. Include at least one possessive or other free-standing pronoun and one durative or habitual aspect marker.

Exercise 3. Possessive pronouns

Choose six nouns from any of the vocabulary lists and use them with each of the possessive pronouns. Remember that kinship terms already have possession built in.

𐓂𐒰

Nouns

𐒻𐒿𐓂́𐒰𐓩	ihkówa	friend
𐒿𐓂́𐓲𐓩	hkóða	friend

Verbs

𐒰́𐓮𐓪𐓘	átǫpe (strong-stem)	raise, take care of
𐒻́𐒼𐒻𐓮𐓪𐓘	íkihtǫpe (a-ða)	visit one's family
ō𐓻ú	oožú (a-ða)	pour or put into
𐓯𐒼𐒰́𐓟𐒰	škáce (a-ða)	play
𐓲ā𐒰𐓲𐓪𐒰́𐒼𐒰	ðaaxtáke (br-šc)	bite
𐓲𐒻𐒼'𐒻́𐓲𐒰	ðikʼíðe (br-šc)	scratch

Adjectives

𐒼'𐒰́𐓮𐒰́𐒼𐒻	kʼą́saaki	fast
𐒻𐒰́𐒼𐒰 𐓲𐒻	hcéka xci	brand new

Other

𐒰́𐓯𐒰	áha	whenever
𐓷𐒰́𐓪 𐓛𐒰́𐓚𐒻	hą́ąpa záani	all day

ᔐᎨᏁ	háahci	all the time, continually
ᏂᎮᏁᏍᎸ	íkiha	repetitively, every time
ᏝᎸᎨᎸ	nąka	maybe
ᎠᎪᎦᎠᎠᎸ	tookétą	in the summer
ᏔᎭᏍᎸ	ðáha	when, as soon as

Notes for Chapter 13

The form ᏈᏁ ᏍᎠ [pi che], in sentence 9 of the dialogue, is an evidential. It means something like *so I know what I'm talking about* and shows that the speaker has knowledge that makes him confident in what he is saying.

Chapter 14

Motion Verbs

Oȟná

Oȟpíko ʌẖẖʌ Oɔ́ẖʌ ʌɾő ʌẖẖʌ.

1. Oɔ́ẖʌ 7ʌ́ɔʌ, ẖóẖʌ, ʌDópa ẖɠn.
2. Þʌɔuoɔñ̃ Þáψaɔñ̃ ʌẖń, DoDʌ́ʌ ʌʌÐʌ́ẖʌ, DoDʌ́ʌ ɔńẖʌẖn ẖɠn.
3. ʌʌẖʌẖoɔñ̃ Þáψaɔñ̃ ʌẖń, DoDʌ́ʌ ʌʌÐʌ́ẖʌ, DoDʌ́ʌ ɔńẖʌẖn ẖɠn.
4. 7ñ̃ɾóɔñ̃ Þáψaɔñ̃ ʌẖń, DoDʌ́ʌ ʌʌÐʌ́ẖʌ, DoDʌ́ʌ ɔńẖʌẖn ẖɠn.
5. 7ʌ́ɔn ʌʌʌńʌoÐn.
6. ʌʌẖő ʌńÐʌ 7ʌ́ɔn ʌʌʌ̃ɾnÐn Þa óʌaɔʌ ʌDẖʌʌ́a.
7. ẖaẖőÞa, ɔʌ́ɔa Dóa ʌ́Þʌ ʌDẖʌʌ́a.
8. Þʌɔuoɔñ̃ Þáψaɔñ̃ ʌẖń.
9. ʌʌẖʌẖoɔñ̃ Þáψaɔñ̃ ʌẖń.
10. 7ñ̃ɾóɔñ̃ Þáψaɔñ̃ ʌẖń.
11. ʌʌ̃ńÞẖʌ.
12. ʌʌɔʌ́ẖa.
13. Oɔ́Þʌ, ẖẖóẖʌ, ẖ́7aɔẖʌ, ɔʌɔúʌu ẖẖn Þáψaɔñ̃ ʌ́zu ʌʌʌẖẖna ʌDẖʌʌ́a.
14. ẖʌẖóɔʌ́.

Grandpa addresses Ilonshka.

1. All Ilonshka, singers, and onlookers.
2. Gray Horse Drumkeeper, Head Committeeman, and Committeemen.
3. Pawhuska Drumkeeper, Head Committeeman, and Committeemen.
4. Hominy Drumkeeper, Head Committeeman, and Committeemen.
5. I respectfully address everyone.
6. I am grateful to everyone that danced on my song.
7. Now, I am going to call a few names (to give them blankets).
8. The Gray Horse Drumkeeper.

9. The Pawhuska Drumkeeper.
10. The Hominy Drumkeeper.
11. The Town Crier.
12. The Whipmen.
13. I will have First Son and Second Son put money and tobacco on the drum.
14. That's all.

At a Giveaway, people who are called will receive something, usually a blanket. This dialogue is an example of how you might address people and call them for a giveaway.

Ṹa ʔʌkŏcᴧꝣɑ

How to think about movement in osage

English speakers are used to using verbs like *come* and *go* in a very loose way—we rely on context to tell us what those words mean. For example, if someone says, "Are you coming to the party?" it is not really different from saying, "Are you going to the party?" In Osage we are very careful about expressing the ideas of *here* versus *there* and of *traveling* versus *arriving*. In this chapter we will learn how to use eight important verbs of motion.

These eight verbs of motion also permit us to make verbs that mean *bring* and *take*. We will make another eight verbs based on the basic motion verbs that give us very fine distinctions in moving and carrying.

Movement toward *here*: ᴧʃú [ahú], ᴧƙú [akú], and the h-stem verb class

The motion verbs ᴧʃú [ahú] and ᴧƙú [akú] both mean *moving here*. In Osage we make another distinction: ᴧʃú [ahú] means *come here* while ᴧƙú [akú] means *come back here*, so it could also be translated *return here*. These verbs are used when motion is underway, so they are almost always used with continuous aspect.

(1) ħaƙǫ́ꝣa ʔʌƙǫ́ʔa ᴧᴅᴧ ħāƙʌ́ **ᴧʃú** ᴧᴅᴧ.
    ðekǫ́ǫce wakǫ́ze apa ðeeká **ahú** apai
    The teacher is **coming here** now.

(2) ƙǫ́ƙa ṹcá́ʔᴧ ᴧᴅᴧ **ᴧƙú** ᴧᴅᴧ!
    šǫ́ke iiséwai apa **akú** apai
    The mean dog is **coming back here**!

The h-stem verb class and ᴧʃú [ahú]

ᴧʃú [ahú] *come here* is a member of a new verb class, the *h-stem class*. In the h-stem class, the pronoun for first-person singular *I* is ᴅƙ [pš] and for second-person *you* (both singular and plural) is ƙ [š]. In ᴧʃú [ahú] these pronouns replace the first two sounds.

(3) ᏇᎮᎤ ᎯᏍᎠ.
   pšu ąhé
   I'm coming here.
(4) ᎮᎤ ᏂᎴᎮᎠ.
   šu ðaašé
   You're coming here.
(5) ᎮᎤ ᏉᎴᎮᎠ.
   šu paašé
   You (plural) are coming here.

As we have done before, we use the aspect marker ᏉᎴᎮᎠ [paašé] to show that *you* is plural in example 5. We will do the same to distinguish first-person dual (we two) ᎯᏂᎠ [ąðé] from first-person plural (we) ᎯᎧᎯᏂᎠ [ąkáðe].

(6) ᎢᎧᎯᏍᎤ ᎯᏂᎠ.
   ąkáhu ąðé
   We two are coming here.
(7) ᎢᎧᎯᏍᎤ ᎢᎧᎯᏂᎠ.
   ąkáhu ąkáðe OR ąkai
   We are coming here.

ᎯᏍᎤ [akú] *come back here*

ᎯᏍᎤ [akú] *come back here* belongs to the a-ða class. The forms for first-person singular *I* and third-person are the same: ᎯᏍᎤ [akú]. We distinguish them with the aspect marker. The first syllable Ꭿ [a] is sometimes omitted from this verb. Another common way to use this word is ᏍᎤᎣ [kuó], the command form for *come here* (which you first saw in the dialogue from chapter 4).

(8) ᎯᏍᎤ ᎯᏍᎠ.
   akú ąhé
   I'm coming back here.
(9) ᎯᏍᎤ ᎯᏉᎯ.
   akú apai
   She's coming back here. ("she" or another third-person)
(10) ᏍᎤᎣ!
   kuó
   Come here!
(11) ᏂᎯᏍᎤ ᏂᎴᎮᎠ.
   ðakú ðaašé
   You're coming back here.
(12) ᏂᎯᏍᎤ ᏉᎴᎮᎠ.
   ðakú paašé
   You (plural) are coming back here.
(13) ᎢᎧᎯᏍᎤ ᎯᏂᎠ.
   ąkáku ąðé
   We two are coming back here.

(14) **ᎧᎧᎶU ᎧᎶᏂᎠ**.
ą̄káku ą̄káðe OR ą̄kai
We are coming back here.

Arrival *here*: ᎪᏃᎾ [achí] and ᎪᏓᎾ [alí]

The motion verb ᎪᏃᎾ [achí] means *arrive here* or *get here*. And ᎪᏓᎾ [alí] means *get back here*, *arrive back here*, or *arrive home*. These are both in the a-ða verb class. The initial sound is very often omitted from ᎪᏃᎾ [achí] in the third-person, as we see in these examples from the dialogue in chapter 4.

ᎪᏃᎾ [achí] *arrive here* or *get here*

(15) ᏂᏂᏐ ᎪᎠ **ᏃᏂ** ᏂᎠ?
ðiihǫ́ apa **chí** ðe
Has your mother **arrived**?

(16) ᏂᎴᏓᎾ **ᏂᎪᏃᎾ** ᏃᎠ.
ðáalį **ðachí** che
It's good **you**'re here.

In usage, this verb is most commonly encountered when we say ᎪᏃᎾ [achí] *I'm here*.

ᎪᏓᎾ [alí] *get back here*, *arrive back here*, *arrive home*

(17) OᏃᎾᏓᎠ ᎪᏓᎾ ᎠᎪ ᏇᏁᎶᎦᎠ.
ohcíle **alí** hta mįkšé
I will arrive home.

The third-person form of ᎪᏓᎾ [alí] *arrive back* also loses *a* in most speech.

(18) ᎢᏓᎠᎠ ᎧᏁᎢᎴ OᏃᎾᏓᎠ **ᏓᎾ** ᎠᎠ.
iinąhtą akxa ohcíle **lí** pe
My aunt (mother's older sister) came back home.

(19) ᏥᎠᏐᎠᎶ ᏃᏁᎴᏂᎠ ᎧᏁᎢᎴ OᏃᎾᏓᎠ **ᏓᎾ** ᎠᎠ ᎧᏁᎢᎴ.
kaasį́ta wižį́ðe akxa ohcíle **lí** hta akxai
My brother (male's older brother) will return home tomorrow.

Compare ᎪᏓᎾ [alí] and ᎧᏂ [akú] in 20a and 20b.

(20a) ᏥᎴᎢ ᏂᎠ ᎪᎠ ᏓᎾᏁᎢ **ᏓᎾ** ᎠᎠ.
hkáwa ðe apa ną́ą́ke **lí** pe
That horse ran back here (and it arrived).

(20b) ᏥᎪᏯᎸ ᏋᎠ ᎠᏫᎸ ᏌᎵᎦ **ᎸᎦᎤ** ᎠᏫᎸ.
hkáwa ðe apa ną́ąke **akú** apai
That horse is running back here (and it has not yet arrived).

When ᎸᏌᏁ [ali] and other short verbs are the last word in the sentence, as in 21a, the pronunciation is often altered. Many people will add an α [e] to make ᏋᎸᏌᏁα [ðalíe] rather than ᏋᎸᏌᏁ [ðalí]. In 21b, the sentence ends with the aspect marker, so ᏋᎸᏌᏁ [ðalí] is not the last word, and no α [e] is added.

(21a) ᏕᎭᎠᏛᏉᏋᏅ **ᏋᎸᏌᏁα**?
haatxą́ci **ðalíe**
When did you come back?

(21b) ᏕᎭᎠᏛᏉᎠᏛᎸ **ᏋᎸᏌᏁ** ᎧᎸ ᏌᏁᎦᎠ́?
haatxą́ta **ðalí** hta nįkše
When will you come back?

Movement toward *there*: ᎸᏋᎠ̋ [aðée] and ᎸᏌᎠ̋ [alée]

The motion verbs ᎸᏋᎠ̋ [aðée] *go there* and ᎸᏌᎠ̋ [alée] *go back there* are used for movement away from the speaker—moving *there*. It's easiest for us to think of these as *go* and *go back*. These are used when we talk about movement that is underway, but we do not assume that the one going arrived. This is a somewhat difficult concept for English speakers, since we assume that if someone went somewhere, he or she arrived.

ᎸᏋᎠ̋ [aðée] *go there*

ᎸᏋᎠ̋ [aðée] is in the brush verb class. Like other motion verbs, the first sound is dropped when we use the pronouns ᏒᎠ [br] *I* and ᏍᏣ [šc] *you*, giving us ᏒᎠ̋ [brée] *I go* and ᏍᏣᎠ̋ [šcée] *you go*, singular and plural. ᎸᏌᎠ̋ [alée] is in the a-ða class.

(22) ᎼᏁᏫᎸ ᎸᏍᏉᎸ ᏌᏂᎠ́ᎠᏫ ᏂᏍᏁ́ **ᎸᏋᎠ̋** ᎠᎠ.
míɣa akxa niitáahpa įkší **aðáa** pe
The duck **went** to the pond.

In example 22, we are saying that the duck moved toward the pond, but not whether it arrived.

(23) ᏕᎣᏯ́ᏍᏅ **ᏍᏣᎠ̋**?
hową́įki **šcée**
Where are **you** going?

(24) ᒐᎾᏌᎷᏴᏁ **ᎦᏛᏥᏛᎠ**?
howáįki štáape
Where are **you (plural)** going?

The form for *you (plural) go*, ᎦᏛᏥᏛᎠ [štáape], may be puzzling at first since it comes from ᎦᏃᎠ̋ [šcée]. There is a brief explanation for this in the notes at the end of this chapter.

The form for first-person dual *we two*, ᎠᎦᎵᏂᎠ [ąkáðe], is interesting because it is the same as the first plural continuous aspect marker. Historically, the aspect marker ᎠᎦᎵᏂᎠ [ąkáðe] evolved from this movement verb, which is why it is also pronounced the same way.

(25) ᏣᎠ̋ᏴᎠ ᏂᎦᏁᏌᎠ ᎠᎦᏴᏬᏨᎦᎠ ᏃᏁ **ᎠᎦᎵᏂᎠ** ᏃᏴᎠ.
hą́ąpa íkiha taapóska ci **ąkáðe** nąpe
We two go to school every day.

(26) ᏒᏁᏨᎣ́ᎠᏃᏁ̓ ᎠᏴᎠ ᏒᎠᎦ̧ᎣᎠᎠᏃ ᏃᏁ ᎹᎠᏂ̌ ᎠᏂᎠ̋ ᎠᏴᎠ.
wisǫ́eži ąpa wahkǫ́tahci ci mąðį́ aðée ąpai
My brother (female's younger brother) is walking to church.

(27) ᏌᎠ̋ ᎧᎦᏁ ᎹᎠᏂ̌ ᏇᎠ̋ ᎠᏌᎠ̋.
žą́ą kši mąðį́ brée ąhé
I am walking to the forest.

In 26 and 27 above, we have both ᎹᎠᏂ̌ [mąðį́] *walk* and ᎠᏂᎠ̋ [aðée] *go*. It is very common to say ᎹᎠᏂ̌ ᎠᏂᎠ̋ [mąðį́ aðée], literally *go by walking*.

ᎠᏃᎠ̋ [alée] *go back there*

ᎠᏃᎠ̋ [alée] *go back there* uses the same form, ᎠᏃᎠ̋ [alée], for both first-person singular *I* and third-person. This is also true for ᎠᎦᎤ́ [akú], ᎠᏃᏂ [achí], and ᎠᏃᏂ́ [alí]. We distinguish the two meanings by using different aspect markers as shown in 28 and 29 below.

(28) ᎠᏃᎠ̋ **ᎠᏌᎠ̋**.
  alée **ąhé**
  I am returning there.
(29) ᎠᏃᎠ̋ **ᎠᏴᎠ**.
  alée **ąpai**
  He is returning there.
(30) **ᎠᎦᏃᎠ** **ᎠᏂᎠ̋**.
  ąkále aðé
  We two are returning there.
(31) **ᎠᎦᏃᏃᎠᏴᎠ**.
  ąkálape
  We (plural) returned there.
(32) **ᎠᎦᏃᎠ ᎠᎦᎵᏂᎠ**.
  ąkále ąkáðe
  We (plural) are returning there.

Arrival *there*: ᎠᏏ [ahí] and ᎠᎩᏏ [akší]

We use ᎠᏏ [ahí] to mean arriving at or being at a place that is not here. It is often used to express *stop by* or *stop in at*. It is an h-stem verb, so it will have the pronouns �pᏍ [pš] *I* and Ꮝ [š] *you*. Not only the initial ᎠᎳ [a] but also the Ꮫ [h] in the stem is deleted in first- and second-person forms: ᏪᏍᏏ [pší] and ᏍᏏ [ší]. If the verb is in completive aspect, speakers usually add the sound [e] to the end of the verb if it's at the end of a sentence: ᏪᏍᏏᎠ [pšíe] and ᏍᏏᎠ [šíe], as in examples 35 and 36. If the future marker or other aspect marker is used, no [e] is needed, as in example 33.

(33) **ᏪᏍᏏ** ᏪᎳ ᎼᏂᎩᏏᎠ.
 pší hta mįkšé
 I'll be there.

(34) Ꮒꮒ **ᎠᏏ** Ꮒα.
 hci **ahí** pe
 She stopped by the house.

(35) **ᏍᏏα**.
 šíe
 You got there.

(36) **ᏪᏍᏏα**.
 pšíe
 I got there.

Because ᎠᏏ [ahí] has the sense of *get somewhere*, it has an important second use as *become*, *start to*, and *get*, such as *get old*, *get sick*.

(37) ᏍᏏᏪᎳᎩᎳ **ᏪᏍᏏα**.
 šįhtąką **pšíe**
 I got fat.

(38) ᎳᎣᏪᎳ **ᎠᏏ** Ꮒα.
 hóohtą **ahí** pe
 He started to shout.

ᎠᎩᏏ [akší] *arrive back there* or *return there*

ᎠᎩᏏ [akší] is an a-ða verb, and it means *arrive back there* or *return there*. It has a second meaning of *return home*, often used if there has been a period of absence from one's home.

(39) ᏍᎣᎩα ꮒᏍαᏚᎳ ᎠᏪᎳ ᎠᎩᏏ ᎠᏪᎳ!
 šóke iiséwai apa akší apai
 The mean dog is back there! (It came back to where it was before.)

(40) ᎫᏍꮐα ᏍᎩᏂᎳ ᎠᎩᎳᎩᏂα.
 tooké íkiha ąkákšipe
 We returned home every summer.

Bringing and taking with ᎭᏂ [aðį́] *have*

The verb ᎭᏂ [aðį́] is used to mean possession, the basic sense of English *have*. (Be careful. English has secondary uses for this verb, such as *have a baby* or *have fun*, but Osage uses other verbs for these meanings.) ᎭᏂ [aðį́] is a brush verb, and the continuous aspect marker will usually be left out. This is because possession is, by its nature, a state, so it will most often be understood with continuous aspect. We saw this with stative verbs in chapter 10.

(41) ᏂᎭᏞᎦ ᎠᏘ ᎤᎭᏆᏞ ᎭᎤᏘᎠ **ᎭᏂ**.
    iðáce apa oðíhtą ðǫǫpá **aðį́**
    His father **has** two cars.

(42) ᎹᏃᎦᏍᎦᏞ ᎠᎠᏞᎦ **ᎳᏍᏂ**?
    mą́zeska háaną **ašcį**
    How much money do **you have**?

(43) ᎹᏃᎦᏍᎦᏞ ᎠᎠᏞᎦ **ᎳᏍᏂ ᏆᏍᎦᎠ**?
    mą́zeska háaną **ašcį paašé**
    How much money do **you (plural) have**?

Bringing and taking

The eight motion verbs discussed above form another eight verbs that have to do with carrying something while moving or arriving. These will correspond to English *bring* and *take*, but you can already guess that English meanings are much broader than the Osage ones. In English, *bring* and *take* can often be used interchangeably, but here we will use *bring* for verbs that mean *carry here* and *take* to translate verbs that mean *carry there*.

All the *bring* and *take* verbs are compounded with the verb for *have* (ᎭᏂ [aðį́]). Both parts of the compounded verb use the pronouns for their own verb class. This will make some very interesting forms in some cases.

Bring here: ᎭᏂᎡᏌᎤ [aðįahu], ᎭᏂᎡᏆᎤ [aðįaku], ᎭᏂᎡᏃ [aðįachi], ᎭᏂᎡᏞᏃ [aðįali]

The uses of ᎭᏂᎡᏌᎤ [aðįahu] *bring here but not arrive* are somewhat more limited than those of the other carrying verbs because there are fewer situations when we would just talk about the motion underway. One way to translate this might be *on the way*.

ᎭᏂᎡᏌᎤ [aðįahu]

(44) ᏂᏞᎦ ᎠᏘ ᎤᎦᎤᏆᎦ **ᎭᏂᎡᏌᎤ** ᎠᏘ.
    iiná apa ónǫbre **aðįahu** apai
    My mother is bringing food (here). (My mother is on the way here with the food.)

The form for *I'm bringing it here* is ᎭᏒᏂᏆᎰ [abrípšu]. Since ᎭᏂ [aðį́] is a brush verb, we need to use the first-person pronoun Ꮢ [br], and because ᎠᎰ [ahú] is an h-stem verb, we also need the first-person pronoun ᏆᎰ [pš].

(45) Ǫ́žu ðóžo wį **abrípšu** ąhé.
óžu htóho wį **abrípšu** ąhé
I'm bringing a blue bowl **here**. (I'm on my way with a blue bowl.)

The form for *you're bringing it here* is ᎪᏥᏁᏒᎤ [aščíšu].

(46) ᎰᏛ **ᎪᏥᏁᏒᎤ** ᏠᎠᏒᎠ.
hó **aščíšu** ðaašé
You are bringing fish **here**. (You are on the way with the fish.)

ᎪᏍᏁᎳᎩᎤ [aðíaku]

We use ᎪᏍᏁᎳᎩᎤ [aðíaku] *bring back here* often to mean *bring back home*. The shortened form ᎪᏍᎳᎩᎤ [áðįku] is often used. ᎳᎩᎤ [akú] is an a-ða verb. This could be translated as *on the way back*.

(47) Óðaake waléze **aðíaku** apai. OR Óðaake waléze **áðįku** apai.
óðaake waléze **aðíaku** apai OR óðaake waléze **áðįku** apai
She's bringing the newspaper **back**.
(48) Óðaake waléze **abríaku** ąhé.
óðaake waléze **abríaku** ąhé
I'm bringing the newspaper **back**.
(49) waléze **aščíðaku** ðaašé.
waléze **aščíðaku** ðaašé
You're bringing the book **back**.

ᎪᏍᏁᎴᏁ [aðíachi]

ᎪᏍᏁᎴᏁ [aðíachi] is used to mean *bringing something and arriving at a place*, very often home.

(50) Hą́apa ðe iiną́ akxa ówe **aðíachi** pe.
hą́apa ðe iiną́ akxa ówe **aðíachi** pe
Mother **brought** groceries **home** today.
(51) Mázeska **aščíðachi** ðe?
mázeska **aščíðachi** ðe
Did **you bring** any money? (and arrive with it)

In example 51, because the event has already occurred, we understand that you brought money and arrived here with it. Notice again that we use pronouns on both ᎪᏍᏁ [aðí] and ᎴᏁ [achí] for second-person *you*.

𐒰𐓵𐓣́͘𐓘𐓧𐓣 [aðįali]

𐒰𐓵𐓣́͘𐓘𐓧𐓣 [aðíali] is used when we mean we brought something back, often home, and arrived with it.

(52) 𐒻𐓧𐓪́͘𐓟𐓻𐓣͘ 𐓷𐓣́𐓱𐓘 𐓪𐓞𐓣́𐓧𐓟 **𐒰𐓜𐓣́͘𐓘𐓧𐓣**.
ilǫ́ežį wíhta ohcíle **abrįali**
I brought my cat back (**home**).

Take there: **𐓘𐓵𐓣́͘𐓘𐓵𐓟 [aðįaðe], 𐓘𐓵𐓣́͘𐓘𐓧𐓟 [aðįale], 𐓘𐓵𐓣́͘𐓘𐓡𐓣 [aðįahi], 𐓘𐓵𐓣́𐓘𐓤𐓯𐓣 [aðíakši]**

Just as we saw with the four *bring* verbs, another four motion verbs could be thought of as *take somewhere not here*. We will use the English *take* for these verbs.

𐒰𐓵𐓣́͘𐓘𐓵𐓟̄ [aðįaðee]

𐒰𐓵𐓣́͘𐓘𐓵𐓟̄ [aðíaðee] expresses the concept of carrying something without saying if someone arrived. One good way to say this is *take away*. Remember that both 𐓘𐓵𐓣́͘ [aðį́] and 𐓘𐓵𐓟̄́ [aðée] belong to the brush class, and each part needs to have its own pronouns.

(53) **𐒰𐓵𐓣́͘𐓘𐓵𐓟̄** 𐓱𐓘 𐓘𐓤𐓸𐓘.
aðįaðee hta akxa
He will **take** it (**away**).
(54) 𐓨𐓘́͘𐓺𐓟𐓮𐓤𐓘 **𐓘𐓯𐓝𐓣́͘𐓯𐓝𐓟̄** 𐓵𐓘̄𐓯𐓟́?
mą́zeska **ašcį́šcee** ðaašé
Were **you taking** the money **there**? (Were you on your way there with the money?)
(55) 𐓷𐓘𐓤𐓪́͘𐓺𐓟 𐓷𐓣́𐓱𐓘 𐓷𐓘𐓮𐓤𐓶́𐓟 **𐓘́𐓜𐓣͘𐓜𐓟̄** 𐓘𐓡𐓟́.
wakǫ́ze wíhta waskúe **ábrįbree** ahé
I am taking sweets to my teacher. (I'm on my way there with the sweets for the teacher.)

𐒰𐓵𐓣́͘𐓘𐓧𐓟̄ [aðįalee]

𐒰𐓵𐓣́͘𐓘𐓧𐓟̄ [aðíalee] means *carry something back or return with it*, especially back home.

(56) **𐒰𐓜𐓣́͘𐓘𐓧𐓟̄** 𐓘͘𐓡𐓟́.
abrįalee ąhé
I'm taking it **back home**. (I'm on my way back home with it.)
(57) 𐓷𐓘𐓮𐓤𐓶́𐓟 **𐓘͘𐓤𐓘́𐓵𐓣͘𐓘͘𐓤𐓘𐓧𐓟̄** 𐓘͘𐓤𐓘́𐓵𐓟.
waskúe **ąkáðįąkalee** ąkáðe
We are on our way **back home** with the sweets. (We are taking sweets back home.)

𐓪𐓸𐓘𐓵𐓣 [aðįahi]

𐓪𐓸𐓘𐓵𐓣 [aðįahi] means *carry something somewhere and arrive with it*. This is probably the most commonly used of the carry verbs. Remember that the first part of the verb is a brush verb and the second part an h-stem verb. In all of these sentences, there is an assumption that the subject of the sentence both took something and arrived with it.

(58) 𐓣𐓪𐓰𐓘𐓻𐓣 𐓘𐒼𐓸𐓘 𐓵𐓣𐒷𐓣𐒼𐓪 𐒷𐓣 𐓂𐓘𐓂𐓰𐓻𐓶 **𐓪𐓸𐓘𐓵𐓣** 𐓷𐓘.
ihtáci akxa wihcíko hci nąnúhu **aðįahi** pe
Father **took** tobacco to Grandpa's house.

(59) 𐓂𐓻𐓣𐒷𐓪 𐓂𐓂𐓪𐓻𐓘 **𐓘𐓻𐒷𐓂𐓸𐓣** 𐓱𐓘 𐓸𐓘?
ókizo ónǫbre **ašcíši** hta ðe
Are **you taking** food to the party?

Example 60 shows that we can take people as well as things.

(60) 𐒻𐒼𐓂 𐓷𐓘𐓸𐓂𐓰𐓘𐓻𐓣 𐒷𐓣 **𐓘𐓻𐒷𐓂𐓸𐓣** 𐓱𐓘 𐓷𐓘𐓸𐓂?
iikó wahkótahci ci **ašcíši** hta paašé
Will **you (plural) take** my grandmother to church?

𐓪𐓸𐓘𐓸𐒼𐓸𐓣 [aðįakši]

𐓪𐓸𐓘𐓸𐒼𐓸𐓣 [aðįakši] means *take something somewhere* or *return something somewhere*. This is often for taking something home.

(61) 𐒼𐓂𐒼𐓘 𐓣𐓻𐓘𐓵𐓘 𐓘𐓷𐓘 𐓵𐓘𐓱𐓶 **𐓪𐓸𐓘𐓸𐒼𐓸𐓣** 𐓷𐓘.
šǫ́ke iiséwai apa wahú **aðįakši** pe
The mean dog **took** a bone **back** (**there**).

𐓂𐓸'𐓶𐒷𐓘

Exercise 1. Do you understand?

What does this conversation mean in English?

A: 𐓱𐓂𐓷𐓘 𐓱𐓘 𐓰𐓘𐓵𐓘 𐓸𐒼𐓣 𐒼𐒷𐒽 𐓷𐓘 𐓻𐓣𐒼𐒽𐓂?
B: 𐓱𐓂𐓸𐓂𐓰𐓘? 𐓰𐓣𐓰𐓘 𐒼𐓂𐒽𐒼𐓰𐓘 𐓻𐓣𐒼𐒽𐓂?
A: 𐓻𐓣𐒼𐓸𐓰𐓴𐓪𐒼𐓘 𐓘𐒼𐒷𐓂𐓸𐓱𐓸𐓘𐒼𐓶.
B: 𐓱𐓂𐓵𐓘𐒼𐓣 𐒼𐒽 𐓷𐓘 𐓵𐓱𐒽?
A: 𐓂𐓵𐓘𐒷𐓣 𐒷𐓘𐒼𐓸 𐓸𐓘.

Exercise 2. Composition

Write an Osage composition of six sentences. Include at least one motion verb.

Exercise 3. Verb practice

Give the Osage verbs for the following:

1. you came back here
2. I arrived there
3. you (plural) have
4. she is bringing something here
5. I am taking something there
6. we are bringing something back
7. we two went there
8. he is going there
9. you (plural) returned back there
10. he began to cry

Exercise 4. Make a chart of the eight movement verbs

Go back over the chapter and list the singular forms (*I*, *you*, and *he*, *she*, or *it*) for the eight movement verbs: *moving toward here*, *arriving here*, *moving there*, and *arriving there*. Next, add in the plural forms (*we two*, *we plural*, *you plural*, and *they*). Finally, write out the secondary meanings for the *arrive there* verbs.

Exercise 5. Make a chart of the eight *bring* and *take* verbs

Again, go over the chapter and list all the forms for the eight *bring* and *take* verbs, as you did with exercise 4.

ṅa

Nouns

óƕn7o	ókizo	party
óħʌƙα ɥʌcá7α	óðaake waléze	newspaper, magazine, or newsletter
ᴅʌħά	paðé	winter
ᴘα̋	pée	spring
ᴅōƙα	tooké	summer
ᴆʌ̄ᴅʌ́	htaatá	autumn

Verbs

ʌʃń	ahí (h-stem)	arrive there (ALSO begin, get)
ʌʃú	ahú (h-stem)	come here
ʌƙɕń	akší (a-ða)	arrive back there
ʌƙú	akú (a-ða)	come back/return here

ᎪᏓᎬ	alée (a-ða)	go back/return there
ᎪᏓᎲ	alí (a-ða)	arrive back here
ᎪᏋᎲ	achí (a-ða)	arrive here
ᎪᏂᎬ	aðée (br-šc)	go there
ᎪᏂᎲ	aðį́ (br-šc)	have, possess
ᎪᏂᎲᎪᏌᏁ	aðį́ahi (br-šc + h-stem)	take there, bring there
ᎪᏂᎲᎪᏌᎤ	aðį́ahu (br-šc + h-stem)	bring here
ᎪᏂᎲᎪᏞᏍᏁ	aðį́akši (br-šc + a-ða)	take back there, take home
ᎪᏂᎲᎪᏞᎤ	aðį́aku (br-šc + a-ða)	bring back here
ᎪᏂᎲᎪᏓᎬ	aðį́alee (br-šc + a-ða)	take back, take home
ᎪᏂᎲᎪᏓᏁ	aðį́ali (br-šc + a-ða)	bring back here, bring home
ᎪᏂᎲᎪᏋᏁ	aðį́achi (br-šc + h-stem)	bring here, arrive with
ᎪᏂᎲᎪᏂᎬ	aðį́aðee (br-šc)	carry, take there

Adjectives

ᏍᎲᎠᎪᏝᎪ	šį́htąką	fat

Notes for Chapter 14

The form for *you (plural) go* [štáape] may be puzzling at first since it comes from [šcée], but it can be explained by two simple pronunciation rules of Osage. First, remember that the plural marker [pe] causes the vowel [e] of a preceding verb to become [a], so that [šceepe] becomes [šcaape]. Next, the sound [c] usually only appears before the vowels [i] and [e], so [c] reverts to [t] when it comes before the vowels [a, o, u]. Thus, [šcaape] becomes [štaape]. The form [štáapaži] *you (plural) don't go* behaves similarly.

Chapter 15

Connectors and Nasal-Stem Verbs

ᎤᎦᏛᎦᎾ

1. **ᏅᏟᎸᎠ:** ᏐᏂᏃᎦ ᏗᎦᏊᎧ ᎤᎯᏃᎩ ᎤᎦᎱᎷᎠ ᎤᎤᎴ ᏞᏃᎦᏂᎴᎩ'ᏂᎦᎩᏂᎬ'ᏂᎠᎴ ᎴᎦᎱᎧ.
2. **ᎤᏐ:** ᏙᎭᏣᎢᎢᎢᎢᎠᎾᎠᏙᎴ ᎨᎧᏟ ᎴᎦᎱ.
3. ᏙᎭᏣᎢ ᏓᎴᎷᏈ'ᏂᏉᎢᎾᏂ ᏐᏎᎠᏂᏃᏪ ᎴᎧᎴᏟ ᎴᏟᏂᎨᎦ, ᏃᎷᎴᎲ ᎦᎧᏂ.
4. ᎳᎦᏂᎣᎸᎠ ᎨᎧᏟ, ᎤᎴᎱᎦᎦᏃᎠᏗᏂᏐᏂ, ᎴᎠᎣ, ᎴᏟᎤᏃᏂᏓᎴ.
5. **ᏅᏟᎸᎠ:** ᎣᎮᎾᏂ ᏃᎴᎨᎦᏟ ᎴᎧᎣᎴᎠᎴ ᎴᏟᏂᎨᎦ.
6. **ᎤᏐ:** ᏃᎴᎷᏈ'ᏂᎴᎦᎦᏃᏪᎠ ᎴᎾᎦᎦ, ᎠᎤᎴ ᏟᏂᏞᎴᎠ ᎦᎧᏂ.
7. ᏃᏂᏐᏟ ᎦᎦᏍᏂ ᎣᎴᎷᎠ, ᏐᏂᏊᏂ ᎦᎦᎾᎪᎠ, ᎴᎠ ᎦᎨᎦ ᎠᎴ ᎾᏂᎨᎦ.
8. **ᏅᏟᎸᎠ:** ᎫᎦ ᏐᎯᎦ ᎦᎶᎸᎠ?
9. Supernaw's ᏐᎯᎦ ᎴᎦᎧᏟ ᎴᏟᎦ ᏟᎯᎴᎦ.
10. ᎧᏣᎮᎠᎴ Supernaw's ᎴᏂ ᎴᏂ ᎾᎦ ᎠᎴ ᎾᏂᎨᎦ.
11. **ᎤᏐ:** ᏃᏂᏐᏟᎦ ᎦᎦᏫᎠᎠ ᎳᎶᏟᏂ ᏟᏂᎦᏟ.

1. **Father:** Sonny is going to carry Grandpa's fan and mirror board.
2. **Mother:** Sonny wants eight new shirts.
3. We have lots of scarves that he can choose from, and scarf slides too.
4. We will buy new armbands, bells, and earrings.
5. **Father:** We will look for all new things.
6. **Mother:** I will make his choker and bandoleros.
7. I will ask Older Sister to make the streamers and garters.
8. **Father:** Who will make the moccasins?
9. Supernaw's might have new moccasins.
10. I will go to Supernaw's tomorrow.
11. **Mother:** Don't forget Sonny's belt.

Supernaw's Indian Store is a well-known store in Skiatook, and it is often referred to as Supernaw's. All of the things mentioned here will be used or worn in the dances. Sonny wants eight shirts because he'll wear a new shirt each time he dances.

ña ʌkńcλ₂a

Up until now, most of our sentences have been made up of one clause, which is a simple sentence such as "My grandmother helped a child." But many sentences are made up of more than one clause. In this chapter, we will learn how to put together clauses to make longer and more natural sentences.

In English, for example, we might say something like "My dog knows that I will feed him," or "My dog wants to go outside." In the first example, the clause *my dog knows* is put together with *I will feed him* using the connector *that*. In the second example, the clause *my dog wants* is put together with *go outside* using the connector *to*.

We already have some examples of putting Osage clauses together. When we use ƙóħa [kóða] *want* with a verb, we are using two clauses (chapter 8). The adverbs ʎʌ [áha] *whenever* and ħʎʌ [ðáha] *when* connect clauses, and so does the adverbial particle ʂo [šǫ] when it means *while* (see chapter 13). Some writers call these a type of *conjunction* or *subordinator*. In this book we will call all the types of words that connect clauses *connectors*.

In this chapter we will learn how to make longer Osage sentences and how to use the connectors that put them together when necessary. We will discuss joining noun phrases in a later chapter.

Clauses joined by word order (no connector)

Some clauses in Osage do not need a connector when they are joined. When we join two simple sentences together in English we would do this with *and*, or we would just pronounce one right after the other. This is often how we do it in Osage; we simply put one clause after the other.

(1) Oħńᴆʌ ʎńᴆʌ ʌƙʌʌ zúꝣa ʌƙʌʌ oħńᴆʌ ħńᴆʌ ʌƙʌʌ ᴆóʎo ʌƙʌʌ.
    oðíhtą wíhta akxa žúuce akxa oðíhtą ðíhta akxa htóho akxa
    My car is red (and) your car is blue.

Clauses that permit subject pronouns on both verbs

There are many Osage verbs, such as ƙóħʌ [kóða] *want* and ńƙ'uꝣa [ík'uce] *try* that do not use a connector between clauses. For verbs like these, we can put subject pronouns either on both verbs or only on the main (final) verb. This is a speaker's choice. So examples 2 and 3 are both correct.

(2) ʎʌꝣúa ħʌꝣá ƙóʀʌ.
    wacúe ðaaché **hkǫ́**bra
    I want to eat bread.

(3) ʎʌꝣúa ʀʎꝣa ƙóʀʌ.
    wacúe **br**áache hkǫ́bra
    I want to eat bread.

In example 2, only 𝐤ó𝐑⋀ [hkǫ́bra] *I want* includes the first-person pronoun. In example 3, though, both ᏏᏞᏃᎯ [ðaaché] *eat* and 𝐤óᏏ⋀ [kǫ́ða] *want* have first-person pronouns.

(4) Þ₅𝐧 𝐧ᏏᏞ𝐤′𝐔ᏃᎯ.
    pši iðák'uce
    I tried to go there.

Í𝐤′𝐔ᏃᎯ [ík'uce] *try* (or *practice* or *study*) is an i-stem verb (see chapter 8), so the pronouns for *I* and *you* are both Ꮒ⋀ [ða]. The difference is where the accent goes: 𝐧ᏏᏞ𝐤′𝐔ᏃᎯ [iðák'uce] for *I* versus í𝐧ᏏᏞ𝐤′𝐔ᏃᎯ [íðak'uce] for *you*.

(5) Î𝐤ó oᏏᏞ𝐤⋀ íᏏᏞ𝐤′𝐔ᏃᎯ ⷰ⋀ ∠𝐧𝐤₅ǫ́?
    iihkó oðáhkǫ **íð**ak'uce hta nįkšé
    Will **you** try to help Grandma?

Clauses with different subjects

Often clauses that use no connectors such as 𝐤óᏏ⋀ [kǫ́ða] *want* have different subjects. An example of this in English is "**He** wants **me** to eat dinner." *He* is the subject of the main clause and *me* is the subject of the second clause. Notice that *me* is the subject of *eat*, even though it appears with the pronoun we usually use for objects. We will do something similar in Osage.

(6) ᎼᏞᏃÁᏃᎯ íᎯ ÞÍỌ́ ᎼᏞ𝐤ọ𝐑⋀.
    wažáže íe hpíǫ **wá**hkǫbrą
    I want **them** to know the Osage language.

In example 6, the subject of the main verb is *I*, indicated by the [h] and the [br] of 𝐤ó𝐑⋀ [hkǫ́bra] *I want*. The subject of the second clause is *them*, indicated by Ꮝ⋀ [wá]. So we say Ꮝ⋀𝐤ọ𝐑⋀ [wáhkǫbra] *I want them*, where Ꮝ⋀ [wá] *them* is the subject of the second clause. Note that, just like we do in English, Ꮝ⋀ [wá] *them* appears in the object position of the main verb [hkǫbra]. (See chapter 9.)

(7) ÓᏍᴀ ₅ᏃÚᏍ𝐧 Ꮒ𝐧𝐤óᏏ⋀ ⋀𝐤ᏂᎯ⋀.
    ówe **šc**úwį **ð**ikǫ́ða akxa
    He wants **you** to buy groceries.

In example 7, we say Ꮒ𝐧𝐤óᏏ⋀ [ðikǫ́ða] *he wants you* using Ꮒ𝐧 [ði] *you*, and we also put the subject marker ₅Ꮓ [šc] on the verb ᏏᏌᏍ𝐧 [ðuwį́], giving ₅ᏃÚᏍ𝐧 [šcúwį] *you buy*.

Joining clauses using verbs of motion

Another way to join clauses is by using verbs of motion (see chapter 14) with another verb. In these sentences we only put subject pronouns on the motion verb, the verb of the main clause. Motion verbs are often used with another verb to express a purpose.

(8) ᏌᎶᏂ ᎥᎨᎶᏂᏄᎠ.
waachí ąkáchipe
We came to dance.

(9) ᏌᎶᏀᎧ ᎠᏛᏂᎠ.
waaðǫ́ pšíe
I went to sing.

In examples 8 and 9, only the main verbs ᎥᏃᏂ [achí] and ᎥᏍᏂ [ahí] have subject pronouns. One very common construction is to use ᛈᎥᏀᎧ [mąðį́] *walk* with a motion verb. We usually just say this in English with *walk*.

(10) ᏌᎥᎨᎧᏔᎠ ᎥᎨᎧᏛᎥᏐᏂ ᎥᏛᎥ ᎠᎥᏛᎧᏏᎥ ᛈᎥᏀᎧ ᎥᏀᎧ ᎠᎠ.
wakǫ́ze ąkǫ́htapi apa taapǫ́ska mąðį́ aðáa pe
Our teacher walked (went by walking) to school.

(11) ᎠᎧᏐᎥ ᏦᏐᏁ ᛈᎥᏀᎧ **ᎡᎧ** ᎠᎥ ᎥᏍᎧ.
htą́wą kši mąðį́ **br**ée hta ąhé
I'm going to walk to town.

Clauses joined with connectors

Now let's look at some clauses that are joined with connectors.

ᏃᎠ [che] *that*

An important connector is ᏃᎠ [che], which is not to be confused with the evidential marker of the same form. It is very much like English *that* in sentences such as "My neighbor thinks that his house is too big" or "I know that summer will be here soon." There are several things to know about how to make this kind of sentence. Let's begin by looking at example 12.

(12) ᏒᏂᎧᎥ ᎥᎨᎧᎥ **ᏁᏃᏂᎨᎠ ᎠᎧ ᏁᏁᎠ ᏃᎠ** ᎠᏁᎠ ᎥᎨᎧᎥ.
níhka akxa **ižį́ke htáa íiðe che** éðe akxa
The man thinks **that his son saw a deer**.

First, one of the clauses is actually embedded in the other, the main clause. This embedded clause, shown in bold font above, appears before the main verb. We will see this embedding when both the clauses have a noun phrase subject. In this sentence, the main clause is ᏒᏂᎧᎥ ᎥᎨᎧᎥ ᎠᏁᎠ ᎥᎨᎧᎥ [níhka akxa éðe akxa] *the man thinks*. The embedded clause is ᏁᏃᏂᎨᎠ ᎠᎧ ᏁᏁᎠ [ižį́ke htáa íiðe] *his son saw a deer*. The connector ᏃᎠ [che] separates the clauses by showing where the embedded clause ends.

We place ᏃᎠ [che] at the end of the embedded clause, separating it from the clause that contains the main verb.

The subject of the embedded clause does not take a subject marker, and the verb of the embedded clause does not take an aspect marker.

In the next example, the subject of the main verb is a pronoun, not a noun phrase. In sentences like this, where the main verb has a pronoun subject, 𝐞𝐚 [che] will still show us where the embedded clause ends.

(13) **𝐰𝐢𝐳𝐨́𝐤𝐞 𝐥𝐢́ 𝐜𝐡𝐞** íhpahǫ mįkšé
   wižǫ́ke lí che íhpahǫ mįkšé
   I know **that my daughter returned (home)**.

In this sentence the embedded clause is 𝐰𝐢𝐳𝐨́𝐤𝐚 𝐥𝐢́ [wižǫ́ke lí] *my daughter returned home*. The main clause is íhpahǫ mįkšé [íhpahǫ mįkšé] *I know*. Again, we do not use a subject marker with the subject of the embedded clause, wižǫ́ke [wižǫ́ke] *my daughter*.

Clauses with the indefinite question words *what* and *who*

We also use 𝐞𝐚 [che] in clauses with indefinite *what* and *who* as in example 14. An *indefinite* is when we use question words such as *what* and *who* without asking a real question. Examples in English are "I remember **what** you said" and "The boy knows **who** helped him." Although we would not use *that* to connect these clauses in English, we will use 𝐞𝐚 [che] to connect them in Osage.

(14) **𝐭𝐚́𝐚𝐭ą š𝐤ǫ́š𝐭𝐚 𝐜𝐡𝐞** íhpahǫ mįkšé
   táatą škǫ́šta che íhpahǫ mįkšé
   I know **what you want**.

(15) **𝐩𝐞́𝐞 𝐡𝐤ą𝐚𝐜𝐨́𝐨𝐥ą 𝐳𝐚́𝐚𝐧𝐢 ð𝐚𝐚𝐜𝐡𝐞́ 𝐜𝐡𝐞** ípahǫ akxa
   pée hkąącóolą záani ðaaché che ípahǫ akxa
   He knows **who ate all the pie**.

ᎪᏃᏅ [aži] *but*

The connector ᎪᏃᏅ [aži] is used very much like English *but*. (Do not confuse it with ᎪᏃᏅ [aži] *not*.) It appears between full clauses. Both clauses will have subject markers and aspect markers when these are needed.

(16) **wað́úwį brée hkóbra mįkšé aži mázeska ąðį́įke**
   wað́úwį brée hkóbra mįkšé **aži** mázeska ąðį́įke
   I want to go shopping, **but** I don't have any money.

(17) **šǫ́ke ąkóhtapi akxa oðúuc'aka pe aži hcíle akxa kíoxta šǫ akxa**
   šǫ́ke ąkóhtapi akxa oðúuc'aka pe **aži** hcíle akxa kíoxta šǫ akxa
   Our dog is lazy, **but** the family still loves him.

ᏦᎠ [kóe] *and* and ᏦᎥᏲ́ [kaðǫ́] *and then*

We use ᏦᎠ [kóe] to connect full sentences, the way we would use *and* in English, and we use ᏦᎥᏲ́ [kaðǫ́] when connecting two sentences, especially when one happens in sequence, immediately after the other.

(18) ᪽᪽᪽᪽᪽ **kaðǫ́** ᪽᪽᪽ ᪽᪽᪽᪽᪽.
      ąwanóbrape **kaðǫ́** waachí ąkáhipe
      We ate dinner, **and then** we went to dance.
(19) ᪽᪽ ᪽᪽ ᪽᪽᪽᪽᪽ ᪽ ᪽᪽ ᪽᪽ **kóa** ᪽᪽ ᪽᪽ ᪽᪽᪽ ᪽ ᪽᪽ ᪽᪽.
      iihkó apa wahkǫ́tahci ci aðée apai **kóe** iiną́ apa ówehci ci aðée apai
      Grandma is going to church, **and** Mother is going to the grocery store.
(20a) ᪽᪽ ᪽᪽᪽ ᪽᪽᪽᪽ ᪽᪽᪽᪽ ᪽᪽ ᪽᪽᪽ **kóa** ᪽᪽ ᪽᪽᪽᪽᪽ ᪽᪽ ᪽᪽᪽.
      iiną́ akxa ohkúlą ðiiškí hta akxa **kóe** hci ðuuwásu hta akxa
      Mother will wash clothes, **and** she will clean the house.
(20b) ᪽᪽ ᪽᪽᪽ ᪽᪽᪽᪽ ᪽᪽᪽᪽ ᪽᪽ ᪽᪽᪽ **kaðǫ́** ᪽᪽ ᪽᪽᪽᪽᪽ ᪽᪽ ᪽᪽᪽.
      iiną́ akxa ohkúlą ðiiškí hta akxa **kaðǫ́** hci ðuuwásu hta akxa
      Mother will wash clothes, **and then** she will clean the house.

In example 20a, Mother might be cleaning the house while she is washing clothes. In 20b, Mother will first wash clothes and then clean the house after that.

Examples of Osage connected sentences

Here are examples of sentences using all the ways we can make connected sentences that we have discussed so far.

Clauses joined by word order

(21) ᪽᪽᪽ ᪽᪽᪽ ᪽᪽᪽ ᪽᪽᪽᪽ ᪽ ᪽᪽᪽᪽᪽ ᪽᪽᪽ ᪽᪽᪽ ᪽᪽᪽᪽ ᪽.
      sǫ́ke wíhta akxa ðáalį pe ilǫ́ežį wíhta akxa iiséwai pe
      My dog is nice (and) my cat is mean.

Clauses that permit subject pronouns on both verbs

(22) ᪽᪽᪽᪽ ᪽᪽᪽ **᪽᪽᪽᪽** **᪽᪽᪽᪽**?
      wacúe skúe štáache **škǫ́šta**
      Do **you** want to eat cake?

Clauses with different subjects

(23) ᪽᪽᪽᪽᪽ ᪽᪽᪽ ᪽᪽᪽ **ą**᪽᪽᪽ ᪽᪽᪽.
      wihcíko akxa oáhką **ą**kǫ́ða akxa.
      Grandfather wants **me** to help him.

Joining clauses using verbs of motion

When we join clauses with verbs of motion, *only* the verb of motion has a pronoun, as in this case:

(24) ᒐᐣᕼᐞ ᕂᒉᾰ?
hiiðá šcée
Are **you** going swimming?

Examples of clauses joined by connectors

ᕼᐞᔎᐊ [ðáha] *when, as soon as* (at some moment in time)

(25) Ꮓᐣᕃᐞ ᐊᕃᕼᐞ ᐊᒉᕵ ᐅα **ᕼᐞᔎᐊ** ᒉᐣ ᴏᑲᕵ ᐅα.
níhka ðe akxa achí pe **ðáha** hci ohpá pe
When that man arrived, he went into the house.

ᕵᔎᐊ [áha] *whenever*

(26) ᒉᕵ7α ᐊᏃᕼα **ᕵᔎᐊ** ᐅᕵ7ᕵᏃᕠ ᕃᕵᐅᐞ.
hcéze ąníe **áha** paazénii bráahtą
My stomach hurts **whenever** I drink milk.

(27) ᕠᕃᕵ ᕠᕼᕵᕼα ᐊᔎᕵ **ᕵᔎᐊ** ᕵ7ᴏ.
iihkó iiðáðe ąhé **áha** ą́ązo
Whenever I see my grandmother, I am glad.

(28) ᔈᐊᕃᕵ7α ᐊᕃᴏᕅᐊᐅᕠ ᐊᐅᐞ ᴏᔈᐊᕃᐞᐅᕠ **ᕵᔎᐊ** ᐊᕃᴏᕼᐊ ᐊᕃᕵᕼα.
wakóze ąkóhtapi apa ówahkąpi **áha** ąkóða ąkáðe
Our teacher helps us **whenever** we want.

ᕂᴏ· [šǫ] *while*

(29) ᕼᐊᒉᕵᔎα **ᕂᴏ·** Ꮓᕠᕃᕵ ᕂᴏᕃα ᕼᕵᐅᐞ ᐊᐅᐞ ᕵᕵᓯᵾ ᐊᕃᴏᕵᐊ ᕼᕵᒉᕵ ᐊᐅᐞ.
ðažį́įhe **šǫ** nįkšé sǫ́ke ðíhta apa htóožu ąkóhta ðaaché apai
While you were sleeping, your dog was eating our meat pie.

(30) ᒉᕵᏃα ᐊᐅᐞ ᔈᐊᏃᴏᕃα **ᕂᴏ·** ᐊᐅᐞ ᕼᐊᒉᕵᔎα ᓫᕵᕃᕵα.
hcíle apa wanǫ́bre **šǫ** apa ðažį́įhe žą́kše
While the family was eating dinner, you were sleeping.

(31) ᐊᒉᕵᔎα **ᕂᴏ·** ᒧᕠᕃᕵ ᓫᕠᕃᕵᒉᕠ ᐊᐅᐞ ᕂᕃᒉα ᐊᐅᐞ.
ažį́įhe **šǫ** mįkšé žįkážį apa škáce apai
While I was sleeping, the children were playing.

ᒉα [che] *that*

(32) ᔈᐊᕃᕵ7α ᕼᕵᐅᐞ ᐊᕃᕼᐞ ᓫᕠᕃᕵᒉᕠ ᔈᕵᏃᕠ ᔈᐊᕼᕵᐅᐞ **ᒉα** ᐊᒉᕵ ᐅα.
wakóze ðíhta akxa žįkážį wáli wadíhta **che** ąží pe
Your teacher believes **that** the children work hard.

(33) ᐅᕵᐅᐞ ᕃᕵᕃᐞ **ᒉα** ᕵᕂᐅᐊᔎᴏᓯ.
táatą hkóbra **che** íšpahǫži
You don't know **what** I want.

ᎪᏃᏂ [ąži] *but*

(34) ᏋᏓᏝ ᏲᏅᎮᎠ ᎠᎩᎶᎠ ᏕᎠᏲᏌᏂᎢ ᏆᏐᏲᎠ ᎠᎩᎶᎠ **ᎪᏃᏂ** ᏲᏃᏕᏫᎿᎦ ᎬᏂᎦᎻᎠ́.
hcíle ðíhta akxa waðúwį kóða akxa **ąži** ðískike nįkšé
Your family wants to shop, **but** you are tired.

Ⱪóα [kóe] *and*

(35) ᏊᏃᎻᏂᎯᏂ' ᎠᎠᎠ ᎠᎠᎠᎰᏕᏆᎠᏂ ᏃᏂ ᎠᏲᎦ̋ ᎠᎠᎠ **Ⱪóα** ᏂᏆ̋Ꮼ ᎠᎠᎠ Supernaw's ᏃᏂ ᎠᏲᎦ̋ ᎠᎠᎠ.
šįmįžį apa taapóskahci ci aðée apai **kóe** iihkó apa Supernaw's ci aðée apai
The girl is going to school, **and** her grandmother is going to Supernaw's.

ⰔᎪᏲó' [kaðǫ́] *and then*

(36) ᎪᏕᎠᏞᎰᏞᎠᎠ **ⰔᎪᏲó'** ᏕᎦ̋Ჲó' ᎠᎩᎠᏕᏂᎠᎠ.
ąwanǫ́brape **kaðǫ́** waaðǫ́ ąkáhipe
We ate dinner, **and then** we went to sing.

Henry Pratt wearing men's clothes, view from the front. Photo by Butch DeLong.

Henry Pratt wearing men's clothes, view from the back. Photo by Butch DeLong.

Learn the difference: ᎪᏃᏛ [ažį́], ᎪᏃᏂ [ąži], ᎪᏃᏂ [aži]

Students will need to learn the difference between three Osage words that are very close in pronunciation but very different in meaning.

The verb ᎪᏃᏛ [ažį́] *think, believe* has an accented and nasal [į́].

(37) ÓᏓᎣ ᎪᏃᏛ.
  ékǫ ažį́
  She thinks so.

The connector ᎪᏃᏂ [ąži] *but* has a nasal ą, and no accented vowels.

(38) ᏍᏛᏇᎠᏃᏁ ᎪᏓᏊᎪ ᏚᎠᏛ ᏥᏘᎪᏞᏁ ᎪᏓᏊᎪ, ᎪᏃᏂ ᏍᏛᏫᎠᏃᏁ ᎪᏓᏊᎪ ᏥᎾᏑᎠ ᏥᏘᎪᏞᏁ ᎪᏓᏊᎪ.
  šį́tožį akxa wašį́ kíðalį akxa ąži šį́mižį akxa hką́ące kíðalį akxa
  The boy likes bacon, but the girl likes fruit.

The negator ᎪᏃᏂ [aži] *not* has no nasal vowels and no accented vowels. It is a suffix on the verb.

(39) ᏞᏎᏥᎪᏃᏂ ᎪᏓᏊᎪ.
  nąąkaži
  He didn't run.

Here is a sentence with all three forms.

(40) ᏥᏂᏥᎪᏑᎠ ᎪᏓᏊᎪ ᏥᎾᏑᎠ Ú ᏥᎠᏞᏁ ᏠᎠ ᎪᏃᎾᎪᏃᏂ ᎪᏓᏊᎪ, ᎪᏃᏂ ᏥᎶᏛᎠ ᏍᎠᎤᏚᏁ.
  ðiðáce akxa hką́ące žúe ðáalį che ažį́aži akxa ąži šáhpe šcúwį
  Your father doesn't think that the tomatoes are good, but you bought six.

Nasal-stem verbs

The nasal-stem verb class has fewer members than others, but these verbs are commonly used. Five important verbs in this class are ᎠᎣ [éǫ] *do* (not in the presence of others or for others), ᎠᏓᎣ [ékiǫ] *do* (in the presence of others), ᎪᏃᏛ [ažį́] *think, believe*, ᏉᏛᎣ [hpį́ǫ] *know, be skillful*, and Ꮒ [į] *wear*. Of course, many Osage verbs have nasal vowels, so just because a verb has a nasal vowel does not mean that it is in this class.

In this verb class, the pronoun for first-person singular, *I*, is Ꮢ [m]. The pronoun for second-person singular, *you*, is Ꮕ [ž]. These pronouns will appear before the nasal vowel. The other pronouns work as we have seen before.

(41) ᏚᏊᏃ ᏥᎠ ᎪᏓᏊᎪ ᏚᏛᏓᎪᏞᏁ ᎣᏠᎠᎪᎪ Ꮒ ᎪᏓᏊᎪ.
  wak'ó ðe akxa wéehkilį ohtáza į akxa
  That woman **is wearing** pretty Osage clothes.

(42) 𐓈𐓘𐓯𐓤𐓘𐓫𐓣 **𐓄𐓣** 𐓘𐓯𐓘́.
haaskámį **mį** ahé
I'm wearing a shawl.

(43) 𐓈𐓘𐓯𐓤𐓘𐓫𐓣 𐓏𐓣́𐓡𐓘 **𐓻𐓣** 𐓡𐓘𐓘𐓮𐓟́.
haaskámi wíhta **ži** ðaašé
You're wearing my shawl.

(44) 𐓈𐓘𐓯𐓤𐓘𐓫𐓣 𐓪𐓬𐓘́𐓰𐓘 **𐓘𐓤𐓣** **𐓘𐓤𐓘́𐓺𐓟**.
haaskámi ohtáza **akį akáðe**
We are wearing beautiful shawls.

(45) 𐓏𐓘𐓻𐓘́𐓻𐓟 𐓊𐓪̄𐓄𐓟́ 𐓡𐓘́𐓘𐓬𐓣 **𐓻𐓣** **𐔁𐓘𐓘𐓮𐓟́**.
wažáže hoopé ðáali **ži paašé**
You (plural) are wearing fine Osage moccasins.

Using 𐓟́𐓪̄ [éǫ] and 𐓟́𐓤𐓣𐓪̄ [ékiǫ]

𐓟́𐓪̄ [éǫ] *do it, do something* (not in the presence of others / not for others)

The verb 𐓟́𐓪̄ [éǫ] means *do it, do something* (not in the presence of others / not for others). (Note that some writers may insert 𐓏 [w] between the vowels 𐓟 [e] and 𐓪̄ [ǫ] in spelling, 𐓟́𐓏𐓪̄ [ewǫ].)

(46) 𐓟́𐓪̄ 𐓻𐓘 𐓟́𐔁𐓘.
éǫ che ébre
I think that he did it (not in the presence of others).

(47) 𐓟́𐓫𐓪̄.
émǫ
I did it (not in the presence of others).

(48) 𐓟́𐓻𐓪̄?
éžǫ
Did you do it? (not in the presence of others)

𐓟́𐓪̄ [éǫ] does not have plural forms.

𐓟́𐓤𐓣𐓪̄ [ékiǫ] *do* (in the presence of others)

The verb 𐓟́𐓤𐓣𐓪̄ [ékiǫ] means *do* (in the presence of others).

(49) 𐓟́𐓤𐓣𐓫𐓪̄. OR 𐓟́𐓤𐓣𐓫𐓘.
ékimǫ OR ékimą
I do (it).

(50) 𐓟́𐓤𐓣𐓻𐓪̄.
ékižǫ
You do (it).

(51) 𐓘𐓮́𐓤𐓵𐓪. or 𐓘𐓤𐓵𐓪 𐓛𐓤𐓬́𐓷𐓘.
eą́kią or ékią ąkáðe
We do (it).

The plural form of 𐓘𐓤𐓵𐓪 [ékią] in example 51 is not always used. Speakers often prefer to just use plural aspect markers: 𐓘𐓤𐓵𐓪 𐓛𐓤𐓬́𐓷𐓘 [ékią ąkáðe] *we do it*, or 𐓘𐓤𐓵𐓰𐓪 𐓬𐓛𐓧𐓘 [ékižǫ paašé] *you (plural) do it*.

Using 𐓄𐓵́𐓪 [hpíǫ] *know how, be skillful at something*

This verb means both *know how* and *be skillful at something*. It is slightly different from the other nasal-stem verbs because the second-person singular *you* uses both the pronouns 𐓰 [ž] and 𐓧 [š].

(52) 𐓷𐓛𐓰𐓘́𐓰𐓘 𐓵́𐓘 𐓄𐓵́𐓟𐓪 𐓟𐓵𐓤𐓧𐓘́.
wažáže íe hpímǫ mįkšé
I know the Osage language.

(53) 𐓷𐓛𐓰𐓘́𐓰𐓘 𐓵́𐓘 𐓧𐓄𐓵́𐓰𐓪 𐓜𐓵𐓤𐓧𐓘́?
wažáže íe špížǫ nįkšé
Do **you** know the Osage language?

(54) 𐓪𐓶𐓵́ 𐓄𐓵́𐓪 𐓬𐓘.
oohǫ́ hpíǫ pe
She's good at cooking. (She's a good cook.)

(55) 𐓷𐓛𐓮𐓵́ 𐓄𐓵́𐓪 𐓬𐓘.
waachí hpíǫ pe
She's good at dancing. (She's a good dancer.)

(56) 𐓷𐓛𐓮𐓵́ 𐓛𐓄𐓵́𐓪 𐓛𐓤𐓛𐓬𐓧𐓵́.
waachí **ąhpíǫ ąkatxą́**
We know how to dance.

Using 𐓛𐓰𐓵́ [ažį́] *think, believe*

This verb has a similar meaning as the verb 𐓘́𐓷𐓘 [éðe]. These words don't mean exactly the same thing in Osage, but they have a meaning like *think* or *believe* in English. In the first- and second-person, we use the forms 𐓛𐓰𐓘́𐓟𐓵 [ažámį] and 𐓛𐓰𐓘́𐓰𐓵 [ažážį].

(57) 𐓘́𐓪 𐓰𐓘 𐓛𐓰𐓘́𐓟𐓵.
éǫ che ažámį
I believe that he did it.

(58) 𐓷𐓘́ 𐓛𐓰𐓘́𐓰𐓵?
ðée ažážį
Do **you** believe that?

(59) 𐓵𐓜𐓶𐓘𐓰𐓵 𐓱𐓶𐓱𐓘𐓤𐓛 𐓰𐓘 𐓛𐓤𐓛𐓰𐓵́ 𐓛𐓷𐓘́.
ilǫ́ežį húheka che **ąkažį́ ąðé**
We two think that the cat is sick.

Ǫk'uẓa

Exercise 1. Do you understand?

What does this short story mean in English?

Ǫxó lpi eŋ sacúšuzŋ ẓa áħa lpi ḳaħǫ́ ą́ eŋ ħūsácu lšǫ́ lpi.
Ħūsácu ɸǫ́ǫ ɸa.
Oħűẓ'lḳazŋ!
Ą́ šǫ́ẓazŋ ħūzá lpi ḳaħǫ́ ōšǫ́eŋ ħūsácu lpi.
Ǫxó ḳą̄sḳǫ́ḳa ẓa lzǫ́ǫŋ!

Exercise 2. Composition

Write a composition of at least six Osage sentences. Include at least two sentences with more than one clause.

Exercise 3. Practice

1. Use ɸǫ́ǫ *be good at, know how to* in three sentences with different pronouns.
2. Use a verb of motion to make a sentence with two clauses.
3. Write a sentence using the connector ẓa.
4. Write a sentence using the connector lzŋ.
5. Write two sentences, one using the connector ḳóa and the other using ḳaħǫ́.

Ǫa

Nouns

ḳašṗáoɔpa	kašpéǫpa	quarter (coin)
ḳą̄ẓóɔa	hkąącóolą	pie
oḳúɔa	ohkúlą	clothes
saħása ɔáʀa	waðáawa lébrą	dime

Verbs

lzǫ́	ažį́ (nasal-stem)	believe, think
áḳŋo	ékiǫ (nasal-stem)	do (in the presence of others)
áo	éǫ (nasal-stem)	do (not in the presence of or for others)
áħa	éðe (br-šc)	thinking that way, consider, believe
ǫ	į (nasal-stem)	wear (clothes)
ḳą̄sḳǫ́ḳa	kaaskíke (ki-stative)	be tired (physically)
oħűẓ'lḳa	oðúuc'ake (br-šc)	be lazy
ožáħa	ožéðe (stative)	be tired (mentally)

ÞήƠ	hpíǫ (nasal-stem)	know (how to), be skillful at
ŦñʂḳΠ	ðiiškí (br-šc)	launder, wash (someone else's clothes)
ŦūzȎ	ðuuzé (br-šc)	choose, select, take

Adjectives

ñsȎɥʌŦα	iiséwaðe	mean
ñsȎɥʌ	iiséwai	mean (variant)
óɹαsʌzп	óhesaži	fast
sńsп	sísi	energetic

Other

άḳσ	ékǫ	like that
zλ̰ℓп	záani	all

Notes for Chapter 15

Good English-Osage correspondences for *think*, *believe*, *believe in*, *consider*, and *think about* are not easily prescribed and depend in some ways upon speaker preference.

The word [iiséwaðe] *mean* is often pronounced as [iiséwai]; we list it both ways in our glossary.

Chapter 16

Using the ᏦᏂ [ki] Pronouns

ᎣᏥᏂᎠ

1. ᎠᎳᏍᎪᎠ, ᏐᏪᎠ ᏂᎿᎴᎠ ᎣᏦᏥᏑ ᎴᏦᏂᎢᎠᏒ ᏗᎥ.
2. ᎤᏗᎸ ᎴᏦᏔᎴ ᎣᏦᏥᏑ ᏚᏂᎢᎠ ᎥᎢᎠᏒ ᏗᎥ.
3. ᎤᏗᎸ ᎴᏦᏔᎴ ᏚᏂᎠᏍᏂ ᏐᏂᏛᎴ ᏦᏌᏛᎠ ᏦᎴᎰ ᎴᏛᏦᏔᎴ ᏍᎾᎢᎠ ᏦᏌᏫᎠ.
4. ᎹᏂᎣᏛᎵᏦᎠ ᏢᎠᏛᎣᎠᎵ ᎣᏦᏍᏒᎠ ᎠᎴ ᏐᏂᏗ ᏐᏂ ᎴᏳᏃᏑ ᏦᎴᎰ ᎣᎹᏂᎠ ᎣᎵᏦᏂᎢᎠᏒ ᏗᎥ.
5. ᎤᎠᏒᏂ ᎴᏦᏔᎴ "ᏐᏂ ᏖᎵᏧᏃᏑ?" ᎵᏓᏔᎣᎹᎠ ᎦᎠᎵ.
6. ᏐᏂ ᎠᎴ ᎵᏗᎢᏈᎤᏌᎠ ᎠᎴ ᏓᏂ ᎠᏌᏂ ᏛᎠᏎᏈᎤᏒ ᎠᏃᎤ ᏗᎥ.
7. ᏗᏂᏌᎷᎠ ᎠᎴ ᎤᏗᎸ ᏐᎴᏂᏂ ᎦᎠᎢ ᏐᏂ ᎶᎠ ᎠᏢᎦᎠ ᎴᏃᏂ ᎹᏂᏦᎢᎠ ᎠᎴ ᎴᏍᏂᎢᎠ ᏒᎤᎡ'ᎵᏦᎠ.
8. ᎹᏂᎣᏛᎵᏦᎠ ᏦᏂᎠᏓᎱᎵ ᎣᏦᏍᏒᎠ ᏒᏂ ᎠᏌᏂ ᏦᎴᎰ ᎤᏗᎸ ᎴᏦᏔᎴ ᎠᏓᏛᏦᎴ ᏛᎢᎠᏍᏂ ᏗᎥ.
9. ᎤᏗᎸ ᎴᏦᏔᎴ ᎣᏛᎵᏦᎠ ᏐᏂ ᎴᏛᎰᎠᏂ ᎠᏌᏂ ᎹᎠᏃᎠ ᎣᏦᏂᎠ ᏦᏂᏛᎵᎠ ᎠᎴ ᎴᏍᏂᎢᎠ ᏢᎦᏂ ᏗᎥ.

1. First, I pick out my clothes for the next day.
2. Sometimes Mom picks out my clothes for me.
3. Mom gives Little Sister a bath and then gets her ready to lie down and sleep.
4. When it's 7:30 I take a bath and brush my teeth and put on my pajamas.
5. Dad always asks, "Did you brush your teeth?"
6. In case I get thirsty during the night I set water beside my bed.
7. If it's cold I ask Mom for another blanket, but I can't sleep when it's hot.
8. I lie down at 8:30, and Mom turns off the lights.
9. Sometimes Mom reads me a story or watches her phone until I go to sleep.

ᏂᎠ ᏌᎴᏦᏂᏓᎵᏒᎠ

We have learned to use many pronouns, for subjects and objects and possessives. Here we will learn another group of pronouns that are related by their form and meaning: they are all a form of ᏦᏂ [ki] and they all have to do with *doing to*, or *for*, *someone* or *oneself*.

There are three ᏦᏂ [ki] pronouns: ᏦᏂ [kí], ᏦᏂ [ki], and ᏦᏂ [hki], and each one has many forms. Briefly, ᏦᏂ [kí] means *to or for someone*, ᏦᏂ [ki] means *do to or for one's own*, and ᏦᏂ

[hki] means *do to or for oneself* or, in plural forms, *to or for each other*. Because these sound so similar, we need to take care to understand their differences. We will describe them one by one with examples.

ᖴń [kí] *to or for someone (else)*

The accented pronoun ᖴń [kí] (called the *dative* in grammar books) is used when we need to name someone who receives, benefits from, or is affected by something. For instance, in English we might say "My uncle gave me some money," where *me* tells us who received the money. Or "We bought a new hat for Grandpa," where *Grandpa* is the one who got the hat. We call this form accented ᖴń [kí] because it is usually accented.

In example 1, accented ᖴń [kí] lets us know that Mother bought a shawl for someone (in this case, *the cook*).

(1) Ĩɀʌ ʌᖴʀʌ **óʃơ** ʃāсᖴʌ́ᴦп· **ᖴńħuɤп·** ᴘα.
    įiná akxa **óohǫ** haaskámį **kíðuwį** pe
    Mother bought a shawl **for the cook.**

(2) ʃāсᖴʌ́ᴦп· **ᖴńħuɤп·** ᴘα.
    haaskámį **kíðuwį** pe
    She bought a shawl **for her.**

(3) ᴦ́ʌ7α ʃń̃ᴢαᴢп· ɤп· **ᖴńʀuɤп·**.
    máze híįcežį wį **kí**bruwi
    I bought a metal bowl **for him.**

It is important to note that accented ᖴń [kí] is only used when the subject and the object (the recipient) of the verb are both third-person.

When we use object pronouns for first- and second-person (for me, for you, for us) and third-person plural (for them), ᖴń [kí] is *replaced with an accent* on the object pronoun (see chapter 9 for object pronouns). For example, in example 4, instead of ᖴń [kí], we see an accent on the object pronoun ń́ [ą́] in ń́ħuɤп· [ą́ðuwį].

(4) ɤáõʃơ ᴢáᖴʌ **ń́ħuɤп·** ᴘα.
    wéoohǫ hcéka **ą́ðuwį** pe
    She bought new cooking utensils **for me.**

(5) Õʃơ ɤáᖴʌʃп **ħńħuɤп·** ᴘα.
    óohǫ wékahi **ðíðuwį** pe
    She bought a cook-paddle **for you.**

(6) ᴦ́ʌ7α ʃń̃ᴢαᴢп· ɤп· **ɤńʀuɤп·**.
    máze híįcežį wį **wí**bruwi
    I bought a metal bowl **for you.**

Remember that ɤń [wí], in example 6, is used when the subject is *I* and the object is *you singular* or *you plural*.

(7) ᒪᐦᐠᐊᓴ ᐋᥫᒍᐃᖮ.
    mąhkása ą́šcuwį
    You bought **me** coffee.

(8) Ꮜᑐᐅᐃᖮ ᑊᐊ.
    wáðuwį pe
    She bought it **for us**.
    OR She bought it **for them**.

(9) ᒍᥫᒉᒣᐧᐠᖮ Ꮜᥫᒉᐅᐃᖮᑊᐊ.
    hįįcežį **wášcuwįpe**
    You bought plates **for us**.

(10) ᐊᗦᖫᑐᐅᐃᖮᑊᐊ.
    ąðíðuwįpe
    We two bought it for **you (plural)**.
    OR We (plural) bought it for **you (singular)**.

Again, note that in example 10 the ᑊᐊ [pe] could pluralize either the subject ᐱ [ą] (making *we* plural) or the object ᗦᖫ [ðí] (making *you* plural). Context tells us which way to interpret it.

Verbs that include Ꮶᐠ [ki] in their structure

Recall that in chapter 10 we learned about ki-stative verbs such as ᏦᖫᏃ [kízo] *like, enjoy*. Those verbs only included Ꮶᐠ [ki] in the third-person, just as we have seen above. In all other persons, the Ꮶᐠ [ki] was deleted, and the accented stative subject pronoun was used.

(11) **ᏦᖫᏃ** ᑊᐊ.
    kízo pe
    He had fun.

(12) Ꮜᐱᒉᖫ **ᗦᏃ**
    waachí **ą́**zo
    I enjoy the dancing.

The verb Ꮉ'ᐅ [k'u] *give*

Ꮉ'ᐅ [k'u] *give* is an a-ða verb that builds in the meaning of the recipient and so does not need a Ꮶᐠ [ki] pronoun. It uses the regular pronouns from the a-ða class.

(13) ᒪᖫᐠᐱ ᗷᖫᒪᐠ ᗦᐊ ᐱᐠᗷᐱ Ꮉ'ᐊᏌ ᒪᏌᖫ Ꮉ'ᐅ ᑊᐊ.
    níhka ðáalį ðe akxa hkáwa mąąhį́ k'u pe
    That good man gave hay to the horse.

(14) ᒍᐱᗷᖫ Ꮜᐠ ᐱᏦ'ᐆ ᑊᐊ.
    haxį́ wį ąk'ú pe
    He gave **me** a blanket.

(15) ᒉᖫᒉᐠ ᏌᐠᏦ'ᐆ.
    níini wik'ú
    I gave **you** cold water.

ᏃᏂ [ki] *do to or for one's own*

The unaccented ᏃᏂ [ki] pronoun is frequently used to talk about one's own possessions or family. ᏃᏂ [ki] takes on many different forms, depending on the first consonant of the verb it is used with. We will show this below. It is important to know that the meaning includes the subject as well as the possessed object: *I do for my own, you do for your own*, and so on. This ᏃᏂ [ki] pronoun has the meaning of *both* the subject and the object. Because of this, the usual subject pronoun is replaced by the ᏃᏂ [ki] pronoun. The forms of this ᏃᏂ [ki] pronoun replace the pronouns normally used with all verb classes.

This ᏃᏂ [ki] is different from the one above because it does not have an inherent accent, but sometimes the accent will shift onto it anyway, particularly if it is the second syllable. Osage speakers commonly use forms of [ki] to talk about possession instead of the possessive pronouns that we studied in chapter 13. You will see this in sentences 16–18.

As we said above, this pronoun has many forms and pronunciation rules, depending on which consonant appears first in the verb stem. We shall begin with the pronoun forms that are used with verbs whose first consonant is Ꭰ [p], Ꭲ [t], or Ꭹ [k], such as ᎣᎠᎠᎭᎦ [opétxa] *tie up, wrap up*; ᎠᎣᎠ [tópe] *watch, look*; or ᏹᎸᎠ [káaye] *make*. Notice that when we say the first consonant of a verb, we can still talk about verbs that begin with a vowel, like ᎣᎠᎠᎭᎦ [opétxa]. The first sound is Ꭳ [o], but the first consonant is Ꭰ [p].

Forms of ᏃᏂ [ki] in verbs whose first consonant is Ꭰ [p], Ꭲ [t], Ꭹ [k]

There are four forms shown below. All four end in Ꭻ [h] in the Osage alphabet, but the Ꭻ [h] never appears. Instead, it makes the following [p, t, k] preaspirated: Ꭰ [hp], Ꭲ [ht], Ꭹ [hk].

ᎠᏃᏂᎫ [akih]

For first-person singular, we use ᎠᏃᏂᎫ [akih] *I do to or for my own.*

(16) ᎠᎴᎦ ᏌᎸᏐᎳᎠ **ᎠᏃᎾᏹᎸᎠ** ᎠᎠᎭᎴᎦ.
    hpáze wanǫ́bre **akíh**kaaye ątxahé
    I'm making **my own** supper.

(17) ᏂᎠ ᎣᎠᏃᏂᎠᏌᎠ.
    íe o**ákih**pše
    I keep **my** word.

In the example above, the first consonant of the verb ᎣᎠᏌᎠ [opšé] *obey, follow*, is Ꭰ [p].

ᏛᎠᏃᏂᎫ [ðakih]

For second-person, we use ᏛᎠᏃᏂᎫ [ðakih] *you do to or for your own.*

(18) ᏃᏂᎸᏃᏂᎢ **ᏛᎠᏃᏂᎠᎣᎠ** ᏞᏃᏌᎠ.
    žįkážį **ðakíh**tǫpe nįkše
    You are watching **your own** children.

Notice that ᑐᑖ [tópe] is a strong-stem verb that would take ṡ [š] as the pronoun for *you* (see chapter 8). However, when using [ki] pronouns, the normal subject pronouns, like ṡ [š], are replaced by the ᖴᑎ [ki] pronouns—in this case, ᚁᐱᖴᑎᔑ [ðakih].

ᖴᑎᔑ [kih]

For third-person, we use **ᖴᑎᔑ [kih]** *one does to or for one's own*.

(19) ᔑᐱᚏᐣ oᖴᐣᑊᑕᚁᚏᔑ ᐱᖴᚏᐱ.
    haxį o**kíh**petxą akxai
    He's tying up **his own** blankets.

Notice in example 19 that the ᖴᑎᔑ [kih] comes right before the first consonant, ᑊ [p].

ᐱᖴᑎᔑ [ąkih]

For first-person dual and plural, we use **ᐱᖴᑎᔑ [ąkih]** *we do to or for our own*.

(20) ᔑᐱᚏᐣ **ᐱᖴ**óᖴᑎᑊᑕᗪᚏᐱ ᐱᖴᗪᚏᔑ.
    haxį **ąkókih**petxa ąkatxá
    We are tying up **our own** blankets.

Recall from chapter 7 that the first-person plural form ᐱ [ą] or ᐱᖴ [ąk] appears first on most verbs while the other subject pronouns are infixed (see chapter 5). We illustrate this with ᐱᖴᑎᔑ [ąkih]—we will move ᐱᖴ [ąk] to the beginning of the verb but keep the ᖴᑎᔑ [kih] part to the left of the first consonant. This makes a very interesting form! You may notice that we actually have ᐱᖴ-o-ᖴᑎᔑ [ąk-o-kih].

Forms of ᖴᑎ [ki] in verbs whose first consonant is ᚁ [ð]

With verbs whose first consonant is ᚁ [ð], such as ᚁūᘮᐱ [ðuužá] *wash* and ᚁñḁᖴᑎ [ðíiški] *launder*, ᚁ [ð] is replaced by ᒪ [l] in all forms.

ᐱᒪ [al]

For first-person singular, we use **ᐱᒪ [al]** *I do to or for my own*.

(21) ᑎᘁά ᐱᒪűᘮᐱ.
    įcé **al**úuža
    I washed **my** face.

Notice that ᚁūᘮᐱ [ðuužá] is a brush-class verb that would usually use ᖴ [br] for *I*. Again, remember that the ᖴᑎ [ki] pronouns *replace* the usual subject pronouns, so we get **ᐱᒪ**űᘮᐱ [**al**úuža].

ᏏᎲᏞ [ðal]

For second-person singular and plural, we use ᏏᎲᏞ [ðal] *you do to or for your own*.

(22) ᏍᏂ ᏏᎲᏞúžᏁ ᏞᏂᏦᏍá?
   híi **ðal**úuža nįkšé
   Are **you** brushing **your** teeth? (*LITERALLY* Are you washing your teeth?)

Ꮡ [l]

For third-person singular and plural, we use Ꮡ [l] *one does to or for one's own*.

(23) ᏍᎭᏚᏦᎪ ᏞᏂᏍᏦᏂ Ꮅα.
   haaská **l**íiški pe
   She laundered **her own** shirts.

ᎪᏞ [ąl]

For first-person dual and plural, we use ᎪᏞ [ąl] *we do to or for our own*.

(24) ᏅᎲᏍú ᎪᏞᏂᏍᏦᏂ ᎪᏛᏏᎪ.
   hpahú **ąl**íiški ątxá
   We two are washing **our (own)** hair.

ᏦᏂ [ki] in verbs whose first consonant is anything other than Ꮅ [p], Ꮅ [t], Ꮠ [k], or Ꮏ [ð]

Verbs that do not fit into the previous two groups, such as Ꮠ'ú [k'ú] *give*, óᏦᎪ [óhką] *help*, and ōᏍó [oohó] *cook*, use the forms shown below. (Remember that Ꮠ' [k'] and Ꮠ [hk] are not the same as Ꮠ [k].)

ᎪᏦᏂ [aki]

For first-person singular, we use ᎪᏦᏂ [aki] *I do to or for my own*.

(25) ᏅᏂᏞα ᎪᏦᏂᏦ'ᏌᏂ.
   hcíle **akí**k'u
   I gave it to **my own** family.

ᏏᎪᏦᏂ [ðaki]

For second-person singular and plural, we use ᏏᎪᏦᏂ [ðaki] *you do to or for your own*.

(26) ᏦóᏏᎪ oᏏᎪᏦᏂᏦᎪ.
   hkóða o**ðáki**hką
   You helped **your own** friends.

𐓘𐓟 [ki]

For third-person singular and plural, we use 𐓘𐓟 [ki] *one does to or for one's own*.

(27) 𐓘𐓘𐓯𐓣𐓘𐓧𐓟𐓟 𐓯𐓘𐓧𐓘𐓪𐓴𐓘 ō𐓘𐓣𐓯𐓪 𐓮𐓘.
kaasį́exci wanǫ́bre oo**kí**hǫ pe
He cooked **his own** breakfast.

𐓘̨𐓘𐓟 [ąki]

For first-person dual and plural, we use 𐓘̨𐓘𐓟 [ąki] *we do to or for our own*.

(28) 𐓟𐓯𐓧𐓘 𐓘̨𐓘ó𐓘𐓟𐓘̨𐓘𐓘𐓟.
hcíle **ąkó**kih**ką**pe
We helped **our own** family.

Notice again how we split 𐓘̨𐓘𐓟 [ąki] into 𐓘̨𐓘 [ąk] and 𐓘𐓟𐓴 [kih] so that 𐓘̨𐓘 [ąk] could appear first and 𐓘𐓟 [ki] could appear before the first consonant in the verb stem.

𐓘𐓟 [hki] *do to or for oneself or each other*

The last group of 𐓘𐓟 [ki] pronouns are the ones that mean *do to oneself* or *for oneself* (called reflexive in grammar books) or *each other* (called reciprocal). Plural forms have two possible interpretations: reflexive *yourselves, ourselves, themselves*, or reciprocal *each other*. Like the previous set, the forms of 𐓘𐓟 [hki] depend on the first consonant of the verb.

Forms of 𐓘𐓟 [hki] in verbs whose first consonant is 𐓘 [p], 𐓘 [t], 𐓘 [k]

There are four 𐓘𐓟 [hki] forms for verbs whose first consonant is 𐓘 [p], 𐓘 [t], 𐓘 [k]. These forms end in 𐓴 [h] in the Osage alphabet, so as we saw earlier, they make the following [p, t, k] preaspirated: 𐓘 [hp], 𐓘 [ht], 𐓘 [hk].

𐓘̨𐓘𐓟𐓴 [ahkih]

For first-person singular, we use 𐓘̨𐓘𐓟𐓴 [ahkih] *I do to or for myself*.

(29) 𐓘̨𐓘𐓯𐓘𐓪𐓘𐓘 𐓘𐓟𐓘̨𐓧á.
ahkíhtǫpe mįkšé
I'm looking at **myself**.

𐓽𐓘̨𐓘𐓟𐓴 [ðahkih]

For second-person, we use 𐓽𐓘̨𐓘𐓟𐓴 [ðahkih] *you do to or for yourself*.

(30) ᏂᎶᏦᎼᎣᏆ ᏞᏁᏦᎦᎠ.
    ðahkíhtǫpe nįkšé
    Are **you** looking at **yourself**?

(31) ᏂᎶᏦᎼᎣᏆ ᏆᎶᎦᎠ.
    ðahkíhtǫpe paašé
    Are **you (plural)** looking at **each other**?
    OR Are **you (plural)** looking at **yourselves**?

ᏫᏁ [hkih]

For third-person, we use **ᏫᏁ** [hkih] *one does to or for oneself*.

(32) ᏋᎶᏋᎾ ᏕᏦᎾ ᏦᏁᏦᎶᏇᎶ ᏆᎠ.
    wacúe skúe **hkih**káaɣa pe
    She made a cake **for herself**.

ᎶᏦᏁᎷ [ąhkih]

For first-person dual and plural, we use **ᎶᏦᏁᎷ** [ąhkih] *we do to or for ourselves or each other*.

(33) ᏋᎠᎦᎶ ᎼᎶᏞᏂ **ᎶᏦᏁᏦᎶᏇᎶᎠ**.
    hcéwai htaaníi **ąhkíh**kaaɣape
    We made yonkapin soup **for ourselves**.
    OR **We** made yonkapin soup **for each other**.

Forms of ᏫᏁ [hki] in verbs whose first consonant is Ꮒ [ð]

This group of verbs will have the same sound change as the ᏫᏁ [ki] pronouns above: the Ꮒ [ð] will be replaced by Ꮑ [l].

ᎶᏦᏁᏞ [ahkil]

For the first-person singular, we use **ᎶᏦᏁᏞ** [ahkil] *I do to or for myself*.

(34) ᏃᎼᎠ **ᎶᏦᏁᏞ**ᎤᎦᏁ.
    hǫopé **ahkíl**uwį
    I bought shoes **for myself**.

ᏂᎶᏦᏁᏞ [ðahkil]

For second-person, we use **ᏂᎶᏦᏁᏞ** [ðahkil] *you do to or for yourself*.

(35) ᎣᏂᎾᎠᏁ **ᏂᎶᏦᏁᏞ**ᎤᎦᏁ ᏆᎶᎦᎠ.
    oðíhtą **ðahkíl**uwį paašé
    You (plural) are buying a car **for yourselves**.

ᏦᏁᏞ [hkil]

For third-person, we use **ᏦᏁᏞ [hkil]** *one does to or for oneself*.

(36) **ᏦᏁᏞ**ñꭺᎠᏯ ᎠᏦᎻᎠ.
 hkilíištą akxai
 He's getting **himself** ready.

In example 36, the verb ᏂñꭺᎠᏯ [ðiistą́] *finish* takes on the meaning *get ready* when used with ᏦᏁᏞ [hkil].

ᎠᏦᏁᏞ [ąhkil]

For first-person dual and plural, we use **ᎠᏦᏁᏞ [ąhkil]** *do to or for ourselves or each other*.

(37) **ᎠᏦᏁ́Ꮞ**ñꭺᎠᏯ ᎠᏂá.
 ąhkíliištą ąðé
 We two are getting **ourselves** ready.

ᏦᏁ [hki] in verbs whose first consonant is anything other than Ꮄ [p], Ꮀ [t], Ꮓ [k], or Ꮒ [ð]

ᎠᏦᏁ [ahki]

For first-person singular, we use **ᎠᏦᏁ [ahki]** *I do to or for myself*.

(38) ᎤᎠᏦᏁᏦᏯ.
 o**áhki**hką
 I helped **myself**.

ᏂᎠᏦᏁ [ðahki]

For second-person, we use **ᏂᎠᏦᏁ [ðahki]** *you do to or for yourself*.

(39) **ᏂᎠᏦᏁ́**ᏓʼᎤ.
 ðahkík'u
 You gave it to **yourself**.

ᏦᏁ [hki]

For third-person, we use **ᏦᏁ [hki]** *one does to or for oneself*.

(40) ᏆáᎠᎠ ᏃáᏞᎠ ᎠᎢ ᎤᏦń⸌Ꭳʼ Ꮄa.
 hpáata žéelą wį oo**hkí**họ pe
 He cooked **himself** an omelet.

ᎪᏊᏂ [a̧hki]

For first-person dual and plural, we use **ᎪᏊᏂ** [a̧hki] *do to or for ourselves or each other*.

(41) **ᎪᏀóᏊᏂᏊᎪ.**
a̧kóhkihka̧
We two helped **ourselves**.
OR **We two** helped **each other**.

The verb oᏊńα [ohkíe] *speak with someone, converse, call on the phone* has *each other* built into it. We also have the full form, oᏊńᏊα [ohkíhkie], which means *hold a conversation, generally with more than two persons*. We will look at this again in chapter 20.

(42) **ᎪᏀóᏊᏂᏊα ᎪᏊᎪᎠᕁá.**
a̧kóhkihkie a̧katxái
We are having a conversation.

ńᏊ'uᴇα

Exercise 1. Do you understand?

What does this conversation mean?

A: ÞᎪᏕú ᎪᏞńᏊᏊᏂ ᒼᏂᏊᏕá. ᏕᎪᏕúᏕuᏃᏂ ᎪᏊᐊᎪ.
B: ᒼńoᏂᎪᏊα ᏕᎪᏞᎪ ᏊᴇńᏊᎠᎪ ÐᎪ ᏞᏂᏊᏕá? OᎪᏂᎪᏊᎪ ᏊóᏊᎪ ᒼᏂᏊᏕá.
A: ᒼńoᏂᎪᏊα ᏊᏂαᎠőÞᎪ ᴇᏂ ᏞᎪᏊᎪ ᏇńᏊᎠᎪ.
B: ᏂᏕńᏂᎪÞα ÐᎪ ᒼᏂᏊᏕá.

Exercise 2. Composition

Write a composition of six Osage sentences. Include at least one use of a verb with any ki- pronoun.

Exercise 3. Put it in Osage

Give the Osage for:

1. He's looking for his (own) cat.
2. We washed our faces.
3. He bought it for me.
4. Are you getting yourself ready?
5. I'm making myself a sandwich.

Exercise 4. Practice ki- verbs

Using the verbs ꝺóꝺa, ħūzá, and ōꞌó, give the verb forms with all pronouns in all three ki- groups.

ńa

Nouns

ꞌńꞃazɴ	hį́įcežį̇	plates
ꞌōꝺá	họopé	shoes
ᵯǎ7a ꞌńꞃazɴ	máze hį́įcežį̇	metal bowl
ʟńʟɴ	nį́įni	cold water
ōꞌó ꞌáꝅʌꞌɴ	óoho͎ wékahi	cook-paddle
ꝺǎꝺʌ zǎcʌ	hpáata žéeḻą	fried egg or omelet
ꝺǎ7a ꞌʌcóra	hpáze wanó̧bre	supper
ꝺǎza ᵯʌǯʌcʌ ʟǎᴪa	hpéže mąhkása ną́ye	ice tea
ꝅǎꝅa ńꝺuꝅᴧʌ	šáake ípukxa	hand towel
ꞃáꞌʌ ꝺǎʟń	hcéwai htaanį́į	yonkapin soup
ꞃúꝅa	hcúke	spoon
ꞌáōꞌo	wéooho͎	cooking utensils
ꞌáꝺuꝅᴧʌ	wépukxa	towels

Verbs

ɴħʌꝺa	iðáhpe (i-stem)	wait for
ꝅꞌú	k'ú (a-ða)	give
ʟńꝅń	liiškí (ki-ð-stem)	wash (own hair or laundry)
ʟūzá	luužá (ki-ð-stem)	wash (own body or things)
oꝅńꝅɴa	ohkíhkie (a-ða)	hold a conversation
oꝺǎꝺᴧʌ	opétxą (strong-stem)	tie up
oꝺꝅá	opšé (a-ða)	obey, follow
ħɴꝅń	ðiiškí (br-šc)	wash clothes

Adjectives

ꝺǎꞌń	hpaahį́	sharp

Other

ńa oꝅńꝺꝅa	íe okípše (a-ða)	keep one's word

Notes for Chapter 16

Quintero argues for [ki], [kik], and [hkik] as underlying forms for *dative*, *suus*, and *reflexive* morphemes. We have chosen to present these forms without the final [k] for pedagogical reasons. This is because, though the final [k] has a historical status, it never surfaces.

Chapter 17

Building Words with Prefixes

Oǧná

This Oǧná section was written by author Stephanie Rapp.

When the drum is passed to the new drumkeeper his family will help pay for this position by the giving of gifts to the former drumkeeper and his family. This ceremony is referred to as paying for the drum. In 1963 my cousin Stephen Cody Tucker accepted the drum for the Gray Horse district. He came to my home to tell us the good news. He wanted me to help pay for the drum at the following June dance. My family soon started gathering the Osage clothes that I would be wearing to be given away. The wedding coat and hat are special items of clothing that are worn by women on this day. When Cody paid for the drum, these are the clothes I wore.

1. ⟨Osage text⟩
2. ⟨Osage text⟩
3. ⟨Osage text⟩
4. ⟨Osage text⟩
5. ⟨Osage text⟩
6. ⟨Osage text⟩
7. ⟨Osage text⟩
8. ⟨Osage text⟩

1. I gave these Osage clothes away.
2. The skirt was blue broadcloth.
3. The shirt was gold.
4. One of the finger woven belts was red, yellow, blue, and green with beads, and the other belt was left unfinished.
5. Ribbons, three shirt pins, and a (shiny) brooch.
6. A bead necklace and earrings too.
7. Moccasins.
8. Red wedding coat and wedding hat.

On this day my Aunt Louise 𐓏𐓣𐓩𐓛𐓮𐓣 [wihcími] dressed me in these Osage clothes. Before entering the dance arbor, the women wearing these clothes lined up and followed the drumkeeper into the arbor. After entering the arbor, the names of the women to receive these clothes were called. After being called, the women came and took us to where they were sitting and began to undress us. After being undressed, the women gave us shawls to wear, and we returned to our seats. Photo from Stephanie Rapp's personal collection.

𐓁𐓘 𐓏𐓘𐓸𐓣𐓵𐓣𐓬𐓘

All students of the Osage language now know that verbs have many prefixes that serve many purposes. Up to now, most of these have been pronouns. Now we will introduce two other kinds of prefixes. One group gives information such as *with*, *for*, and *to*. The other group, called the *instrumental prefixes* are a hallmark of Siouan languages. They tell us the manner of an action, such as *using the hands*.

The prefixes ɩ, o, ʌ́ [i, o, á]

The prefix ɩ [i] *with, about, a means to*

The prefix ɩ [i] is used when we want to introduce an instrument, such as *make **with** wood* or *eat **with** a spoon*. The prefix ɩ [i] appears on the verb before the subject pronouns. Notice that with the prefix ɩ [i] we do not need a preposition like *with* the way we would in English. The meaning is also different from English *with* since it is *not* used to express accompaniment. That is done with a special verb zóʌa [žóle] *accompany* or *be with*, which is discussed below. This prefix ɩ [i] is usually accented.

(1) 𐒹𐓴𐓤𐓟 𐓣𐓩𐓘𐓮𐓘 𐓛𐓘.
     hcúke íðaacha pe
     She ate it **with** a spoon.

(2) Žáą **íkąąγe** akxai.
žą́ą **íkaaγe** akxai
He's making it **with** (out of) wood.

(3) Ówe **mázaska** íhta **íbruwį**.
ówe **mázeska** íhta **íbruwį**
I bought groceries **with** his money.

The Prefix o [o] *location, goal*

The prefix **o** [o] or long **ō** [oo] is placed on verbs to signal a location or a goal. We see it in verbs like ósi [ósi] *get off, get down from* and olį́į [olį́į] *sit (somewhere), sit in, ride in, live in*. Again, when we place the prefix **o** [o] on a verb, we do not need to use a preposition.

The prefix **o** [o] comes before pronouns. But remember from chapter 5 that when we use ąk [ąk] *we*, it comes first, before **o** [o].

(4) Hkáwa **o**ási.
hkáwa **o**ási
I got **off** the horse.

(5) Páce ąk**ó**si.
páce ąk**ó**si
We two got **out of** the boat.

(6) Hową́įki **o**ðálįį škóšta?
hową́įki **o**ðálįį škóšta
Where do you want to sit?
OR Where do you want to live?

In example 6, *where* means *which location*, which is why it takes **o** [o].

O [o] is built into many verbs we have already learned, including ōhó [oohó] *cook*, océ [océ] *look for*, and óhką [óhką] *help*. In many cases, it is no longer clear just how the meaning of *a place* or *a goal* is included in the verb. We can simply learn these verbs as a single word.

(7) Níi céγe **ōžú** akxa.
níi céγe **oožú** akxa
He **pours** water **into** the bucket.

(8) Mąhkása céγeska **ōážu** ątxahé.
mąhkása céγeska **ooážu** ątxahé
I'm pouring coffee into the cup.

(9) Paazénįį **ō**žu ąk**ó**župe.
paazénįį **óo**žu ąk**óo**župe
We poured milk into the bowl.

Notice that the word for *bowl*, ṓžu [óožu], is similar to *pour into*, ōžú [oožú]. See chapter 19 for more discussion of this.

The prefix ʌ́ [á] *on, upon, over, for the benefit of*

We learned to use ǩń [kí] in chapter 16 to show that someone benefitted from some action (as in example 10 below). And we also learned that with object pronouns like *me* or *you*, the [ki] changed to accented [á] (as in example 11 below).

(10) Ųzʌ́ ʌǩʌʌ **ǒsơ** sʌcǩʌ℘ń **ǩńħuʌń** Þα.
    įįná akxa **óohǫ** haaskámį **kíðuwį** pe
    Mother bought a shawl **for the cook**.

(11) ʌ́αǒsơ ɛ́αǩʌ **ʌ́ħuʌń** Þα.
    wéoohǫ hcéka **áðuwį** pe
    She bought new cooking utensils **for me**.

The prefix ʌ́ [á] provides a second way to show that someone benefited from some action. Ʌ́ [á] appears at the beginning of the verb and is almost always accented. We can use ʌ́ [á] when the object is third-person. Let us look at some examples.

Using ħuʌń [ðuwį] once more as our example, we will place ʌ́ [á] before the subject pronouns.

(12a) ÞʌDʌ Ųzʌ́ **ʌ́ʀuʌń**.
    hpáata įįná **ábruwį**
    I bought eggs **for my mother**.

(12b) ℘ʌ́sń ÞʌsŃ ʌń **ʌ́ʀuʌń**.
    máąhį hpaahí wį **ábruwį**
    I bought a sharp knife **for him/her**.

(12c) ʌ́αÞuǩʌʌ **ʌ́ŝcuʌń**.
    wépukxa **áščuwį**
    You bought towels **for him/her**.

(12d) **ʌ́ħuʌń** Þα.
    áðuwį pe
    He/she bought it **for him/her**.
    OR They bought it **for him/her**.

Note that in 12d we could have used ǩńħuʌń [kíðuwį], like in example 10, instead of ʌ́ħuʌń [áðuwį]. Speakers have the option to use either form when both the subject and the object are third-person. There is a subtle difference in meaning. If we use [kí], then we are in the presence of other people, but if we use [á], we are not in the presence of others.

(12e) **ʌ̨́ħuʌń**.
    áąðuwį
    We bought it for **him/her**.

When we add ʌ́ [á] to a form that begins with a nasal vowel like ʌ [ą] in 12d, the accented ʌ́ [á] will become nasal too.

Á [á] is also used to mean *on, upon, over*. Like the prefix o [o], it is placed before the pronouns.

(13) Ðá apa óžąke **á**nąąke apai.
htáa apa óžąke **á**nąąke apai
The deer ran **on** the road.

By itself, ᏡᎾᏓ [wísi] just means *jump*. We might use this if someone were jumping up and down. Usually though, we mean that someone is jumping from one spot to another. This is why we have learned oᏡᎾᏓ [owísi], with the prefix [o], as the basic verb for *jump*. We can also use the prefix [á] with ᏡᎾᏓ [wísi] to form ᎪᏡᎾᏓ [áwisi] *jump over* as in 14.

(14) Ðá apa ápahta **á**wisi pe.
htáa apa ápahta **á**wisi pe
The deer jumped **over** the fence.

Just as we saw with the prefixes ᎾᎾ [i] and o [o], there are many verbs that include Á [á] to make new meanings. Two of these have similar meanings, such as ÁᏟa [ále] *put on top of* and Ázu [ážu] *set items out on something*.

(15) ᏡᎪᎦ'ó ᎪᎩᎳ ᏃáᏇa ᕐᎪᏃa ᏡáõᏚᕐ **ÁᏟ** pe.
wak'ó akxa céɣe máze wéoohǫ **á**la pe
The woman **put** the pot **on top of** the stove.

(16) ᎷᎾ̨ea ÁᏡᎪᏟoᏒa ÁᏂᎪ**zu**?
hį́įce áwanǫbre **á**ðažu
Did you **set** the plates **on** the table?

In the previous example, the word for *table*, ÁᏡᎪᏟoᏒa [áwanǫbre], literally means *eat dinner on*.

ZóᏟa [žóle] *accompaniment with*

In English, the preposition *with* has many meanings. Two of the most important are *instrumental with* (as in "He hit the bug with his shoe.") and *accompaniment with* (as in "We always eat lunch with our parents."). We have learned to make *instrumental with* using Osage ᎾᎾ [i]. For the meaning of accompaniment, Osage has a special verb, zóᏟa [žóle], that means *go with, be with, accompany*.

We most often will use another verb, especially a verb of motion, along with zóᏟa [žóle]. The pronouns come after the o [o] in zóᏟa [žóle]. This is an a-ða verb.

(17) ZóᏟa ᕐᎪᏂᏏ́ apa.
žóle mą̨ðį́ apai
He's walking with her.

As with many examples in Osage, we need to use context to understand the meanings of the third-person forms. Example 17 could also mean, for instance, *she's walking with him*, and so forth.

(18) 𐒹ó𐒼𐒰𐒿𐒰 𐒶𐒿𐒷𐒻 𐒶𐒰?
žóðale ðachí ðe
Did **you** come with her?

Notice that we put the pronoun 𐒶𐒿 [ða] *you* on both 𐒹óla [žóle] and 𐒿𐒷𐒻 [achí].

(19) 𐒻𐒹𐒰𐒷𐒻 𐒿𐒰𐒷 𐒹ó𐒼𐒰 𐒿𐒷𐒻 𐒿𐒰𐒷.
ihtáci apa žóale achí apa
Father came here **with me**.

𐒹óla [žóle] can also be used to talk about things that accompany each other. In the dialogue of chapter 6 we see the sentence:

(20) 𐒽𐒿𐒼ń 𐒿ā́𐒾𐒿 **𐒹ó𐒿𐒰** ō𐒾𐒻𐒿 𐒿𐒾𐒶𐒿𐒻ā́.
wašį́ hpáata **žóle** ooáhą atxąhé
I am cooking bacon and eggs.
(I am cooking bacon **with** eggs. OR I am cooking bacon **along with** eggs.)

Recall from chapter 6 that *I cook* is pronounced ō𐒾𐒻𐒿 [ooáhą] rather than ō𐒾𐒻𐒿 [ooáhǫ].

In 21–23, notice the difference in meaning between the 𐒻 [i] prefix for *instrumental with* and the verb 𐒹óla [žóle] for *accompaniment with*.

(21) 𐒾ā𐒿ń 𐒷ú𐒼𐒰 ń𐒶𐒿𐒷𐒿 𐒾𐒰.
htaaníi hcúke íðaacha pe
He ate soup **with** a spoon.

(22) 𐒾ā𐒿ń ñ𐒿ó𐒾𐒿 **𐒹ó𐒿𐒰** 𐒶𐒿𐒷ā́ 𐒾𐒰.
htaaníi iihǫ́htą **žóle** ðaachá pe
He ate soup **with** his aunt. (his mother's older sister)

(23) **𐒹ó𐒿𐒰** 𐒿𐒷ń 𐒾𐒰.
žóle achí pe
He came here **with her**.

Special Siouan instrumental prefixes

All the Siouan languages use special prefixes to talk about the way an action occurs—usually the kind of instrument that is used to perform an action. Body parts are often considered kinds of instruments. Many of the verbs we have already learned have instrumental prefixes. Fluent Osage speakers can use the instrumental prefixes to make new words, but the words most

Michaela Pratt wearing women's clothes, view from the front. Photo by Butch DeLong.

Michaela Pratt wearing women's clothes, view from the back. Photo by Butch DeLong.

modern speakers use are already in the vocabulary. As the vocabulary has evolved, the original meanings of the prefixes are often no longer apparent, just as we saw with the ᓂ [i], ᓄ [o], ᐤ [á] prefixes.

ᖮᓃ / ᖮᑐ [ðii / ðuu] *by hand, using the hands*

The original form of this prefix is ᖮᓃ [ðii], but it has changed into ᖮᑐ [ðuu] in many words. You will see both forms. Almost all verbs that include this prefix are in the brush verb class. There are a number of nouns that also are formed with this prefix.

(24) ᒡᓂᖬᐱ ᐱᖬᔨᐱ ᓃᖬᐅᐁᐳᕐᐱ ᓴᓂ ᖮᑐᖬᐠᕐᐱ ᐳᓇ.
    níhka akxa íikaahtamą wį ðuuhkáamą pe
    The man rang a bell.

ᖮᑐᖬᐠᕐᐱ [ðuuhkáamą] means *ring a bell or doorbell*. It includes the ᖮᑐ [ðuu] prefix because the action is performed with the hand.

(25) íikaahtamą wį bruuhkáamą
I rang a bell.

(26) máze įįštóolą wíhta ðiixǫ́ pe OR ðuuxǫ́ pe
He broke my glasses (using his hands).

(27) ðuuhpéece wį ąščí nįkšé
Do you have a lighter?

The noun ðuuhpéece *lighter* is made by putting ðuu before hpéece *fire*. A lighter is fire that is produced using the hand.

ðaa *by mouth, using the mouth*

ðaa shows up on verbs such as ðaaškíke *chew*, ðaaxtáke *bite*, and ðaahtą́ *drink*. Almost all verbs that begin with this prefix are in the brush verb class.

(28) wakǫ́ze akxa mįįhtǫ́eli ðaaškíke akxai
The teacher is chewing gum.

(29) mįįhtǫ́eli štáaškike nįkšé?
Are you chewing gum?

(30) šįtóžį akxa ítaeži ðaaxtáka pe
The boy bit his little sister.

(31) wibráaxtake hta mįkšé.
I'm going to bite you.

(32) šǫ́žį akxa níi ðaahtą́ akxai
The puppy is drinking water.

(33) mąhkása ąðáahtą ąðįkšé.
We two are drinking coffee.

(34) hpéženii bráahtą mįkšé.
I am drinking tea.

(35) hą́ąci niikáapxohke štáahtą.
You drank pop last night.

⌐ᴋ̃ [naa̧] *by foot, using the foot*

⌐ᴋ̃ [naa̧] appears on verbs like ⌐ᴋ̃ᴢп [náa̧ží̧] *stand up*, ́⌐ᴋ̃ᴢп́ ánaa̧ží̧ *step on*, and ⌐ᴋ̃ʜᴏ́ [naa̧xó] *break (using the foot; stomp or kick apart)*. These are usually in the a-ða class.

(36) ⌐ᴋ̃ᴢп́!
    naa̧ží̧
    Stand up!

(37) ʌ⌐ᴋ̃ᴢпᴆα.
    anáa̧žipe
    We stood up.

Note that the accented ́ [á] in the verb ́⌐ᴋ̃ᴢп́ [ánaa̧ží̧] means *on*. As above, accented ́ [á] appears first on the verb, so the a-ða pronouns come after it, as in 38 and 39.

(38) ᵐпᴆóαⲥп ́⌐ᴋ̃ᴢп́.
    mii̧htóeli áanaa̧ží̧
    I stepped on some gum.

(39) пⲥóαᴢп́ ⲥñᵮα ́ᴛʌ⌐ᴋ̃ᴢп́.
    ilóeží̧ sii̧ce áðanaa̧ží̧
    You stepped on the cat's tail.

(40) ⸮пᴢá ńᴆʌ ⌐ᴋ̃ʜᴏ́ ᴆα.
    hcižé íhta naa̧xó pe
    He broke her door (by using the foot).

(41) ʐᴋ̃ʜα ʌ⌐ᴋ̃ʜᴏ.
    žáa̧xe anáa̧xo
    I broke the stick (by foot).

The next examples include verbs like ⌐ᴋ̃ᵴᴅʌ [náa̧šta̧] *stop (walking or running)*, ⌐ᴋ̃ⲥá [naa̧sé] *cut the grass*, and ᴏ⌐ᴋ̃ᴢп́ [onáa̧ží̧] *attend*. In these cases, the meaning of ⌐ᴋ̃ [naa̧] may not be clear, but, for example, we need to use our feet to stop ourselves when walking or running, and when we cut grass, the grass is at our feet. For *attend*, we add [o] to [náa̧ží̧] to mean something like to stand somewhere (on your feet), which is often what we are doing when we attend something.

(42) ᵐʌʁń ʌ⸝α ҟʌᵮó ʌ⌐ᴋ̃ᵴᴅʌ.
    ma̧brí a̧hé kaðǫ́ anáa̧šta̧
    I was walking and then I stopped.

Because stopping is completive by its nature, it will always take completive aspect. In the following example, even though third-person completive (he stopped) should take ᴆα [pe], speakers almost never use it because it's not necessary.

(43) ᒣ኿Ꮤᐩ ᐱᐊ ᏦᎵᏔᏬ ᏗᎾᎦᎠᏗ.
mąðí apai kaðǫ́ ną́ąštą
He was walking and then he stopped.

(44) ᎦᎭᐳᏣᏦᎵ ᎥᎦᏬᎠᐱᐞ ᎥᎦᏬᏗᎾᏃᐩ ᎥᎦᎠᎦᎭᎵ.
taapóska ąkóhtapi ąkóną́ąžį ąkatxái
We attend Our School (name of the school).

ÞᎵ [paa] *by pushing away, down, or on*

ÞᎵ [paa] appears on verbs such as ÞᎵᏫᏬᎠ [paaγóe] *push* and ÞᎵᎭᏃᎠ [paaxcé] *tie down*. It is also used with the important word for cutting ÞᎵᏣᎠ [paasé]. This is because cutting usually uses the action of pushing down. Almost all verbs that begin with this prefix are in the strong-stem verb class.

(45) ᏃᎠᏦᎵᏗᏬ ᐱᐊ ᎤᏔᏁᐱᎵ ÞᎵᏫᏬᎠ ᐱᐊ.
hcékanǫ́ǫ apa oðíhtą paaγóe apai
The teenager is pushing the car.

(46) ᎤᏔᏁᐱᎵ ÞᎵᏫᎠ.
oðíhtą hpáaγoe
I pushed the car.

(47) ᎵᎦÞᎵᏫᎠ.
ą́špaaγoe
You pushed me.

(48) ᏃᎠᏫᎠᏗᏃ ÞᎵᎭᎠᎵ.
céγenii paaxtá
Tie (down) the drum!

In example 48 ÞᎵᎭᏃᎠ [paaxcé] becomes ÞᎵᎭᎠᎵ [paaxtá] because it is a command. We saw this change with ᏬᏃᎠ [óce] *look for* in chapter 12. In the command form, if a verb ends in ᏃᎠ [ce] (or ᏃᎠ [hce]), we replace it with ᎠᎵ [tá].

(49) ᏃᎠᏫᎠᏗᏃ ÞᎵᎭᏃᎠ ᒣᏁᏦᎦᎠ.
céγenii hpaaxcé mįkšé
I'm tying (down) the drum.

(50) ᒣᏁᏦᎵᏦ'Ꭰ ᎤᏁᎤᏃᎠ ÞᎵᏣᎠ ᎥᏦᎭᎵ.
mihkák'e ohkísce paasé akxai
She's cutting the mushrooms in half.

(51) ᏍᎵᎦᏯ ᎦÞᎵᏣᎠ.
wašį́ špaáse
You cut the bacon.

ÞᎵ [pá] *by cutting with something sharp*

A second instrumental that is very close in sound to ÞᎵ [paa] is ÞᎵ [pá]. It is very easy to get these two instrumentals confused. Two important verbs with the ÞᎵ [pá] instrumental are ÞᎵᏣᎠ [páse] *cut with a sharp edge* and ᏢᎯᏚᏋᎪ [pascé] *cut into strips* or *cut up*. Many speakers do not really differentiate these forms from ᏢᎰᏚᎪ [paasé], which we saw above. The most important thing about the ᏢᎯ [pá] instrumental is that its members are in the a-ða verb class, with the pronouns occurring after ᏢᎯ [pá].

(52) ᎷᎾᏦᎯᏦ'Ꭰ ᎤᏦᎱᏚᏋᎪ ᏢᎯᏚᎪ ᎯᏦᏬᎵ.
mihkák'e ohkísce páse akxai
She's cutting the mushrooms in half.

(53) ᏌᎯᏣᎴ ᏢᎯᏬᎯᏚᎪ.
wašį pa**ð**áse
You cut the bacon.

(54) ᏌᎯᏋᎤᎪ ᏚᏦᎤᎪ ᏢᎰᏚᎪ.
wacúe skúe pá**a**se
I cut the cake.

Notice the form for *I cut*: ᏢᎰᏚᎪ [páase]. The pronoun Ꭰ [a] comes after the ᏢᎯ [pá] instrumental, making it sound very similar to *she cuts*: ᏢᎰᏚᎪ [paasé], from example 50 above. The same situation applies with the verb ᏢᎯᏚᏋᎪ [pascé] *cut into strips* in 56 below; ᏢᎰᏚᏋᎪ [pá**a**sce] *I'm cutting up (the onion)*.

Some people have begun to use both ᏢᎯᏚᏋᎪ [pascé] (short [pa]) and ᏢᎰᏚᏋᎪ [paascé] (with a long [paa]).

(55) ᎣᏲᎴ ᎯᏦᏬᎵ ᎠᎰ ᏢᎯᏚᏋᎪ ᎯᏦᏬᎵ.
oohǫ́ akxa htáa pascé akxai
The cook is cutting the meat into strips.

(56) ᎷᎰᏃᎵᏬᎪ ᏢᎰᏚᏋᎪ ᎷᎾᏦᎦᎡ.
máąžąxe páasce mįkšé
I'm cutting up the onion.

(57) ᏦᎰᏚᏋᎪ ᏃᎤᎪ ᎯᏢᎯᏚᏋᎪ ᎠᎵ ᎯᏦᎯᏬᎪ.
hką́ące žúe ąpásce hta ąkáðe
We are going to cut up the tomatoes.

ᏦᎰ [kaa] *by striking* or *with sudden quick action*

The prefix ᏦᎰ [kaa] appears in verbs like ᏦᎰᏬᎤ [káaxǫ] *break* and ᏦᎰᏋᎤᏬᎪ [kaacúxe] *sweep*. We need to be careful with words that begin with ᏦᎰ [kaa] because, in many instances, ᏦᎰ [kaa] is not actually the instrumental prefix—for example, ᏦᎰᏫᎡ [kaayé] *make* or ᏦᎰᏚᎴ [kaasí] *tomorrow*.

(58) ᏐᎯᏋᎪ ᏌᎮ ᏦᎰᏬᎤ ᏢᎪ.
hį́įce wį káaxǫ pe
He broke a dish.

In 26 above, we used ᏬᎯᏬᎤ [ðíixǫ] *break with the hands*. Here, ᏦᎰᏬᎤ [káaxǫ] means that he broke the dish with some sudden action, perhaps using his hands or perhaps not. The emphasis with ᏦᎰᏬᎤ [káaxǫ] is on the striking or a sudden action.

This prefix behaves differently from the others when using first- and second-person singular pronouns (I and you). In many but not all cases the 𐓐𐒰̄ [kaa] prefix is deleted. (We saw this earlier in the case of ki-stative verbs.)

(59) 𐒼́𐒰̨𐓓𐒰 𐒻̨𐓍𐓈𐓊́𐓊𐓜𐓜 𐓏𐒻́𐓐𐓜 𐓂́𐓑𐓂̨?
máze įįštóolą wíhta ðáaxǫ
Did you break my glasses?

Notice that the verb is 𐓂́𐓑𐓂̨ [ðáaxǫ], not 𐓂́𐒼𐓑𐓂̨ [ðakáaxǫ]. The 𐓐𐒰̄ [kaa] has been deleted.

(60) 𐓏𐒰𐓐'𐓂́ 𐓏𐒻́𐓐𐓜 𐒰𐒼𐒼𐒰 𐒰́𐓇𐒰̄𐓐𐓂𐒰 𐓐𐒰̄𐓂́𐓍𐒰 𐓊𐒰.
wak'ó wíhta akxa ánąąhkoe kaacúxa pe
My wife swept the floor.

Some people say 𐓏𐒻𐓏𐒰𐓐'𐓂 [wiwák'o] for *my wife*. This term may convey a greater degree of endearment.

(61) 𐒰́𐓇𐒰̄𐓐𐓂𐒰 𐒰́𐓂𐓈𐓂̨𐒰.
ánąąhkoe áacuxe
I swept the floor.

Again, in example 61 the 𐓐𐒰̄ [kaa] prefix has been deleted in first-person.

𐓄𐓎 [pu] *by pressing*

This prefix is not common, but it does appear on the useful verbs 𐓄𐓎́𐒼𐓑𐒰 [púkxa] *wipe* and 𐓄𐓎𐓇𐓓𐒰́𐓊𐒰 [puštáha] *iron*.

(62) 𐓆𐓂́𐒼𐒰 𐓏𐒻́𐓐𐒰 𐒰𐒼𐒼𐒰 𐓊𐒰́𐒰̨𐓇𐒰𐒼𐒰 𐒻́𐓊𐒰 𐓄𐓎𐓇𐓓𐒰́𐓊𐒰 𐒰𐒼𐒼𐒰́𐓊𐒰 𐒰𐒼𐒼𐒰.
níhka wíhta akxa háabrehka íhta puštáha ąkǫ́ða akxa
My husband wants me to iron his ribbons. (Osage dance ribbons)

(63) 𐓆𐓂́𐒼𐒰 𐓏𐒻́𐓐𐒰 𐓊𐒰́𐒰̨𐓇𐒰𐒼𐒰 𐒻́𐓊𐒰 𐓄𐓎𐓇𐓓𐒰́𐓊𐒰 𐒰𐓓𐒼𐒰́.
níhka wíhta háabrehka íhta hpuštáha ątxąhé
I'm ironing my husband's ribbons.

(64) 𐓇𐒰́𐓐𐒰̨𐓂̄ 𐒰𐓄𐒰 𐒰́𐓏𐒰̨𐓇𐒼𐒰 𐓄𐓎́𐒼𐓑𐒰 𐒰𐓄𐒰𐒻.
hcékanǫǫ apa áwanǫbre púkxa apai
The teenagers are wiping the table.

(65) 𐒰́𐓈𐒻̄ 𐒰𐓄𐓎́𐒼𐓑𐒰.
áalįį ąpúkxa
We two wiped the chairs.

𐓄𐒻 [pi] *by blowing*

This is another instrumental with few verb forms. They are in the strong-stem verb class.

A useful expression is ÞΛ ÞṅΨΛ [hpá píɣą] *blow one's nose*.

(66) ÞΛ ₷ÞṅΨΛ.
 hpá špíɣą
 Did you blow your nose?

Þo [po] *by shooting*

This is another rare instrumental prefix. It appears in verbs like ÞóϹa [póse] *cut by shooting* and Þó₷Þa [póšpe] *shoot a piece out*.

(67) ⌐áħᴨ˙ ÞóϹΛ Þa.
 wéðį pósa pe
 He cut the rope by shooting it.

(68) Žã ħa ÞoħΛ₷Þa?
 žą́ą ðe poðášpe
 Did you shoot a piece out of that tree?

DÃ [taa] *by heat*

Most of the verbs that take the DÃ [taa] instrumental are only used with things, not with people. So they only appear in the third-person. There is one common verb that takes human subjects: DÃ₷ΛƧa [táahkace] *be hot*. Some speakers use this verb with stative pronouns and others just use the continuous aspect marker to tell us which person they mean.

(69) ÁDÃ₷ΛƧa. OR DÃ₷ΛƧa ᴍηk₷á.
 ą́taahkace OR táahkace **mįkšé**
 I'm hot.

(70) DÃħṅ₷ΛƧa? OR DÃ₷ΛƧa ∠ηk₷á?
 taaðíhkace OR táahkace **nįkšé**
 Are **you** hot?

Some common DÃ [taa] verbs are DÃϹ₷Λ [táaską] *melt*, DÃϹᴨ˙ [táalį] *burn*, and DÃÞuƧa [táapuze] *dry*.

(71) Ó₷uϹΛ Λ₷ħΛ DÃÞuƧa Λ₷ħΛ.
 óhkula akxa táapuze akxai
 The clothes are drying.

(72) ∠ʎΨa Λ₷ħΛ DÃϹ₷Λ Þa.
 ną́ɣe akxa táaską pe
 The ice melted.

(73) ÞÃ Λ₷ħΛ DÃϹᴨ˙ Þa.
 htáa akxa táalį pe
 The meat burned.

𐒻𐓄'𐓂𐓤𐒷

Exercise 1. Do you understand?

What does this story mean?

𐓹𐓂𐓤𐓯𐓶 𐓍𐓘𐓸 𐓏𐓄𐓘 𐓍𐓘𐓧𐓲𐓘𐓸 𐓞𐓘𐓺𐓘 𐓯𐓻𐓘𐓤𐓬𐓤 𐓞𐓤𐓭𐓸 𐓹𐓶.
𐓘̨ 𐓬𐒻𐓷𐓘 𐓧𐓞𐓛𐓂𐓅𐓄𐓧 𐓡𐓞𐓻𐓂𐓅𐓘 𐓅𐓟𐓶 𐓤𐓂𐓯.
𐓬𐓲𐓻𐓞𐓤𐓘 𐓿𐓛𐓧𐓘 𐓤𐓂𐓯.
𐓂𐓶𐓜𐓘𐓨 𐓩𐓨𐓄𐓫𐓛𐓤𐓘 𐓞𐓘𐓸 𐓬𐓂𐓗𐓛𐓧 𐓺𐓘 𐓫𐓡𐓲𐓛𐓶 𐓫𐓡𐓶𐓟.

Exercise 2. Composition

Write a composition of six Osage sentences. Include at least one use of the prefixes 𐓂, 𐓋, or 𐓁, and one use of a verb containing an instrumental prefix.

Exercise 3. Prefixes

Go through the vocabulary lists and find four verbs that contain instrumental prefixes. Describe how the instrument forms part of the meaning. Do not use verbs that we have discussed already in this chapter.

Exercise 4. Instrumental 𐓂

Write four sentences, two of which use the instrumental 𐓂 *with* and two that use the accompaniment verb 𐓺𐓂𐓧𐓘.

𐒻𐓘

Nouns

𐓘̋𐓧𐒻̈	áalįį	chair
𐓡𐓘̋𐓘𐓬𐓤𐓯	háabrehka	ribbon, ribbons sewn on Osage clothing
𐓡𐒻̋𐒻𐓯𐓤𐓘 𐓷𐓘𐓬𐓂́𐓄'𐒻̨	hį́įska wanǫ́p'į	bead necklace
𐒻̋𐒻𐓤𐓘̈𐓘𐓅𐓞𐓘𐓨	íikaahtamą	bell
𐓨𐓘́𐓺𐓟 𐒻̨𐒻̋𐒻𐓯𐓬𐓛𐓪𐓘	máze įįštóolą	eyeglasses
𐓨𐓘́𐓺𐓟 𐓷𐓘̋𐓛𐓬̂𐓟𐓂̨	máze wéoohǫ	stove
𐓨𐒻̨𐒻𐓡𐓬𐓂́𐓟𐓧𐒻	mįįhtǫ́eli	gum
𐓂𐓡𐓤𐒻́𐓲𐓟	ohkísce	half (of anything)
𐓄𐓘́𐓲𐓟	páce	boat
𐓄𐒻́𐒻𐓲𐓟	hpéece	fire
𐓄𐓘́𐓺𐓟 𐓨𐓘̨𐓡𐓤𐓘́𐓲𐓘	hpéže mąhkása	tea
𐓄𐓘́𐓺𐓟𐓨𐒻̋𐒻	hpéženii	tea

𐓲𐓟́𐓹𐓟𐓩𐓣̄	céɣenii	drum
𐓲𐓟́𐓹𐓟𐓮𐓤𐓘	céɣeska	cup (variant)
𐓲𐓟́𐓹𐓟𐓮𐓤𐓘𐓻𐓣͘	céɣeskažį	small cup, tea cup
𐓳𐓟́𐓡𐓟𐓮𐓤𐓘	hcéheska	cup
𐓵𐓶̄𐓭𐓟̋𐓲𐓟	ðuuhpéece	lighter
𐓷𐓘́𐓬𐓘𐓹𐓘 𐓵𐓣𐓧𐓣́𐓧𐓣𐓟	wápaɣa ðilílie	brooch (sparkly pin for ribbon)
𐓷𐓘̋𐓴𐓟	wáache	skirt
𐓷𐓘̄𐓴𐓟́	waaché	skirt (variant)
𐓷𐓟́𐓵𐓣͘	wéðį	rope
𐓻𐓘̋𐓸𐓟	žą́ąxe	stick, pole

Verbs

𐓘́𐓧𐓟	ále (a-ða)	put on top of
𐓘́𐓻𐓶	ážu (a-ða)	set items out on something
𐓤𐓘̄𐓲𐓶́𐓸𐓟	kaacúxe (kaa-delete)	sweep
𐓩𐓘̋𐓯𐓰𐓘	ną́ąšta (a-ða)	stop (when walking or running)
𐓩𐓘̋𐓻𐓣͘	ną́ąžį (a-ða)	stand, stand up, step on
𐓩𐓪̋𐓭𐓟	nǫ́ǫhpe	(stative) be afraid (of)
𐓪̄𐓻𐓶́	oožú (a-ða)	pour/put into
𐓬𐓘𐓮𐓲𐓟́	pascé (a-ða)	cut into pieces, slices, strips
𐓬𐓘̄𐓸𐓲𐓟́	paaxcé	(strong-stem) tie down, gather in a bundle
𐓬𐓘̄𐓹𐓪́𐓟	paaɣóe (strong-stem)	push something or someone
𐓬𐓣́𐓹𐓘͘	píɣą (strong-stem)	blow on something
𐓬𐓪́𐓮𐓟	póse (a-ða)	cut by shooting
𐓬𐓪́𐓯𐓬𐓟	póšpe (a-ða)	shoot a piece out (of something)
𐓬𐓶́𐓤𐓸𐓘	púkxa (a-ða)	wipe something off, erase
𐓬𐓶𐓯𐓰𐓘́𐓡𐓘	puštáha (strong-stem)	iron (clothes)
𐓰𐓘̋𐓥𐓘𐓲𐓟	táahkace	(single-form/stative) be hot
𐓰𐓘̋𐓧𐓣͘	táalį (single-form)	burn
𐓰𐓘̋𐓬𐓶𐓺𐓟	táapuze (single-form)	dry
𐓰𐓘̋𐓮𐓤𐓘͘	táaską (single-form)	melt
𐓵𐓘̄𐓯𐓤𐓣́𐓤𐓟	ðaaškíke (br-šc)	chew
𐓵𐓣̄𐓯𐓶́𐓬𐓟	ðiišúpe (br-šc)	unlock, open
𐓵𐓣̄𐓸𐓪́͘ / 𐓵𐓶̄𐓸𐓪́͘	ðiixǫ́ / ðuuxǫ́ (br-šc)	break something with the hands
𐓵𐓶̄𐓥𐓘̋𐓨𐓘͘	ðuuhkáamą (br-šc)	ring a bell or doorbell
𐓻𐓪́𐓧𐓟	žóle (a-ða)	be with, accompany

Notes for Chapter 17

The linguistic term for the prefixes [i], [o], and [á] is *applicatives*. Quintero uses the term *locative* for these, although she acknowledges that usually they are not locatives in the typical way this term is used. We have avoided using any linguistic term for them.

In most forms, the prefixes [ðaa], [ðii], and [ðuu] seem to have been reanalyzed as belonging to the stem of brush verbs.

In addition to instrumentals, there are a number of derivational affixes in Osage that we did not have room to include.

The phrase [céɣenii paaxtá] means *tying a hide on a drum by pushing down on a rope*. Though this could be translated as *tie up* in English, in Osage there is a meaning of pushing *down* on the ropes.

We have listed *teenager* as a single word [hcékanǫǫ], but it appears in Quintero's dictionary as two words, [hcéka nǫ́ǫ].

Chapter 18

More about Plurals

Oꜧṅꜧna

1. **ꜱʌꜧóƺa:** Þǎ, ᴅōꜧǎ, ÞⱭᴅʌ́, ÞʌꜧⱭ́—ᒍóꜱʌ ꜧṅᒍō ÞʌꜧⱭ́?
2. **ꜱʌꜧṅOÞᴧʌꜧa 1:** Þǎ ʌ́ᒍō. ÞⱭᴅʌ Ɫñᴢu ꜧᴅʌ. ĈōᒍōÞʌ ʌ́ⱫʌꜧÇ'ơ ꜧóa ⱫŐ ꜱʌⱫⱭ́ƺa ÞóÞa ʌ́ᒍō. ℱʌ́ᴢʌ ℱʌ́ᒍṅ ÞóᒍO ʌᒍṅ ꜧꜧп.
3. **ꜱʌꜧṅOÞᴧʌꜧa 2:** ᴅōꜧǎ ʌ́ᒍō. ᴅʌÞóᴄꜧʌ ÞʌⱫǎ ꜧóa ℱʌ̄ꜧƺǎ ʌꜧᴧʌ. ʌ́ꜧOᴅʌ ʌꜧꜧʌƺa ʌ́ᒍō ʌᒍṅꜧʌ ꜧꜧп.
4. **ꜱʌꜧóƺa:** ᒍóꜱʌ ꜧṅᒍō ⱫOꜧꜧǎ?
5. **ꜱʌꜧṅOÞᴧʌꜧa 3:** ÞⱭ̄ᴅʌ́ ᴢʌ́Þa ʌÞʌ OÞʌ́ƺʌ ꜧṅꜧa ⱫʌÞa. ꜧʌ́ƺaⱫ̄ ᴅʌ̄ꜧƺÚƺa ꜧṅꜧʌ ʌ́ᒍō.
6. **ꜱʌꜧṅOÞᴧʌꜧa 4:** ꜱṅa ℱOꜧꜧǎ. ÞʌꜧⱭ́ ʌ́ᒍō. Ɫṅꜱʌƺa ǎᴅᴧʌ ꜧóa ÞʌᒍÚꜧa ʌ́ᒍō. ᒍʌ̄ᴄꜧʌ́ ꜧōꜧʌ́ ꜧƺÚƺa ℱп ꜧóa Þʌ ʌꜧṅꜧꜧʌƺa.

1. **Teacher:** Spring, summer, fall, winter—which do you all like?
2. **Student 1:** I like spring. It rains a lot. I like listening to the thunder and looking at the lightning. And the land becomes green.
3. **Student 2:** I like summer. School is out and it's hot and sunny. I like to play outdoors and swim.
4. **Teacher:** Which do you like?
5. **Student 3:** In the fall the leaves become beautiful. I like smelling warm apple cider.
6. **Student 4:** It's my turn and I like winter. I like when it's cold and snowing. I wear my warm sweatshirt and play in the snow.

Ṅa ꜱʌꜧṅᴄʌ̄ƺa

Students have probably noticed that in Osage we do not mark nouns with anything that makes them plural, the way we do with the letter *s* in English. We have stated that nouns can be interpreted as either singular or plural depending on context, and we can use aspect markers to tell us whether subjects are singular and plural. We have introduced many plural pronouns. But we have not talked about ways that noun phrases may be plural besides context. (A noun phrase is a noun and the words that go with it. For example, *cat* is a noun, and *the big cat* is a noun phrase.) In this chapter we will learn three ways to do this. One is by joining noun phrases. Another is by adding words that name quantity: numbers like *two* or *three*, or words like *some* and *many*. A third is to use a very special kind of Siouan construction, *position markers*, which will be explained below.

Joining noun phrases

In English we have the very handy word *and* that allows us to put together long strings of noun phrases and sentences. In Osage we may simply put one noun phrase after the other, as in examples 1 and 2.

(1) háaci wihcíko iihkó apa waachí apai
Last night, my grandfather and my grandmother were dancing.

(2) šítoži šímįžį apa ilóeži óžąke áðuuhta ðuxí apai
The boy and the girl were chasing the cat across the road.

Using ški [ški] *also, too, as well as*

We sometimes use ški [ški] to join noun phrases. This word will appear after the nouns (or noun phrases), not between them.

(3) tóoleži máążąxe **ški** brúwį
I bought carrots **as well as** onions.

When we use ški [ški], we are saying something like English *and*, so we could also put example 3 into English as *carrots and onions* or *carrots and onions too* or *carrots and also onions*.
Many speakers use ški [ški] by placing it at the end of a sentence, as an afterthought, as shown in 4.

(4) mąhkása hkóbra mįkšé wacúe skúe **ški**
I want coffee, and cake **too**.

ški [ški] can also be used in strings of adjectives, as in example 5.

(5) wažíka ðe akxa ska ohtáza **ški** akxai
That bird is white **and also** beautiful.

Recall from chapter 17 that the verb žóla [žóle] *be with* is also used to join noun phrases.

Words that name quantity: numbers, 𝈓𐒵𐓧𐒹 [háaną], 𐓏𐓘 [wį], 𐓈𐓪𐓘 [tóe], forms of 𐓍𐓰 [húu], 𐓛𐓧𐓶 [záani]

Numbers

If we use a number greater than one with a noun, that noun will of course be plural. In Osage, we have different ways of treating plurals depending on whether the plural noun is definite, meaning pointed out, or not definite, meaning not specific. In examples 6 and 7, the plural nouns are not specific.

(6) 𐒻𐒽𐓋𐒿𐓧 𐒹𐓘𐒰𐒼𐓘 𐒻𐒹𐓧𐒹𐓘.
    ichóka ðáabri iiðáðe
    I saw three mice.

(7) 𐓮𐒻𐓈𐓪𐓲𐓘 𐒹𐓬𐓀𐓧 𐓈𐒰𐒹𐓘𐓲𐒰 𐒹𐓶𐒼𐒻 𐓧𐓬𐓧.
    šítoži ðǫ́ǫpa htáhtaze ðuxí apai
    Two boys were chasing grasshoppers.

Notice that in example 7, we do not use the subject marker 𐓧𐓬𐓧 [apa] with the subject 𐓮𐒻𐓈𐓪𐓲𐓘 𐒹𐓬𐓀𐓧 [šítoži ðǫ́ǫpa] *two boys*. This is because Osage subject markers are used for definite noun phrases. In example 7, we are just saying that there were two boys who were chasing the grasshoppers. If we had already been talking about the two boys, as in the following example, we do use a subject marker.

(8) 𐓮𐒻𐓈𐓪𐓲𐓘 𐒹𐓬𐓀𐓧 𐓧𐓬𐓧 𐓈𐒰𐒹𐓘𐓲𐒰 𐒹𐓶𐒼𐒻 𐓧𐓬𐓧.
    šítoži ðǫ́ǫpa apa htáhtaze ðuxí apai
    The two boys were chasing the grasshoppers. (Context: we have been talking about the two boys already.)

When we add the subject marker 𐓧𐓬𐓧 [apa] to the same sentence, we now say that there are two boys already mentioned or known: **the** *two boys*. This is similar to what we would do in English: *two boys* versus *the two boys*. We show this again in 9 and 10.

(9) 𐓮𐓪𐒼𐓘 𐒹𐓘𐒰𐒼𐓘 𐓫𐓧𐓮𐓲𐓀𐒼𐓧𐓲𐓘 𐒹𐓘𐒰𐒼𐓘 𐒹𐓶𐒼𐒻 𐓧𐓬𐓧.
    šóke ðą́ąbri mąšcíkaži ðáabri ðuxí apai
    Three dogs were chasing three bunnies.

(10) 𐓮𐓪𐒼𐓘 𐒹𐓘𐒰𐒼𐓘 𐓧𐓬𐓧 𐓫𐓧𐓮𐓲𐓀𐒼𐓧𐓲𐓘 𐒹𐓘𐒰𐒼𐓘 𐒹𐓶𐒼𐒻 𐓧𐓬𐓧.
    šóke ðą́ąbri apa mąšcíkaži ðáabri ðuxí apai
    The three dogs were chasing three bunnies. (Context: we have been talking about the three dogs already.)

𝈓𐒵𐓧𐒹 [háaną] *how many*

Question words like 𝈓𐒵𐓧𐒹 [háaną] *how many* are asking about something plural. If 𝈓𐒵𐓧𐒹 [háaną] is asking about the subject of a sentence, like 11 below, we treat it like a plural subject, as above (without a subject marker). Remember from chapter 12 that sentences with question words do not need an aspect marker.

(11) ᏩᎫᏤᎦ **ᎭᎠᏁ** ᏛᎠ ᎣᏏᏂᎦᎠ?
wakóze háaną pa ođíhką
How many teachers helped you?

We can answer this question with a plural subject too, as in 12 below.

(12) ᏩᎫᏤᎦ ᏂᎤᏛᎠ ᎣᎪᎦᎠ ᏛᎠ.
wakóze ðǫǫpá oáhką pe
Two teachers helped me.

ᏥᏂ [wį] *a, one of*

We have been using ᏥᏂ [wį] *a* throughout this book, but we have not used it yet to mark a subject. Because ᏥᏂ [wį] is not definite, subjects with ᏥᏂ [wį] will not use a subject marker.

(13) ᎣᏏᏂᎠᎠ ᏥᏂ ᎢᏛᎦᎠ ᏛᎠ.
ođíhtą wį ípša pe
A car came by.

If we do use a subject marker with ᏥᏂ [wį], it will pick out one from a group, as in the following example.

(14) ᏩᎫᎣ ᏥᏂ ᎠᎦᎠᎠ ᎣᏥᎦ ᎣᏐ ᎠᎦᎠᎠ.
wak'ó wį akxa ówe oohǫ́ akxai
One of the women is cooking vegetables.

ᏙᏍᎦ [tóe] *some*

One very common way to mark plural noun phrases is with ᏙᏍᎦ [tóe] *some*. By its meaning, it is always plural and never definite, so when it is used in the subject, it will not take a subject marker. Do not confuse ᏙᏍᎦ [tóe] with ᏙᏍᎠ [tówa] *that one* or *those* from chapter 13.

(15) ᏎᏂᏮᏁᏃ **ᏙᏍᎦ** ᎩᏂᎦᏁᏃ ᏂᎤᎲᎥ ᎠᏛᎥ.
šímižį **tóe** kįįkįįežį ðuxí apai
Some girls chased butterflies.

(16) ᏞᏁᎦᎴᏁᎦ **ᏙᏍᎦ** ᎥᎠ ᎥᎡᎠᏛ ᎦᎥᎣᏛᎠᎠ.
níhkašie **tóe** íe íhtapi kíopxa
Some people understand their language.

(17) ᏎᎭᎣᏃᎦ **ᏙᏍᎦ** ᎥᏂᎠᎭᎦ
héeoce **tóe** iiðáðe
I saw **some** monkeys.

ᏑᎤ [húu] and its variants ᏑᎤᎠᏰᎵᎠ [huuhtáka], ᏑᎤᏥᏓᏂ [huuwáli], ᏑᎤᏃ [húuži]

There are several ways to say *many* or *a lot*. They are based on ᏑᎤ [húu], which can be used alone or compounded with ᎠᏰᎵᎠ [htáka] *really big* or ᏥᏓᏂ [wáli] *very much*. These words can be used with nouns or can stand by themselves.

(18) ᎹᏎᏍᎧᎠ **ᏑᎤ** ᎠᏍᏥᎢ.
    mázeska **húu** ąscį́
    You have **a lot of** money.

(19) **ᏑᎤᎠᏰᎵᎠ** ᎣᎲᎵᎲᎠ ᎠᎻᎠ.
    huuhtáka ohkíhkie apai
    A lot of them were talking.

(20) ᏃᎬᎪᏃ **ᏑᎤᏥᏓᏂ** ᎠᎦᎼᏍᎧᎠ ᏏᏂ ᎹᏗᎢ ᏂᎢ ᏓᎠᎠ.
    žįkážį **huuwáli** taapóska ci mądį́ ðée nape
    Many / a lot of children (usually) walk to school.

As we have seen previously, if we place a subject marker in a phrase with a ᏑᎤ [húu] word, we make the subject definite.

(21) ᏂᎠ ᏃᎬᎪᏃ ᏑᎤᏥᏓᏂ **ᎠᎻᎠ** ᎠᎦᎼᏍᎧᎠ ᏏᏂ ᎹᏗᎢ ᏂᎢ ᏍᎠᎻ.
    ðe žįkážį húuwali **apa** taapóska ci mądį́ ðée štą
    That bunch of children always walks to school.

ᏑᎤᏃ [húuži] means *a little bit* or *a few*.

(22) ᏥᏂᎢᏥᎠᏃ **ᏑᎤᏃ** ᎠᏒᎢ
    waðáawažį **húužį** abrį́
    I have **a little bit** of change.

ᏃᎢᏂ [záani] *all, everyone, everything*

(23) ᎧᏍᏪᎣᎦᎠ **ᏃᎢᏂ** ᎪᏗᎠ ᎠᎧᎻᎠ.
    kašpéǫpa **záani** kǫ́ða akxai
    He wants **all** the quarters.

(24) ᏓᎻᎯᎧᎠ **ᏃᎢᏂ** ᎢᏏᎠᏑ?
    lápxąąke **záani** íiðaðe
    Did you see **all** the mosquitoes?

(25) **ᏃᎢᏂ** ᎠᏏ ᎠᎠ.
    záani aðáa pe
    Everyone went there.

The adverbs ᏥᏓᏂ [wálį] and ᏍᏏᏂ [xci]

These two adverbs are both used to mean *very* and *really* and other similar emphatic expressions. ᏥᏓᏂ [wálį] and ᏍᏏᏂ [xci] can both be used in verb phrases or with adjectives that are in the predicate. The difference between them is that ᏎᎯᏓᏗ [wáli̧] is placed before the verb, and ᏣᏴᏂ [xci] is placed after the verb or adjective.

(26) ᏣᎤᎩᎸ ᏍᎠ ᎪᎩᏣᎸ **ᏎᎯᏓᏗ** ᏎᎯᏂᎤ ᏣᎯᏓᏗ ᎪᎩᏣᎸ.
xóhka ðe akxa **wáli̧** waaðǫ́ ðáali̧ akxai
Those singers are **really** singing well.

(27) ᏧᎯᏴ ᏎᎪᏴᏌ ᏣᏛᏁᏍᎩᎸ ᏣᎯᏴᏌ **ᏎᎯᏓᏗ** ᎥᏣᎯᏓᏗ
háazu wacúe ðubráaska ðaaché **wáli̧** ą́ðali̧
I **really** like to eat grape dumplings.

(28) ᏞᏂᎩᎸ ᏎᏁᎠᎸ ᎪᎩᏣᎸ **ᏎᎯᏓᏗ** ᏃᏲᏌ ᏞᎪ.
níhka wíhta akxa **wáli̧** ží̧i̧he ną
My husband sleeps **a lot.**

(29) ᏎᎯᏂᎤ ᏣᎯᏓᏗ **ᏣᏴᏂ** ᎪᎩᏣᎸ.
waaðǫ́ ðą́ali̧ **xci** akxai
She sings **extremely** well.

(30) **ᏎᎯᏓᏗ** ᏞᏂᏎᎸᏴᎠ ᎪᎩᏣᏆ.
wáli̧ níwahce akxái
It's **very** cold (weather).

(31) ᏧᎯᎠᎸ ᏍᎠ ᎶᎯᏫᎠ ᎦᎠᎩᎩ **ᏣᏴᏂ** ᎪᎩᏣᎸ.
hą́apa ðe mą́aye štáke **xci** akxa
It was **very** mild weather today.

Note that only ᏣᏴᏂ [xci] can be used with adjectives in a noun phrase. It is placed after the adjective. In 32, ᎶᎯᏣᎠᎠ ᎦᎸᏴᎠ **ᏣᏴᏂ** ᏎᏂ [máxpu šápe **xci** wi̧] *a very dark cloud*, is a noun phrase, and in 33, ᏦᎪᏎᎸ ᏎᎪᏧᎤᎦᎩᏴᎸᏍ **ᏣᏴᏂ** ᏎᏂ [hkáwa wahóščaži̧ **xci** wi̧] *a very tiny horse* is a noun phrase.

(32) ᎶᎯᏣᎠᎠ ᎦᎸᏴᎠ **ᏣᏴᏂ** ᏎᏂ ᏂᏣᎸᏣᎠ.
máxpu šápe **xci** wi̧ iiðáðe
I saw a **very** dark cloud.

(33) ᏦᎪᏎᎸ ᏎᎪᏧᎤᎦᎩᏴᎸᏍ **ᏣᏴᏂ** ᏎᏂ ᎶᎪᏧᏂ ᏣᎯᏴᎠ ᎪᏆᎥ.
hkáwa wahóščaži̧ **xci** wi̧ mą́ahí̧ ðaaché apai
A **very** tiny horse was eating hay.

αᏴᏂ [ecí] *there is, there are, be or exist here/there*

An important verb is αᏴᏂ [ecí], which usually corresponds to English *there is* and *there are*. This verb only has a single-form verb since it does not ever use pronouns. We don't use a subject marker with αᏴᏂ [ecí].

(34) ᎠᎯᏃᎯᏞᏂ ᏞᎯᏫᎠᎣᏃᏴ αᏴᏂ ᏴᎠ.
paazénii ná̧yeoožu ecí che
There is milk in the refrigerator. (I have evidence of this.)

(35) 𐓋𐓘𐓤𐓘 𐓪𐓂𐓬𐓘́ 𐓘́𐓮𐓣𐓩𐓯𐓘 𐓜𐓎𐓣́ 𐓘𐓬𐓘.
   máka ðǫǫpá ášihta ecí apa
   There are two skunks outside.

𐓜𐓎𐓣́ [ecí] can also mean *be there*. In the following example, we understand *you* from the aspect marker 𐓩𐓣𐓤𐓮𐓘́ [nįkšé] because 𐓜𐓎𐓣́ [ecí] takes no pronouns.

(36) 𐓜𐓎𐓣́ 𐓬𐓘 𐓩𐓣𐓤𐓮𐓘́?
   ecí hta nįkšé
   Will you be there?

Position markers

The Siouan languages all have position markers that are used to note the position that something is in, and in many cases, whether that thing is animate (alive) or inanimate (not alive). Osage has many of these, though some have been let go as the language evolved. The position markers are optional, but they are very much part of the language of fluent speakers, and they help comprehension. Note that they are not used with subjects of sentences—for those we use the subject markers 𐓘𐓤𐓬𐓘 [akxa] and 𐓘𐓬𐓘 [apa]. Another fact about position markers is that their use is evolving.

Osage position markers

𐓣𐓤𐓮𐓘́ [įkšé] (or 𐓭𐓣𐓤𐓮𐓘́ [ðįkšé])	sitting, round	animate and inanimate
𐓊𐓬𐓘 [txą]	standing	animate
𐓮𐓘 [che]	standing, upright, vertical	inanimate
𐓤𐓮𐓘 [kše]	lying, horizontal, long, spread out	animate and inanimate
𐓬𐓘 [pa]	plural sitting, standing, moving	animate
𐓤𐓘 [ke]	plural scattered, dispersed	animate and inanimate

You may find that the position markers remind you of the continuous aspect markers. There is a historical connection in the development of the aspect markers from the position markers, but their uses have diverged greatly. You have probably also noticed that the location words from chapter 4 sometimes are based on position markers.

Also note that we have a third use for 𐓮𐓘 [che]. Do not confuse the position marker 𐓮𐓘 [che] with the evidential marker (chapter 2) or the connector (chapter 15).

In the old usage for Siouan languages, inanimate objects were classified according to their shape, and assigned a position marker. But modern Osage speakers do not use the position markers to classify all objects. Instead, speakers use the position markers only when they need to contrast an object with others or to clarify which object they refer to. Fluent speakers can use position markers to express a large range of subtle differences in how they perceive a situation. This communication is about how the speaker wishes the hearer to interpret a situation, not about classifying objects.

Let's look at some examples of sentences with position markers and their contexts. In 37 and 38, the speaker is using position markers in order to point out a man who might not be known and can be contrasted with other people who are also in the area.

(37) ⌇ńƙʌ **ⁿƙႽȧ** ńꝁʌꝁɑ.
níhka **įkšé** íiðaðe
Do you see the man **sitting there**?

(38) ⌇ńƙʌ **ᴅ⋔ⱴ** ńꝁʌꝁɑ.
níhka **txą** íiðaðe
Do you see the man **standing there**?

In the example below, ⁿƙႽȧ [įkšé] is used to pick out and indicate the position of a noun *that is not the subject*. So position markers always pick out a thing and give more information about it.

(39) ⱴʌƙʌႽᴅơ **ⁿƙႽȧ** ƙʌⱴʌ ⱴ⌇ʌ.
wákaštǫ **įkšé** hkáwa áala
Put the saddle blanket (**sitting there**) on the horse.

In the following example, **ɛɑ** [che], the standing position marker for inanimate things might be used if there is a saltshaker among some other things far down the table.

(40) ⌇ńcƙuɑ **ɛɑ** ⌇úƙāψʌ.
níiskue **che** húkaaɣa
Pass me the salt (**standing**).

ƘႽɑ [kše], like ⁿƙႽȧ [įkšé] and ꝁⁿƙႽȧ [ðįkšé], can be used for both animate and inanimate things.

Contrast the situations in the following two examples. In 41, I'm describing my own dog using the verb [óžą] *lie on*. In 42, the use of ƘႽɑ [kše] points out an unknown dog that is lying down. There may be other dogs, or ƘႽɑ [kše] may simply emphasize that the dog is unknown.

(41) Mick Ⴝóƙɑ ⱴńᴅʌ ʌƙ⋔ʌ ʌ⌇ʌƙoɑ ʌzʌ ʌƙ⋔ʌ.
Mick šǫ́ke wíhta akxa ánąąhkoe ážą akxai
My dog Mick is lying on the porch.

(42) Ⴝóƙɑ **ƘႽɑ** oⱼʌ!
šǫ́ke **kše** olá
Chase away the dog **lying there**!

The two position markers Þʌ [pa] and Ƙɑ [ke] are always plural. Þʌ [pa] is used with objects that are alive, in any position. In example 43, Þʌ [pa] makes ⱴʌƙ'ó [wak'ó] *woman* plural. Context may also tell us that the noun phrase is plural.

(43) wak'ó **pa** óhką hkóbra mįkšé
    I want to help those **women**.

In 44, ke [ke] indicates that the objects are both plural and distributed or scattered. If we leave out ke [ke], we might be talking about a single blanket.

(44) haxį **ke** opetxá
    Wrap up **those** blankets (that are lying around)!

Painting pictures with position markers

Remember that the position markers are typically used in a context where both the speaker and the hearer can see the situation. This allows speakers to use position markers to paint a picture of the idea the speaker wants to communicate.

Returning to the example of blankets, and in the context of two speakers in a room with a blanket or blankets, a speaker could say [haxį įkšé] to point out a particular blanket, *the blanket sitting there*. If there were multiple blankets, the speaker could say [haxį che]. This would indicate that the blankets were stacked up and formed a vertical, standing pile. The speaker could also say [haxį ke] as we saw above, meaning that blankets were scattered around.

Using position markers this way can become metaphorical for some speakers. For example, we typically use [kše] for something horizontal or long like a *stick*; however, if we bundled sticks together, we might end up with a round bundle of sticks, and we could express that by using [įkšé], which is used for round or sitting things: [žáą įkšé], *a bundle of sticks*. We typically use [che] for standing things, like a house, but if we use [kše] with the word *house*, [hci kše], we are suggesting that there is a row or line of houses or that the house is perceived as particularly long and rectangular.

Modern speakers are far less likely to use a single position marker to classify a word and far more likely to describe an object's position as they perceive it in context.

Exercise 1. Do you understand?

What does this short story mean?

Exercise 2. Composition

Write a composition of six Osage sentences. Include at least three uses of plural noun phrases.

Exercise 3. Sentences

Write a sentence using each of these Osage words:

1. ᏍᏬᎾ
2. ᏏᏫ
3. ᎠᎣᎠ
4. a form of Ꮝᘆ
5. ᎶᘆᏞᎾ
6. ᏍᎯᏞᏫ
7. ᎶᏜᎾ

Exercise 4. Context

Give the context for what a speaker might mean in using these position markers in these sentences.

1. ÓᏞᎣᎦᎪ ᎯᎠ ÁᎬᎤ.
2. ᏍᎶÓᎦᎪ ᎠÓᏍᘆ Ꭰᘆ ÁᎭᘆᏞᎾᎽᘆᎬᎾ.

ńa

Nouns

Ꮝṍ	hóo	voice
ᏍűᎬᏫ	húužį	a bit, a few
ᏦᘆᏍᎠᎣᎠᘆ	kašpéǫpa	quarter (coin)
ᎿÁᎻᎠ	máxpu	cloud
ᏞÁᏪᎠōᎬᎤ	náɣeoožu	refrigerator
ᏞńᏍᘆᏍᎣ	níhkašie	person, people, human
ᏞńᏍᘆᏍᎾ	níhkaši	person, people, human (variant)
óᎬᘆᏦᎠ	óžąke	road
ᏍÁᏦᘆᏍᎠᏫ	wákaštǫ	saddle blanket
ᏍᘆᎲÁᏍᘆᎬᏫ	waðáawažį̨	coins, change
ᎬᘆᏞᎽᎣ	žą̄ąníe	sugar (variant)

Verbs

ÁᎬᘆ	ážą (a-ða)	lie on
ᏍᎤᏦÁᏪᎠ	hukáaɣe (strong-stem)	pass (e.g., the salt)

ÍԺᏕα	ípše (i-stem)	come by, pass by
ḳÍOÞʌʌ	kíopxa (ki-stative)	understand
ᄂՈʌᎿα	níwahce (single-form)	it's cold (weather)

Adjectives

ᏕΛÞα	šápe	dark
ᏕÐΛḳα	štáke	mild

Other

ΛᏕՈƉΛ	ášihta	outside
ΛᏕḳΛ	áška	nearby
ΛᏕḳΛ ᏃՈ	áška ci	near (something)
ΛħŪƉΛ	áðuuhta	across
ᒍű	húu	many, lots
ᒍŪƉΛḳΛ	huuhtáka	a large number of
ᒍŪʌΛᏟՈ	huuwáli	a lot of
ᒍűᏃՈ	húuži̧	a bit of, a few of
ᏕḳՈ	ški	also, too, and
ÐÓα	tóe	some, any
ʌΛᏟՈ	wáli̧	very, really
ʌՈ	wi̧	a
ħᏃՈ	xci	real, very, precisely

Notes for Chapter 18

Recall from chapter 4 that location words have to reflect the position of objects. So the location word [i̧kši] *in* was needed for objects that are round, like ponds. [i̧kši] is based on [i̧kšé] *round* or *sitting*.

Historically, Siouan languages, including Osage, had a paradigm for marking plurals by repurposing position markers. For example, singular objects taking [i̧kšé] would use [che] for plural. This system requires that speakers know the assigned position marker for objects. In Osage, this system is no longer robust.

Chapter 19

More about Word Formation: Causatives, ϟʌ [wa], and Compounding

Oꝁńꝁnɑ

1. **ϟnɾá:** ɾʌ̋ᵽʌ ϟʌꝁʌ̇ᴅʌ́ƙn ńɱʌƨɑ ϟnƶńƙɑ n̄ᴅʌ́Ћʌᵽɑ ɑ́ƙnᴅфʌ̇ ʌƙфʌ.
2. ϟnƨńɱn ʌᵽʌ ꞩʌ̋ƙɑōɕʌ̇ƙ'ȯ ƙꞩńψɑ Ɖʌ ʌᵽʌ.
3. Ōɾȯ́ ϟʌƉʌ́ƙʌ ɱnƙꞩɑ́ ƨɑ ɑ̋ ʌᵽʌ.
4. Ɑ̋ n̄Ћʌ́ɕʌ̇ɾn.
5. ʌ̋Ћnфoᵽɑ ʌƙфʌ ϟɑ̋ʌɕʌ̇ ɱnƙꞩɑ́.
6. **ʌϛńƙʌ:** ᴅʌ̋ᴅʌ̇ ōЋʌ́ɾʌ̇ Ћnƙȯ́Ћʌ?
7. **ϟnɾá:** ϟʌƨúɑ ƙʌ̄ϛƨú, Ɖʌ̋ϟɑɕn, ϛúꝁʌ Ɖʌ̄ɕn̋ ϟʌƨúɑ ϛʌ́ϛʌ ƶóɕɑ, ɾʌ̋ʔu ϟʌƨúɑ Ћuʁʌ̋ϛƙʌ, ɾȯʁńƙɑ Ɖóɾo.
8. n̄ɕʌ̇́ ʌƙфʌ ɾʌ́ᵽʌ ƙʌ̋ψɑ ƨɑ ɱȯ́ᵽꞩɑ ƙnϛúЋɑ ʌᵽʌ ɑ́ƙnʌ ᵽɑ.
9. Ɑ̋ᴅʌɕʌ ᵽʌ̄ꞩᵽú ōɾȯ́ ꝁȯ́ʁʌ ɱnƙꞩɑ́.
10. n̄ɾȯ́ ʌƙфʌ ᵽɑ́ƶɑƉoɾo ʌЋńʌƨn ɑ́ƙnɑ, ƙóɑ n̄ꝁó ϟʌƨúɑ ϛƙúɑ ƙʌ̋ψɑ Ɖʌ ʌƙфʌ.
11. **ʌϛńƙʌ:** Ᵽɑ̋ óꝁʌ̇ ƨɑ ɑ́ꞩɑ?
12. **ϟnɾá:** ϟnƶȯ́ʌ̇ Ɖʌ̋ϟɑɕn, ɾȯʁńƙɑ Ɖóɾo ƙʌ̋ψɑ ƨɑ ɑ́ᵽꞩɑ Ɖʌ ɱnƙꞩɑ́.
13. ϟnƶȯ́ƙɑ ϟʌƨúɑ ƙʌ̄ϛƨú ƙʌ̋ψɑ ꝁȯ́ʁʌ.
14. ϟnƉʌ́ɑƶn̈ ϛúꝁʌ Ɖʌ̄ɕn̋ ϟʌƨúɑ ϛʌ́ϛʌ ƶóɕɑ ꞩƙʌ̋ψɑ?
15. **ʌϛńƙʌ:** ʌ̋ɾʌ́.
16. **ϟnɾá:** Ᵽʌ̄ꞩᵽú ɾʌ̋ʔu ϟʌƨúɑ Ћuʁʌ̋ϛƙʌ ᵽʌ̋ψɑ Ɖʌ ɱnƙꞩɑ́.
17. Ꞩńɱnƶn̈ ʌᵽʌ ɾn̋ƨɑ ʌ́ƶu Ɖʌ ʌᵽʌ.
18. Ћʌ̋ɕn̈ Ɖʌ ʌƙфʌ.

1. **Second daughter:** Next week it's Sonny's birthday.
2. Our aunt (father's side) is going to have a handgame for him.
3. She asked me to be the head cook.
4. I agreed (to that).
5. She honored me, and I am thankful.
6. **Third daughter:** What does she want you to cook?

7. **Second daughter:** Frybread, steam fry, chicken and dumplings, grape dumplings, and green beans.
8. Mama said to make a corn dish in remembrance of our ancestors.
9. So, I want to cook ᏯᏁᎦᏮᎿ. (ᏯᏁᎦᏮᎿ [paašpú] is a corn dish.)
10. His mother said she is going to bring a salad, and his grandmother is going to make the cake.
11. **Third daughter:** Who are you going to ask to help?
12. **Second daughter:** I am going to ask (older) sister to make the steam fry and green beans.
13. I want my daughter to make frybread.
14. Younger Sister, will you make chicken and dumplings?
15. **Third daughter:** Yes.
16. **Second daughter:** I will make the ᏯᏁᎦᏮᎿ and grape dumplings.
17. The girls are going to set the table.
18. It will be good.

A handgame is a guessing game that also involves dancing and food. It is for lifting our spirits and celebrating important occasions. Here, a family is preparing to celebrate a birthday.

Ńa ᏑᏁᏦńᏓᏁꝫα

We often need to talk about making or causing something to happen. In English, we can add a suffix such as *-ize* to a word like *random*, giving us *randomize*, meaning *to make random*. We can also build a phrase like *make X do Y*, as in "Fred made me spill my soup." And in some words the causation is inherent. For example, *kill* means *cause to die*.

Osage has two primary ways to form a sentence with a causative meaning. One way is with the use of a causative marker ᏂᎪ [ðe], which will create a new verb. The second way is with the use of verbs that mean *make* or *allow*, like what we do in English.

In this chapter we also discuss how to use ᏄᏁ [wa] with verbs to build sentences that do not need to have an object. We briefly introduced this concept when we talked about the uses of ᏄᏁ [wa] in chapter 9.

Finally, we look at ways of making new words by changing them from verbs to nouns and also by combining two words.

Causatives

Verbs made with causative ᏂᎪ [ðe]

One way that Osage makes words that have causative meanings is by placing ᏂᎪ [ðe] as the final syllable of a verb. We have seen this in the verb ꞌᎪᏂᎪ [cʼéðe] *kill*, which combines ꞌᎪ [cʼe], meaning *die*, with causative ᏂᎪ [ðe]. Do not confuse causative ᏂᎪ [ðe] with ᏂᎪ [ðe] *that* or the declarative evidential ᏂᎪ [ðe]. The following example is from chapter 3.

(1) ᏞᏁᏦᏞ ᏞᏥᏂᏞ ᎠᏁ Ꭼ'ᎠᏂᎠ ᏞᎠᏞ.
    níhka akxa htáa c'éðe apai.
    The man is killing the deer.

Other Ꮒα [ðe]-causative verbs are ᏂᎠᏂα [ðeeðe] *send* and ᏕᎤᏂα [húðe] *hand over, pass*.

(2) ᎢᎠᏞᎬᎾ ᏞᎠᏞ ᏫᏞᏣ7α ᏫᎢ ᏂᎠᏂα ᎠᏞ ᏞᎠᏞ.
    i̧htáci apa waléze wi̧ ðeeðe hta apa
    My father will send a letter.
(3) ᏫᏞᎬᎤα ᏕᎤᏂᎠ.
    wacúe huðá
    Pass the bread.

The Ꮒα [ðe]-causative verb class

It is important to note that Ꮒα [ðe]-causative verbs form their own verb class. They use ᏞᏂᏞ [a-ða] pronouns, but those pronouns appear right before Ꮒα [ðe], not at the start of the verb. We show this in the following examples.

(4) ᏬᎾᎴᎾᏦᏞᏕα ᏫᎢ Ꭼ'αᏞᏂα.
    šǫmi̧hkase wi̧ c'eaðe
    I killed a coyote.
(5) ᏫαᏂᎤᏬᎤᎠα ᏕᎤᏂᏞᏂα.
    wéðušupe huðaðe
    Did **you** hand me the keys?
(6) ᏫᏞᏣ7α ᏂᎠᏂᏂα ᎠᏞ ᎿᎾᏦᏣα.
    waléze ðeeáðe hta mi̧kšé
    I will send the letter.
(7) ᏫᏞᏣ7α ᏕᎤ ᏂαᏞᏂᏞᎠα.
    waléze húu ðeáðape
    We sent a lot of letters.

One interesting example of a Ꮒα [ðe]-causative verb is the relationship between the stative verb ᎣᏂᎠᏞᏂα [oxpáðe] *get lost, be lost* and its causative partner ᎣᏂᎠᏞᏂαᏂα [oxpáðeðe] *lose something*. We can see that to lose something is to cause it to be lost.

(8) ᎣᏂᎠᏞᏂᏞ Ꭰα.
    oxpáða pe
    She got lost.

Remember that the stative pronouns appear after the first o, as we see below.

(9) ᎣᏞᏂᎠᏞᏂα.
    oáxpaðe
    I got lost.

(10) 𐓀𐓧𐓄𐓘𐓧𐓐𐓘.
    oðíxpaðe
    You got lost.

However, be careful to place the pronouns for the causative 𐓀𐓘𐓄𐓧𐓐𐓘𐓧𐓐𐓘 [oxpádeðe] *lose something* before the final 𐓐𐓘 [ðe]-syllable.

(11) 𐓷𐓟𐓧𐓤𐓱𐓯𐓟 𐓀𐓘𐓄𐓧𐓐𐓘𐓧𐓐𐓘.
    wéðušupe oxpádea**ð**e
    I lost the keys.

(12) 𐓍𐓘𐓘𐓰𐓴𐓬𐓲𐓟 𐓷𐓲𐓬𐓘 𐓀𐓘𐓄𐓧𐓐𐓘**𐓐**𐓧𐓐𐓘.
    haaskámį wíhta oxpáde**ð**aðe
    You lost my shawl.

(13) 𐓣𐓘𐓰𐓟𐓯𐓤𐓧 𐓰𐓘𐓘𐓠𐓲 𐓀𐓘𐓄𐓧𐓐𐓘**𐓧**𐓐𐓧**𐓄**𐓘.
    mázeska záani oxpádea̜ða**pe**
    We lost all the money.

Causatives made with clauses

Osage also forms causative expressions with clauses, like we do in English. This means the sentence will have two clauses, one with the causative verb, usually *make* or *have*, and one that says what was made to happen. This kind of sentence is done with no connectors between the clauses, as explained in chapter 15.

Three common Osage verbs that make causative clauses are 𐓤𐓘𐓘𐓻𐓘 [káaɣe] *make*, which we are already familiar with, 𐓤𐓮𐓲𐓐𐓘 [kšíðe] *have someone (not one's own relatives) do something*, and 𐓤𐓲𐓐𐓘 [kíðe] *have (one's own relatives) do something*.

𐓤𐓘𐓘𐓻𐓘 [káaɣe] *make*

Here are some sentences with 𐓤𐓘𐓘𐓻𐓧 [káaɣe].

(14) 𐓮𐓘𐓤𐓘𐓧𐓛 𐓧𐓤𐓲𐓘 𐓺𐓲𐓤𐓘𐓺𐓲 𐓻𐓘𐓘𐓤𐓟 𐓤𐓘𐓘𐓻𐓧 𐓄𐓘.
    hcékanǫǫ akxa žį́káži̜ ɣaaké káaɣa pe
    The teenager made the child cry.

Here, the first clause is [hcékanǫǫ akxa ... káaɣa pe] *the teenager made*. And the second one is [žį́káži̜ ɣaaké] *the child cry*. Notice that there are no connecting words between these clauses, no subject marker on 𐓺𐓲𐓤𐓘𐓺𐓲 [žį́káži̜], and no aspect marker on 𐓻𐓘𐓘𐓤𐓘 [ɣaaké].

The following sentences show how this works when we use pronouns. In the next example, the one who is being made to do something, *me*, appears as the pronoun 𐓘 [a̜] on 𐓘𐓤𐓘𐓘𐓻𐓘 [a̜káaɣe], meaning *made me*.

(15) ᏃᏇᎧᏃᏂ ᏂᎠ ᎠᎦᏂᎠ ᏍᎤᏍᎠᎦᎠ **ᎠᎦᎠᏪᎠ** ᏇᎠ.
    žíkáží ðe akxa húheka **a̧**káaye pe
    That child made **me** sick.

If both the subject and the object are pronouns, we follow the rules we discussed in chapter 9. In this next example, remember that ᏎᏇ [wi] means *I-you*, so **ᏎᏇᏇᎠᏪᎠ** [wihpáaye] means *I make you*. Also remember that ᎦᎠᏪᎠ [káaye] has an irregular first-person singular form, ᏇᎠᏪᎠ [hpáaye].

(16) ᏍᎤᏍᎠᎦᎠ **ᏎᏇᏇᎠᏪᎠ** ᎠᎠ ᎹᏇᎦᎬᎠ.
    húheka **wi**hpáaye hta mi̧kšé
    I'm going to make **you** sick.

In the next example, [a̧ðikáaye] means *we make you*.

(17) ᏎᎠᏃᏇ **ᎠᏂᏇᎦᎠᏪᎠ** ᎠᎠ ᎠᏂᏇᎬᎠ.
    waachí **a̧ði**káaye hta að̧ikšé
    We two will make **you** dance.

ᎦᎬᏇᎾ [kšíðe] *allow, have something done* (non-relatives)

ᎦᎬᏇᎾ [kšíðe] *allow* is a milder causative than ᎦᎠᏪᎠ [káaye]. We might say this as *have (someone do something)*. This verb belongs to the a-ða class, and it is used for people who are not one's own relatives.

(18) ᎯᏁᏏ ᏎᎠᎠᎠ ᎠᎦᎾᎠ ᏃᏇᎧᏃᏂ ᏂᎠ ᏎᎠᏂᎣ ᎦᎬᏇᎾ ᏇᎠ.
    hcíle wíhta akxa žíkáží̧ ðe waaðó̧ kšíða pe.
    My family had that child sing.
(19) ᏂᏇᎦᎦᏇ ᎣᎠᎠ ᎠᏂᎠᎠᎾ **ᎠᎦᏇᎾ**.
    ðicéki ówe aðía̧ðe **a**kšíðe
    I had your uncle carry the groceries.

ᎦᎠᎾ [kíðe] *allow, have something done* (relatives)

If we are speaking about our own relatives, we use the verb ᎦᎠᎾ [kíðe], which also belongs to the a-ða class. In the following example, I had my own son carry groceries, so we use ᎦᎠᎾ [kíðe] rather than ᎦᎬᏇᎾ [kšíðe].

20) ᏎᏇᏃᎦᎦᎠ ᎣᎠᎠ ᎠᏂᎠᎾᎾ **ᎠᎦᎠᎾ**.
    wižíke ówe aðía̧ðe **a**kíðe
    I had my son carry the groceries.

The third-person pronoun 𐓷𐓘 [wa]: uses of definite 𐓷𐓘́ [wá] and indefinite 𐓷𐓘 [wa]

Osage has two third-person 𐓷𐓘́ [wa] pronouns. We call the first one definite 𐓷𐓘́ [wá] and the second one indefinite 𐓷𐓘 [wa]. We will begin with definite 𐓷𐓘́ [wá], which we saw in chapter 9.

Definite 𐓷𐓘́ [wá], which is usually accented, means *them*, where context lets us know what *them* refers to. It is one of the object pronouns, as shown in 21b and 22.

(21a) 𐓇𐓣́𐒰𐒼𐓣̄ 𐒰𐒿𐒰 𐓎𐓪 𐓏𐓘́𐓬𐒰̄ 𐓆𐓣̄𐓒𐒰́ 𐓷𐒰.
šítožį akxa ho ðǫǫpá ðuuzá pe
The boy took two fish.

(21b) 𐓇𐓣́𐒰𐒼𐓣̄ 𐒰𐒿𐒰 𐓷𐓘́𐓆𐓣̄𐓒𐒰 𐓷𐒰.
šítožį akxa **wá**ðuuza pe
The boy took **them**.

(22) 𐓊𐓶́𐓎𐒰𐒼𐒰 𐓪𐒼𐓘́𐓇𐓣 𐒰𐒿𐒰 𐓪𐓷𐓘́𐒼𐒰 𐓷𐒰.
húheka okášą akxa o**wá**hką pe
The nurse helped **them**. (where *them* is known from context)

Note that in 23, with no third-person object pronoun, the sentence means *he took it*, where *it* means something definite, which we would know from context.

(23) 𐓇𐓣́𐒰𐒼𐓣̄ 𐒰𐒿𐒰 𐓆𐓣̄𐓒𐒰́ 𐓷𐒰.
šítožį akxa ðuuzá pe
The boy took **it**.

In chapter 9, we also briefly introduced the idea of another 𐓷𐓘 [wa], called indefinite 𐓷𐓘 [wa], to talk about an indefinite object. By this, we mean objects that are not known from context and that can be thought of as *stuff* or *folks*.

(24) 𐓇𐓣́𐒰𐒼𐓣̄ 𐒰𐒿𐒰 𐓷𐓘𐓆𐓣̄́𐓒𐒰 𐓷𐒰.
šítožį akxa **wa**ðúuza pe
The boy took **stuff**.

If we have a verb that takes an object, we have three options.
First, we can name the object with a noun phrase or a pronoun, as in 25.

(25) 𐓍𐒰𐓵𐓶́𐓎𐓶 𐓆𐓘́𐓇𐓪𐒰 𐒰𐒿𐒰𐓣.
nąnúhu ðáašoe akxai
He's smoking tobacco.

Second, we can leave out the pronoun, as in 26. Then the sentence will be interpreted as having a definite object like *it*.

(26) ᏔᏦᏌᎣᏌ ᕍα.
ðáašoa pe
He smokes **it**.

Third, we can place indefinite ᏌᏃ [wa] on the verb, as in 27. With ᏌᏃ [wa], we get the general meaning of *he smokes*, without a specific sense of *what* he is smoking.

(27) ᏌᏃᏔᏦᏌᎣα ᏦᏗᏃ.
waðáašoe štą
He smokes.

Indefinite ᏌᏃ [wa] provides a similar meaning in 28. Here, the sense is that the dog regularly bites people. The ᏦᏗᏃ [štą] aspect marker lets us know that this is habitual.

(28) ᏦᎤᏦα ᏔαᏃᏦᏃᏃ ᏌᏃᏔᏦᏃᏗᏦα ᏦᏗᏃ.
šóke ðe akxa waðáaxtake štą
That dog bites.

This means that we can make many verbs that have general meanings, like in 27 and 28, by adding ᏌᏃ [wa].

ᏌᏃ [wa] followed by O [o] produces Ó [ó]

There is a special rule for indefinite ᏌᏃ [wa] when used with verbs that begin with O [o]. In these cases, when ᏌᏃ [wa] is placed at the beginning of the verb, the ᏌᏃ [wa] and the O [o] will merge to become an accented Ó [ó]. Notice in 30 that the verb *to hunt* or *look for*, OᏒα [océ], changes to ÓᏒα [óce] when we don't name an object. If the O [o] on the verb is already accented, the accent stays, as in 31.

(29) ᏃᏁᏦᏃ ᏃᕍᏃ ᕍᏁ OᏒα ᏃᕍᏃ.
níhka apa htáa océ apai.
The man was hunting deer.

(30) ᏃᏁᏦᏃ ᏃᕍᏃ ÓᏒα ᏃᕍᏃ.
níhka apa óce apai (óce, *not* waocé)
The man was hunting (stuff).

(31) ᏒᎤᏒαᏦᏃ OᏦᏃᏦᏃ ᏃᏦᏃᏃ ᏌᏁᏁᏦo ÓᏦᏃ ᕍα.
húheka okášą akxa wihcíko óhką pe
The nurse helped my grandfather.

(32) ᏒᎤᏒαᏦᏃ OᏦᏃᏦᏃ ᏃᏦᏃᏃ ÓᏦᏃ ᏃᏃ.
húheka okášą akxa óhką ną (óhką, *not* waóhką)
The nurse helps (folks).

The use of this ᏌᏃ [wa] is so common that we can make many vocabulary words with it. For example, ᏔᎤᏌᏁ [ðuwį́] *buy* becomes ᏌᏃᏔᎤᏌᏁ [waðúwį̀] *shop* (buy stuff).

(33) Óʂa ʀúʂṅ ᴧᴅṁᴧʃá.
    ówe brúwi̧ atxa̧hé
    I'm buying vegetables.
(34) ʂᴧʀúʂṅ ᴧʃá.
    wabrúwi̧ a̧hé
    I'm shopping.

Remember, of course, not every word that begins with ʂᴧ [wa] contains the indefinite ʂᴧ [wa].

Verbs into nouns

You have probably already noticed that many Osage nouns have the same form as the verb. Since we do this all the time in English, it is not surprising.

Some verb-noun pairs that we have seen:

ńa	íe	to speak; a word
ʂᴧᶻń	waachí	to dance; a dance
ᴸńzu	níižu	to rain; rain
ʂᴧᴛó	waaðǫ́	to sing; a song

Verbs made with ʂᴧ [wa] are very frequently converted into nouns. We have already seen ʂᴧᴸóʀa [wanǫ́bre] *eat a meal* and *dinner*, and áʂᴧᴸoʀa [áwanǫbre] *eat something on* and *table*. The word ʂᴧᴘ̌ᴸaza [wapáaleze] *writing instrument* works like this too. We can see the instrumental ᴘā [paa] *by pushing* and ᴸaza [leze] *marks*. As a verb this would mean *make marks on stuff by pushing down*, but of course we really only use this word as the noun *writing instrument* (usually a *pen* or *pencil*).

Many other nouns have been made from verbs that begin with o [o]. This is because of what happens when we combine ʂᴧ [wa] and o [o] (as above). For example, őzu [óožu] *a bowl* comes from ʂᴧ [wa] plus ōzú [oožú] *to pour or put into*, and őʃσ [óoho̧] *a cook* comes from ʂᴧ [wa] plus ōʃó [oohó̧] *to cook*.

Making new nouns using compounding

You have probably already noticed that many Osage words seem to be made from two other words. For instance, ʂᴧᶻúa ᴄ̌ḵúa [wacúe skúe] *cake* is made of the words for *bread* and *sweet*. We also have ʃᴧᴘᴧ ʂᴧᶻúa [hápa wacúe] *cornbread*, ʂᴧᶻúa ŧuᴅ̌ᴧᴘᴧ [wacúe ðutáahpa] *biscuit*, and ʂᴧᶻúa ʂácᴧ [wacúe wéli] *frybread*. Some compounds are written as a single word, such as ᴘᴧᴸń [htaaníi] *soup*, made from the words for *meat* and *water*.

The rules for making compound nouns are quite simple. If the compound is made from two nouns, the main noun comes second, just as is done in English. So ʃᴧᴘᴧ ʂᴧᶻúa [hápa wacúe] *corn + bread* is a type of bread made from corn. ᏂᏁᏃᏃᎠ ᏁᎠ ᏂᏁᏝᎠᏃᎠ [wažáže íe waléze] combines three words the same way to mean *Osage language book*.

If the compound noun is made from a noun and an adjective or verb, the noun comes first. So the word for *cake* is ᏂᎪᏌᎠ ᏎᏸᎠ [wacúe skúe] *bread + sweet*. The word for *pie* is ᏸᎶᏃᎠ ŌᏝᏸ [hkáące oolá] *fruit + put into* (sometimes shortened to ᏸᎶᏃᏝᏸ [hką́ącóolą]).

Compounding verbs in Osage is very rare. Even though we see some compounded verbs such as ᏙᏞᎾᎸᏁ [aðį́achi] *arrive with* (see chapter 14), most Osage verbs are formed through the many roots and prefixes that we have been studying.

ńk'uꮓa

Exercise 1. Do you understand?

What does this short story mean?

ᏂᏁᏸáᏸᏁ ᎴᏰᎵ óᏃᎠ ᏸóᏞᎵ ᎴᏰᎵ ᏸóᎠ ᏰᎵᏟó ᎴᏝᏋᎠ ᏖᏁ ᏬᎴᏞú ᎴᏞά ᎴᏰᎵ.
ᏂᎴᏃúᎠᎵ ᏕᎲ ᏃᏲ Ꭰᏸú ᏸᎠ ńᎴᎮᏳ ᎴᏰᎵ.
Ōα ᎼóᏟᏁᏸᎴᏋᎠ ᏂᏁ ᎴᎴᏸ'ó ᏸᎠ άᏞᎴ ᎲᎠ.
ᎷᎴᎵᏸńᏸᎴ ᎴóᏰᎵ ᏂᎠᏃńᏸᎴ ᏕᏩᏃᏁ ᎵᏸᏁ ńᏞᎴ ᎲᎠ άᏃᏁ ᎴáᎴᎵ ᏞᏁᏸá ᏃʼάᏞᎴᏃᏁ.

Exercise 2. Composition

Write a composition in Osage of at least six sentences. Include at least one kind of causative sentence and one use of indefinite ᏂᎴ.

Exercise 3. Short phrases

Give the Osage for these phrases:

1. you lost it
2. he made me cry
3. I mailed it
4. you had your uncle do it
5. the chief had me do it

Exercise 4. Finding ᏂᎴ

Go through the vocabulary lists and find six words that include the indefinite ᏂᎴ marker. Remember that not every word that begins with ᏂᎴ is in this group.

ŋa

Nouns

ÁDΛƵΛ	átahką	lights
ÁZΛ	ážą	bed
ƘÃƵα ŌᏞΛ	hką́ące oolą́	fruit pie
ᏮΛ7α OƵŃα	máze ohkíe	telephone
OᏮŃZα	omíže	pajamas, bedding
ÞΛ7ΑᏞÑ ᏎΑᏞႶ	paazénii wéli	butter, cream

Verbs

ᏙÚℏα	húðe (ð e-causative)	hand over, pass
ƘŃℏα	kíðe (a-ða)	allow (own relatives) to
ƘᏕŃℏα	kšíðe (a-ða)	allow, have something done
OᏢÞᎳℏα	oxpáðe (stative)	get lost, be lost
OᏢÞᎳℏαℏα	oxpáðeðe (ð e-causative)	lose (something)
ℏᎳᏕOα	ðáašoe (br-šc)	smoke
ℏᎲℏα	ðéeðe (ð e-causative)	send
ℏŪDΛZႶ	ðuutáaži (br-šc)	turn off

Notes for Chapter 19

With respect to ðe-causatives, we are not claiming that ℏα [ðe] is a productive morpheme. It is only minimally productive now.

Chapter 20

Final Topics: Useful Expressions, Verbs for Speaking, Relative Clauses

ᎣᏏᏲᏂᎠ

The family is finishing up preparations for the meal after the handgame.

1. **ᏐᏁᏚᎦ:** ᏣᎸᎦᎥᏣᎸᏫᎶ'ᏃᏅ ᏲᏐᎠ ᏎᏈᎦᎠᎢ.
2. **ᎠᏍᎦᏯᎢ:** ᏣᎸᏂᎻᏅᏃᎾ ᎠᎠᎢ ᏐᏂᏛᎠ ᎢᏃᎤ ᏎᏈᎦᎠᎢ ᎠᎠ.
3. **ᏐᏁᏚᎦ:** ᏞᏣᏂᎠᎠ ᎠᎨᎠ ᎹᎢᏎᏅ. ᏐᏂᏃᎦᎦ ᎠᎠᎢ ᏐᎠᏛᏌᎠ ᏥᎠᏣᎤ ᏲᏐᎠ ᎦᎠᏃ ᏎᏈᎦᎠᎢ.
4. ᎠᎠᎴᎻ, ᏍᎤᏣᎦ ᎠᎵᎦᏁ ᏐᎠᏛᏌᎠ ᏣᎵᏣᎠ ᏃᏓᏣ, ᏐᎠᎥᎤ ᏐᎠᏛᏌᎠ ᏎᎤᏘᏍᏣᎦ, ᎠᎠᏐᎠᎵᏅ, ᏝᎠᎠᎠ ᎠᏎᎠᏣᎤ ᏣᎠᏎᏅ ᏐᏂᏛᎠ ᎣᏣᎥᎠᎤ ᏣᎥᏩᎠ.
5. **ᎠᏍᎦᏯᎢ:** ᎠᎠᏌᎠᏪᏐᎥ ᏞᎠᎥᎠᎥᎤ ᎠᏛᏁ ᎠᏣᎻᎠ, ᏣᎥᎠ ᏞᏔᏎᎤ ᏲᏐᎠ ᏎᏈᎦᎠᎢ.
6. ᏐᏂᏃᎥᎾ ᎠᏤᏫᎠ ᏐᎣᏂᏣᎦ ᎠᎠᏃ ᎣᎭᎣᎦᎠᎠᏅ ᏣᎠ ᎠᏤᏫᎠ, ᎠᏌᏅ ᏎᏐᎠ ᏎᏈᎦᎠᎢ.
7. **ᏐᏁᏚᎦ:** ᎿᎠᏣᎵᏐᎠ ᎠᏣᎥᎠᎠ?
8. **ᎠᏍᎦᏯᎢ:** ᎠᎾᎠ ᏝᎠᎥᎠᎠ ᎠᎠᎠᎣᎠᏐᎠ.
9. **ᏐᏁᏚᎦ:** ᏐᎠᏛᏌᎠ ᏤᏥᎠᎠ ᎠᏐᎠᎶᏣᎠ ᎠᎢᎤᎠᎠ, ᏞᏃᏌᎤ ᎣᏣᎥᎠᎤ ᎠᏤᏫᎠ.
10. ᎠᎶᏣᎠ ᎠᎠ ᎠᏐᎠᎶᏣᎠ ᎠᎢᎤ ᎠᎠ.

1. **Second daughter:** The handgame is almost finished.
2. **Third daughter:** The girls have finished setting the tables.
3. **Second daughter:** Go outside and look. Daughter is almost finished cooking the frybread.
4. It's time to bring in the chicken and dumplings, grape dumplings, and steam fry, and fill the serving bowls.
5. **Third daughter:** The salad is in the refrigerator, and the ᏞᏔᏎᎤ is finished cooking.
6. Older Sister is still stirring the green beans, but they are almost done.
7. **Second daughter:** Did we make coffee?
8. **Third daughter:** I'll make some.
9. **Second daughter:** The cake is set on the table, and the pitchers are full.
10. Let's set the food on the table.

ńα ᏕᏗᏕńᏗᏗᏕα

In this last chapter, we will discuss some topics that are very important to understanding Osage but that did not fit into earlier chapters. We have gathered them here, even though they are not related to each other. We will look at one last evidential marker ẮᏗα [áape], three useful grammatical words (ᏕᏗ [ši], ᏕᏗᏕά [ðąącé], ᎠᏕ [tą]), five verbs for speaking (ńα [íe], ắ [ée], áᏕnα [ékie], óᏕnα [óhkie], and oᏕńᏕnα [ohkíhkie]), and three types of relative clauses.

Evidential marker ẮᏗα [áape]

Beginning in chapter 2 we have used the evidential markers ꜧα [ðe] and ᏕΑ [che]. Recall that ꜧα [ðe], the declarative evidential, is generally built into the aspect markers Ꭰα [pe], ΛᏕᏕΛ [akxai], and ΛᎠΛ [apai]. And the ᏕΑ [che] evidential means the speaker has evidence for a statement.

ẮᏗα [áape] (reportive evidential)

The evidential ẮᏗα [áape] is used when a speaker does not know something directly but rather because others have reported it. A good way to put this in English is *they said* or *it is said*.

A place setting like this can be found at dinners for many Osage occasions. Photo by Butch DeLong.

Let's examine the same sentence with three evidentials—ħα [ðe], ɛα [che], and ΛÞα [áape].

(1) ᏎΛᵬόɔα ΛᵬόÐΛÞɒ Λᵬ⋔Λ ⋒Λɔαςᵬ̣Λ ᒉűᴏᒉń Þα.
wakóze akóhtapi akxa mázeska húu ohí pe ([pe] includes [ðe])
Our teacher won a lot of money. (I am declaring this as a fact.)

(2) ᏎΛᵬόɔα ΛᵬόÐΛÞɒ Λᵬ⋔Λ ⋒Λɔαςᵬ̣Λ ᒉűᴏᒉń ɛα.
wakóze akóhtapi akxa mázeska húu ohí che
Our teacher won a lot of money. (I have evidence for it.)

(3) ᏎΛᵬόɔα ΛᵬόÐΛÞɒ Λᵬ⋔Λ ⋒Λɔαςᵬ̣Λ ᒉűᴏᒉń ΛÞα.
wakóze akóhtapi akxa mázeska húu ohí áape
Our teacher won a lot of money. (They said.)

Expressions for *again*, *possibly*, and *if*

ᏕɩΠ [ši] *again*

The adverb ᏕɩΠ [ši] *again* is placed right before the verb it modifies in a sentence.

(4) ɔΛ̋ᒐΠ **ᏕɩΠ** ᏎΛ̃ɛń ᵬόħΛ Λᵬ⋔Λ.
záani **ši** waachí kóða akxai
Everyone wants to dance **again**.

Here is a sentence from the ᴏᵬ̣ńα [ohkíe] in chapter 11.

(5) ΠÐό ħαᒉΛ ᏎΛɔΛ́ɔα ńα **ᏕɩΠ** ᴏᵬ̣ńα ΛᒐΛᵬ̣'ᴏ ᵬόᵬΛ ⋒ΠᵬᏕά.
ihtói ðeha wažáže íe **ši** ohkíe ánąk'o hkóbra mikšé
In the future, I want to hear the Osage language being spoken **again**.

ᏕɩΠ [ši] can also be used to mean *more* or *another* as in this sentence from the dialogue in chapter 16.

(6) ᒐńᏎΛɛα ᴅᴧ ṇ́ᒐᴋ́ ᒉΛ⋔ń̋ **ᏕɩΠ ᏎΠ** ɛα άÞᏕα.
níwahce tą iiną haxí **ši wį** hce épše
If it's cold I ask Mom for **another** blanket.

While this literally means *ask again for a blanket*, ᏕɩΠ ᏎΠ [ši wį] is often used where, in English, we would use *another*.

ħΛ̃ɛά [ðąąché] *can, could, possibly*

ħΛ̃ɛά [ðąąché] is placed after the verb in a sentence to give the meaning of possibility. It can be given as *can* or *could* as well as *possibly* or *might*. A continuous aspect marker usually follows.

(7) 𐒻𐒰𐓓𐓶 𐓐𐒰𐒿𐓍𐒰́ 𐒹𐓤𐒼𐒰𐒻.
   níižu **ðąąché** akxai
   It **might** rain.

(8) 𐓂𐒰́𐓐𐒰𐒻𐓐𐒼 𐓐𐒰𐒿𐓍𐒰 𐒻𐓂𐒼𐓤𐒰́?
   oáðahką **ðąąché** nįkšé
   Could you help me?

We can place the negation marker 𐒰𐓓𐓂 [aži] on 𐓐𐒰𐒿𐓍𐒰́ [ðąąché] to get 𐓐𐒰𐒿𐓍𐒰́𐓓𐓂 [ðąącháži] *can't, couldn't,* or *not possible*. We do not use the special negative forms 𐒿𐒰𐓓𐓂 [maži] and 𐓉𐒰𐓓𐓂 [paži] when negating 𐓐𐒰𐒿𐓍𐒰́ [ðąąché].

(9) 𐒻𐓐𐒰́𐓓𐓂 𐒿𐓤𐒼𐒰 𐓂𐓐𐒻́𐓃𐓐𐒰 𐓅𐒰́𐓤𐒿 𐓐𐓊𐓓𐒻́ **𐓐𐒰𐒿𐓍𐒰́𐓓𐓂** 𐒿𐓤𐒼𐒰𐒻.
   įhtáci akxa oðíhtą hcéka ðuwí **ðąącháži** akxai
   Father **couldn't** buy a new car.

(10) 𐒻𐓊𐓉𐒰́ 𐓐𐒻𐓃𐓐𐒰 𐒻𐓐𐒰́𐓐𐒰 **𐓐𐒰𐒿𐓍𐒰́𐓓𐓂** 𐒿𐓂𐓤𐓤𐒰́.
   hǫǫpé ðíhta iiðáðe **ðąącháži** mįkšé
   I **can't** find your shoes.

𐒑𐒿 [tą] *if, when* (at whatever time), *since*

𐒑𐒿 [tą] implies something that might happen in the future. This connecting word is placed after its clause. In example 11, 𐒑𐒿 [tą] is put after the clause 𐒻𐒻𐓓𐓶 [níižu] *it rains*.

(11) 𐒻𐒻𐓓𐓶 **𐒑𐒿** 𐓂́𐓅𐒰𐓓𐓂 𐓅𐒑́𐓉𐒰𐓓𐓂.
   níižu **tą** ówehci štáapaži
   If it rains, you (plural) won't go to the store.

(Refer to chapter 14 for how 𐓅𐒑́𐓉𐒰𐓓𐓂 [štáapaži] is formed from [šcée] + [paži].)

(12) 𐓆𐓃𐓅𐒑𐒿 **𐒑𐒿** 𐓂𐓃𐓊𐒼𐒰 𐒑𐒿 𐒿𐓂𐓤𐒼𐒰́.
   bríištą **tą** owíhką hta mįkšé
   When I get finished, I will help you.

Verbs for speaking: **ńα** [íe], **𐒰́** [ée], **ákna** [ékie], **óna** [óhkie], and **oknína** [ohkíhkie]

Osage has a number of verbs that refer to speaking and conversation. They have subtle differences and are easy to confuse. We are already familiar with **ńα** [íe], an i-stem verb that means *speak* or *talk*. It is the most common of the speaking verbs and also makes up many compound nouns, such as 𐓄𐒰𐓓𐒰́𐓓𐒰 ńα [wažáže íe] *Osage language*.

(13) 𐓄𐒰𐓓𐒰́𐓓𐒰 ńα **𐒰𐓉𐒰́𐒰** 𐒰𐓤𐒰́𐓐𐒰.
   wažáže íe **ąnáe** ąkáðe
   We are **speaking** Osage.

ǧ [ée] *say that (reported speech)*

ǧ [ée] is an h-stem verb that is usually used to report speech that has already occurred. In the examples below, we usually put the connector ʔa [che] (which corresponds to English *that*) between the two clauses (see chapter 15).

(14) ՐᴎDó ᴧᴊúᴊakᴧ ʔa **áɾꙅa**
   sitǫ́i ahúheka che **épše**
   I said that I was sick yesterday.

(15) ԵᴧḳńDᴧᴊa ʔa **áꙅa**.
   ðakítahe che **éše**
   You said that you got better.

Third-person ǧ [ée] becomes ᴧɒa [áape], which is the same form as the reportive evidential marker from above. Students can see that the rule that changes the sound of ǧ [ée] to ᴧ [aa] before ɒa [pe] is at work here: ᴧ ɒa [áa pe] is written as ᴧɒa [áape].

We do not need the connector ʔa [che] when using ᴧɒa [áape].

(16) 7ᴧᴌᴨ ḳń7o ᴧɒa.
   záani kízo áape
   He said that everyone had a good time.
   OR It was said (OR they said) that everyone had a good time.

We also use ǧ [ée] for the expression *how does someone say?* In example 17, don't confuse the emphatic pronoun ǧ [ée] (see chapter 13) with the verb ǧ [ée] *say*. They are pronounced and spelled the same.

(17) ǧ ᴊᴧḳɒ **áꙅa**.
   ée háakǫ **éše**
   How do **you say** that?

Recall from chapter 1 that we can also use ᴊᴧḳɒ ꙅDᴧʔa [háakǫ štáace], meaning *how do you pronounce* (or *how do you say*). This is because Եᴧʔa [ðáace] can also mean *pronounce*.

ʔa ǧ [hce ée] *(telling or asking someone to do something)*

In chapter 12 we learned that ʔa [hce] can be used for English *let's*, or it can be used for *let* as one of the command forms.

ʔa [hce] is also used with ǧ [ée] to mean *tell or ask someone to do something*. These two words are always pronounced together as ʔǧ [hcée] but we will write them as separate words to be clearer. The aspect marker ᴧɒᴧ [apa] is preferred for third-person sentences. This expression is only used with another clause: the main clause is ʔa ǧ [hce ée] and the embedded clause says what is requested.

There is no connector between the two clauses, and there is no subject marker on the embedded clause (see chapter 15). In example 18, Ꭸᴧḳóʔa ᴧḳᴊᴧ . . . ʔa ǧ ᴧɒᴧ [wakóze akxa

... hce ée apa] is the main clause, and ᏕᎱᏂᎾᎠᎧᎯᎯ ᏕᎯᏟᏂ ᏁᏧ'ᎤᏃᎠ [waðíopxai wálį ík'uce] is the embedded clause.

(18) ᏕᎯᏦᏃᎠ ᎯᏧᎯᎯ ᏕᎱᏂᎾᎠᎧᎯᎯ ᏕᎯᏟᏂ ᏁᏧ'ᎤᏃᎠ **ᏃᎠ ᎨᏨ** ᎯᎠᎯ.
wakóze akxa waðíopxai wálį ík'uce **hce ée** apa
The teacher **told** the student to study a lot.

(19) ᏃᏂᏧᎯᏃᏂ ᎯᏧᏧᏂ **ᏃᎠ ᎨᎠᎧᏂᎠ**.
žįkážį akší **hce épše**
I **told** the child to go back home.

ᏃᎠ ᎨᏨ [hce ée] is very commonly used in the sense of *to be asked*.

(20) ᏧᎯᏐᏂᏧᎠ ᏁᎠ **ᏃᎠ ᎨᏨ** ᎯᎠᎯ.
kahíke ie **hce ée** apa
The chief **was asked** to speak.

We can also use the verb ᏁᏐᏟ [íihǫ] *ask as a request* with **ᏃᎠ** [hce] instead of **ᎨᏨ** [ée]. ᏁᏐᏟ [íihǫ] is an i-stem verb.

(21) ᏕᏂᏃᏬᏧᎠ ᏁᏧᏬ ᏬᏧᎯ **ᏃᎠ ᏁᏂᎯᏐᏟ**.
wižǫ́ke iihkǫ́ óhką **hce iiðáhǫ**
I **asked** my daughter to help Grandma.

ᎨᏧᏂᎠ [ékie] *say* (to others in their presence)

While ᏁᎠ [íe] means *speak* in a general way, ᎨᏧᏂᎠ [ékie] means *speak in the presence of others*. A student might say that most all speaking is done in the presence of others, but ᎨᏧᏂᎠ [ékie] emphasizes this point. ᎨᏧᏂᎠ [ékie] is an h-stem verb.

Here is a sentence from chapter 11.

(22) ᎠᎯᏐᏟᏂᎠ, ᏕᎯᏟᎠᏃᎠ ᏂᎠ ᏁᎠ ᎠᏬᎠ **ᎨᏧᏂᎠᎧᏂᎠ** ᏧᏬᏂᎯ.
hpahále waléze ðe íe tóe **ékipše** hkǫ́bra
First, I want to **say** a few words about this book.

(23) ᏧᎯᏐᏂᏧᎠ ᎯᏧᎯᎠ ᏁᎠ ᎠᏬᎠ **ᎨᏧᏂᎠᏂᎠ** ᏂᏂᏧᏬᎱᎯ ᎯᏧᎯᎯ.
kahíke akxa íe tóe **ékiše** ðikǫ́ða akxai
The chief wants **you** to **say** a few words.

(24) ᏃᏁᏟᎠ **ᎨᎯᏧᏂᎠ** ᎠᎯ ᎯᎱᏂᏧᏨᎠ.
hcíle **éąkie** hta ąðįkšé
Are **we two** going to **speak** to the family?

OᏧᏁᎠ [ohkíe] and oᏧᏁᏧᏂᎠ [ohkíhkie] *talk to* or *converse with*

These verbs are used when people are talking back and forth with each other. In modern use, oᏧᏁᎠ [ohkíe] can also mean *calling on the telephone*. It tends to be used in a conversation between two people. When there are a number of speakers, oȟńȟna [ohkíhkie] is preferred. These verbs are both in the a-ða verb class.

(25) 𐓎𐓟𐓇𐓘𐓪 𐓘𐓤𐓬𐓘 𐓺𐓆𐓒𐓇𐓘 **oȟńa** 𐓘𐓤𐓬𐓘.
ihcíko akxa wižįke **ohkíe** akxai.
His grandfather is **talking to** my son.

(26) **O𐓺ńȟna** ȟóʀ𐓘 𐓤𐓆ȟ𐓟á.
owíhkie hkǫ́bra mįkšé
I want to **talk to you**.

(27) 𐓞𐓒𐓣𐓘 𐓦𐓇𐓒𐓣 𐓘𐓒𐓘 **oȟńȟna** 𐓘𐓒𐓘.
hcíle záani apa **ohkíhkie** apai
The whole family was **talking to each other**.

The following example is from chapter 16.

(28) **Ňȟóȟnȟna** 𐓘ȟ𐓘𐓒ȟá.
ąkóhkihkie ąkatxái
We are having a conversation.

Relative clauses

The last topic we will discuss is the way to make *relative clauses*. One of the trickiest parts of learning to make these is being able to identify them! Here is an example of a relative clause in English: "The cat **that bit me** ran away." The clause *that bit me* describes the *cat*, and the whole noun phrase *the cat that bit me* is the subject of the sentence. Here is another example: "The community appreciates the women *who helped the children*." The clause *who helped the children* describes *women*, and the entire noun phrase *the women who helped the children* is the object of the sentence. In short, a relative clause describes a noun that is inside a noun phrase in a sentence.

Osage does not make relative clauses the way English does, but there are a few basic types of sentences that you can learn and practice.

In the first type, the relative clause is in the subject of the sentence. There are two important things to note about this type of relative clause. First, there is no subject marker 𐓘𐓤𐓬𐓘 [akxa] or 𐓘𐓒𐓘 [apa] in the relative clause—not on the noun and not at the end of the relative clause. Even if the subject is definite, we use 𐓺𐓣 [wį] if singular or 𐓪óa [tóe] if plural. Second, the relative clause does have an aspect marker.

(29) 𐓎𐓦óazn 𐓺𐓣 𐓘ȟá𐓆ȟ𐓒𐓘 𐓒𐓘 ȟóʀ𐓆𐓘 𐓒𐓘.
ilǫ́eži wį ąðáaxta pe hkóopša pe
The cat that bit me ran off.

(30) 𐓎𐓦óazn 𐓪óa 𐓘ȟá𐓆ȟ𐓒𐓘 𐓒𐓘 ȟóʀ𐓆𐓘 𐓒𐓘.
ilǫ́eži tóe ąðáaxta pe hkóopša pe
The cats that bit me ran off.

(31) 𐓁𐒿𐓂́𐒰𐓊𐒻 𐓏𐒻̨ 𐓂̈𐓍𐒰́𐓄𐒰 𐓒𐓂́𐓐𐒰 𐒷𐓘𐓓𐓊𐒾.
ilóeži wį iiðáðe žį́įhe akxai
The cat that I saw was sleeping.

In the second type, the relative clause is in the object of the sentence.

There are three things to remember about this type of relative clause. First, if the subject is a noun phrase (not a pronoun), that subject will take a subject marker, 𐒷𐓘𐓓𐓊𐒷 [akxa] or 𐒷𐓄𐒷 [apa]. Second, the relative clause usually comes first in the sentence (as we saw above). These two points are illustrated in the following examples.

(32) 𐓁𐒿𐓂́𐒰𐓊𐒻 𐓏𐒻̨ 𐒷𐓍𐒰́́𐓊𐓄𐒷 𐓄𐒰 **𐓁𐒻́𐓊𐓂𐓓𐒻̨ 𐒷𐓘𐓓𐓊𐒷** 𐒻̈𐓊𐒷 𐓄𐒰.
ilóeži wį ̨aðáaxta pe **šį́toží akxa** íiða pe
The boy saw the cat that bit me.

(33) 𐓁𐒿𐓂́𐒰𐓊𐒻 𐓏𐒻̨ 𐒷𐓍𐒰́́𐓊𐓄𐒷 𐓄𐒰 **𐒻̈𐓊𐒷𐓍𐒰**.
ilóeži wį ̨aðáaxta pe **íiðaðe**
You saw the cat that bit me.

A third way to make a relative clause is to use position markers. We do this by adding a position marker at the end of the relative clause. In the following example, we might have said 𐓧𐒷𐓊𐒻́ 𐓓𐒰 [haxí che] to talk about a stack of blankets (see chapter 18). In a relative clause, that position marker, 𐓓𐒰 [che], is placed *at the end of the clause* rather than directly after the noun, 𐓧𐒷𐓊𐒻́ [haxí] blanket.

(34) 𐓧𐒷𐓊𐒻́ 𐒷𐓍𐒰́𐓐𐓂𐓐'𐓊 𐓓𐒰 𐒷́𐓍𐒰𐒿𐒻̨ 𐒻̈𐓂𐓐𐓒𐒰́.
haxí ̨aðákik'u che ̨áðaalį mįkšé
I like **the blankets that you gave me**.

How do we go forward from here?

Congratulations on making it this far! We have covered a lot of material. But despite the amount of work we have done in learning Osage, we are far from finished. There are many grammar topics that we have left unexplained, often because they are more complicated than we can manage in a beginning grammar book, and sometimes because those topics are much more rarely used in modern speech. And, of course, our glossary contains only a fraction of the Osage vocabulary.

Some students will want to progress in their Osage language studies. At this time there are no advanced language books, but students can do a number of things to maintain and expand their language knowledge and fluency.

First, students can get together with other Osage students and speakers and speak together. This is, perhaps, the most important thing a learner can do. Second, students can help Osage teachers form advanced classes. Third, some students will want to read parts of Carolyn Quintero's *Osage Grammar*. Those students should probably discuss this material with an Osage teacher. Fourth, students should continue to learn Osage words from a source such as Carolyn

Quintero's *Osage Dictionary*. This will help to add to their vocabulary. Fifth, students can seek out online sources such as videos, audio content, websites, and apps that feature Osage being spoken. Last, students should support any language programs that exist now and those that will be formed in the future.

𐓂𐓊'𐓶𐒷𐓘

Choosing from all the vocabulary words and grammar lessons in this book, write a thoughtful Osage composition of twelve sentences.

𐓂𐓘

Nouns

    𐓤𐰱𐓂𐓊𐓘   kahíke   chief

Verbs

𐰱	ée (h-stem)	say
𐰱𐓊𐓘	ékie (h-stem)	say to others
𐓤𐓘𐓄𐓯𐓘	hkóopše (a-ða)	run away, flee
𐓂𐱂𐓬𐓘	íðǫye (br-sc)	ask for information
𐓂𐰱𐓯	íihǫ (i-stem)	ask as a request
o𐓊𐓂𐓘	ohkíe (a-ða)	talk to someone, talk on telephone

Notes for Chapter 20

The verb [ée] is virtually never used with plural forms.

Appendix A

APA Dialogues and Stories

Chapter 7 ohkíhkie

1. **A:** mąhkása tóe káaɣe htai
2. **B:** ąháį mąhkása hkóbra mįkšé
3. **C:** tóe hpáaɣe hta mįkšé mąhkása oohǫ́ ðiištą́
4. **D:** mąhkása oožú ðéka
5. **C:** oowížu hce pée hpaazénii žąąníi kǫ́ða
6. **A:** mąhkása akxa hpa wálį akxa
7. **B:** hpaazénii tóe hkóbra mįkšé
8. **D:** mąhkása skúe ądǎalį žąąníi tóe ąk'ú
9. **C:** mąhkása sápe éena bráahtą
10. **A:** mąhkása ðáalį akxa

1. **A:** Let's fix some coffee.
2. **B:** Yes, I want coffee. (woman speaking)
3. **C:** I'll make some. . . . The coffee is ready.
4. **D:** Here is a coffee mug.
5. **C:** Let me pour for you. Who wants cream and sugar?
6. **A:** This coffee is really strong.
7. **B:** I want some cream.
8. **D:** I like sweet coffee. Give me some sugar.
9. **C:** I only drink mine black.
10. **A:** The coffee is good.

Chapter 8 ohkíhkie

1. **wihé:** iihkó, hpasú olį́į ilǫ́ǫška ąkáðe hta
2. **iihkó:** ąhą́ haatxą́ta scée škóšta

3. **wihé:** mįįðóhta ðiištą́ waachí brée hkǫ́bra
4. **iihkó:** wéhkilį okíhpaahą škǫ́šta
5. **wihé:** ąhą́ iihkó wéhkilį okíhpaahą hkǫ́bra
6. **wak'óhpa:** hą́ąhkaži wéhkilį okípą́ąhą hkǫ́bramąži
7. **iihkó:** ehtą́ haaskámį aðíaðaa
8. **ilǫ́ohpa:** hą́ąðe waachí hkǫ́bra
9. **iihkó:** ðáalį wižį́ke haaská ðíhta hpuštáha hta mįkšé

1. **Second daughter:** Grandma, are we going to the Gray Horse dances?
2. **Grandmother:** Yes, when do you want to go?
3. **Second daughter:** I want to go to the afternoon dance.
4. **Grandmother:** Do you want to dress?
5. **Second daughter:** Yes, Grandma, I want to dress.
6. **First daughter:** No, I don't want to dress.
7. **Grandmother:** Well then, take your shawl.
8. **First son:** I want to dance tonight.
9. **Grandmother:** Good, Sonny, I will iron your shirt.

Chapter 9 ohkíhkie

1. mįįðohta ðiištą́ waachí álįįha hcíle apa hpáze wanǫ́bre ci ðe hta apa
2. **wihé:** nǫhpéąhi hową́įki hpáze wanǫ́bre ądáache hta ąkatxą́
3. **wak'óhpa:** hcíle ąkóhtapi zącólį céɣenii aðį́ ímą žówale ąwanǫ́bre hta ðe
4. **ílǫ́ǫhpa:** táatą oohǫ́ apai
5. **iihǫ́:** htáa lįkó wacúe kaascú
6. **wak'óhpa:** ðáalį
7. **ílǫ́ǫhpa:** ą́hǫǫ
8. **wihé:** mį́įoðaake háaną ąkáðe hta
9. **iihǫ́:** mį́įoðaake tóopa tą ąkáðe hta akxai hpáze wanǫ́bre mį́įoðaake sáhtą akxai
10. **iðáce:** éetxą háhahkiðapi

1. After the afternoon dance, the family will be going to supper.
2. **Second daughter:** I'm hungry. Where will we eat supper?
3. **First daughter:** Are we going to eat with our family or with the Hominy drumkeeper?
4. **First son:** What are they cooking?
5. **Mother:** Meat gravy and frybread.
6. **First daughter:** Good!
7. **First son:** I really like that!
8. **Second daughter:** What time will we go?
9. **Mother:** When it's 4:00, we will leave. Supper is at 5:00.
10. **Father:** Everybody be ready.

Chapter 10 ohkíhkie

1. **iihkó:** kaasį́tą akxa waníðe hta
2. **iihǫ́:** wapáaxce ąkóhtapi ąkáaɣe htai
3. **iihkó:** haxį́ ðe che haaskámį ški níąðe hta ąkatxái
4. **iðáce:** wiškítą mázeska tóe nąnúhu ški céɣenii ažu abrį mįšké
5. **iihkó:** ðáalį hta akxa
6. **iihǫ́:** ðekǫ́oce pée waníðe paaxcé
7. **ilǫ́ǫhpa:** wie ékimǫ
8. **iihkó:** kaasį́tą pée wapáaxce k'įahi
9. **kšǫ́ka:** wíe ékimǫ
10. **iihǫ́:** šį́mįžį mį́waapaache lúustako
11. **wak'óhtą:** mį́waapaache žúuce alúustako
12. **wihé:** mį́waapaache htóho alúustako
13. **iihkǫ́:** ðáalį ąhkíliištąpe

1. **Grandma:** Tomorrow is Giveaway.
2. **Mother:** Let's make our bundles.
3. **Grandma:** These are the blankets and shawls we are going to give away.
4. **Father:** I also have some money and tobacco to put on the drum.
5. **Grandma:** It'll be good.
6. **Mother:** Now, who is going to tie up the giveaway?
7. **Eldest son:** Me, I will do it.
8. **Grandma:** Tomorrow, who will carry the bundle?
9. **Second son:** Me, I will do it.
10. **Mother:** Girls, get your blankets ready.
11. **First daughter:** I have my red blanket ready.
12. **Second daughter:** I have my blue blanket ready.
13. **Grandma:** Good. . . . We are ready.

Chapter 11 ohkíe

1. záani wawíhǫipi hkǫ́bra.
2. wižǫ́ą wihtáežį wihcį́to wižį́ðe
3. hpahą́le waléze ðe íe tóe ékipše hkǫ́bra
4. ée wažáže íe che wažáže ók'ą ški oðáake hta akxa
5. wažáže íe íðai ðiópxąį škǫ́štapi ðáha waléze ðe oðíhkąpi hta akxa
6. ðekǫ́oce oáhkilake mįkšé
7. Stephanie Rapp įįštáxį žáže abríe
8. xuðátǫmį wažáže žáže abríe
9. Tulsa htą́wą owálįį mįkšé
10. hašíhta apa htaasíle htą́wą ðaatá pe
11. hcížo waštáke htą́wąla mįkšé

12. hpasú olį́į aníhkašie
13. wižǫ́ke ðǫ́ǫpa iitáðe
14. žį̱ká owáhkihą ðǫ́opa abrį́ mį̱kšé
15. ðe waléze akxa žį̱ká owáhkihą wíhta wažáže íe hkihpíǫ óhką hta akxai che ékǫ ažámį̱ mį̱kšé
16. wažáže íe hpíǫ wahkǫ́bra
17. ihtǫ́į̱ ðéha wažáže íe ohkíhkie ši ánąk'ǫ hkóbra hta mį̱kšé
18. wažáže níhkaši apa wažáže íe wažáže óhk'ą ą̱kóhtapi šǫǫšówe mą̱ðį́ ðée kǫ́ða hta apai
19. éetana záani waašką́ htai.

1. I wish to address all of you with respect.
2. Older sisters, younger sisters, older brothers, younger brothers.
3. First, I want to say a few words about this book.
4. It is going to tell you about the Osage language and Osage ways.
5. This book is going to help those of you who want to know and understand the Osage language.
6. Now I'm going to tell about myself.
7. Stephanie Rapp is my (English) name.
8. My Osage name is Xuðátǫmį̱.
9. I live in Tulsa.
10. The ones before me called it Htaasíle Htą́wą (Deer Tracks Town).
11. My clan is Hcížo Waštake.
12. I belong to the Gray Horse district.
13. I have two daughters.
14. I have four grandchildren.
15. I believe this book will help my grandchildren to learn the Osage language.
16. I want them to learn the Osage language.
17. In the future, I want to hear the Osage language being spoken again.
18. Osage people want the Osage language and our Osage ways to go on forever.
19. Therefore, everybody, let's do our best!

Chapter 12 ohkíhkie

1. waníðe ékitxą ahí akxai
2. **iihkó:** áhcihtą kši ą̱káðe htai
3. **iihǫ́:** xóhka apa waaðǫ́ ðǫ́ha éetxą pe
4. waðáachi hta níhkašie íihkimą̱į̱ níðe wak'ó waaðǫ́ ímą wák'u
5. šáake oðį́į̱ke kaðǫ́ mázeska wák'u
6. **iihkó:** íciko waaðǫ́ íhta ðǫ́ha éetxą ahí akxai
7. **wak'óhpa:** háhahkiða wihcíko hcéka waachí tą ą̱kóðaha
8. **iihkó:** ihcíko waaðǫ́ ðiištą́ tą wapáaxce ą̱kóhtapi ą̱hkíliiški hta ą̱káðe
9. **iihǫ́:** ihcíko akxa íe tóe ékie kaðǫ́ žáže kípą́ áwawak'u hta

10. hpáhąle ée céɣenii aðį̄ ðáabrį kípą kaðǫ́ hkóða ąkóhtapi wéenį ąkóða hta
11. alį́įha ihcíko haxį́ haaskámį ški į kšiðé, záanii šáake oðį́įke
12. kaðǫ́ ilǫ́ǫhpa akxa kšǫ́ka éeðǫǫpa mą́zeska ninúhu ški céɣenii ážu

1. It's time again for Giveaway.
2. **Grandma:** Let's go to the arbor.
3. **Mother:** It's almost time for the singers to start.
4. When you dance, give to the visitors or women singers.
5. Shake hands and give them money.
6. **Grandma:** It's almost time for Grandpa's song.
7. **First daughter:** Get ready. When Grandpa starts dancing we will follow him out.
8. **Grandma:** When Grandpa's song ends we will gather together with our bundles.
9. **Mother:** Grandpa will say a few words and then call out the names we are giving to.
10. He will call the three drumkeepers first, and then our friends we want to show our appreciation to.
11. Shake hands with everybody after Grandpa puts blankets and shawls on them.
12. And then First Son and Second Son will both put money and tobacco on the drum.

Chapter 13 ohkíhkie

1. **iihǫ́:** tookétą wižį́ke akxa ilǫ́ǫška ohpé hta akxai
2. **iðáce:** ékǫ éetxą́ ahí akxa
3. **iihǫ́:** táatą záani ąká ðį che ąpáahi hce kaðǫ́ táatążiški ą́ðúwį waðílą ąhkíhkaaɣe
4. įcéki akxa xúða mą́šǫ wį akíðį akxai
5. **iðáce:** ðáalį
6. **iihǫ́:** htaasį́įce wapúške ški ą́ðuwį hta ąkatxái
7. **iðáce:** htaasį́įce wahú haaléžowaake toe abrį́
8. **iihǫ́:** ihcími akxa wažáže wéehkilį kšíɣe hta akxai
9. **iðáce:** wapáache ðáalį káaɣa pi che
10. **iihǫ́:** húuįke híðaxa húðaxe sce kšíɣe hta eená táatą ðáalį hta akxai
11. ée htónįke káaɣe ški

1. **Mother:** In the summer Sonny will go into the dance.
2. **Father:** It is time.
3. **Mother:** Let's gather up everything we have, and then decide what else we will buy.
4. Uncle has an eagle feather for him.
5. **Father:** Good.
6. **Mother:** We will buy him a roach headdress and drop feathers too.
7. **Father:** I have a roach spreader and some handkerchiefs.
8. **Mother:** Aunt will make his Osage clothes.
9. **Father:** She makes good ribbon work.
10. **Mother:** She is going to make leggings, breechcloth, and a tail piece for him. Therefore, his things will be good.

11. She will make his otter too.

Chapter 14 ohkíe

ihcíko akxa ilǫ́ǫška wahǫ́ǫ akxa

1. ilǫ́ǫška záani xóhka watópe ški
2. hpásuolįį céɣenii aðį́ totą́ha wahtą́ka totą́ha níhkaši ški
3. waxákolįį céɣenii aðį́ totą́ha wahtą́ka totą́ha níhkaši ški
4. zą̄ącólįį céɣenii aðį́ totą́ha wahtą́ka totą́ha níhkaši ški
5. záani wawíhǫįpi
6. waaðǫ́ wíhta záani awáachipi hce ówenį atxą́hé
7. ðekǫ́ǫce žáže tóe áapą atxą́hé
8. hpásuolįį céɣenii aðį́
9. waxákolįį céɣenii aðį́
10. zą̄ącólįį céɣenii aðį́
11. wacípxąį
12. waną́še
13. ilǫ́ǫhpa kšǫ́ka mą́zeska nąnúhu ški céɣenii ážu áwakšie atxą́hé
14. kakóną

Grandpa addresses Ilonshka.

1. All Ilonshka, singers, and onlookers.
2. Gray Horse Drumkeeper, Head Committeeman, and Committeemen.
3. Pawhuska Drumkeeper, Head Committeeman, and Committeemen.
4. Hominy Drumkeeper, Head Committeeman, and Committeemen.
5. I respectfully address everyone.
6. I am grateful to everyone that danced on my song.
7. Now, I am going to call a few names (to give them blankets).
8. The Gray Horse Drumkeeper.
9. The Pawhuska Drumkeeper.
10. The Hominy Drumkeeper.
11. The Town Crier.
12. The Whipmen.
13. I will have First Son and Second Son put money and tobacco on the drum.
14. That's all.

Chapter 15 ohkíhkie

1. **iðáce:** wižį́ke akxa íhciko íhkuaci íhta niióhkiac'į ški k'įhta akxai
2. **iihǫ́:** haaská hcéka hkietǫ́ǫpa kǫ́ða akxa

3. haaská wanóp'į huuwáli ðuuzé che ąkáðį ąðįkšé wápaɣa ški
4. áapiolą hcéka mązéštahižį íįhtǫ ądúwį tą
5. **iðáce:** záani wahcéka ąkóhce hta ąðįkšé
6. **iihǫ́:** wanóp'į akšíɣe hta mįkšé tóoce ðiláace ški
7. wižǫ́ą hcéehį ópahtą hįúni kšíɣe hce éepše hta mįkšé
8. **iðáce:** pée hǫǫpé káaɣe
9. Supernaw's hǫǫpé hcéka aðį́ ðą́ąche
10. kaasíta Supernaw's hci ci brée hta mįkšé
11. **iihǫ́:** wižį́ke íišupe áalǫðį ðįká

1. **Father:** Sonny is going to carry Grandpa's fan and mirror board.
2. **Mother:** Sonny wants eight new shirts.
3. We have lots of scarves that he can choose from, and scarf slides too.
4. We will buy new armbands, bells, and earrings.
5. **Father:** We will look for all new things.
6. **Mother:** I will make his choker and bandoleros.
7. I will ask Older Sister to make the streamers and garters.
8. **Father:** Who will make the moccasins?
9. Supernaw's might have new moccasins.
10. I will go to Supernaw's tomorrow.
11. **Mother:** Don't forget Sonny's belt.

Chapter 16 ohkíe

1. hpahą́le hą́ąpa ímąche ohkúlą akíhpaahi ną
2. iiną́ akxa ohkúlą wíhta ápaahi ną
3. iiną́ akxa wihtéžį hiiðá kšíðe kaðǫ́ áðiikxą žį́įhe kšíɣe
4. mį́įoðaake hpeðópa ohkísce tą híibrą híi alúuža kaðǫ́ omíže oákihpaahą ną
5. įhtáci akxa híi ðalúuža ąną́ðǫɣe štą
6. hą́ą tą ąną́puze tą níi ážą páskuha áažu ną
7. níwahce tą iiną́ haxį́ ši wį hce épše ąži mą́ąšcé tą ažį́įhe brúuc'ake
8. mį́įoðaake hkietóopa ohkísce ci áažą kaðǫ́ iiną́ akxa átahką ðuutáži ną
9. iiną́ akxa óðaake wį ąðáace ąži máze ohkíe kihtópe tą ažį́įhe pši ną

1. First, I pick out my clothes for the next day.
2. Sometimes Mom picks out my clothes for me.
3. Mom gives Little Sister a bath and then gets her ready to lie down and sleep.
4. When it's 7:30 I take a bath and brush my teeth and put on my pajamas.
5. Dad always asks, "Did you brush your teeth?"
6. In case I get thirsty during the night I set water beside my bed.
7. If it's cold I ask Mom for another blanket, but I can't sleep when it's hot.
8. I lie down at 8:30, and Mom turns off the lights.
9. Sometimes Mom reads me a story or watches her phone until I go to sleep.

Chapter 17 ohkíe

1. wažáže wéhkilįౖ ðe niáðe
2. wáache akxa haaštáha htóho akxa
3. haaská akxa mązeska zi ékǫ akxa
4. hceehįౖ́ wįౖ akxa žúuce zi mąąhį́ htóho hį́įska žóle akxa hcehį́į́ ímąkše ðiištą́ ðįké
5. háabreka wápaɣa ðáabrįౖ wápaɣa ðilílie
6. hą́ąska wanǫ́p'įౖ į́įhtǫ ški
7. hǫǫpé
8. ákahamįౖ žúuce lǫǫhúu

1. I gave these Osage clothes away.
2. The skirt was blue broadcloth.
3. The shirt was gold.
4. One of the finger woven belts was red, yellow, blue, and green with beads, and the other belt was left unfinished.
5. Ribbons, three shirt pins, and a (shiny) brooch.
6. A bead necklace and earrings too.
7. Moccasins.
8. Red wedding coat and wedding hat.

Chapter 18 ohkíhkie

1. **wakǫ́ze:** pée tooké htąątą́ paðé hówa ðíhǫǫ paašé
2. **waðíopxaðe 1:** pée ą́hǫǫ péetą níižu štą lǫǫhóohtą ánąk'ǫ kóe lǫ́ǫ waléze htǫ́pe ą́hǫǫ mą́žą mąąhį́ htóho ahí ški
3. **waðíopxaðe 2:** tooké ą́hǫǫ taapóska panąą́ kóe mąąšcé akxa ášihta aškáce ą́hǫǫ ahíibra ški
4. **wakǫ́ze:** hówa ðíhǫǫ nįkšé
5. **waðíopxaðe 3:** htąątą́ žą́ape apa ohtáza hkíðe nąpe hką́ącenii taašcúce bríbrą ą́hǫǫ
6. **waðíopxaðe 4:** wíe mįkšé paðé ą́hǫǫ níwahce éetxą kóe pahúðe ą́hǫǫ hą́ąská šooká šcúuce mįౖ kóe pa akíškace

1. **Teacher:** Spring, summer, fall, winter—which do you all like?
2. **Student 1:** I like spring. It rains a lot. I like listening to the thunder and looking at the lightning. And the land becomes green.
3. **Student 2:** I like summer. School is out and it's hot and sunny. I like to play outdoors and swim.
4. **Teacher:** Which do you like?
5. **Student 3:** In the fall the leaves become beautiful. I like smelling warm apple cider.
6. **Student 4:** It's my turn and I like winter. I like when it's cold and snowing. I wear my warm sweatshirt and play in the snow.

Chapter 19 ohkíhkie

1. **wihé:** háapa wahką́htáki ímąche wižį́ke iitáðape ékitxą akxai
2. ihcími apa šáakeoolą́k'o kšíγe hta apa
3. oohǫ́ wahtą́ka mįkšé hce ée apa
4. ée iiðánąhi
5. ą́ðixope akxa wéeaną mįkšé
6. **asíka:** táatą ooðáhą ðikóða
7. **wihé:** wacúe kaascú htáaweli súhka htaaníi wacúe sása žóle háazu wacúe ðubráaska hǫbríke htóho
8. iiną́ akxa hápa káaγe hce mǫ́pše kisúðe apai ékia pe
9. éetana paašpú oohǫ́ hkǫ́bra mįkšé
10. iihǫ́ akxa hpéžehtoho ą́ðíachi ékie kóe iihkó wacúe skúe káaγe hta akxa
11. **asíka:** pée óhką hce éše
12. **wihé:** wižǫ́ą htáaweli hǫbríke htóho káaγe hce épše hta mįkšé
13. wižǫ́ke wacúe kaascú káaγe hkǫ́bra
14. wihtáežį súhka htaaníi wacúe sása žóle škáaγe
15. **asíka:** ąháį
16. **wihé:** paašpú háazu wacúe ðubráaska hpáaγe hta mįksé
17. šímįžį apa híįce ážu hta apai
18. ðáalį hta akxa

1. **Second daughter:** Next week it's Sonny's birthday.
2. Our aunt (father's side) is going to have a handgame for him.
3. She asked me to be the head cook.
4. I agreed (to that).
5. She honored me, and I am thankful.
6. **Third daughter:** What does she want you to cook?
7. **Second daughter:** Frybread, steam fry, chicken and dumplings, grape dumplings, and green beans.
8. Mama said to make a corn dish in remembrance of our ancestors.
9. So, I want to cook ᏢᎪᏍᏢᎤ. (ᏢᎪᏍᏢᎤ [paašpú] is a corn dish.)
10. His mother said she is going to bring a salad and his grandmother is going to make the cake.
11. **Third daughter:** Who are you going to ask to help?
12. **Second daughter:** I am going to ask (older) sister to make the steam fry and green beans.
13. I want my daughter to make frybread.
14. Younger Sister, will you make chicken and dumplings?
15. **Third daughter:** Yes
16. I will make the ᏢᎪᏍᏢᎤ and grape dumplings.
17. **Second daughter:** The girls are going to set the table.
18. It will be good.

Chapter 20 ohkíhkie

1. **wihé:** šáakeooląk'ǫ ðǫ́ha ðiištą́
2. **asį́ka:** šį́mįžį́ apa hį́įce ážu ðiištą́ pe
3. **wihé:** ášihta tópe mąðį́ wižǫ́ke apa wacúe kaascú ðǫ́ha oohǫ́ ðiištą́
4. éetxą súhka htaaníi wacúe sása žóle háazu wacúe ðuubráaska htáaweli hcíhta ąðį́ku kaðǫ́ hį́įce okúhpu káaɣa
5. **asį́ka:** hpéžehtoho ną́ɣeoožu ecí akxa kóe paašpú oohǫ́ ðiištą́
6. wižǫ́e akxa hǫbrį́ke htóho oðókahi šǫ akxa ąži ðǫ́ha ðiištą́
7. **wihé:** mąhkása ąkáaɣe
8. **asį́ka:** tóe hpáaɣe atxąhé
9. **wihé:** wacúe skúe áwanǫbre ážupe níioožu okúhpu akxai
10. ónǫbre che áwanǫbre ážu htai

1. **Second daughter:** The handgame is almost finished.
2. **Third daughter:** The girls have finished setting the tables.
3. **Second daughter:** Go outside and look. Daughter is almost finished cooking the frybread.
4. It's time to bring in the chicken and dumplings, grape dumplings, and steam fry, and fill the serving bowls.
5. **Third daughter:** The salad is in the refrigerator, and the ÞʌꜱÞú is finished cooking.
6. Older Sister is still stirring the green beans, but they are almost done.
7. **Second daughter:** Did we make coffee?
8. **Third daughter:** I'll make some.
9. **Second daughter:** The cake is set on the table, and the pitchers are full.
10. Let's set the food on the table.

Appendix B

Verb Classes

This appendix illustrates the person marking for ten verb classes. It does not include the way plural forms change with aspect marking. Please refer to the chapters for that information.

The third-person forms could be given as *he, she, it,* or *they.*

a-ða

ᏌᏋᏅ	waachí	dance	ᎣᎦᎸ	óhką	help
ᎠᏌᏋᏂ	awáachi	I dance	ᎣᎠᎸᎦ	oáhką	I help
ᏌᎮᏋᏂ	waðáachi	you dance	ᎣᎮᎠᎸᎦ	oðáhką	you help
ᏌᏋᏅ	waachí	(third-person)	ᎣᎦᎸ	óhką	(third-person)
ᎠᏌᏋᏂ	ąwáachi	we dance	ᎠᎪᎣᎦᎸ	ąkóhką	we help

brush

ᏌᎮᎮᎣ	waaðǫ́	sing	ᎮᏄᎦᎠᎸ	ðiištą́	be finished
ᏌᎠᎣ	waabrǫ́	I sing	ᎡᏄᎦᎠᎸ	bríištą	I am finished
ᏌᎮᎠᎠᎣ	waaštǫ́	you sing	ᎠᏴᏄᎦᎠᎸ	scíištą	you are finished
ᏌᎮᎮᎣ	waaðǫ́	(third-person)	ᎮᏄᎦᎠᎸ	ðiištą́	(third-person)
ᎠᏌᎮᎮᎣ	ąwáaðǫ	we sing	ᎠᎮᏄᎦᎠᎸ	ąðiištą	we are finished

stative

ᏌᎤᏍᎠᎦᎸ	húheka	be sick	ᏞᏄᎹᎠ	níhce	be cold
ᎠᏌᎤᏍᎠᎦᎸ	ąhúheka	I am sick	ᏞᏄᎸᎹᎠ	níąhce	I am cold
ᎮᏅᏌᎤᏍᎠᎦᎸ	ðihúheka	you are sick	ᏞᏄᎮᏅᎹᎠ	níðihce	you are cold
ᏌᎤᏍᎠᎦᎸ	húheka	(third-person)	ᏞᏄᎹᎠ	níhce	(third-person)
ᏌᎠᏌᎤᏍᎠᎦᎸ	wahúheka	we are sick	ᏞᏄᎠᏌᎹᎠ	níwahce	we are cold

ki-stative

ᎩᏂᏔᎸᏗ	kídali̥	feel good, like	ᎩᏂᏃ	kízo	enjoy
ᎭᏔᎸᏗ	ádali̥	I feel good	ᎭᏃ	ázo	I enjoy
ᏏᏂᏔᎸᏗ	ðídali̥	you feel good	ᏏᏂᏃ	ðízo	you enjoy
ᎩᏂᏔᎸᏗ	kídali̥	(third-person)	ᎩᏂᏃ	kízo	(third-person)
ᏩᏔᎸᏗ	wádali̥	we feel good	ᏩᏃ	wázo	we enjoy

strong-stem

ᏙᏆ	tópe	watch, look at	ᎢᏆᏍᎣ	ípaho	know
ᏇᏆ	htópe	I watch	ᎢᏥᏆᏍᎣ	íhpaho	I know
ᏍᏙᏆ	štópe	you watch	ᎢᏍᏆᏍᎣ	íšpaho	you know
ᏙᏆ	tópe	(third-person)	ᎢᏆᏍᎣ	ípaho	(third-person)
ᎠᏙᏆ	atópe	we watch	ᎠᎾᏆᏍᎣ	ąnápaho	we know

variations on strong-stem

ᎩᎸᏯ	káaɣe	make	ᎪᏔᎸ	kóda	want
ᏉᎸᏯ	hpáaɣe	I make	ᎪᏒᎸ	hkóbra	I want
ᏍᎩᎸᏯ	škáaɣe	you make	ᏍᎪᏍᏗᎸ	škóšta	you want
ᎩᎸᏯ	káaɣe	(third-person)	ᎪᏔᎸ	kóda	(third-person)
ᎠᎩᎸᏯ	ąkáaɣe	we make	ᎠᎪᏔᎸ	ąkóda	we want

i-stem

ᏈᏥᎸ	íixa	laugh	ᏈᎬꞌᎤᏎ	íkꞌuce	study, try
ᏈᏔᎸᏥᎸ	iiðáxa	I laugh	ᏈᏔᎸᎬꞌᎤᏎ	iðákꞌuce	I try
ᏈᏔᎸᏥᎸ	iiðaxa	you laugh	ᏈᏔᎸᎬꞌᎤᏎ	íðakꞌuce	you try
ᏈᏥᎸ	íixa	(third-person)	ᏈᎬꞌᎤᏎ	íkꞌuce	(third-person)
ᎠᎾᏥᎸ	ąnáxa	we laugh	ᎠᎾᎬꞌᎤᏎ	ąnákꞌuce	we try

h-stem

ᎸᏏ	ahí	arrive there	ᎠᎬᎾ	ékie	speak to someone
ᏉᏍᏂ	pši	I arrive there	ᎠᎬᏉᏍᎠ	ékipše	I speak to someone
ᏍᏂ	ši	you arrive there	ᎠᎬᏍᎠ	ékiše	you speak to someone
ᎸᏏ	ahí	(third-person)	ᎠᎬᎾ	ékie	(third-person)
ᎠᎬᎸᏏ	ąkáhi	we arrive there	ᎠᎸᎬᎾ	éąkie	we speak to someone

nasal-stem

ᏞᏃᎅ	aží	believe	Ꮎ	į	wear
ᏞᏃᎷᎾ	ažámį	I believe	ᎷᎾ	mį	I wear
ᏞᏃᎳᏃᎾ	ažáží	you believe	ᏃᎾ	ží	you wear
ᏞᏃᎅ	aží	(third-person)	Ꮎ	į	(third-person)
ᎬᎳᏃᎾ	ąkáží	we believe	ᎬᎾ	ąkí	we wear

ðe-causative

ɂ'áħa	c'éðe	kill	ħáħa	ðéeðe	send
ɂ'áʌħa	c'éaðe	I kill	ħaʌħa	ðeáðe	I send
ɂ'áħʌħa	c'éðaðe	you kill	ħaħʌħa	ðeðáðe	you send
ɂ'áħa	c'éðe	(third-person)	ħáħa	ðéeðe	(third-person)
ɂ'áʌħa	c'éąðe	we kill	ħaʌħa	ðeą́ðe	we send

𐓇𐓘𐓓𐓘𐓓𐓘 𐒻𐓘-English Glossary

ד́. ą́ą. yes (used by women)
ᐊᔅᐱ. áha. whenever
ᐱᔅᐠ. ąhą́į. yes (used by women)
ᐱᔅń. ahí (h-stem). arrive there
ᐱᔅú. ahú (h-stem). come here
ák̨ᐱᔅᐱ𐒼ń. ákahamį. Osage wedding coat
ᐱk̨ń. akší (a-ða). arrive back there
ᐱk̨ú. akú (a-ða). come back, return here
ᐱᓚᐊ. ále (a-ða). put on top of
ᐱᓚᐊ́. alée (a-ða). go back, return there
ᐊ́ᓚń. áalįį. chair
ᐱᓚń. alí (a-ða). arrive back here
ᐊ́ᓚñᔅᐱ. álįįha. after, afterward
ᐊ́ᓚOħń. áaloðį (br-šc, a-ða). leave behind, forget
ᐊ́ᓚñk̨Oᐊ. ánąąhkoe. floor, porch
ᐊ́ᑭOᓚᐱ. áapiolą. armband
ᐱᔅńᘛñ. asížį. one's fourth-born (and beyond) daughter
ᐱk̨ᑎᗞᐱ. ášihta. outside
ᐱk̨ᐠ ᘛñ. áška ci. near (something)
ᐱk̨ᐠᐱ. áška. nearby
ᐱᗞᐱk̨ᐱ. átahką. lights
ᐱᗞOᑭᗞ. átǫpe (strong-stem). raise, take care of
ᐱᔅᑎᗞᐱ. asíka. one's third-born daughter
ᐱᘛᑎᗞᐱ. áhcihtą. arbor
ᐱᘛń. achí (a-ða). arrive here
ᐱħą́. aðée (br-šc). go there
ᐱħń. aðį́ (br-šc). have, possess
ᐱħńᔅñ. aðį́ahi (br-šc + h-stem). take there, bring there
ᐱħńᔅú. aðį́ahu (br-šc + h-stem). bring here

ᴧᏖᎶᴧᏕᏥᑎ. aðį́akši (br-šc + a-ða). take back there, take home
ᴧᏖᎶᴧᏕU. áðįaku (br-šc + a-ða). bring back here
ᴧᏖᎶᴧᏓᾱ. aðį́alee (br-šc + a-ða). take back, take home
ᴧᏖᎶᴧᏓᑎ. aðį́ali (br-šc + a-ða). bring back here, bring home
ᴧᏖᎶᴧᏖᾱ. aðį́aðee (br-šc). carry, take there
ᴧᏖᎶᴧᏉᑎ. aðį́achi (br-šc + h-stem). bring here, arrive with
ᴧᏖñᏦᏥᴧ. áðiikxą. lying down
ᴧᏖŪÐᴧ. áðuuhta. across
ᴧ५ᴧᏓOᎡᾱ. áwanǫbre. table
ᴧZᴧ. ážą (a-ða). lie on
ᴧZᴧ. ážą. bed
ᴧZń. ažį́ (nasal stem). believe, think
ᴧZU. ážu (a-ða). set items out on something
ᏒᴧᏜᏥᾱᏦᾱ. brápxąąke. mosquito
ᏒᾱᏟᏦᴧ. bráaska. flat
ᏒÓᏦᴧ. bróka. dollar
GÓÐᴧ. čóopa. small amount, few (also a noun)
ᾱ̋. ée (h-stem). say
áᏦnᾱ. ékie (h-stem). say to others
áᏦnᴏ̇. ékįǫ (nasal stem). do (in the presence of others)
áᏦᴏ. ékǫ. like that
ᾱ̋ᏓΛ. éena. therefore, that's why
áᴏ̇. éǫ (nasal stem). do (not in the presence of others, not for others)
áÐΛ. étą. therefore
ᾱ̋ÐᏥΛ. éetxą. it is time to
áᏖᾱ. éðe (br-šc). thinking that way, consider, believe
ᾱ̋ᏖŌÐᴧ. éeðǫǫpa. both, both of them
Ꮛ̋. hą́ą. night
ᏕᾴᏒᾱᏦᴧ. háabrehka. ribbon, ribbons sewn on Osage clothing
ᏕᾴᏦᴏᎠᴧ. háakǫta. why?
ᏕᾴᏦᴧZᑎ. hą́ąhkaži. no (used by men and women)
ᏕᴧᏓáZO५ᾱᏦᾱ. haaléžowaake. handkerchief
Ꮛ̋ᏁᴧᏆ Ðᴧ५ᴧ. hą́ąmąðį htą́wą. Hominy (city in Oklahoma)
ᏕᾴᏓᴧ. háaną. how many?
ᏕᾴÐᴧ Ꮖᾱ. hą́ąpa ðe. today
ᏕᾴÐᴧ ५ᴧᏦᴧÐᾴᏦᑎ. hą́ąpa wahkątáki. week
ᏕᾴÐᴧ Zᾱ́Ꮣᑎ. hą́ąpa záani. all day
ᏕᾴÐᴧ. hą́ąpa. day
ᏕᴧÐᴧ ५ᴧᏬÚᾱ. hápa wacúe. cornbread (general)
ᏕᴧÐᴧ. hápa. corn
ᏕᴧᏟᏦᴧ. haaská. shirt
ᏕᴧᏟᏦᴧᏁᑎ̇. haaskámį. lightweight shawl
ᏕᴧᏕᎠÐᴧᏕᴧ. haaštáha. a woolen broadcloth
ᏕᴧᎠÐᏥᾴÐᴧ. haatxą́ta. when (in the present or future)?

haatxáci. when (in the past)?
háace. last night
háaci. last night (variant)
háahci. all the time, continually
háaðe. tonight
hawé. hello
haxį́. blanket
háazu wacúe ðubráaska. grape dumplings
héeoce. monkey
híi. teeth
híihką. ankle
hį́iska wanóp'į. bead necklace
hį́iska. beads, often for dance clothes
hį́ice. plate, dish
hį́icežį. plates
hiiðá (br-šc). swim, bathe
híðaxa. breechcloth
híðe (ðe-causative). send there
hiúni. garter
ho. fish
hóo. voice
hǫbríke htóho. green beans
hǫbríke. beans
hǫǫpé. shoes
hóohtą (a-ða). shout, bark, howl
hóohtą. animal noise
hówa. which?
howáįki. where?
howé. yes (used by men)
húu. many, lots
húhaska íe. English language.
húheka (stative). be sick
húuįke. leggings
hukáaɣe (strong-stem). pass (e.g., the sugar)
huuhtáka. a large number of
húðe (ðe-causative). hand over
huuwáli. a lot of
húužį. a bit of, a few of
į (nasal stem). wear (clothes)
íe (a-ða). talk, speak
íe. word, speech, vocabulary
íe okípše (a-ða). keep one's word
íe wahkílaace. grammar
íihǫ (i-stem). ask as a request

ⁿsó. iihǫ́. his/her or an/the aunt (mother's elder; short form)
ⁿsóðʌ. iihǫ́htą. his/her or an/the aunt (mother's elder)
ⁿsóziⁿ. iihǫ́žį. his/her or an/the aunt (mother's younger; žį form)
ik'uce. ík'uce (i-stem). practice, study, try
ik'uce. ík'uce. practice
ikáðʌmʌ. íikaahtamą. bell
ikiha. íkiha. repetitively, every time
ikihtope. íkihtope (a-ða). visit one's family
ikǫ́. iihkǫ́. grandmother (any side; ALSO his/her grandmother)
ikówa. ihkówa. friend
ikuaci. íhkuaci. fan
ilóeži. ilǫ́eží. cat
ilǫ́hpa. ilǫ́ǫhpa. one's firstborn son
imą. ímą. one or the other
imąkše. ímąkše. other
imache. ímąche. the next one
iiná. iiną́. (our) mother
iináhi. iiną́hi (i-stem). agree
iinához. iiną́htą. (our) aunt, mother's older sister
iinához. iiną́htą. my aunt (mother's elder)
iináží. iiną́žį. (our) aunt, mother's younger sister
ipaho. ípahǫ (i-stem, strong). know
ipše. ípše (i-stem). come by, pass by
ihpią. íhpią. belt
iisewaðe. iiséwaðe. mean
iisewai. iiséwai. mean (variant)
iištáxi íe. įįštáxį íe. English language
iišupe. íišupe. men's belt
iðǫye. íðǫye (br-šc). ask a question
ihtáci. įhtáci. (our) father
ihtácihta. įhtácihtą. (our) uncle, father's older brother
ihtáciži. įhtácižį. (our) uncle, father's younger brother
iihto. íįhtǫ. earrings
ihtóį ðéha. ihtǫ́į ðéha. future, the future
iceki. icéki. his/her or a/the uncle (mother's brother)
ihciko. ihcíko. his/her or a/the grandfather (any side)
ihcimi. ihcími. his/her or an/the aunt (father's sister; any)
ihcošpa. ihcóšpa. his/her or a/the grandchild (general)
ichoka. ichóka. mouse
iðahpe. iðáhpe (i-stem). wait, wait for
iðace. iðáce. his/her father (ALSO his/her father's brother)
iðaceži. iðácežį. (someone else's) uncle (father's brother)
iiðe. íiðe (i-stem). see, find
iðǫye. íðǫye (br-sc). ask for information

íixa (i-stem). laugh
ižíke. his/her or a/the son (any; general term)
ižóke. his/her or a/the daughter (any; general term)
k'ąsaaki. fast
k'ú (a-ða). give
kahíke. chief
kaasį́. tomorrow
kaasį́tą. tomorrow (variant)
kaasįexci wanóbre. breakfast (morning meal)
kaasįexci. morning, in the morning
kaaskíke (ki-stative). be tired (physically)
kašpéopa. quarter (coin)
kaacúxe (kaa-delete). sweep
kaðǫ́. and (sequential) . . . and then.
káxa. creek
káaɣe (strong-stem). make
kaažį́ (a-ða). drive (something, e.g., a car)
kíhoǫ (ki-stative). like, like to do things
kįíkįįežį́. butterfly
kíkxo. feast (noun)
kíopxa (ki-stative). understand.
kíoxta (ki-stative). like or love someone
kípą (strong-stem). call, invite
kisúðe (a-ða). remember
kítąhe (a-ða). get better
kíðalį (ki-stative). be glad, be pleased, like
kíðe (a-ða). allow (own relatives) to
kįįðe (a-ða). throw
kízo (ki-stative). enjoy, like
kóða (strong, br-šc). want
kšáka. one's second-born son
kšíðe (a-ða). allow, have something done
kšíɣe (a-ða). make for
kšǫ́ka. second son (variant)
kxáke. third son
kxážį. one's third-born (and beyond) son
hkąą́ce hį́įšce. peach
hkąą́ce žúe. tomato
hkąą́ce. apple or fruit
hkąą́cenii. juice
hkąą́cóolą. pie
hkáwa. horse
hkée. turtle
hkietóopa. eight

ʰōᴅ₍ₐ. hkoopšé (a-ða). run away, flee
ʰóʰʌ. hkóða. friend
ʟʌᴅʜʌ̃ᵏa. lápxąąke. mosquito
ʟʌ̃ʰa. ḷą́ąðe. big
ʟʌzʌ̃. lažį́į. thin, skinny, slender
ʟⱯʀʌ ᴇᴀ̨ʌ̃̃ᵏa. lébrą hcewį́įke. nine
ʟⱯʀʌ. lébrą. ten
ʟʌ̃ⓢʙʌ̃. liiškí (ki-ð-stem). wash own hair or laundry
ʟőʾ ↯ʌʟá7a. ḷǫ́ǫ waléze. lightning
ʟō̃ɾőᴅʌ. ḷǫǫhóohtą. thunder
ʟōɾᴜ̃́. ḷǫǫhúu. Osage wedding hat
ʟūzʌ́. luužá (ki-ð-stem). wash own body or things
ʟúzn. lúži. slowly
ᴍʌ̃ɾń. mąąhį́. grass or hay
ᴍʌ̃́ɾn̄. mą́ąhį. knife
ᴍʌ́ᵏʌ. mą́ka. skunk
ᴍʌʙ́ʌ. mąhká. medicine
ᴍʌʙ́Ɐᴅʌ. mąhkáhpa. pepper
ᴍʌʙ́ʌ́ᴄʌ. mąhkása. coffee
ᴍʌ́ʂo. mą́šǫ. feather
ᴍʌ̃ʂᴇá. mą́ąšcé. hot weather
ᴍʌʂᴇń́ᵏʌ. mąšcį́ka. rabbit
ᴍʌʂᴇń́ᵏʌzn̄. mąšcį́kažį. bunny
ᴍʌʰń. mąðį́ (br-šc). walk
ᴍʌ́ʜᴅᴜ. mą́xpu. cloud
ᴍʌ́̃ɥa. mą́ąɣe. weather
ᴍʌ́7a ɾń̄ᴇazn̄. mą́ze hį́įcežį. metal bowl
ᴍʌ́7a n̄̃ⓢᴅő́ʟʌ. mą́ze įįštóolą. eyeglasses
ᴍʌ́7a oʙ́nα. mą́ze ohkíe. telephone
ᴍʌ́7a ↯Ɐōɾoʾ. mą́ze wéoohǫ. stove
ᴍʌ́7aōɾoʾ. mą́zeoohǫ. oven
ᴍʌ́7aᴄʙʌ 7n á̃ᵏoʾ. mą́zeska zi ékǫ. gold color
ᴍʌ́7aᴄʙ́ʌ. mą́zeska. money
ᴍʌ́7aⓢᴅʌɾn̄zn̄. mą́zeštahižį. bells for men's dance clothes
ᴍʌ́7a ᴇúʙα. mą́ze hcúke. spoon (metal)
ᴍʌ́zʌ. mą́žą. land
ᴍʌ̃́zʌʜα. mą́ążąxe. onion
ᴍn̄. mį. blanket or robes (general term)
ᴍń̄. mį́į. sun
ᴍń̃oᴅʌ. mį́įǫpa. moon
ᴍń̃oʰʌᵏa ɾʌ́ʟʌ. mį́įǫðaake háaną. what time?
ᴍń̃oʰʌᵏa. mį́įǫðaake. clock, o'clock, time of day
ᴍń̃ᴅóαʟn̄. mįįhtǫ́eli. gum
ᴍń̃ʰoᴅʌ ʰn̄ⓢᴅʌ́. mį́įðohta ðiištą́. afternoon

𐒼𐓣́𐓧𐓪𐓰𐓣. míįðohta. noon, midday
𐒼𐓣́𐓶𐓘𐓩𐓘𐒿𐒷. míwaapaache. blanket (a woman's)
𐒼𐓣́𐓲𐓧. míɣa. duck
𐒼𐓪́𐓬𐓦𐓘. mópše. ancestors
𐓩𐓧𐒼'𐓟́. nąk'ǫ́ (a-ða). hear
𐓩𐓧𐒼𐓧. nąka. maybe
𐓩𐓬́𐒼𐓘. ną́ąke (a-ða). run
𐓩𐓧𐓩𐓶́𐓯𐓶. nąnúhu. tobacco
𐓩𐓬́𐓻𐓷𐓧. ną́ąšta (a-ða). stop (when walking or running)
𐓩𐓬́𐓺𐓘 𐒼𐓣́𐓬𐓦𐓘. náɣe kípše. ice cream
𐓩𐓬́𐓺𐓘 𐓬𐓘𐓻𐓟́𐓩𐓣. náɣe paazénii. ice cream
𐓩𐓬́𐓺𐓘. náɣe. ice
𐓩𐓬́𐓺𐓘𐓪𐓻𐓶. náɣeoožu. refrigerator
𐓩𐓬́𐓻𐓣. ną́ąží (a-ða). stand, stand up, step on
𐓩𐓣́𐓟. níe (stative). be hurt, in pain
𐓩𐓣𐒼𐓬́𐓬𐓦𐓪𐒼𐓘. niikáapxohke. soda, pop
𐓩𐓣́𐒼𐓧. níhka. man
𐓩𐓣́𐒼𐓧𐓦𐓣. níhkaši. person, people, human (variant)
𐓩𐓣́𐒼𐓧𐓦𐓣𐓘 𐓣́𐒼𐓣𐓶𐓧. níhkašie íikimą̨į. visitors
𐓩𐓣́𐒼𐓧𐓦𐓣𐓘. níhkašie. person, people, human
𐓩𐓣́𐓧𐓣. níini. cold water
𐓩𐓣́𐓪𐒼𐓣𐓧𐒿'𐓣. nióhkiac'į. mirror board
𐓩𐓣́𐓪𐓻𐓶. níioožu. pitcher
𐓩𐓣́𐓯𐒼𐓶𐓘. níiskue. salt
𐓩𐓣𐓰𐓬́𐓦𐓧. niitáahpa. pond
𐓩𐓣́𐓻𐓘. níhce (stative). be cold
𐓩𐓣́𐓴𐓘. níðe (ðe-causative). give away
𐓩𐓣́𐓶𐓧𐒿𐓘. níwahce (single-form). it's cold (weather)
𐓩𐓣́𐓻𐓶. níižu. rain
𐓩𐓣́𐓻𐓶𐒿𐓘. níižuuce. river, especially the Arkansas River
𐓩𐓪́. nǫ́ǫ. old, elderly
𐓧𐓪𐓬𐓟́𐓯𐓣. nǫhpéhi (stative). be hungry
𐓧𐓪́𐓬𐓘. nǫ́ǫhpe (stative). be afraid (of)
𐓪́𐓯𐓘𐓯𐓧𐓻𐓣. óhesaži. fast
𐓪́𐓯𐓪 ́𐓘́𐒼𐓧𐓯𐓣. óohǫ wékahi. cook-paddle
𐓪́𐓯𐓪́. oohǫ́ (a-ða). cook, prepare
𐓪́𐓯𐓪. óohǫ. a cook
𐓪𐓯𐓪́𐒿𐓣. oohǫ́hci. kitchen
𐓪𐒼𐓣́𐓬𐓬𐓬𐓘𐓬𐓧. okíhpaahą (a-ða). dress oneself
𐓪𐒼𐓶́𐓬𐓶. okúhpu (stative). be full
𐓪́𐒼𐓬. óhką (a-ða). help
𐓪́𐒼𐓣𐓘. óhkie (a-ða). talk to someone, talk on telephone, a talk
𐓪́𐒼𐓣𐓘. óhkie. a talk
𐓪𐒼𐓣́𐒼𐓣𐓘. ohkíhkie (a-ða). hold a conversation

okíhkie. a conversation
óhkihpaache. blanket (a man's)
ohkísce. half (of anything)
ohkúlą. clothes
omíže. pajamas, bedding
ónǫbre. food
op'ą́ða. steam, fog on water
opétxą (strong-stem). tie up
opšé (a-ða). obey, follow
ohpé (a-ða). enter, go in
ohtáza. beautiful, pretty
océ (a-ða). look for, search for, hunt
oðáha (br-šc). follow
óðaake waléze. magazine, newspaper, or newsletter
óðaake. story
oðį́įke (br-šc). catch, hug
oðíhtą. car
oðíhtą k'ą́saaki. train
oðóhake. last, final
oðúuc'ake (br-šc). be lazy
ówe. vegetables, groceries
ówehci. grocery store
owísi (a-ða). jump
oxpáðe (stative). get lost, be lost
oxpáðeðe (ðe-causative). lose (something)
óžąke. road
ožéhci. bathroom
ožéðe (stative). be tired (mentally)
oožú (a-ða). pour or put into
óožu. bowl
pa. snow
paahí (strong-stem). gather up
pahúðe (single-form). to snow
páaleze (strong-stem). write
panąą́. adjourned, let out
paasé (strong-stem). cut (something up)
pascé (a-ða). cut into pieces, slices, strips
paašpú. corn dish
páce. boat
paðé. winter
paaxó. hill, mountain
paaxcé (strong-stem). tie down, gather in a bundle
paagóe (strong-stem). push something or someone
paazénii saakí. cheese

Osage-English Glossary

ÞĀZÁLÑ ˇSALN. paazénii wéli. butter, cream
ÞĀZÁLÑ. paazénii. milk
Þǽ. pée. spring
Þǽ. pée. who?
Þǽ ŦNǨÁ. pée ðiké. no one (not anyone)
ÞŃΨΛ. píγą (strong-stem). blow on something
ÞÓCA. póse (a-ða). cut by shooting
ÞÓ§ÞΛ. pószpe (a-ða). shoot a piece out (of something)
ÞÚǨⱮΛ. púkxa (a-ða). wipe something off, erase
ÞU§DΛˇSA. puštáha (strong-stem). iron (clothes)
ÞΛ. hpa. nose or bitter
ÞΛˇSÍLA. hpahále. first, at the outset
ÞĀˇSŃ. hpaahí. sharp
ÞΛˇSÚ. hpahú. hair
ÐΛˇSÚCǨΛ. hpahúska. Pawhuska
ÐΛCUOLÑ. hpásuolį̃. Gray Horse
ÞǼDΛ ZǼLΛ. hpáata žéelą. fried egg or omelet
ÞǼDΛ. hpáata. eggs
ÞΛ7A ˇSLÓⱤA. hpáze wanóbre. supper
ÞΛ7A. hpáze. evening
ÞÁZA ⱤΛǨÁCΛ LŃΨA. hpéže mąhkása náγe. ice tea
ÞǼ₽A ZǼ. hpéece žą́ą́. firewood
ÞǼ₽A. hpéece. fire
ÞǼŦŌÞΛ. hpéeðǫǫpa. seven
ÞÁZA ⱤΛǨÁCΛ. hpéže mąhkása. tea
ÞÁZALÑ. hpéženii. tea
ÞÁZAÐOˇSO. hpéžehtoho. lettuce, salad
ÞΉ. hpį́ (nasal stem). know (how to), be skillful at
ÞŃCU. hpísu. acorns
ÞŃZΠ. hpííži. bad
ÞŃZΠ. hpííži (stative). feel bad
ÐÓǨΛ. hpǫ́hka. Ponca
CΛÞA. sápe. black
CΛĐΛ. sáhtą. five
CŃ. síi. foot
CŃǨΛ. síka. squirrel
CŃCΠ. sísi. energetic
CΠDÓ. sitǫ́į. yesterday
CŃ₽A. síįce. tail piece
CǨΛ. ska. white
CÚǨΛ. súhka. chicken
CÚDΛ. súutą. ripe
§ΛǨA ŃÞUǨⱮΛ. šáake ípukxa. hand towel
§ΛǨA. šáake. hand

ᘂ́ḳaōᴧḳ'ǫ. šáakeoolą̄k'ǫ. handgame
ᘂ́ᴧᴅa. šápe. dark
ᘂ́ᴧᴅa. šáhpe. six
ᘂ́ᴨᴜzᴨ. šímįžį. girl
ᘂ́ᴨᴅozᴨ. šítožį. boy
ᘂ́ᴨᴅᴧ. šíhtąą. fat (adjective)
ᘂḳᴧzа. škáce (a-ða). play
ᘂḳᴨ. ški. also, too, and
ᘂōḳᴧ. šooká. thick
ᴊṓ. hóo. yes (used by men)
ᘂóḳa. šǫ́ke. dog
ᘂóḳaᴅᴧ. šǫ́kehtą. wolf
ᘂóᴨḳᴧca. šǫ́mįhkase. coyote, fox, wolf, canine
ᘂózᴨ. šǫ́žį. puppy
ᘂᴅáḳa. štáke. mild
ᘂzúza. šcúuce. warm (said of clothes)
ᴅᴧᴊá. tąhé (stative). be fine
ᴅáḳᴧza. táahkace (single-form/stative). be hot
ᴅáᴧᴨ. táalį (single-form). burn
ᴅáᴅóᴄḳᴧ(zᴨ). taapóska(hci). school (building)
ᴅáᴅᴜza. táapuze (single-form). dry
ᴅáᴄḳᴧ. táaską (single-form). melt
ᴅáᘂzúa. taašcúe. warm
ᴅáᴅᴧ. táatą. what?
ᴅáᴅᴧ ᵴᴨḳá. táatą ðįké. nothing (not anything)
ᴅóa. tóe. some, any
ᴅōḳá. tooké. summer
ᴅōḳaᴅᴧ. tookétą. in the summer, summertime
ᴅóᴄazᴨ. tóoleži. carrot
ᴅóᴅᴧ. tóopa. four
ᴅóᴅа. tǫ́pe (strong-stem). watch, look at
ᴅóᴄḳᴧ. tóoska. potato
ᴅoᴅáᴊᴧ. totą́ha. committeeman
ᴅóza ᵴᴨᴄᴧza. tóoce ðiláace. bandolero
ᴅóza. tóoce. throat
ᴅᴛáᴊᴧ. txą́ha. until, from
ᴆá ᴄᴨḳó. htáa lįkó. meat gravy
ᴆá. htáa. deer or meat
ᴆᴧᴄáḳ'ᴧ ńᴅᴜḳᴛᴧ. htaną́k'a ípukxa. paper napkin.
ᴆᴧᴄáḳ'ᴧ. htaną́k'a. paper
ᴆáᴄń. htaaníi. soup
ᴆáᴅá. htaapé. ball
ᴆáᴄńza ᵴᴧᴊú. htaasį́įce wahú. roach spreader
ᴆáᴄńza. htaasį́įce. headdress

𐓰𐓠𐓯𐓘. htaaská. sheep
𐓰𐓠𐓪𐓘́. htąątá. autumn, in the autumn
𐓰𐓘𐓰𐓬𐓟𐓘. htáhtaze. grasshopper
𐓰𐓠𐓣𐓘́. htaacé. windy
𐓰𐓠́𐓵𐓘𐓷𐓡. htáaweli. steam fry
𐓰𐓪́𐓡𐓂. htóho. blue
𐓰𐓪́𐓷𐓡. htóolą. sandwich
𐓰𐓪́𐓷𐓡𐓤𐓘. htónąke. otter, otter hide, otter hide garment
𐓰𐓪́𐓻𐓤. htóožu. meat pie
𐓣'𐓘́𐓭𐓘. c'éðe (ðe-causative). kill
𐓣𐓘. ce. lake
𐓣𐓘𐓷𐓟́𐓯𐓤𐓡𐓻𐓡. cexéskažį. cup
𐓣𐓘́𐓺𐓘. céγe. bucket, pail, kettle, pot
𐓣𐓘́𐓺𐓘𐓡𐓻 𐓡𐓭𐓡́. céγenii aðį. drumkeeper
𐓣𐓘́𐓺𐓘𐓡𐓻. céγenii. drum
𐓣𐓪́𐓰𐓡𐓻. cúutaži. raw
𐓣𐓪́𐓣𐓘. cúuce, súutą. ripe
𐓣𐓘́. hcée. buffalo
𐓣𐓘́𐓯𐓘𐓯𐓤𐓡. hcéeheska. cup
𐓣𐓘́𐓯𐓘𐓻𐓡. hcéhežį. dishes, plates, cups, bowls
𐓣𐓠𐓯𐓡́. hceehį́į. streamers, yarn belt
𐓣𐓘́𐓤𐓡 𐓸𐓣𐓡. hcéka xci. brand new
𐓣𐓘́𐓤𐓡. hcéka. fresh, new
𐓣𐓘́𐓽𐓡 𐓰𐓠𐓻𐓡́. hcéwai htaaníi. yonkapin soup
𐓣𐓘́𐓬𐓘. hcéze. stomach
𐓣𐓡́. hcí. house
𐓣𐓡́𐓤𐓂. hcíko. my grandfather (any side)
𐓣𐓡́𐓷𐓘. hcíle. family
𐓣𐓡́𐓪𐓤𐓡. hcíohka. room
𐓣𐓡́𐓰𐓡. hcíhta. inside
𐓣𐓪́𐓤𐓘. hcúke. spoon
𐓭𐓠́𐓪𐓡𐓻. ðáabrį. three
𐓭𐓠́𐓯𐓡. ðáha. when, as soon as
𐓭𐓠́𐓷𐓡𐓻. ðáalį. good
𐓭𐓠́𐓯𐓤𐓡́𐓤𐓘. ðaaškíke (br-šc). chew
𐓭𐓠́𐓰𐓘́. ðaahtá (br-šc). drink
𐓭𐓠́𐓣𐓘́. ðaacé (br-šc). call, pronounce, read
𐓭𐓠́𐓣𐓘́. ðaaché (br-šc). eat
𐓭𐓠́𐓱𐓪𐓘. ðáašoe (br-šc). smoke
𐓭𐓠́𐓻𐓰𐓠́𐓤𐓘. ðaaxtáke (br-šc). bite
𐓭𐓘𐓤𐓪́𐓣𐓘. ðekǫ́ǫce. now
𐓭𐓘́𐓭𐓘. ðéeðe (ðe-causative). send
𐓭𐓡𐓬𐓡́. ðibrą́ (br-šc). smell
𐓭𐓡𐓯𐓪́. ðiihǫ́. your mother

ᎮᏂᏐᎣᎠᏗ. ðiihǫ́htą. your aunt (mother's elder)
ᎮᏂᏐᎣᏃᏁ. ðiihǫ́žį. your aunt (mother's younger; žį form)
ᎮᏁᎦ'ᏅᎻᎠ. ðik'íðe (br-šc). scratch
ᎮᏂᎩᎠ. ðįké (stative). have none, lack, not have anything
ᎮᏁᎩᎠ. ðįké. none, no, not any, there is no
ᎮᏂᎬó. ðiihkó. your grandmother (any side)
ᎮᏂᏐᎩᏅ. ðiiškí (br-šc). launder, wash clothes or hair
ᎮᏂᏐᎠᏗ. ðiištą́ (br-šc). be finished
ᎮᏂᏐᎤᏆᎠ. ðiišúpe (br-šc). open, unlock
ᎮᏁᏆᏞᎠᏃᏁ. ðihtáežį. your younger sister
ᎮᏁᏃᎶᎬᏁ. ðįcéki. your uncle (mother's brother)
ᎮᏁᏃᏅᎬᎣ. ðihcíko. your grandfather (any side)
ᎮᏁᏃᏅᏠᏁ. ðihcími. your aunt (father's sister; any)
ᎮᏁᏃóᎩᏆᎳ. ðihcóšpa. your grandchild (general)
ᎮᏁᎮᏞᏃᎠ. ðiðáce. your father (ALSO your father's brother)
ᎮᏁᎮᏞᏃᎠᏃᏁ. ðiðácežį. your uncle (father's brother; žį form)
ᎮᏂᎮó / ᎮᎤᎮó. ðiixǫ́ / ðuuxǫ́ (br-šc). break something with the hands
ᎮᏁᎮóᏆᎠ. ðixópe (br-šc). honor
ᎮᏁᏃᏅᎩᎠ. ðižį́ke. your son (any; general term)
ᎮᏁᏃóᎩᎠ. ðižǫ́ke. your daughter (any; general term)
ᎮóᏐᏞ. ðǫ́ha. almost
ᎮōᏆᏞ. ðǫǫpá. two
ᎮóᎮᎣ. ðóðo. greasy
ᎮᎤᎩᏞᎻᏞ. ðuuhkáamą (br-šc). ring a bell or doorbell
ᎮᎤᏆᎦᏃᎠ. ðuuhpéece. lighter
ᎮᎤᎠᏞᏃᏁ. ðuutáaži (br-šc). turn off
ᎮᎤᏃ'ᏞᎩᎠ. ðuuc'áke (br-šc). be unable to
ᎮᎤᏐᎠᏕᎤ. ðuuwásu (br-šc). clean, clean up
ᎮᎤᏐᏅ. ðuwį́ (br-šc). buy
ᎮᎤᎻᏅ. ðuxí (br-šc). chase
ᎮᎤᏃᎠ. ðuuzé (br-šc). take, choose, select
ᎮᎤᏃᏞ. ðuužá (br-šc). wash (dishes, a car, etc.; not one's own)
ᏕᏐó. wahǫ́ǫ. address (at an Ilonshka)
ᏕᏐók'Ꮥ. wahók'a. young
ᏕᏐóᎩᏃᎠ. wahóšce. small
ᏕᏐóᎩᎠ. wahǫ́įke. an orphan, without family
ᏕᏐúᎩᏞ. wahúhka. fork
ᏕᏞk'ó. wak'ó. woman
ᏕᏞk'óᏆᏞ. wak'óhpa. first daughter
ᏕᏞk'óᎠᏗ. wak'óhtą. one's firstborn daughter
ᏕᏞᎩᏐᎠᎣ. wákaštǫ. blanket (folded to cushion a seat), saddle blanket
ᏕᏞᎩᎠᏃᏁ. wakáaži (a-ða). drive
ᏕᎩᏁᏆᏕᎻᏞ. wáakipetxą. a wrap-around skirt
ᏕᏞᎩóᏃᎠ. wakóze. teacher

𐓏𐓘𐒻𐓐𐓪𐓰𐓘𐒳𐓈. wahkǫ́tahci. church
𐓏𐓘𐒷𐓘𐓓𐓘. waléze. newspaper, book, printed material
𐓏𐓘𐒷𐓘𐓓𐓘𐓣𐓒𐓘. walézeaace. class
𐓏𐓘𐒷𐓈𐓁. wálį. very, really
𐓏𐓘𐓇𐓘𐓪𐓷𐓘. wanáše. whipman
𐓏𐓘𐓇𐓪𐓤𐓘. waníðe. giveaway items gifted at the dances OR the Giveaway event itself
𐓏𐓘𐓇𐓪𐓐𐓬𐓘. wanǫ́bre (a-ða). to dine (ALSO dinner)
𐓏𐓘𐓇𐓪𐓐'𐓁. wanǫ́p'į. medallion
𐓏𐓘𐓘𐓬𐓘𐓒𐓘. waapáache. ribbon work
𐓏𐓘𐓬𐓘𐓭𐓒𐓘. wapáaxce. bundle
𐓏𐓘𐓬𐓘𐓷𐓘 𐓷𐓣𐓡𐓣𐓡𐓡𐓘. wápaɣa ðilílie. brooch (sparkly pin for ribbon)
𐓏𐓘𐓬𐓘𐓷𐓘. wápaɣa. brooch, scarf slide
𐓏𐓘𐓬𐓘𐓤𐓮𐓊𐓒. wapúška. beads
𐓏𐓘𐓬𐓘𐓤𐓮𐓊𐓘. wapúške. drop feathers
𐓏𐓘𐓇𐓘𐓬𐓘. wasápe. bear
𐓏𐓘𐓇𐓡𐓇𐓈𐓊𐓘. wasísike. energetic, strong
𐓏𐓘𐓇𐓤𐓯𐓘 𐓇𐓘𐓬𐓘. waskúe sápe. blackberry
𐓏𐓘𐓇𐓯𐓒𐓺. wasúhu. clean
𐓏𐓘𐓇𐓯𐓒𐓺𐓞𐓁. wasúhuži. dirty
𐓏𐓘𐓮𐓁. wašį́. bacon or fat
𐓏𐓘𐓮𐓪𐓮𐓘. wašóše. brave
𐓏𐓘𐓪𐓪𐓘𐓒𐓈. watǫ́ehci. store
𐓏𐓘𐓪𐓪𐓬𐓘. watǫ́pe. onlookers
𐓏𐓘𐓪𐓪𐓒𐓈. watǫ́įhci. store (variant)
𐓏𐓘𐓬𐓘𐓊𐓒. wahtą́ka. head (or chief)
𐓏𐓘𐒷𐓁𐓬𐓞𐓤. wacípxaį. town crier
𐓏𐓘𐒷𐓯𐓘 𐓊𐓘𐓇𐒷𐓯. wacúe kaascú. frybread (slit)
𐓏𐓘𐒷𐓯𐓘 𐓇𐓘𐓇𐓒. wacúe sása. dumplings
𐓏𐓘𐒷𐓯𐓘 𐓇𐓊𐓯𐓘. wacúe skúe. cake (common alternative)
𐓏𐓘𐒷𐓯𐓘 𐓇𐓊𐓯𐓤𐓘. wacúe skúðe. cake
𐓏𐓘𐒷𐓯𐓘 𐓪𐓘𐓓𐓁𐓮𐓁. wacúe taazíhi. toast
𐓏𐓘𐒷𐓯𐓘 𐓤𐓺𐓪𐓘𐓬𐓒. wacúe ðutáahpa. biscuit
𐓏𐓘𐒷𐓯𐓘 𐓏𐓘𐓈𐓁. wacúe wéli. frybread (general)
𐓏𐓘𐒷𐓯𐓘 𐓩𐓘𐓒𐓒. wacúe žéela. deep-fried frybread (cornbread)
𐓏𐓘𐒷𐓯𐓘. wacúe. bread (any kind)
𐓏𐓘𐒷𐓯𐓬𐓒. wacúhta. animal
𐓏𐓘𐒷𐓯𐓬𐓒𐓈. wacúhtahci. barn
𐓏𐓘𐒷𐓘. wáache. Osage skirt
𐓏𐓘𐒷𐓘. waaché. Osage skirt (variant)
𐓏𐓘𐒷𐓁. waachí (a-ða). dance
𐓏𐓘𐒷𐓁. waachí. a dance
𐓏𐓘𐓡𐓘𐓯𐓘 𐓒𐓘𐓈𐓒. waðáawa lébra. dime
𐓏𐓘𐓡𐓘𐓯𐓘𐓓𐓁. waðáawaží. coins, change
𐓏𐓘𐓡𐓁𐓒𐓒 𐓊𐓘𐓷𐓘. waðílą káaɣe (strong-stem on káaɣe). make a decision, decide

𐓇𐒰𐓘𐓣𐓪𐓄𐓬𐓘𐓠𐓘. waðíopxaðe. student
𐓇𐒰𐓘𐓣𐓪𐓄𐓬𐓘𐒷. waðíopxai. student (variant)
𐓇𐒰𐓘𐓣. waaðǫ́ (br-šc). sing
𐓇𐒰𐓇𐒰𐓬𐓣. wáwalį. stingy
𐓇𐒰𐓬𐒰𐓗𐓪𐓬𐓣. waxákolįį. Pawhuska District
𐓇𐒰𐓥𐓣𐓗𐒷. wažį́ka. bird
𐓇𐒰́𐓗𐓯𐓬𐓣. ok͟hį́pa-ᶻ. wéhkilį okíhpaahą (a-ða). dress oneself in one's own clothes
𐓇𐒰́𐓗𐓯𐓬𐓣. wéhkilį. traditional clothes
𐓇𐒰́𐓬𐒰𐓛𐒰. wéleze. pen or pencil
𐓇𐒰́𐓬𐓣. wéeli. head
𐓇𐒰́𐓬𐓣. wéli. oil, pork fat
𐓇𐒰́𐓫𐓛𐓪. wéoohǫ. cooking utensils
𐓇𐒰́𐓄𐓶𐓗𐓬𐓬. wépukxa. towels
𐓇𐒰́𐒻'𐓬. wéc'a. snake
𐓇𐒰́𐓗𐓣. wéðį. rope
𐓇𐒰́𐓗𐓶𐓙𐓶𐓄𐒰. wéðušupe. keys
𐓇𐒰́𐓥𐒰𐓬𐓣. wéžeelą. skillet
𐓇𐓣. wį. a
𐓇𐓣𐓯𐒰́. wihé. second-born daughter
𐓇𐓣𐓬𐓪𐒰́𐓥𐓣. wisǫ́ežį. a woman's younger brother
𐓇𐓣𐓬𐓪́𐓗𐓬. wisǫ́ka. a man's younger brother
𐓇𐓣𐓑𐓬𐒰𐓥𐓣. wihtáežį. my younger sister
𐓇𐓣𐓑𐒰́𐓗𐒰. wihtą́ke. a man's older sister
𐓇𐓣𐓑𐒰́𐓥𐓣. wihtéžį. a younger sister
𐓇𐓣𐓓𐒰́𐓗𐓣. wįcéki. (our) uncle, on our mother's side
𐓇𐓣𐓓𐒰́𐓗𐓣. wįcéki. my uncle (mother's brother)
𐓇𐓣𐓓𐒻́𐓗𐓪. wihcíko. our grandfather
𐓇𐓣𐓓𐒻́𐓳𐓣. wihcími. (our) aunt (father's sister; any)
𐓇𐓣𐓓𐒻́𐓑𐓪. wihcįhto. a woman's older brother
𐓇𐓣𐓓𐓪́𐓯𐓄𐓬. wihcóšpa. our grandchildren
𐓇𐓣́𐓬𐓓𐒷. wį́xce. one
𐓇𐓣𐓥𐒻́𐓗𐒰. wižį́ke. son (any; general term)
𐓇𐓣𐓥𐒻́𐓗𐒰. wižį́ðe. a man's older brother
𐓇𐓣𐓥𐓪́𐓬. wižǫ́ą. a woman's older sister
𐓇𐓣𐓥𐓪́𐓗𐒰. wižǫ́ke. (my) daughter
𐓬𐓪́𐓗𐒰. xóhka. singers and drummers (traditional)
𐓬𐒷𐓣. xci. real, very, precisely
𐓬𐓶́𐓗𐓬. xúða. eagle
𐓷𐒰́𐓗𐒰. ɣaaké (a-ða). cry
𐓜𐒰́𐓬𐓣. záani. all
𐓜𐒰́𐓬𐓪𐓬𐓣. zą̄ącólįį. Hominy district
𐓜𐓣. zi. yellow
𐓜𐓣́𐓥𐓷𐓰𐒰 𐒰́𐓗𐓪. zížuuce ékǫ. orange
𐓥𐒰́. žą́ą. forest, woods, wood

𐓓𐓘𐓵𐓪𐒰. žą́ąhkoe. trunk, box (variant)
𐓓𐓘𐓵𐓪𐓵𐒰. žą́ąhkoke. trunk, box
𐓓𐓘𐓣𐓘. žąąníi. sugar
𐓓𐓘𐓣𐓘𐒰. žaaníe. sugar or candy (variant)
𐓓𐓘𐓣𐒰𐓣𐓓𐒷. žąąníeži. candy
𐓓𐓘𐓩𐒰́. žąąpé. leaf
𐓓𐓘́𐓪𐒰. žą́ąxe. stick, pole
𐓓𐒰́𐓓𐒰. žáže. name
𐓓𐒰𐓵𐒰́. žeká. leg
𐓓𐒰́𐓣𐓪. žéelą. fried
𐓓𐓣́𐓱𐒰. žį́įhe (a-ða). sleep
𐓓𐓣𐓵𐒰́ 𐓪𐓷𐒰́𐓵𐓣𐓱𐒰. žįká owáhkihą. a grandchild
𐓓𐓣𐓵𐒰́. žįká. small
𐓓𐓣𐓵𐒰́𐓓𐒷. žįkáži. child
𐓓𐓪́𐓧𐒰. žóle (a-ða). be with, accompany
𐓓𐓲́𐓷𐒰. žúuce. red

English-𐓏𐓘𐓻𐓘𐓻𐓟 𐒻𐓟 Glossary

a. 𐓏𐓣. wį
acorns. 𐓡𐓷𐓣𐓢𐓲. hpísu
across. 𐓘𐓱𐓴𐓹𐓻𐓘. áðuuhta
address (at an Ilonshka). 𐓏𐓘𐓦𐓷̣. wahǫ́ǫ
adjourned (let out). 𐓷𐓘𐓻𐓮̣. paną́ą
after (afterward). 𐓘𐓲𐓣̨𐓶𐓘. álįįha
afternoon. 𐓯𐓣̨𐓣̨𐓱𐓬𐓹𐓘 𐓱𐓣𐓣𐓮𐓹𐓮̣. mį́įðohta ðiištą́
agree. 𐓣̨𐓲𐓘̣𐓶𐓣. iiną́hi (i-stem)
all day. 𐓷𐓘́𐓘𐓹𐓘 𐓻𐓘́𐓘𐓲𐓣. hą́ąpa záani
all the time, continually. 𐓷𐓘́𐓘𐓶𐓣. háahci
all. 𐓻𐓘́𐓘𐓲𐓣. záani
allow (have something done). 𐓤𐓯𐓣̨́𐓱𐓘. kšį́ðe (a-ða)
allow (own relatives) to. 𐓤𐓣̨́𐓱𐓘. kį́ðe (a-ða)
almost. 𐓱𐓬́𐓶𐓘. ðǫ́ha
also, too (see chap. 18). 𐓮𐓤𐓣. ški
ancestors. 𐓯𐓬́𐓷𐓮𐓘. mǫ́pše
and (and then; sequential). 𐓤𐓘𐓱𐓬́. kaðǫ́
animal noise. 𐓷𐓬́𐓹𐓶. hóohtą
animal. 𐓏𐓘𐓻𐓲́𐓹𐓶. wacúhta
ankle. 𐓶𐓣́𐓶𐓤𐓶. hííhką
any (some). 𐓹𐓬́𐓘. tóe
apple (fruit in general). 𐓤𐓘́𐓻𐓘. hką́ące
arbor. 𐓘́𐓻𐓹𐓹𐓶. áhcihtą
armband. 𐓘́𐓷𐓹𐓬𐓲𐓶. áapiolą
arrive back here. 𐓘𐓲𐓣́. alí (a-ða)
arrive back there. 𐓘𐓤𐓮𐓣́. akší (a-ða)
arrive here. 𐓘𐓻𐓣́. achí (a-ða)
arrive there. 𐓘𐓶𐓣́. ahí (h-stem)
ask (as a request). 𐓣̨́𐓶𐓬. íihǫ (i-stem)

ask (for information). íðǫγα. íðǫγe (br-sc)
ask a question. íðǫγα. íðǫγe (br-šc)
aunt (father's sister; see chap. 11). wihcími
aunt (mother's older sister; see chap. 11). iináhtą
aunt (mother's younger sister; see chap. 11). iinážį
autumn. htaatá
bacon (or fat). wašį́
bad. hpíiži
ball. htaapé
bandolero. tóoce ðiláace
bark (howl, shout). hóohtą (a-ða)
barn. wacúhtahci
bathe. hiiðá (br-šc)
bathroom. ožéhci
be afraid (of). nǫ́ǫhpe (stative)
be cold (stative). níhce (stative)
be fine (stative). tąhé (stative)
be finished. ðiištą́ (br-šc)
be full. okúhpu (stative)
be glad (like). kíðalį (ki-stative)
be hot. táahkace (single-form/stative)
be hungry. nǫhpéhi (stative)
be hurt, in pain. níe (stative)
be lazy. oðúuc'ake (br-šc)
be sick (stative). húheka (stative)
be tired (mentally). ožéðe (stative)
be tired (physically). kaaskíke (ki-stative)
be unable to. ðuuc'áke (br-šc)
be with (accompany). žóle (a-ða)
bead necklace. híįška wanóp'į
beads (often for dance clothes). híįska
beads. wapúška
beans. hǫbríke
bear. wasápe
beautiful. ohtáza
bed. ážą
bedding (bundle of bedding, pajamas). omíže
believe (think that way, consider). éðe (br-šc)
believe (think). ažį́ (nasal stem)
bell. íikaahtamą
bells (for men's dance clothes). mázeštahižį
belt. íhpią
big. lą́ąðe
bird. wažį́ka

biscuit. ⺊⼈ᔕᎤα ᏂᑌᎠɅÞɅ. wacúe ðutáahpa
bit (a bit of; a few of). ᒍⓊZᑎ. húužį
bite. ᏂɅʌᎠʎ̧α. ðaaxtáke (br-šc)
bitter. Þʌ. hpa
black. ⊂ʎÞα. sápe
blackberry. ⺊ʌ⊂ḱύα ⊂ʎÞα. waskúe sápe
blanket (a man's; see chap. 11). óⱩɳÞʎ̧ℰα. óhkihpaache
blanket (a woman's; see chap. 11). ᵚή⺊ʎ̧ÞʎℰΑ. mį́waapaache
blanket (see chap. 11). ᒍʌ⼾ή́. haxį́
blow on something. Þή̧Ψʌ. píγą (strong-stem)
blue. ÞóᒍO. htóho
boat. ÞʎᎯα. páce
book (printed matter in general). ⺊ʌᏣή́7α. waléze
both, both of them. ά̧ᏂŌÞʌ. éeðǫǫpa
bowl. ő̧Zᑌ. óožu
box (trunk). Z̧ά̧ḱokα. žą́ąhkoke OR Z̧ά̧ḱoα. žą́ąhkoe
boy. ⱩήᎠOZᑎ. šį́toží
brand new. ℰά̧ḰΛ ⼾ℰᑎ. hcéka xci
brave. ⺊Λ⼾óⱩα. wašóše
bread (any kind). ⺊ʌℰύα. wacúe
break (with the hands). ᏂïⱢΧό. ðiixǫ́ OR ᏂÜⱢΧό. ðuuxǫ́ (br-šc)
breakfast (morning meal). ḰɅ⊂ήα⼾ℰᑎ ⺊ɅᏣό̧Ɽα. kaasį́exci wanǫ́bre
breechcloth. ᒍήᏂʌⱢʌ. híðaxa
bring back (here, home). ʌᏂή́ʌᏣɩ. aðį́ali (br-šc + a-ða)
bring back here. ʌᏂή́ʌḱᑌ. áðįaku (br-šc + a-ða)
bring here (arrive with). ʌᏂή́ʌℰᑎ. aðį́achi (br-šc + h-stem)
bring here. ʌᏂή́ʌᒍᑌ. aðį́ahu (br-šc + h-stem)
brooch (scarf slide, or pin). ⺊ʎÞʌΨʌ. wápaγa
brooch (sparkly pin for ribbon). ⺊ʎÞʌΨʌ ᏂᑎᏣή́Ꮳᑎα. wápaγa ðilílie
brother (man's elder brother; see chap. 11). ⺊ɳZή́Ᏼα. wižį́ðe
brother (man's younger brother; see chap. 11). ⺊ɳ⊂ó̧ḰΛ. wisǫ́ka
brother (woman's elder brother; see chap. 11). ⺊ɳℰή́ᎠO. wihcį́hto
brother (woman's younger brother; see chap. 11). ⺊ɳ⊂όαZᑎ. wisǫ́eží
bucket (kettle, pot). ℰά̧Ψα. céγe
buffalo. ℰά̧. hcée
bundle. ⺊ʎÞʎ̧⼾ℰα. wapáaxce
bunny. ᵚʌⱩℰή́ḰʌZᑎ. mą̧scį́kaží
burn. Ꭰά́Ꮳᑎ. táalį (single-form)
butter (cream). ÞʎᏋʎᏣñ ⺊άᏣᑎ. paazénii wéli
butterfly. Ḱή́ḰñαZᑎ. kį́įkįįežį
buy. Ꮒᑌ⺊ή́. ðuwį́ (br-šc)
cake. ⺊ʌℰύα ⊂ḱύᏂα. wacúe skúðe
call (pronounce, read). Ꮒʎℰά. ðaacé (br-šc)
candy. Z̧ά̧ᏣñαZᑎ. žą́ąníežį

car. 𐓂𐓐𐓆𐓠𐓈. oðíhtą
carrot. 𐓊𐓂𐓍𐓘𐓊𐓈. tóoleži
carry (take there). 𐓈𐓐𐓆𐓈𐓐𐓘. aðíaðee (br-šc)
cat. 𐓈𐓍𐓂𐓘𐓊𐓈. ilóeží
catch (or hug). 𐓂𐓐𐓆𐓐𐓰𐓘. oðíįke (br-šc)
chair. 𐓆𐓍𐓆. áalįį
chase. 𐓐𐓎𐓐𐓆. ðuxí (br-šc)
cheese. 𐓑𐓆𐓋𐓘𐓍𐓆 𐓒𐓆𐓐𐓆. paazénii saakí
chew. 𐓐𐓆𐓢𐓐𐓆𐓰𐓘. ðaaškíke (br-šc)
chicken. 𐓒𐓎𐓐𐓈. súhka
chief (or head). 𐓊𐓈𐓠𐓆𐓐𐓈. wahtą́ka
chief. 𐓐𐓈𐓊𐓆𐓰𐓘. kahíke
child. 𐓏𐓊𐓐𐓆𐓍𐓊𐓈. žįkáží
choose (select, take). 𐓐𐓎𐓋𐓆. ðuuzé (br-šc)
church. 𐓊𐓈𐓐𐓏𐓊𐓠𐓈. wahkǫ́tahci
class. 𐓊𐓈𐓍𐓆𐓋𐓘𐓈𐓠𐓘. walézeaace
clean up. 𐓐𐓎𐓊𐓆𐓒𐓎. ðuuwásu (br-šc)
clean. 𐓊𐓈𐓒𐓎𐓑𐓎. wasúhu
clock (o'clock). 𐓮𐓆𐓐𐓐𐓈𐓰𐓘. mį́oðaake
clothes. 𐓂𐓰𐓎𐓍𐓈. ohkúlą
cloud. 𐓮𐓆𐓐𐓑𐓎. máxpu
coffee. 𐓮𐓈𐓰𐓆𐓒𐓈. mąhkása
coins. 𐓊𐓈𐓐𐓆𐓊𐓈𐓊𐓈. waðáawaží
cold water. 𐓍𐓆𐓍𐓈. níini
come (pass) by. 𐓆𐓑𐓰𐓘. ípše (i-stem)
come back (return here). 𐓈𐓰𐓎. akú (a-ða)
come here. 𐓈𐓒𐓎. ahú (h-stem)
committeeman. 𐓊𐓂𐓊𐓆𐓒𐓈. totą́ha
conversation. 𐓂𐓰𐓆𐓰𐓈𐓘. ohkíhkie
cook (prepare). 𐓎𐓒𐓆. oohǫ́ (a-ða)
cook-paddle. 𐓎𐓒𐓆 𐓊𐓆𐓰𐓆𐓒𐓍. óohǫ wékahi
cook. 𐓎𐓒𐓆. óohǫ
cooking utensils. 𐓊𐓆𐓎𐓒𐓆. wéoohǫ
corn dish. 𐓑𐓆𐓢𐓑𐓎. paašpú
corn. 𐓒𐓆𐓑𐓈. hápa
cornbread (general). 𐓒𐓆𐓑𐓈 𐓊𐓈𐓋𐓎𐓘. hápa wacúe
coyote (fox, wolf, canine). 𐓢𐓆𐓮𐓆𐓰𐓈𐓒𐓈. šǫ́mįhkase
cream (butter). 𐓑𐓆𐓋𐓆𐓍𐓆 𐓊𐓆𐓍𐓈. paazénii wéli
creek. 𐓰𐓆𐓑𐓐𐓈. káxa
cry. Ψ𐓆𐓰𐓆. γaaké (a-ða)
cup. ℓ𐓆𐓊𐓂𐓒𐓰𐓈. hcéheska OR ℓ𐓆Ψ𐓂𐓒𐓰𐓈. céγeska OR ℓ𐓆Ψ𐓂𐓒𐓰𐓈𐓊𐓈. céγeskaží
cut (something up). 𐓑𐓆𐓒𐓆. paasé (strong-stem)
cut by shooting. 𐓑𐓆𐓒𐓘. póse (a-ða)
cut into pieces, slices, or strips. 𐓑𐓈𐓒𐓋𐓆. pascé (a-ða)

dance (n). 𐓏𐓘𐓮𐓂́. waachí
dance. 𐓏𐓘𐓮𐓂́. waachí (a-ða)
dark. 𐓮𐓘́𐓤𐓟. šápe
daughter (first-born; see chap. 11). 𐓏𐓎𐓤'𐓘́𐓪𐓯. wak'óhtą
daughter (fourth-born and beyond; see chap. 11). 𐓘𐓯𐓣́𐓮𐓟. asíži̧
daughter (general; see chap. 11). 𐓏𐓣𐓲𐓪́𐓤𐓟. wižǫ́ke
daughter (second-born; see chap. 11). 𐓏𐓣𐓭𐓟́. wihé
daughter (third-born; see chap. 11). 𐓘𐓯𐓣́𐓤𐓟. asíka
day. 𐓩𐓘́𐓪𐓟. hą́ą́pa
decide. 𐓏𐓘𐓱𐓣́𐓮𐓟 𐓤𐓘́𐓯𐓟. waðíla̧ káaye (strong-stem on káaye)
deep-fried frybread (cornbread). 𐓏𐓘𐓮𐓡́𐓘 𐓲𐓘́𐓮𐓟. wacúe žéela
deer. 𐓡𐓓𐓘́. htáa
dime. 𐓏𐓘𐓱𐓘́𐓏𐓘 𐓬𐓘́𐓤𐓟. waðáawa lébra̧
dirty. 𐓏𐓘𐓮𐓡́𐓩𐓡𐓣. wasúhuži
dishes (plates, cups, bowls). 𐓮𐓘́𐓩𐓘𐓲𐓣. hcéheži̧
dine (ALSO dinner). 𐓏𐓘𐓫𐓪́𐓬𐓟. wanǫ́bre (a-ða)
do (in the presence of others). 𐓟́𐓤𐓣𐓪. ékią (nasal stem)
do (not in the presence of others). 𐓟́𐓪. éą (nasal stem)
dog. 𐓮𐓪́𐓤𐓟. šǫ́ke
dollar. 𐓬𐓪́𐓤𐓘. bróka
dress oneself in one's own clothes. 𐓏𐓟́𐓤𐓣𐓬𐓣 𐓪𐓤𐓣́𐓪𐓡𐓘𐓩𐓘. wéhkili̧ okíhpaahą (a-ða)
dress oneself. 𐓪𐓤𐓣́𐓪𐓡𐓘𐓩𐓘. okíhpaahą (a-ða)
drink. 𐓱𐓡𐓓𐓘́. ðaahtá (br-šc)
drive (e.g., a car). 𐓤𐓘𐓲𐓣́. kaaží (a-ða)
drive. 𐓏𐓘𐓤𐓘́𐓲𐓣. wakáaži (a-ða)
drop feathers. 𐓏𐓘𐓪𐓡́𐓮𐓤𐓟. wapúške
drum. 𐓲𐓘́𐓯𐓟𐓬𐓣. céyenii
drumkeeper. 𐓲𐓘́𐓯𐓟𐓬𐓣 𐓘𐓱𐓣́. céyenii aðí
dry. 𐓓𐓘́𐓪𐓡𐓯𐓟. táapuze (single-form)
duck. 𐓬𐓣́𐓯𐓟. míya
dumplings. 𐓏𐓘𐓮𐓡́𐓘 𐓮𐓘́𐓮𐓟. wacúe sása
eagle. 𐓷𐓡́𐓱𐓟. xúða
earrings. 𐓣́𐓓𐓪. íihto̧
eat. 𐓱𐓡𐓓𐓟́. ðaaché (br-šc)
eggs. 𐓡𐓘́𐓓𐓟. hpáata
eight. 𐓤𐓣𐓟𐓓𐓪́𐓟𐓟. hkietóopa
energetic. 𐓮𐓣́𐓮𐓣. sísi
English language. 𐓣𐓓𐓡𐓓𐓘́𐓱𐓣 𐓣́𐓟. ii̧štáxi̧ íe OR 𐓩𐓡́𐓩𐓘𐓮𐓤𐓟 𐓣́𐓟. húhaska íe
enter (go in). 𐓪𐓡𐓟́. ohpé (a-ða)
erase (wipe off). 𐓪𐓤́𐓷𐓟. púkxa (a-ða)
evening. 𐓡𐓘́𐓯𐓟. hpáze
eyeglasses. 𐓬𐓘́𐓯𐓟 𐓣𐓓𐓡𐓓𐓪́𐓪𐓟. má̧ze ii̧štóolą
family. 𐓲𐓣́𐓬𐓟. hcíle
fan. 𐓣́𐓤𐓷𐓘𐓲𐓣. íhkuaci

fast. 𐒼ʼ𐒰𐒖𐒻𐒼𐒿. kʼą́saaki
fast. ó𐒷𐒰𐒖𐒻𐓄𐒿. óhesaži
fat (adjective). 𐓄𐒷́𐓧𐒰̃. šį́htąą
fat (chubby). 𐓄𐒷́𐓧𐒰𐒼𐒰̨. šį́htąką
fat (or bacon). 𐓏𐒰𐓄𐒷́. wašį́
father (our, see chap. 11). 𐓂𐓧𐒰́𐒹𐒿. į̨htáci
feast. 𐒼𐒷́𐒼𐒹𐒰. kíkxo
feather. 𐒼𐒰́𐓄𐒲. mą́šǫ
feel bad (see chap. 10). 𐓄𐒷́𐒻𐓄𐒿. hpíiži (stative)
final (last). 𐒰𐓍𐒷́𐒺𐓧𐒼𐒰. oðóhake
fire. 𐓄𐒰́𐒹𐒰. hpéece
firewood. 𐓄𐒰́𐒹𐒰 𐓅𐒰́. hpéece žą́ą
first. 𐓄𐒰𐓃𐒷́𐓧𐒰. hpahą́le
fish. 𐓃𐒼. ho
five. 𐓧𐒰́𐒹𐒰. sáhtą
flat. 𐒵𐓇𐓈𐒺𐓧𐒰. bráaska
floor (porch). 𐒰́𐒷𐒼𐒺𐓂𐒰. ánąąhkoe
follow. 𐒰𐓍𐒺́𐓧𐒷. oðáha (br-šc)
food. ó𐓧𐒷𐓂𐒵𐒰. ónǫbre
foot. 𐓧𐒷́. síi
forest (woods, wood). 𐓅𐒰́. žą́ą
forget. 𐒰́𐒰𐓧𐒺𐓍𐒷̨. áalǫðį̨ (br-šc, a-ða)
fork. 𐓏𐒰𐒹𐒻́𐒼𐒰. wahúhka
four. 𐓈𐒺́𐓄𐒰. tóopa
fox (coyote, wolf, canine). 𐓄𐒰́𐓃𐒻𐒼𐒰𐓇𐒷. šǫ́mį̨hkase
fried egg (omelet). 𐓄𐒰́𐓧𐒰 𐓅𐒰́𐒷𐓧𐒰̨. hpáata žéelą
fried. 𐓅𐒰́𐒷𐓧𐒰̨. žéelą
friend. 𐒼𐒺́𐓍𐒰. hkóða OR 𐒻𐒼𐒺́𐓏𐒰. ihkówa
frybread (general). 𐓏𐒰𐒹𐒰́ 𐓏𐒷́𐓧𐒻. wacúe wéli
frybread (slit). 𐓏𐒰𐒹𐒰́ 𐒼𐒰́𐒖𐒹𐒰. wacúe kaascú
future (the future). 𐒻𐒹𐓇𐒺́ 𐓍𐒺́𐒹𐒰. ihtǫ́į̨ ðéha
garter. 𐒹𐒻𐒹𐒻́𐓧𐒿. hį̨úni
gather up. 𐓄𐒰𐒹𐒻́. paahí (strong-stem)
get (be) lost. 𐒰𐓇𐓄𐒰́𐓍𐒰. oxpáðe (stative)
get better. 𐒼𐒻́𐓧𐒰𐒹𐒰. kítąhe (a-ða)
girl. 𐓄𐒷́𐓁𐒷𐓅𐒻̨. šį́mį̨žį̨
give away. 𐓧𐒻́𐓍𐒰. níðe (ðe-causative)
give. 𐒼ʼ𐒺́. kʼú (a-ða)
Giveaway (capitalized for the event; lowercased for items gifted at the Giveaway). 𐓏𐒰𐓧𐒻́𐓍𐒰. waníðe
go back (return there). 𐒰𐓧𐒰́. alée (a-ða)
go there. 𐒺𐓍𐒰́. aðée (br-šc)
gold color. 𐒰́𐒰𐓅𐒷𐓇𐒼𐒰 𐓅𐒻 𐒰́𐒼𐒺. mázeska zi ékǫ
good. 𐓍𐒰́𐓧𐒻̨. ðáalį̨

grammar. íe wahkílaace
grandchild (see chap. 11). žįká owáhkihą
grandchildren (see chap. 11). wihcóšpa
grandfather (see chap. 11). hcíko
grandfather (see chap. 11). wihcíko
grandmother (see chap. 11). iihkó
grape dumplings. háazu wacúe ðubráaska
grass (hay). mąąhí
grasshopper. htáhtaze
Gray Horse. hpásuolįį
greasy. ðóðo
green beans. hǫbríke htóho
groceries. ówe
grocery store. ówehci
gum. mįįhtóeli
hair. hpahú
half (of anything). ohkísce
hand over. húðe (ðe-causative)
hand towel. šáake ípukxa
hand. šáake
handgame. šáakeooląk'ǫ
handkerchief. haaléžowaake
have (possess). aðį́ (br-šc)
hay (grass). mąąhí
head. wéeli
headdress. htaasį́įce
hear. nąk'ǫ́ (a-ða)
hello. hawé
help. óhką (a-ða)
hill. paaxó
hold a conversation. ohkíhkie (a-ða)
Hominy (city in Oklahoma). háąmąðį htáwą
Hominy district. ząącólįį
honor. ðixópe (br-šc)
horse. hkáwa
hot weather. mąąšcé
house. hcí
how many? háaną
hug. oðį́įke (br-šc)
hunt (search, look for). océ (a-ða)
ice cream. náγe kípše
ice cream. náγe paazénii
ice tea. hpéže mąhkása náγe
ice. náγe

inside. 𐓞𐓣́𐓱𐓘. hcíhta
invite (call). 𐓤𐓣́𐓬𐓘͘. kípą (strong-stem)
iron (clothes). 𐓬𐓶𐓯𐓰𐓘́𐓡𐓘. puštáha (strong-stem)
it's cold (weather). 𐓩𐓣́𐓷𐓘𐓞𐓟. níwahce (single-form).
juice. 𐓥𐓘̋͘𐓝𐓟𐓩𐓣̄. hkąącenii
jump. 𐓪𐓷𐓣́𐓮𐓣. owísi (a-ða)
keep one's word. 𐓣́𐓟 𐓪𐓤𐓣́𐓬𐓯𐓟. íe okípše (a-ða)
keys. 𐓷𐓟́𐓵𐓶𐓯𐓶𐓬𐓟. wéðušupe
kill. 𐓝'𐓟́𐓵𐓟. c'éðe (ðe-causative)
kitchen. 𐓪̄𐓡𐓪́͘𐓞𐓣. oohǫ́hci
knife. 𐓨𐓘̋͘𐓡𐓣͘. mą́ąhį
know (how to, be skillful at). 𐓭𐓣́𐓪͘. hpíǫ (nasal stem)
know. 𐓣́𐓬𐓘𐓡𐓪͘. ípahǫ (i-stem, strong)
lack (have no). 𐓵𐓣̄͘𐓤𐓟́. ðįįké (stative)
lake. 𐓝𐓟. ce
land. 𐓨𐓘́͘𐓻𐓘͘. mą́žą
language (speech, talk, word). 𐓣́𐓟. íe
large number of. 𐓡𐓶̄𐓱𐓘́͘𐓤𐓘. huuhtą́ka
last (final). 𐓪𐓵𐓪́𐓡𐓘𐓤𐓟. oðóhake
last night. 𐓡𐓘̋͘𐓝𐓟. hą́ące *OR* 𐓡𐓘̋͘𐓝𐓣. hą́ąci
laugh. 𐓣̋𐓸𐓘. íixa (i-stem)
leaf. 𐓻𐓘̄͘𐓬𐓟́. žąąpé
leave behind. 𐓘̋𐓧𐓪͘𐓵𐓣͘. áalǫðį (br-šc, a-ða)
leg. 𐓻𐓟𐓤𐓘́. žeká
leggings. 𐓡𐓶̋𐓣͘𐓤𐓟. húuįke
lettuce (salad). 𐓭𐓟́𐓻𐓟𐓱𐓪𐓡𐓪. hpéžehtoho
lie on. 𐓘́𐓻𐓘͘. ážą (a-ða)
lighter. 𐓵𐓶̄𐓭𐓟̋𐓝𐓟. ðuuhpéece
lightning. 𐓧𐓪̋͘ 𐓷𐓘𐓧𐓟́𐓺𐓟. lǫ́ǫ waléze
lights. 𐓘́𐓰𐓘𐓥𐓘͘. átahką
lightweight shawl. 𐓡𐓘̄𐓮𐓤𐓘́𐓨𐓣͘. haaskámį
like (see chap. 10). 𐓤𐓣́𐓡𐓪̄͘. kíhǫǫ (ki-stative)
like (see chap. 10). 𐓤𐓣́𐓺𐓪. kízo (ki-stative)
like that. 𐓟́𐓤𐓪͘. ékǫ
look for (search). 𐓪𐓝𐓟́. océ (a-ða)
lose (something). 𐓪𐓸𐓬𐓘́𐓵𐓟𐓵𐓟. oxpáðeðe (ðe-causative)
lot (a lot of). 𐓡𐓶̄𐓷𐓘́𐓧𐓣. huuwáli
love someone. 𐓤𐓣́𐓪𐓸𐓱𐓘. kíoxta (ki-stative)
lying down. 𐓘́𐓵𐓣̄𐓤𐓸𐓘͘. áðiikxą
magazine (or newspaper, printed matter). 𐓪́𐓵𐓘̄𐓤𐓟 𐓷𐓘𐓧𐓟́𐓺𐓟. óðaake waléze
make a decision. 𐓷𐓘𐓵𐓣́𐓧𐓘͘ 𐓤𐓘̋𐓹𐓟. waðílą káaɣe (strong-stem on káaɣe)
make for. 𐓤𐓯𐓣́𐓹𐓟. kšíɣe (a-ða)
make. 𐓤𐓘̋𐓹𐓟. káaɣe (strong-stem)
man. 𐓩𐓣́𐓥𐓘. níhka

English-Osage Glossary

many (lots). 𐒻𐒴. húu
maybe. 𐓇𐒰𐓐𐒰. nąka
mean. 𐒻𐒷𐒼𐒴𐓐𐒰. iiséwaðe OR 𐒻𐒷𐒼𐒴𐓐. iiséwai
meat gravy. 𐓄𐒰. 𐒷𐓐𐓄𐒷. htáa ḷikó
meat pie. 𐓄𐒷𐒼𐓔. htóožu
meat. 𐓄𐒰. htáa
medallion. 𐓐𐒷𐒼𐒴𐓐'𐒻. wanǫ́p'į
medicine. 𐒻𐓐𐒼𐒰. mąhká
melt. 𐓄𐒰𐒼𐓄𐒰. táaską (single-form)
men's belt. 𐒻𐒴𐓐𐒴𐒰. íišupe
metal bowl. 𐒻𐒴𐓐𐒼𐒰 𐒼𐒴𐓐𐒷𐒰𐓐. máze hį́icežį
mild. 𐓐𐓄𐒴𐓀𐒰. štáke
milk. 𐒴𐓄𐓐𐒴𐒼𐒴. paazénii
mirror board. 𐒴𐒴𐓐𐓀𐒴𐓔'𐒻. nióhkiac'į
money. 𐒻𐒴𐓐𐒼𐒼𐒰. mázeska
monkey. 𐓐𐒴𐓐𐒼𐒰. héeoce
moon. 𐒻𐒴𐓐𐒴𐒼𐒰. mį́įopa
morning, in the morning. 𐓐𐒴𐒼𐒴𐒼𐒴𐓐𐓔. kaasį́excí
mosquito. 𐓐𐓐𐓐𐒰𐓀𐒰. brápxąąke OR 𐒴𐓐𐒰𐓀𐒰. lápxąąke
mother (our; see chap. 11). 𐒴𐒷𐒰. iiną́
mouse. 𐒻𐒼𐓐𐒴𐒼𐒰. įchóka
my younger sister. 𐒴𐒼𐒴𐓐𐒼𐒴. wihtáežį
name. 𐓔𐒰𐓔𐒰. žáže
near (something). 𐒴𐓐𐒼𐒰 𐓔𐒻. áška ci
nearby. 𐒴𐓐𐒼𐒰. áška
new (fresh). 𐓔𐒰𐓐𐒰. hcéka
newspaper (magazine, newsletter, printed matter). 𐒴𐓄𐒴𐓐𐒼𐒰 𐒴𐓐𐒰𐓔𐒰. óðaake waléze
night. 𐒴𐒰. háą
nine. 𐒴𐒼𐓐𐒴 𐓔𐒰𐒼𐒴𐓐𐒼𐒰. lébrą hcewį́įke
no (used by men and women). 𐒴𐒰𐓐𐒴𐒼𐒴. hą́ąhkaži
no one (not anyone). 𐓄𐒰𐒴 𐓄𐒻𐓀𐒴. pée ðįké
none (not any, there is no). 𐓄𐒻𐓀𐒴. ðįké
noon. 𐒻𐒴𐓐𐓐𐒴𐒴. mį́įðohta
nose. 𐓄𐒰. hpa
nothing (not anything). 𐓄𐒰𐓄𐒰 𐓄𐒻𐓀𐒴. táatą ðįké
now. 𐓀𐒰𐓐𐒼𐒴𐓐𐒰. ðekǫ́ǫce
obey (follow). 𐒴𐓄𐓐𐒰. opšé (a-ða)
oil (fat, grease, lard). 𐓐𐒰𐒴𐒻. wéli
old (elderly). 𐒴𐒰. nǫ́ǫ
one or the other. 𐒴𐒴𐒼𐒴. ímą
one. 𐓐𐒴𐓐𐒴𐓐𐒰. wį́xce
onion. 𐒻𐒴𐓔𐒴𐓐𐒰. máąžąxe
onlookers. 𐓐𐒴𐓄𐒴𐓐𐒰. watópe
open (unlock). 𐓐𐒴𐓐𐒴𐓐𐒰. ðiišúpe (br-šc)

orange. 𐓓𐓣́𐓓𐓶𐓓𐒰 𐒰́𐔄𐓪. zízuuce éko
orphan (without family). 𐓏𐓘𐓯𐓪́𐔄𐒰. wahóike
Osage wedding coat. 𐒰́𐔄𐓘𐓯𐓘𐓭𐓣. ákahami
Osage wedding hat. 𐓶𐓪́𐓯𐓶́. loohúu
Osage skirt. 𐓏𐓘́𐓵𐒰. wáache OR 𐓏𐒰̄𐓵𐒰́. waaché
other. 𐓣́𐓨𐓘𐔄𐓯𐒰. ímakše
otter (otter hide, otter hide garment). 𐒹𐓪́𐓷𐓘́𐔄𐒰. htónake
outside. 𐒰́𐓻𐓣𐒼𐓰𐒰. ášihta
oven. 𐓨𐓘́𐓓𐒰 𐓳𐓯𐓪́. máze oohó
pajamas (bedding, bundle). 𐓪𐓨𐓣́𐓓𐒰. omíže
paper napkin. 𐒹𐓰𐓘𐓵𐒰́𐔄'𐒰 𐓣́𐒹𐓶𐔄𐓷𐒰. htanák'a ípukxa
paper. 𐒹𐓰𐓘𐓵𐒰́𐔄'𐒰. htanák'a
pass (e.g., the sugar). 𐓷𐓶𐔄𐒰́𐓻𐒰. hukáaye (strong-stem)
Pawhuska District. 𐓏𐓘𐔄𐒰́𐔄𐓪𐓵𐓣́𐓣. waxákolii
Pawhuska. 𐒹𐓰𐓘𐓯𐓶́𐔄𐒼𐓰. hpahúska
peach. 𐔄𐒰̄́𐓻𐒰 𐓯𐓣́𐓻𐒰. hkáace híisce
pen or pencil. 𐓏𐓘́𐓶𐓪𐓓𐒰. wéleze
pepper. 𐓨𐓘𐒹𐔄𐒰́𐒹𐓰. mahkáhpa
person (people). 𐓶𐓣́𐒹𐔄𐓘𐓻𐓣𐒰. níhkašie OR 𐓶𐓣́𐒹𐔄𐓘𐓻𐓣. níhkaši
pie. 𐔄𐒰̄𐓓𐓶́𐓵𐓣. hkaacóola
pitcher. 𐓶𐓣́𐓳𐓓𐓶. níioožu
plant (grow). 𐓳𐓓𐓶́. oožú (a-ða)
plate (dish). 𐓯𐓣́𐓻𐒰. híice
play. 𐓻𐔄𐒰́𐓻𐒰. škáce (a-ða)
Ponca. 𐒹𐓪́𐔄𐒼𐓰. hpóhka
pond. 𐓶𐓣̄𐒹𐒰́𐒹𐓰. niitáahpa
potato. 𐒹𐓳́𐓳𐒼𐓰. tóoska
pour (or put) into. 𐓳𐓓𐓶́. oožú (a-ða)
practice (study, try). 𐓣́𐔄'𐓶𐓻𐒰. ík'uce (i-stem)
practice. 𐓣́𐔄'𐓶𐓻𐒰. ík'uce
puppy. 𐓻𐓪́𐓓𐓣́. šóži
push (something or someone). 𐒹𐒰̄𐓻𐓪́𐒰. paayóe (strong-stem)
put on top of. 𐒰́𐓶𐒰. ále (a-ða)
quarter (coin). 𐔄𐒰𐓻𐒹𐓪́𐓳𐒹𐓰. kašpéopa
rabbit. 𐓨𐓘𐓻𐓻𐓣́𐔄𐒼𐓰. maščíka
rain. 𐓶𐓣́𐓓𐓶. níižu
raise (take care of). 𐒰́𐒹𐓳𐒹𐓰. átope (strong-stem)
raw. 𐓻𐓶́𐒹𐓰𐒰𐓻𐓣. cúutaži
real (very, precisely). 𐔄𐓻𐓣. xci
red. 𐓓𐓶́𐓻𐒰. žúuce
refrigerator. 𐓶𐒰́𐓻𐓘𐓳𐓓𐓶. náyeoožu
remember. 𐔄𐓣𐓵𐓶́𐒹𐒰. kisúðe (a-ða)
repetitively (every time). 𐓣́𐔄𐓣𐒹𐓘. íkiha
ribbon (sewn on Osage clothing). 𐒹𐒰́𐒰𐒹𐔄𐒼𐓰. háabrehka

ribbon work. 𐓇𐓘𐓄𐓘́𐓛𐓣. waapáache
ring (ring a bell or doorbell). 𐓠𐓶𐓤𐓘́𐓪𐓣. ðuuhkáamą (br-šc)
ripe. 𐓌𐓴́𐓂𐓣. súutą OR 𐓌𐓴́𐓣. cúuce
river. 𐓆𐓣́𐓰𐓴𐓣. níižuuce
roach spreader. 𐓂𐓘𐓌𐓣́𐓣𐓘 𐓇𐓣𐓒𐓴́. htaasį́įce wahú
road. 𐓂́𐓲𐓘𐓤𐓘. óžąke
robes. 𐓪𐓣. mį
room. 𐓣́𐓪𐓤𐓣. hcíohka
rope. 𐓇𐓘́𐓠𐓣. wéðį
run away (flee). 𐓤𐓪́𐓄𐓦𐓘. hkoopšé (a-ða)
run. 𐓆𐓘́𐓤𐓘. nąąke (a-ða)
saddle blanket. 𐓇𐓘́𐓤𐓘𐓦𐓂. wákaštǫ
salad (lettuce). 𐓄𐓘́𐓲𐓘𐓂𐓒𐓪. hpéžehtoho
salt. 𐓆𐓣́𐓌𐓤𐓶𐓘. níiskue
sandwich. 𐓄𐓴́𐓒𐓣. htóolą
say to others. 𐓘́𐓤𐓣𐓘. ékie (h-stem)
say. 𐓘́. ée (h-stem)
school (building). 𐓂𐓘𐓄𐓴́𐓌𐓤𐓣(𐓣𐓣). taapóska(hci)
scratch. 𐓠𐓣𐓤'𐓣́𐓠𐓘. ðikʼíðe (br-šc)
search (look for, hunt). 𐓪𐓣𐓘́. océ (a-ða)
see, find. 𐓣́𐓠𐓘. ííðe (i-stem)
select (choose, take). 𐓠𐓶𐓰𐓘́. ðuuzé (br-šc)
send there. 𐓒𐓣́𐓠𐓘. híðe (ðe-causative)
send. 𐓠𐓘́𐓠𐓘. ðéeðe (ðe-causative)
set items out on something. 𐓘́𐓰𐓶. ážu (a-ða)
seven. 𐓄𐓘́𐓠𐓪𐓄𐓘. hpéeðǫǫpa
sharp. 𐓄𐓘𐓒𐓣́. hpaahį́
sheep. 𐓂𐓘𐓌𐓤𐓘́. htaaská
shirt. 𐓒𐓘𐓌𐓤𐓘́. haaská
shoes. 𐓒𐓪𐓄𐓘́. hǫǫpé
shoot a piece out (of something). 𐓄𐓴́𐓦𐓄𐓘. póšpe (a-ða)
shout (bark, howl). 𐓒𐓴́𐓂𐓣. hóohtą (a-ða)
sing. 𐓇𐓘𐓠𐓴́. waaðǫ́ (br-šc)
singers and drummers (traditional). 𐓮𐓴́𐓤𐓣. xóhka
sister (man's elder; see chap. 11). 𐓇𐓣𐓂𐓘́𐓤𐓘. wihtáke
sister (woman's elder; see chap. 11). 𐓇𐓣𐓰𐓴́𐓣. wižǫ́ą
sister (younger; see chap. 11). 𐓇𐓣𐓂𐓘́𐓰𐓣. wihtéžį
six. 𐓦𐓘́𐓄𐓘. šáhpe
skillet. 𐓇𐓘́𐓰𐓰𐓣𐓣. wéžeelą
skinny (thin). 𐓆𐓘𐓰𐓣́. lažį́į
skirt. 𐓇𐓘́𐓣𐓘. wáache
skunk. 𐓪𐓣́𐓤𐓘. mą́ka
sleep. 𐓰𐓣́𐓒𐓘. žį́įhe (a-ða)
slowly. 𐓆𐓴́𐓰𐓣. lúži

small amount, few. ᏀᎰᏢᎯ. čóopa
small plate. ᏚᏁᏃᎯᏃᏂ. hį́įcežį̇
small. ᏏᎯᏚᎤᏬᎨᏃᎠ. wahóšce OR ᏃᏁᏍᎯ. žįká
smell. ᏂᏁᏒᎨ. ðibrą́ (br-šc)
smoke. ᏂᎬᏍᏬᎣᎠ. ðáašoe (br-šc)
snake. ᏏᎠᏢ'Ꭿ. wéc'a
snow (verb for to snow). ᏢᎯᏚᎤᏂ. pahúðe (single-form)
snow. ᏢᎯ. pa
soda, pop. ᏞᏁᏍᎯᏢᎱᎣᏍᎨᎠ. niikáapxohke
some (any). ᎠᎣᎠ. tóe
son (first-born; see chap. 11). ᏁᏞᎰᏢᎯ. ilǫ́ǫhpa
son (general; see chap. 11). ᏏᏁᏃᏂᏍᎨᎠ. wižį́ke
son (second-born; see chap. 11). ᏍᏬᎣᏍᎯᎯ (ᏍᏬᎯᏍᎯᎯ). kšǫ́ka (kšą́ka)
son (third-born; see chap. 11). ᏍᎱᎯᏍᎨᎠ. kxáke
son (third-born; see chap. 11). ᏍᎱᎯᏃᏂ. kxážį̇
soup. ᎠᏞᎨᏁ. htaaníi
speak (talk). ᏁᎠ. íe (a-ða)
speech (language, speech, word). ᏁᎠ. íe
spoon (metal). ᎺᎯᏉᎠ ᏢᎤᏍᎨᎠ. máze hcúke
spoon. ᏢᎤᏍᎨᎠ. hcúke
spring. ᏢᎨᎨ. pée
squirrel. ᏚᏁᏍᎯ. sį́ka
stand (stand up, step on). ᏞᎨᏃᏂ. ną́ąžį̇ (a-ða)
steam fry. ᎠᎬᏚᎠᏞᏂ. htáaweli
steam. ᎣᏢ'ᎯᏂᎯ. op'ą́ða
stick (pole). ᏃᎨᎱᎠ. žą́ąxe
stingy. ᏚᏏᏍᎯᏞᏂ. wáwalį̇
stomach. ᏢᎠᏉᎠ. hcéze
stop (when walking or running). ᏞᎨᏍᏬᎠᎯ. ną́ąšta (a-ða)
store (grocery store). ᎣᏚᎠᏢᏁ. ówehci
store. ᏚᎯᎠᎣᎠᏢᏁ. watǫ́ehci
story. ᎣᏂᎯᏍᎨᎠ. óðaake
stove. ᎺᎯᏉᎠ ᏚᎠᎣᏚᏞ. máze wéoohǫ
streamers. ᏢᎠᏚᏁ. hceehį́į
strong (energetic). ᏚᎯᏚᏁᏚᏁᏍᎨᎠ. wasísike
student. ᏚᎯᏂᏁᎣᏢᎱᎯᏂᎠ. waðíopxaðe OR ᏚᎯᏂᎣᏢᎱᎯ. waðíopxai
study (practice, try). ᏁᏍ'ᎤᏉᎠ. ík'uce (i-stem)
sugar. ᏃᎨᏞᏁ. žą́ąníi OR ᏃᎨᏞᏁᎠ. žaaníe
summer. ᎠᎣᏍᎯ. tooké
summertime, in the summer. ᎠᎣᏍᎯᎠᏞ. tookétą.
sun. ᎺᏂ. mį́į
supper. ᏢᎯᏉᎠ ᏚᎯᏞᎣᏍᎨᎠ. hpáze wanǫ́bre
sweep. ᏍᎨᏉᎤᎱᎠ. kaacúxe (kaa-delete)
swim. ᏚᏁᏂᎯ. hiiðá (br-šc)

table. 𐓘𐓯𐓘𐓜𐓂𐓤𐓪. áwanǫbre
tail piece. 𐓯𐓣́𐓜𐓪. síįce
take (bring) there. 𐓘𐓪𐓣́𐓘𐓯𐓫. aðíahi (br-šc + h-stem)
take back (home). 𐓘𐓪𐓣́𐓘𐓜𐓘̄. aðíalee (br-šc + a-ða)
take back there (home). 𐓘𐓪𐓣́𐓘𐓜𐓤𐓯𐓫. aðíakši (br-šc + a-ða)
talk (language, speech, word). 𐓣́𐓘. íe
talk (speak). 𐓣́𐓘. íe (a-ða)
talk to someone (talk on the telephone). 𐓪́𐓤𐓣𐓫. óhkie (a-ða)
talk. 𐓪́𐓤𐓣𐓫. óhkie
tea. 𐓷𐓘́𐓻𐓘 𐓉𐓘𐓤𐓪́𐓯𐓘 or 𐓷𐓘́𐓻𐓘𐓜𐓣́. hpéže mąhkása or hpéženii
teacher. 𐓯𐓘𐓤𐓪́𐓻𐓘. wakóze
teeth. 𐓯𐓣́. híi
telephone. 𐓨𐓘́𐓻𐓘 𐓪𐓤𐓣́𐓫. máze ohkíe
ten. 𐓜𐓘́𐓬𐓪. lébrą
the next one. 𐓣́𐓨𐓘𐓻𐓘. ímąche
therefore (that's why). 𐓘́𐓜𐓪. éena
therefore. 𐓘́𐓜𐓪. étą
thick. 𐓯𐓪́𐓤𐓪. šooká
thin (skinny). 𐓜𐓘𐓻𐓣́. ląžį́į
think (believe). 𐓘𐓻𐓣́. ažį́ (nasal stem)
three. 𐓪𐓘́𐓬𐓣. ðáabrį
throat. 𐓉𐓪́𐓻𐓘. tóoce
throw. 𐓤𐓣́𐓪𐓘. kį́įðe (a-ða)
thunder. 𐓜𐓪𐓪́𐓪𐓪. lǫǫhóohtą
tie down (gather in a bundle). 𐓷𐓘𐓺𐓻𐓘́. paaxcé (strong-stem)
tie up. 𐓪𐓷𐓘́𐓉𐓻𐓘. opétxą (strong-stem)
time to. 𐓘́𐓉𐓻𐓘. éetxą
toast. 𐓯𐓘𐓻𐓤́𐓘 𐓉𐓘́𐓻𐓣́𐓫. wacúe taazíhi
tobacco. 𐓜𐓘𐓜𐓤́𐓯𐓤. nąnúhu
today. 𐓯𐓘́𐓷𐓜 𐓪𐓘. hą́ąpa ðe
tomato. 𐓤𐓘́𐓻𐓘 𐓻𐓤́𐓘. hką́ące žúe
tomorrow. 𐓤𐓘𐓯𐓣́. kaasį́ or 𐓤𐓘𐓯𐓣́𐓉𐓘. kaasį́tą
tonight. 𐓯𐓘́𐓪𐓘. hą́ąðe
too, also (see chap. 18). 𐓯𐓤𐓣. ški
towels. 𐓯𐓘́𐓷𐓤𐓤́𐓻𐓫. wépukxa
town crier. 𐓯𐓘𐓻𐓣́𐓷𐓻𐓘. wacípxaį
traditional clothes. 𐓯𐓘́𐓤𐓣𐓜𐓣́. wéhkilį
train. 𐓪𐓪𐓣́𐓷𐓘 𐓤'𐓘́𐓯𐓘𐓤𐓣. oðíhtą k'ą́saaki
trunk (box). 𐓻𐓘́𐓤𐓪𐓤𐓪. žą́ąhkoke or 𐓻𐓘́𐓤𐓪𐓘. žą́ąhkoe
try (practice, study). 𐓣́𐓤'𐓤𐓻𐓘. ík'uce (i-stem)
turn off. 𐓪𐓉𐓘́𐓻𐓫. ðuutáaži (br-šc)
turtle. 𐓤𐓘́. hkée
two. 𐓪𐓪𐓷𐓘́. ðǫǫpá
uncle (father's younger brother; see chap. 11). 𐓣𐓉𐓘́𐓻𐓣𐓻𐓣. įhtácižį

uncle (father's older brother; see chap. 11). 𐒰𐒷𐒺𐒸𐒻𐒸𐒼. įhtácihtą
uncle (mother's brother; see chap. 11). 𐒽𐒾𐒿𐓀𐓁𐒻. wįcéki
understand. 𐓂𐒻𐒺𐓃𐒾𐒸. kíopxa (ki-stative)
until (from). 𐒸𐒾𐒼𐒽𐒸. txą́ha
vegetables. 𐒺𐒽𐒻. ówe
very (really). 𐒽𐒸𐒾𐒺. wálį
visit (one's family). 𐒻𐓂𐒾𐒸𐒺𐒸𐒻. íkihtǫpe (a-ða)
visitors. 𐒾𐒻𐓂𐒾𐒿𐒸𐒺 𐒻𐓂𐒾𐒺𐒿. níhkašie íikimąį
vocabulary. 𐒻𐒺. íe
voice. 𐒽𐒻. hóo
wait (for). 𐒸𐓃𐒾𐒻𐒺. iðáhpe (i-stem)
walk. 𐒿𐒾𐓃𐒾. mą́ðį (br-šc)
want. 𐒼𐒻𐓃𐒾. kǫ́ða (strong, br-šc)
warm (a room or clothes, not a person). 𐒿𐒻𐒽𐒻𐒺. šcúuce
warm. 𐒸𐒾𐒿𐒻𐒽𐒺. taašcúe
wash (dishes, a car, etc.; not one's own). 𐓃𐒾𐒾𐒿𐒸. ðuužá (br-šc)
wash (own body or things). 𐒾𐒼𐒾𐒿𐒸. luužá (ki-ð-stem)
wash (own hair or laundry). 𐒾𐒺𐒿𐒼𐒾. liiškí (ki-ð-stem)
wash clothes or hair. 𐓃𐒺𐒿𐒼𐒾. ðiiškí (br-šc)
watch (look at). 𐒸𐒻𐒺𐒺. tǫ́pe (strong-stem)
wear (clothes). 𐒻. į (nasal stem)
weather. 𐒿𐒾𐓄𐒺. mą́ąye
week. 𐒽𐒾𐒺 𐒽𐒺𐒼𐒸𐒾𐒼𐒻. hą́ąpa wahkątáki.
what time? 𐒿𐒻𐒺𐓃𐒾𐒼𐒺 𐒽𐒾𐒾𐒺. mį́ioðaake háaną
what? 𐒸𐒾𐒸𐒾. táatą
when (as soon as). 𐓃𐒾𐒺𐒸. ðáha
whenever. 𐒾𐒺𐒸. áha
when (in the past)? 𐒽𐒾𐒸𐒾𐒼𐒻𐒸. haatxą́ci
when (in the present or future)? 𐒽𐒾𐒸𐒼𐒾𐒸𐒸. haatxą́ta
where? 𐒽𐒻𐒽𐒾𐒼𐒸. howáįki
which? 𐒽𐒻𐒽𐒸. hówa
whipman. 𐒽𐒾𐒾𐒼𐒿𐒺. waną́še
white. 𐒻𐒼𐒸. ska
who? 𐒺𐒾. pée
why? 𐒽𐒾𐒼𐒻𐒽𐒸. háakǫta
windy. 𐒺𐒾𐒿𐒾. htaacé
winter. 𐒺𐒸𐓃𐒾. paðé
wipe off (erase). 𐒺𐒾𐒼𐒸𐒸. púkxa (a-ða)
wolf. 𐒿𐒻𐒼𐒸𐒺𐒸. šǫ́kehtą
woman. 𐒽𐒸𐒼'𐒻. wak'ó
woolen broadcloth. 𐒽𐒾𐒿𐒸𐒾𐒽𐒸. haaštáha
word (talk, speech). 𐒻𐒺. íe
wrap-around skirt. 𐒽𐒾𐒼𐓁𐒺𐒸𐒸𐒾. wáakipetxą
write. 𐒺𐒾𐒾𐒾𐓅𐒺. páaleze (strong-stem)

yarn belt. 𐓳𐓟̄𐓡𐓣̋͘. hceehį́į
yellow. 𐓺𐓣. zi
yes (used by men). 𐓡𐓪̋. hóo
yes (used by men). 𐓡𐓪𐓷𐓟́. howé
yes (used by women). 𐓘̋͘. ą́ą
yes (used by women). 𐓘͘𐓡𐓘́͘. ąhą́į
yesterday. 𐓮𐓣𐓰𐓫́. sitǫ́į
yonkapin soup. 𐓳𐓟́𐓷𐓙 𐓱𐓘̄𐓩𐓣̋. hcéwai htaaníi
young. 𐓷𐓘𐓡𐓪́𐓤'𐓘. wahók'a

Index

a-ða verb class, 49, 51–52; paradigms for 78; special case of wa and o verbs, 54. *See also* Appendix B

a, first-person singular pronoun, 51–52; position with wa and o verbs, 54–55. *See also* a-ða verb class

ą: first-person dual and plural subject pronoun, 71–72, 74–75, 77; first-person singular object pronoun, 97; first-person singular stative subject pronoun, 110. *See also* Appendix B

ą...pe, first-person plural pronoun, completive, 72

áape, reportive evidential marker, 223–24

ąðé, first-person dual continuous aspect, moving or have been doing, 75. *See also* 77–79

ąðihé, first-person singular emphatic continuous aspect, moving or have been doing, 61, 64

ąðįkšé, first-person dual continuous aspect, sitting, lying, or ongoing, 74–75. *See also* 77–79

adjective: as modifier, 32–33; as predicate, 33–34

áha, connector, 139, 140, 161. *See* Chapter 13 and 15

ąhé, first-person singular continuous aspect, moving or have been doing, 60–61, 64. *See also* 77–79

ąk, form of first-person dual and plural subject pronoun *ą*, 71–72, 74–75, 77

ąkáðe, first-person plural continuous aspect, sitting, moving, lying, or have been doing, 75–77. *See also* 77–79

ąkatxą́, first-person plural continuous aspect, standing or imminent, 76–77. *See also* 77–79

ąkóe, first-person dual and plural emphatic pronoun, 143

ąkóhta, first-person dual possessive pronoun, 141

ąkóhtapi, first-person plural possessive pronoun, 141

akxa: subject marker, 22; continuous aspect marker, 24, 65. *See* subject marker, aspect

akxai, variation of *akxa* and uses of, 24–25, 65. *See also* 77–79

apa: subject marker, 22; continuous aspect marker, 23–25, 65. *See* subject marker, aspect

apai, variation of *apa* and uses of, 24–25, 65. *See also* 77–79

aspect: definition of, 22; completive, 23; continuous, 23–24; durative, 138; habitual, 136–38

ątxąhé, first-person singular continuous aspect, standing or imminent action, 61–62, 64. *See also* 77–79

ąži, connector, 164. *See* Chapter 15

br-šc (brush) verb class, 51–53; variations 77–79. *See also* Appendix B

br, first-person singular pronoun, 51, 52, 53. *See also* br-šc (brush) verb class

causatives: using ðe-causative verbs, 213–15; using *káaɣe*, *kšíðe*, and *kíðe*, 215–16

che: as connector, 163–64; as evidential, 26; as position marker, 207, 208

clauses, definition of 139, 161; examples of types 166–67. *See* Chapter 15
commands: definition of, 128; 'let's,' 129; negative, 132; plural, 128–29; singular, 128
compound nouns, 219–20
connectors, definition of, 139–40, 161. *See* Chapter 15
converting verbs to nouns, 219

ðá, first-person singular pronoun i-stem class, 88
ða, second-person singular pronoun, 51–52; position with wa and o verbs, 54–55. *See also* a-ða verb class
ðąąché, 'can, could, possibly,' 224–25
ðaašé, second-person singular continuous aspect, moving or have been doing, 62–63, 65. *See also* 77–79
ðáha, connector, 139, 161. *See* Chapters 13 and 15
ðątxąše, second-person singular continuous aspect, standing or imminent, 63, 65. *See also* 77–79
ðe-causative verb class, 214–15. *See also* Appendix B
ðe: as causative marker, 213–214; as demonstrative 'that', 35; as evidential, 24, 25–26; as question marker, 43
dée, as replacement for third-person pronoun, 98
definite. *See* subject marker and *wá*
ðį, the verb 'be,' 65; singular forms, 65–66
ði: second-person singular object pronoun, 97; second-person singular stative subject pronoun, 110, 111
ði...api, second-person plural object pronoun, 100
ðíe, second-person singular and plural emphatic pronoun, 143
ðíhta, second-person singular possessive pronoun, 140
ðíhtapi, second-person plural possessive pronoun, 141

ecí, 'there is, there are,' 206–7
ée, third-person emphatic pronoun, 144
éhtaha, location word. *See* Chapter 4
emphatic pronouns, 142–44. *See* freestanding pronouns

evidential: claim of evidence *che*, 26; declarative *ðe*, 26; definition of, 25–26; reportive *áape*, 223–24

freestanding pronouns, 140–44; emphatic, 142–44; possessive, 140–42
future marker. *See hta*

h-stem verb class, 148. *See also* Appendix B
h, first-person singular pronoun strong-stem class, 91. *See also* Appendix B
háachi, 136, 138. *See* aspect
hki, 'do for oneself, each other,' forms, 179–82
hta, future marker, 79

i-stem verb class, 88–92; paradigms for 89–91; forms with *wa* and *wá*, 101; stative forms, 113. *See also* Appendix B
íe and íiðe, list of completive and continuous forms for, 89–90
íhta, third-person singular possessive pronoun, 141
íhtapi, third-person plural possessive pronoun, 142
íkiha, 136, 138. *See* aspect
įkší, location word. *See* Chapter 4
indefinite: questions, 164; subjects, 203; wa, 98, 217–19
instrumental prefixes: definition of, 190–91; *ðaa*, 'by mouth,' 192; *ðii/ðuu*, 'by hand,' 191; *kaa*, 'by striking,' 195–96; *nąą*, 'by foot,' 193; *pá*, 'by cutting with a sharp thing,' 194–95; *paa*, 'by pushing,' 194; *pi*, 'by blowing,' 196–97; *po*, 'by shooting,' 197; *pu*, 'by pressing,' 196; *taa*, 'by heat,' 197

kaðǫ́, connector, 164–65. *See* Chapter 15
ki pronouns. *See* Chapter 16
ki-stative verb class, 114–16. *See also* Appendix B
ki, 'do for one's own,' forms, 176–79
kí, 'to or for someone (else),' forms, 173–75
kóe, connector, 164–65. *See* Chapter 15
kši, location word. *See* Chapter 4
kšíhtaha, location word. *See* Chapter 4

m, first-person singular pronoun, nasal-stem class, 168

mįkšé, first-person singular continuous aspect, sitting, lying, or ongoing, 59–60, 64. *See also* 77–79
motion verbs. *See* Chapter 14

ną, 136–37, 138. *See* aspect
nasal-stem verb class, 168–70. *See also* Appendix B
negation: with *aží*, 129–30; with commands, 132; with *ðįįké*, 131; with *ðįké*, 131; with future 132
nįkšé, second-person singular continuous aspect, sitting or ongoing, 62, 65. *See also* 77–79
noun phrases: definition of, 32–33, 35; joining, 201–2; plural, 201–5

object, definition of, 31; pronouns. *See* Chapter 9

paašé, second-person plural continuous aspect, 76, 77. *See also* 77–79
pe: as completive aspect marker, 23, 74; for permanent conditions, 33–35; as plural marker, 71–74
plural pronouns. *See* Chapter 7 and 9
position markers: definitions and list of, 207; in relative clauses, 229; use and context, 208–9
possessive pronouns, 140–42. *See* freestanding pronouns
pš, first-person singular pronoun, h-stem class, 148

questions: as indefinites, 164; using question words, 83–88; yes-no questions, 43–44

relative clauses, 228–29

š, second-person singular pronoun, strong-stem class, 91; h-stem class, 148
šc and *št*, second-person singular pronoun, br-šc (brush) verb class, 51–53
ši, 'again,' 224
šǫ, 138–39. *See* aspect
štą, 136–37, 138. *See* aspect
stative verb class, 110–12; i-stem stative verbs, 113; infixing verbs, 112. *See also* ki-stative verb class and Appendix B

Stephen Cody Tucker, 185
strong-stem verb class, 90–91. *See also* Appendix B
subject and object pronouns used together, 101–6
subject marker: definition of, 22, 24–25; deletion with plural and indefinite subjects, 203; deletion with relative clauses, 228. See *akxa* and *apa*
Supernaw's Indian Store, 160

tą, 'if, since,' 225
third-person pronouns: freestanding emphatic, 140, 144; plural object, 100–101; possessive, 140, 141, 142; singular object, 98–99; *tówa*, 144; *wá* definite, 217; *wa* indefinite, 98–99, 217–19; *wé*, 106; unmarked, 50
tówa, third-person freestanding pronoun, 144. *See also* third-person pronouns.

verb classes: a-ða, 49, 51–52; br-šc (brush), 51–53; ðe-causative, 214–215; h-stem, 148; i-stem, 88–92; ki-stative, 114–116; nasal-stem, 168–70; stative, 110–12; strong-stem, 90–91. *See also* Appendix B
verbs in more than one class, 55, 91–92, 154, 157

wá, definite third-person pronoun, 217. *See also* third-person pronouns
wa: first-person dual and plural subject pronoun, stative class, 110; indefinite, 98–99, 217–19; plural object, 100–101. *See also* third-person pronouns
wa…api, first-person plural object pronoun, 99
wálį, 'very,' 205–6. *See also xci*
wé, 106. *See also* third-person pronouns
wíe, first-person singular emphatic pronoun, 142
wíhta, first-person singular possessive pronoun, 140

xci, 'very,' 205–6. *See also wálį*

ž, second-person singular and plural pronoun, nasal-stem class, 168
žą́kše, second-person singular continuous aspect, lying, 63, 65. *See also* 77–79

www.ingramcontent.com/pod-product-compliance
Lightning Source LLC
Chambersburg PA
CBHW081211230426
43666CB00015B/2709